Compressed Development

Compressed Development

Time and Timing in Economic and Social Development

D. HUGH WHITTAKER
TIMOTHY J. STURGEON
TOSHIE OKITA
TIANBIAO ZHU

OXFORD
UNIVERSITY PRESS

OXFORD
UNIVERSITY PRESS

Great Clarendon Street, Oxford, OX2 6DP,
United Kingdom

Oxford University Press is a department of the University of Oxford.
It furthers the University's objective of excellence in research, scholarship,
and education by publishing worldwide. Oxford is a registered trade mark of
Oxford University Press in the UK and in certain other countries

First Edition published in 2020

Impression: 1

Published in the United States of America by Oxford University Press
198 Madison Avenue, New York, NY 10016, United States of America

British Library Cataloguing in Publication Data
Data available

Library of Congress Control Number: 2020931646

ISBN 978–0–19–874494–8

Printed and bound by
CPI Group (UK) Ltd, Croydon, CR0 4YY

Praise for *Compressed Development*

Compressed Development assesses the dynamic interactions between industrial policy, financialization, organization, technological innovation, employment, and automation. It illuminates the tensions between economic, social, and environmental challenges facing contemporary globalization, including climate change, inequality, and vulnerability. It provides an analytical and empirical tour de force, which is essential reading for all scholars and policy actors focused on contemporary industrial and technological innovation, global value chains, and digital platforms. It comes at a pivotal time for assessing seismic geo-political shifts, reflected in US-China trade and technological conflicts, as well as nationalist campaigns for de-globalization. Written before the COVID pandemic, it lays out an essential exploration of the diverse economic and social counter forces that will influence the outcome, whether brutal or benign, and the importance of proactive international policy in shaping any future global recovery.

Stephanie Barrientos, Professor of Global Development,
University of Manchester

Compressed development used to be seen as a special feature of some exceptionally successful countries in late economic development. This book, while not repudiating such views altogether, convincingly leads us to realize that compressed development has long been a generic mode of transformation embedded in the global ecology of industrial, technological, financial, and demographic relations. Even China's recent 'developmental miracle', among other national cases, is forcefully reinterpreted in respect to the opportunities, resources, and pressures from the specific world-era in which developmental compression is as much a requirement as an achievement.

Chang Kyung-Sup, Professor of Sociology, Seoul National University

Bold in its theoretical ambitions and panoramic in its empirical scope, *Compressed Development* breaks new ground in its projections of the global dynamics of development. Moving firmly beyond encumbering old schemas, the authors project a vision of the current global matrix of technological and organizational change, mediated by states and markets, in which the evolution of sectors and strategies is compressed, and China becomes the most telling national case. Any scholar hoping to keep pace with the dizzying world of the

21st century global political economy needs to start by confronting the complexities set out in this book.

Peter Evans, Professor Emeritus of Sociology, University of California, Berkeley and Senior Research Fellow, Watson Institute for International Studies and Public Affairs, Brown University

The tide of globalization, which appeared to be an irresistible force at the turn of the 21st century, splintered into a confusing welter of economic, political, and social scenarios in the 2010s. *Compressed Development* offers a framework that helps explain why the dividing line between early and late developing economies has become blurred, and why the rivalry between the United States and China is likely to define the main features of the global economy in the coming decades. While *Compressed Development* provides no simple answers about the future of development, it gives countries, companies, civil society organizations, and ordinary citizens essential tools needed to navigate the choices and challenges ahead of us. A highly recommended book for decision-makers, scholars, and students.

Gary Gereffi, Professor Emeritus of Sociology and Director, Center on Global Value Chains, Duke University

In this book the authors coin a new term – 'compressed development' – to shed light on what's new and what's different in the development experience after the 1990s; economic change is taking place both at a much faster rate and in an international context that allows states far less control. They explain why today's developing countries are facing challenges that are fundamentally different from any in the past. This is a fascinating synthesis of the technological, institutional, and ideological transformations of our era.

Dani Rodrik, Ford Foundation Professor of International Political Economy, John F. Kennedy School of Government, Harvard University

Compressed Development is an eye-opener for those of us who study capitalism, globalization, and development. The authors present a new approach to understanding economic and social development on a global scale, especially since 1990. Developing countries have faced intense pressure to 'run faster to stand still', meaning to make institutional changes faster and across a wider range of institutions than the 'late developers' of the post-war decades. The book compares Japan earlier and China more recently, with side analyses of the United States and 'emerging Asia', and draws in debates about global value chains, the middle-income trap, the developmental state, health and education, financialization, and the digital economy. It concludes that progress in reducing the enormous differences in living conditions across the world's territories depends on navigating through the new dynamics of 'compressed development'.

Robert H. Wade, Professor of Global Political Economy, London School of Economics and Political Science

Acknowledgements

This book is the product of empirical puzzles, some theoretical unease, and our interdisciplinary predilections. One empirical puzzle was the seemingly simple observation that factories in recent developers that we visited during our field research were using a wide range of technologies and labour processes at the same time, from very old to ultra-modern. Some factories were embedded in global value chains; some were rapidly internationalizing themselves. In some respects they resembled factories in other countries, from multiple time periods. This prompted a set of questions; ultimately, how can we compare the development experiences of, for example, mainland China, Taiwan, Japan, and the U.K.? More importantly, how can we *explain* the differences, and similarities?

Theories help us with explanations, but frequently at a cost; favoured phenomena are highlighted, others disappear. As students we were exposed to competing theoretical explanations of East Asia's (re-)emergence, each highlighting different phenomena. Late development perspectives emphasized the role and capabilities of the state, and state-business interactions, but often with an attenuated view of cross-border interactions. Neoclassical explanations focused on the creation of efficient markets and market allocation, with little or no role for corporate strategy, industrial policy, history, or institutional differences. Institutionalism shed light on business and organization processes, but lost sight of the state and, typically, change. Mostly set in 'national containers', scant attention was paid on any front to the growing importance of subnational and supranational processes, including the cross-border integration of industry-specific business systems and technology ecosystems (i.e., global value chains). Moreover, theories of economic development, at best, treated social development and policy as either historical antecedent or the natural outcome of various development experiences rather than an integral part of development itself.

Hence our attempt to create a framework which brings states and markets, organisations and technology, and the subnational, national, and supranational into a relationship rather than opposition or exclusion. The framework, moreover, needed to accommodate change over time, and to demonstate the importance of time and timing in economic and social development. We cannot claim to have fully succeeded in this endeavour, but this is what we set out to do.

We held our first workshop on compressed development in Beijing in 2007. This resulted in a 2010 piece that set out an initial framing and research agenda. We thought, naively in retrospect, that if we expanded on this skeletal thesis and continued our various research efforts, we could produce a book version by turning the sections of the article into chapters. Alas, in the process we encountered many new challenges and questions which demanded answers. Initially, we expected that we could update and supplement Gerschenkron's notion of 'late development,' for the 1980s onward, using East Asia, especially China, as our emblematic case, as others had done by focusing on the global integration of South Korea and Taiwan in the 1970s and 1980s. But we found ourselves traveling *back* in time, as well as forward, and to countries far from East Asia. Confident that we could meld development and globalization perspectives, we were forced to journey into new conceptual territory. Alexander Pope's *An Essay on Criticism* ('Fools rush in . . . ') springs to mind; the book before you is the product of our decade-long folly, as well as our blind spots and collective predilections.

All this took long enough to bring us to the current moment of turmoil, upheaval, and confusion. The danger of writing a book over a protracted period of time, especially one which seeks to be timely, is that the present keeps changing. Since 2010 digitization has become much more central to economic, political and social processes, and debates about them. The Global Financial Crisis set in motion a series of events which arguably led to Brexit, Trump and an intensification of techno-nationalism, signaling a turn away from the forms globalization and multilateralism that had helped shape the first decades of the compressed development era. Calls for a reform of capitalism and a reining in of 'big tech', and a long-overdue reckoning with the fact that racism and exploitation of vulnerable populations have underpinned capitalist accumulation from the start, have all recently gained momentum. China's rise and the United States' retreat from the global stage suggest a major reshaping of global influences, and a rise in geopolitical tensions. Keeping up with these changes has not been easy; ensuring that our conceptual framework captured and was not over-run by them was even more challenging.

Then, as we were submitting our finished manuscript, a pandemic came which spread with unprecedented speed and ferocity. Would this be the death knell for compressed development? How should we respond? Upon reflection, we are convinced that compressed development as we have depicted it can shed light on the speed of spread and devastating effects of Covid-19, and that the pre-pandemic trajectories of change which we set out in Chapter 9 are likely, if anything, to be hastened in the pandemic's wake. We have therefore left the manuscript unchanged, but have added an Afterword on the effects of Covid-19 as we see them in June 2020. Readers can judge through the passage of time how compressed development has actually changed.

This book is also the product of support and advice from many generous people and organizations. It has been so long in the making, it is not easy to recall all those who have contributed along the way. We particularly wish to acknowledge our colleague Mon Han Tsai, as well as our late friend and colleague Seishi Kimura for their early contributions; Suzanne Berger for introducing us; and Ronald Dore,

Peter Evans and Robert Wade for their encouragement to write the book. Mark Dallas and Ian Neary were excellent first readers.

Warm thanks are also due to Antonio Andreoni, Michael Best, Robert Boyer, Loren Brandt, Dan Breznitz, Ha-Joon Chang, Wan-Wen Chu, Rick Doner, Xiaolan Fu, Kazunori Fujimoto, Gary Gereffi, Chris Gerry, Gary Hamilton, Nigel Haworth, Takashi Hikino, Xiaoming Huang, Takeshi Inagami, Kyle Jaros, Kara Juul, Nahee Kang, Takehiko Kariya, Raphael Kaplinsky, Momoko Kawakami, Matthew Kidder, Sarosh Kuruvilla, Sébastien Lechevalier, Song Lei, Tomoo Marukawa, Matthew McCartney, Yoshifumi Nakata, Sean O'Riain, Bill Pritchard, Eric Protzer, Thomas Rawski, John Ravenhill, Robert Rowthorn, Mari Sako, Diego Sánchez-Ancochea, Jang-Sup Shin, Noël Sturgeon, Eric Thun, Linda Weiss, Eleanor Westney, Toby Whittaker, Nobuo Yokokawa and Ezequiel Zylberberg. All were either instigators, kibitzers, commenters, contributors, or supporters. We acknowledge participants in our Beijing workshop in March 2007, our Compressed Development in Emerging Asia conferences in Auckland and Wellington in December 2012, and our prepublication conference at St Antony's College, Oxford in May 2018.

Financial and material support from the following sources is gratefully acknowledged: Japan Foundation; MEXT 21st Century COE Program, ITEC, Doshisha University; New Zealand Asia Institute; EU's Horizon 2020 research and innovation programme under the Marie Skłodowska-Curie grant agreement No 645763; Asian Studies Centre, St Antony's College, Fell Fund, School of Interdisciplinary Studies, Nissan Institute of Japanese Studies, Oxford University; China's National Social Science Fund (project number 13BJL027) and the Institute for Advanced Study in Humanities and Social Sciences, Zhejiang University.

Finally, Tim would like to thank Richard Lester and Elisabeth Beck Reynolds of MIT's Industrial Performance Center for their unflagging support and encouragement, as well as his wife Judith and daughter Maxine for putting up with his many absences, both geographic and otherwise. Tianbiao would like to thank his wife Shirley and sons Jim and Will for their patience and support, and Toshie and Hugh would like to thank Nina and Toby respectively for their tolerance and good humour throughout this marathon project.

Contents

List of Figures

List of Tables

Compressed Development

An Introduction

Social and economic development is replete with contrasts and paradoxes, rapid change, and inertia. On the one hand, global demographic and population health indicators have shown unprecedented improvement in recent decades (Rosling, 2018). Infant mortality has declined, and life expectancy has increased, and the proportion of the world's population living in extreme poverty has plummeted from 29 per cent to 9 per cent in just two decades.[1] On the other hand, only 13 of the 101 middle-income countries of 1960 reached the high-income level by 2008. Most of those that did were either European or East Asian.[2] The global disparities of 1960 remain essentially intact, 'even after seven decades of self-conscious "development" following the Second World War' (Wade, 2018: 1, 2).

The contrast is evident in Figure 0.1. The upper pair of figures plots fertility rates (Y) against life expectancy (X) for 215 countries in 1970 and 2015 (with only selected countries labelled to avoid overcrowding in the figures). They show a marked shift downwards and to the right—lower fertility rates and longer life expectancy with only few outliers, mainly in sub-Saharan Africa. This is good news for much of the world. However, the lower pair, which plots life expectancy (Y) against per capita gross domestic product (GDP) (X) for the same country panel in the same years, shows the downwards movement of improving life expectancy, but a smaller number of richer countries pulling away to the right, reinforcing Wade's point. And the good news creates the seeds of future challenges, as lower fertility rates and improved life expectancy accelerate demographic ageing. As a result, many countries risk 'going over the hill before getting to the top' (Menon and Melendez-Nakamura, 2009; Morland, 2019).[3]

Critically, the historical *path* of economic development appears to have changed quite dramatically. Industrialization has been seen as *the* path to

[1] Infant mortality in Saudi Arabia declined from 242 deaths per 1000 in 1960 to just thirty-five in thirty-three years, an improvement which took Sweden seventy-seven years. In Iran women had on average six babies in 1984; fifteen years later the figure was three, and now it is 1.6, which is lower than in the United States (Rosling, 2018: 20, 174).

[2] The list of high-income-attaining countries and territories over that time were Equatorial Guinea, Greece, Hong Kong, Ireland, Israel, Japan, South Korea, Mauritius, Portugal, Singapore, Spain, Taiwan, and Puerto Rico (World Bank, 2013: 12).

[3] According to UN forecasts, between 1960 and 2100, the 'median' person age in the world will have doubled from twenty years to older than forty years (Morland, 2019: 274–5).

Compressed Development: Time and Timing in Economic and Social Development. D. Hugh Whittaker, Timothy J. Sturgeon, Toshie Okita, and Tianbiao Zhu, Oxford University Press (2020). © D. Hugh Whittaker, Timothy J. Sturgeon, Toshie Okita, and Tianbiao Zhu. DOI: 10.1093/oso/9780198744948.001.0001

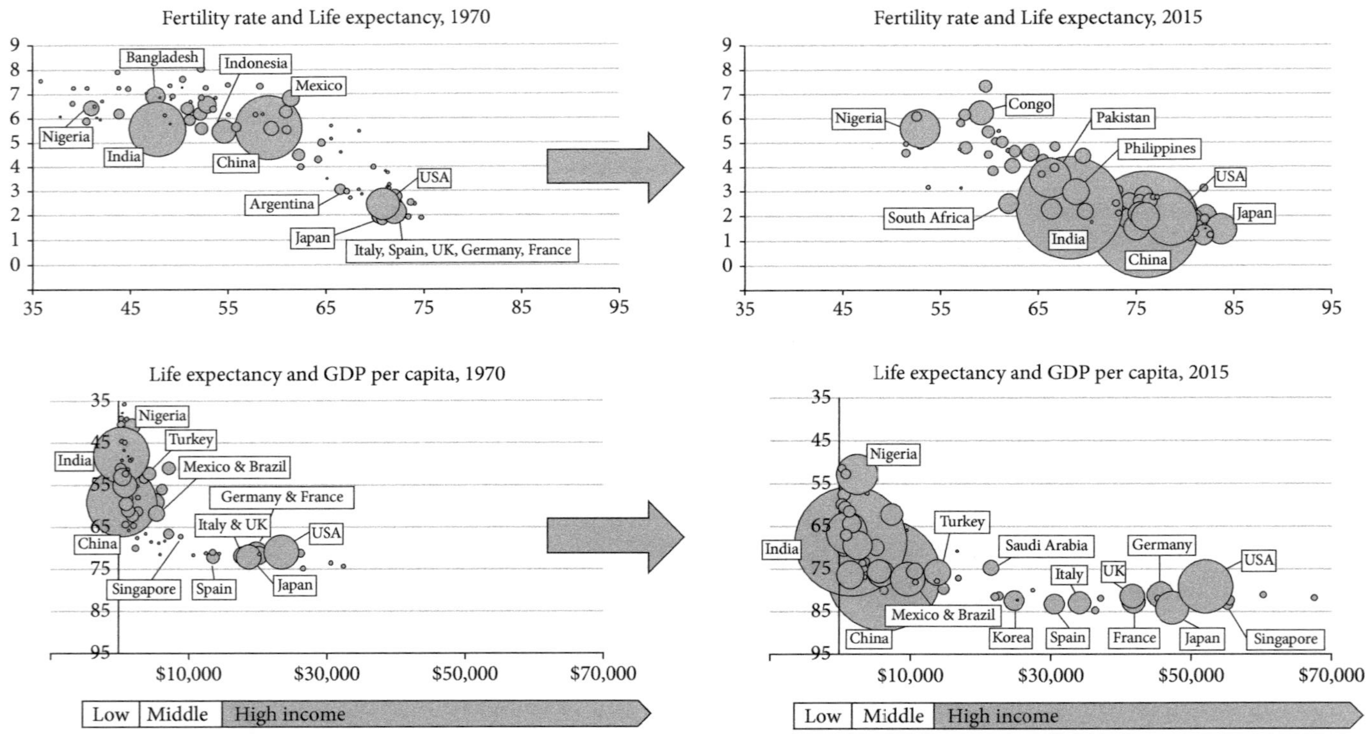

Figure 0.1 Improved public health outcomes are not necessarily associated with the accumulation of wealth

Notes: Countries labelled selectively because of space constraints. GDP per capita figures are in 2010 US dollars.

Source: World Bank Development Indicators, compiled by Eric Protzer.

development for all but the smallest countries, but travelling it has become difficult. As one indicator, whereas the manufacturing sector accounted for a third of employment in many now-developed countries, in recent developing countries, the figure has rarely risen above fifteen per cent. Additionally, qualitative changes within manufacturing, including a narrowing span of manufacturing industries, limited domestic inter-industry linkages, and the decoupling of production and innovation suggest that industrialization has become 'thin'.[4] And, it is not at all clear that other sectors can readily play the same propulsive role as manufacturing did in the past.

This book offers a framework or lens for considering contemporary social and economic development which we call 'compressed development'. It has two critical features, related to time and timing, respectively. The first, as the label suggests, is 'compression' of development experiences. Many writers have noted that later developers, to the extent that they have been able to grow economically, have done so faster than earlier developers, as a result of learning, licensing and investment from earlier developers. Relative to the UK, Germany and the United States grew rapidly, and Japan more rapidly still. Following Japan, South Korea and Taiwan experienced growth that was even more rapid, and, recently, mainland China, despite its vastness, has followed an even-more-rapid economic-growth trajectory.[5]

By the same token, even the most successful countries in terms of rate of growth soon face 'deindustrialization' or postindustrial transitions to services; transitions which are happening increasingly 'prematurely' (Rowthorn and Coutts, 2004; Rodrik, 2015). The UK industrialized over almost two centuries and then started to deindustrialize in the late 1960s. Japan industrialized over the course of a century, but began to deindustrialize in the late 1980s. South Korea and Taiwan began their transitions a mere three to four decades after they embarked on rapid industrialization.

In fact, the most rapid developers today experience industrialization and deindustrialization phenomena simultaneously. Because 'global value chains' (GVCs) shift routine production of goods and services from rich countries to countries that are less developed, while leaving high value-added functions such as innovation and marketing in place, moreover, and because machines rapidly replace workers as the cost of capital equipment falls, industrialization has become 'thin' in terms of employment share, sectoral linkages, and sectoral span.

[4] There is a difference between employment share and GDP share. A growing divergence between the two is also one aspect of 'thin industrialization'.

[5] According to Felipe (2012: 16, 26–7) it took the Netherlands 128 years to cross a lower middle-income zone (per capita income of $2000–7250 in 1990 International GK$), while it took Japan thirty-five years, and China, despite its huge population, a mere seventeen years to do so. He calculates that for every year which passes, it takes a (successful) country seven fewer months to traverse the lower-middle-income zone, and three months less to traverse the upper-middle-income zone ($7250–11,750). The problem, as noted, is that fewer countries are now doing so.

Extreme compression has an impact on social as well as economic development. That which previously unfolded sequentially, over time, is now pressed into virtual simultaneity, putting pressure on the state and other institutions which deliver public services. In health, 'double burdens' see countries grappling with 'rich country' diseases such as type 2 diabetes and obesity at the same time as dealing with communicable diseases and even malnutrition (OWHORC/SDDC, 2006; Stuckler and Basu, 2011). In education, expansion of postgraduate provision and research facilities are pursued while basic education is being consolidated and literacy rates improved. Advanced communications networks are installed while basic transport, sanitation, and energy infrastructure remain incomplete.[6]

The second feature of compressed development interacts with, and intensifies, the first. It refers to the historical time period in which development takes place. The geopolitical, institutional, technological and ideological context for development changes over time. It includes the degree of trade openness, prevailing financial architecture, transformative technologies, and the paradigmatic corporate strategies for organizing industries, production processes, and labour. Together, such '*era*' characteristics have a strong influence on the terms of developing countries' engagement with and integration with global markets, as well as on the formation of domestic industries and institutions.

We define the 'compressed development' era as starting roughly around 1990, and contrast it with development patterns that have come before, especially the postwar decades.[7] The postwar era of 'embedded liberalism' (Ruggie, 1982) saw heightened government intervention and capital controls—both in developed and emerging economies—and at least in developed countries, class compromise and welfare systems built around the goal of full employment, tolerance of controls on trade, and the spread of mass production in vertically integrated enterprises. It was also an era of cheap and stable oil prices. 'Fordism' is one of the many designations for this system of macro- and microeconomic articulation.

To be sure, there were wide variations across countries, and Fordism and embedded liberalism were already under strain in the 1970s. The Bretton Woods institutions were repurposed; national buffers were removed; welfare institutions and class compromises were repudiated; and financial interests became dominant in corporate governance. In the 1980s (and even before) vertical specialization began to replace vertical integration in specific industries, and pioneering discount retailers and manufacturers began to embrace large scale

[6] As Siegel and Stuckler (2011: 221) put it, there is often 'a lack of basic amenities like modern sanitation, hygiene, and safe, paved roadways, while modern conveniences, such as cell phones, televisions and cars, are abundant. For example, one report found that about half of India's population (560 million) were mobile phone subscribers, while only about a third of India's population had access to proper toilets.'

[7] Of course dating complex, multidimensional phenomena like this is problematic, and we recognize the diversity that can readily be viewed in precursors, exceptions, and outliers.

outsourcing and offshoring. The huge firm did not disappear, but became more vertically specialized and global (Feenstra and Hamilton, 2006). Advances in information and communications technology (ICT) facilitated these developments and enabled the emergence of a new, 'networked' business model. By the 1990s, the result could be clearly characterized as a series of sector-specific GVCs, most prominent in complex assembly industries such as apparel, automobiles, and electronics, and extending to software, IT services, and routine back-office functions after 2000. Today, business models may be changing yet again, with ICT even more central in what is emerging as the 'digital economy'.

Often emanating from or through the United States, such developments had a major impact on developing countries and the strategic choices of both the policy makers and entrepreneurs in them. As industries and institutions extended and fragmented across national borders, powerful external actors, over which developing country states could exert only limited control, became more imbricated in the development process. Key aspects of development, including finance, industry organization, technological learning, and market characteristics came to lie beyond the tight control of the nation state. One consequence, as mentioned, is 'thin industrialization'.

The subject matter of this book is how these two features of compressed development, compression and era, intertwine to present new challenges and opportunities for development.

Organizing framework and interdisciplinary approach

The simplest way to explore compressed development would be to limit our consideration to the postwar period, contrasting the eras before and after the 1990s, and to East Asia, where there has been a succession of countries achieving extended periods of high growth. These do figure prominently in this book, but to limit our study in this way would diminish its persuasiveness. Our goals are larger, prompted by questions such as What about other time periods, and other places? Haven't we seen this before?

To the claim that nationally organized industries, and strategies that shape them, have given way to global engagement via GVCs, sceptics could justifiably respond that with some tweaks, this has been seen before (depending on when one starts counting) in the 'first globalization' of the late nineteenth and early twentieth century. If we are comparing recent developers with postwar developers (Kohli, 2004), what about the late developers of the nineteenth century, caught up in the first globalization and financialization? In other words, even if we were to limit our focus to East Asia in the postwar period, we would still need a view of history, and how compression and era have interacted in the past. We attempt to do this by making our *historical* starting point the 'great divergence' that came with the industrial revolution.

We take a similar approach to geographical scope. It is easy enough to point to compression in China, but what about other countries—India, for example? Or Brazil or Iran or South Africa? Are they compressed developers too?[8] While our primary examples come from middle-income countries which have achieved rapid economic growth—and face new challenges and paradoxes as a result—it is not difficult to show that countries which grow slowly or not at all are also influenced by era-related institutions and systems, and experience some aspects of compression, especially when they try to implement strategies to promote industrial upgrading. Why some countries grow economically and not others is obviously important; geopolitics, location, resource endowments, domestic politics, institutional capabilities, and legacies are all crucial. Nonetheless, compression and contemporary era effects are something all countries experience some aspects of.

As this suggests, since compressed development is characterized by processes of global integration, developed countries naturally lie on the other side of the coin, experiencing ongoing structural transformation, outsourcing and offshoring to, and competition with, rising countries. This is especially the case in economically important industries such as automobiles, electronics, and apparel that have historically been large employers—and not coincidentally drivers of GVCs—but it is increasingly so in a wide variety of business functions, from back office services to software coding to research and development. These changes have triggered successive waves of political anxiety and policy responses, the most recent of which have played out, for example, in the guise of Brexit and the Trump Administration's 'America First' mantra.

To cope with the complexity inherent in our conceptual framework, we propose two dyads: states and markets and organization and technology (see Figure 0.2). These are *organizing constructs*, which will be fleshed out in more detail in Chapters 2 and 3, but some preliminary observations are called for. The pairs within each dyad are interlinked, and indeed both are co-dependent and co-evolutionary. The arrows moving in opposite directions indicate that state developments feed into markets, and vice versa, and the same applies to organization and technology.

There are mutual influences *between* the dyad pairs as well, indicated by the vertical arrows. We do not attempt to untangle ultimate causality, and are careful to avoid reductionism or technological determinism. However, in terms of era effects, finance and financial market regulation, which plays an important role in state–market relations, has an impact on the industrial organization–technology dyad through financialization, which is closely associated with marketization (see Chapter 2 and Dore, 2008). Conversely, technology and industry organization influence the state–markets dyad, for example, through their multiple effects on

[8] In fact, we were frequently asked such questions in response to our earlier 'Compressed Development' article (Whittaker et al., 2010). Similar questions were asked about 'late development'.

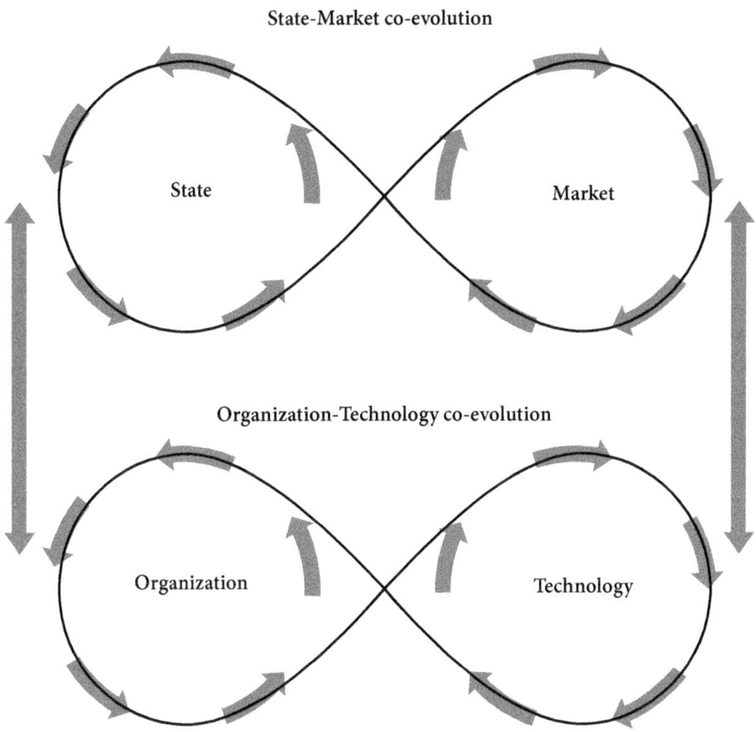

Figure 0.2 State–market and organization–technology dyads

employment and the geography of production systems. In terms of *compression*, organization–technology dynamics may be seen as key *drivers*, while state–market dynamics are better seen as *enablers* or *intensifiers*. The actual *vehicles* of compression are manifold, and include coordinated trade, foreign direct investment by multinationals, technology licensing, codified public knowledge, diaspora returnees and foreign hires, and so on.

Next, and importantly, international geopolitical and economic systems are generated from the dyads in the dominant power(s), and these create a context and powerful set of influences on less-developed countries, especially in the era of compressed development. One result is 'policy compression', or the constriction of policy space through a welter of international agreements and actors (Chang, 2002; Wade, 2003),[9] but such international systems can also be challenged by rising powers, such as Germany in the early twentieth century, Japan in the 1980s, and, more recently, China.

These organizing constructs raise several important issues which underlie our study. First, as noted, '*states*' and '*markets*' may be co-dependent and co-evolving,

[9] Note that this is a different kind of compression from that of time and space.

but there is a tension in their interactions, which have posed particular challenges in different eras. Democracy and capitalism only flourish together when there are restraints on capital; they are not necessarily natural travelling companions. Ruggie's 'embedded liberalism' points to the postwar 'embedding' of markets through laws, policies, and norms, including the institutions of Bretton Woods, which were undermined, dismantled, or repurposed from the 1970s. The concept draws on Polanyi's (1944) analysis of the strife engendered by the 'disembedding' of land, labour, and financial markets in the nineteenth century. It is not difficult to find contemporary parallels, prompting a question of what forms a future 're-embedding' of markets might take.[10]

Second, how are we to situate the *impact of new technology* and *organization forms*, specifically ICT, and the emergence of the 'digital economy'? Do digital platforms (explained later) simply enhance connectivity, and further shrink time and space—the latest wave of technological innovation—or are they more fundamental, like the industrial revolution itself that will radically reorder both the terms and geography of production and innovation? What is the role of technology in 'thin industrialization'? Will new digital tools such as AI-assisted design close off the industrialization path travelled by early, late, and current compressed developers, or open new paths? What are the implications of contemporaneous (if uneven), rather than sequential, adoption of digital technologies across high- and lower-income economies?

Third, concerning the *geopolitical and economic systems* and the *rebalancing of economic activity* between the global North and South, what are the long-term implications of GVCs and the changing global distribution of economic activity? If the 'great divergence' of the late eighteenth century brought about by industrialization resulted in a concentration of wealth and high per capita income in the global North, does the increased concentration of manufacturing activities in the South today represent a 'great convergence'? Or perhaps a partial convergence by a small number of Asian countries, a new phase of core-periphery relations, or a new multipolarity?[11] Or, is all this about to be reversed by neonationalist protectionism and reshoring? *Can* it be reversed? Is it even possible to unwind the elaborate supply chains and technology ecosystems that have emerged with GVCs, and if so, at what cost?

To begin to address such issues requires an interdisciplinary, integrative approach. Inevitably, we are stretched thin in some areas, and our disciplinary

[10] We draw on Polanyi's concepts quite heavily in this book, albeit with some caveats. As numerous writers have pointed out, markets are *always* embedded (cf. Block and Somers, 2014). When we refer to 'disembedding' we are actually referring to embedding in liberal or neoliberal institutions and norms. We also follow Block and Somers in identifying several types of embedding; legal, political and 'ideational' in their case, or broadly speaking, institutional and moral, or ideological.

[11] On the 'great divergence', see Pomeranz (2000). On a 'great convergence', see for example Spence (2012); Baldwin (2016); Grinin and Koroteyev (2015); Mahbubani (2013).

'trespassing' (Hirschman, 1981) may offend specialist sensitivities. However, an integrative approach, we venture, is a useful counter to the academic tendency towards ever finer specialization, which is amenable only to narrow questions, and understandable to ever fewer readers. In particular, we seek an integration, or balance, between the study of development and of globalization. While development scholars have struggled to incorporate globalization into their research, scholars of globalization have struggled with development. The former rightly argue that nation states, politics, and institutions are still important, and that industrial policy, if anything, is on the upswing. The latter argue for the importance of transnational institutions, processes, and communities, and that the current wave of globalization is not simply a pendulum rerun of late nineteenth century internationalization, but a dynamic that is creating a set of new, technologically mediated cross-border structures that are worth identifying and understanding. There is value, we propose, in seeking a reconciliation between these positions.

Late development and compressed development

We are not the first to draw attention to compression in development, of course, or to compression in human experience more generally. In fact, there has been an active socio-cultural discourse on space-time compression for the past century and a half, which explores how our concepts and experience of time and space have undergone profound changes since the Enlightenment with the 'project of modernity', and the rationalities and technological advances of capitalism and industrialization (Harvey, 1989). Previously embedded in 'place' in traditional societies, time and space have become disembedded and available for recombination in a myriad of forms and flows which are increasingly global, and encompass past, present, and even future (Sassen, 1990; Castells, 2009).[12]

Compression has been recognized for almost as long in literature on industrialization and economic development. Veblen (1915) remarked on the rapidity of Germany's catch-up industrialization, and more generally, Trotsky expressed it lucidly in his theory of 'uneven and combined development':

> Although compelled to follow the advanced countries, a backward country does not take things in the same order. The privilege of historic backwardness – and such a privilege exists – permits, or rather compels, the adoption of whatever is ready of any specified date, skipping a whole series of intermediate stages. Savages throw away their bows and arrows for rifles all at once, without traveling

[12] Indeed, while tilting his hat to Marx, Weber, and Durkheim, Giddens (1990) proposes 'time-space distanciation'—perhaps the flip side of compression—as the key to understanding modernity.

> the road which lay between those two weapons in the past ... The fact that Germany and the United States have now outstripped England was made possible by the very backwardness of their capitalist development.
>
> (Trotsky, [1932] 2017: 4)

Backwardness and stage-skipping catch-up were central to Gerschenkron's (1962) 'late-development' thesis, in which later developers were shown to create systematically different institutional features from earlier developers to facilitate rapid, catch-up economic development.[13] Gerschenkron was arguing against the notion that all countries must pass through the same stages of economic development.[14] Although influential, Gerschenkron's late-development thesis has come in for extensive criticism: the elevated role of the state, for example in its ability to direct resources to leading or mid-tech sectors; his downplaying of the role of agriculture, traditional, and small-firm sectors; unproblematic role assigned to finance; neglect of the military and war; and more have been cited.[15] Some of the issues are related to a failure to clearly separate lateness of development and the historical period in question. Our two key features of compressed development, compression and era, enable us to avoid at least this problem, while capitalizing on some of the insights of Gerschenkron and other late-development writers.

The late-development thesis was adapted to explain successive 'miracles' in East Asia, with emphasis on the role of the 'developmental state', in Japan, South Korea, Taiwan, and elsewhere.[16] However, Japan's economic malaise, beginning in the 1990s, the Asian Financial Crisis in the late 1990s, and the US resurgence in the run-up to the 'tech bubble' of 2001 diminished the lustre of the East Asian developmental-state model, and, as a result, interest in late development waned.[17] Instead, institutionalist perspectives gained in popularity, such as 'business systems' and 'varieties of capitalism', approaches that brought (nationally rooted) business and economic institutions to the fore, and moved the state to the background. This had some benefits, but the insights of late development, the perspective of geo-historical change, and the role of the state were often lost in the process. Streeck (2009: 6) laments that, in its reaction against the grand narratives of modernization and Marxist theory, comparative institutional analysis 'lost sight of the two main subjects of social science since its rise in the

[13] It is possible that Gerschenkron was aware of Trotsky's theory, although he did not acknowledge any influence. On the similarities, see Selwyn, 2011.

[14] Specifically, he was critical of Rostow's (1960) five-stage model.

[15] Cole (1978), Herrigel (1996), and more recently Kasza (2018), to mention a few.

[16] Johnson (1982); Amsden (1989); Wade (1990); Woo-Cumings (1999), respectively; also Evans (1995).

[17] Although not necessarily amongst critics of neoliberal development policies. In fact, the state has reappeared, in neo-developmental-state writing, not limited to Asia (see Chapter 8), and some 'state capitalism' writing on China attempts to combine state- and business-level analysis (e.g. Naughton and Tsai, 2015), while interest in the developmental state in general has revived in recent years (Okazaki, 2018).

nineteenth century'—the historical dynamics of the social world (i.e. time), and the evolution of capitalism, producing instead a '*comparative statics* of individual socioeconomic institutions' (emphasis in the original).

Where time and change are missing, so is agency. Neither statist nor institutionalist approaches have dealt well with the roles of technological revolutions, innovation, and management models that come and go in their wake. Addressing this gap, (neo-)Schumpeterian perspectives provide a valuable perspective on change, entrepreneurship, and innovation, usefully drawing attention to the role of technology as an enabler of both globalization and catch-up development.[18] Here entrepreneurs in less developed countries are not simply implementers of state objectives or products of institutional arrangements, but calculative—and affective—agents with a range of motives and strategies. Under pressure from (sometimes global) competition, they may also be influenced by prevailing management fads and ideologies, and pursue objectives broadly consistent with the impetus and logic of catch-up development.

In sum, our interdisciplinary, integrative approach builds on a number of research traditions, which have typically been pursued in isolation or parallel, rather than in dialogue.

Some conceptual refinements

Given the possible ambiguities in the concepts of compression and era, some additional clarification is needed. 'Compression' is, of course, a metaphor for the bringing together of phenomena previously separated by time and/or space, enabled most obviously, but not solely, by new technologies and business models. Later successful developers have generally experienced compression, whether in the nineteenth, twentieth, or twenty-first century, and some aspects of compression can be observed even where there is little growth. Temporal and spatial compression are therefore widespread, in both the past and the present; a general condition of capitalist development.

We make a distinction, however, between eras. With our starting point in the late eighteenth century, we consider Britain as the key early developer. It had embarked on a path of industrialization by the early nineteenth century, and created a scalable geopolitical and economic system to which others had to respond. The group of countries which both achieved national unity and embarked on industrialization and integration into the world economy in the 1860s and 1870s are commonly referred to as 'late developers'. However, another group, which industrialized after World War II, are also commonly labelled as late

[18] Freeman and Soete (1997), and in an Asian context, Mathews (2006) and Lee (2013).

developers. Rather than inventing new labels, we refer to the former as 'early late developers', and the latter, following Kohli (2004) and others, as 'late-late developers' when the distinction is needed. Japan experienced high growth in both eras. In addition, while South Korea and Taiwan fit in the second group, they were still undergoing institutional development as the era of late-late development was giving way to the compressed-development era, in the 1980s. They may be considered transitional cases, but Taiwan in particular owes much of its economic development to its contract manufacturing role in GVCs, and may be considered an early compressed developer.

We designate 1990 onwards as the era of 'compressed development' because compression became (and mostly remains) particularly acute then, and because important changes in geopolitics, ideologies, institutions, technologies, and production systems warrant a different label. It is *not* because it is the only era in which compression has taken place. Our eras are thus historical periods, and not stages. In brief, because of era-related effects, it matters critically *when* a country develops. Observers of organizational transformation have long argued that the external environment and business practices that prevail during an industry's initial high-growth phase and integration into the global economy have a powerful and long-lasting influence on that industry's business systems and routines, and that supporting institutions co-evolve with new high-growth industries. We call this the 'Stinchcombe effect'.[19] The 'liability of newness' of young firms and industries is eventually offset as '... structures become more stable and ties with environments become more durable' (Freeman et al., 1983: 692). By extension, a country's economic institutions, including innovation systems, business culture, corporate governance, industrial organization, and regulation, are also influenced by the business systems of the high-growth industries within their midst. In the context of compressed development, we observe that it matters that high-growth industries, in China for example, are *global* industries.[20]

Strictly speaking, therefore, 'compressed development' refers to the current era, but for the sake of convenience we also refer to compressed developers—countries experiencing rapid development and integration into the global economy from the 1990s onwards, including transition economies—just as it has been common to refer to 'late developers' and 'late-late developers'. It does not mean that all developing or even middle-income countries in this era are experiencing the same rapid growth or the same degree or types of compression. We do pay particular attention to rapidly growing countries such as China. They are

[19] After Arthur Stinchcombe, who observed: 'Organizations which have purposes that can be efficiently reached with the socially possible organizational forms tend to be founded during the period in which they become possible. Then, both because they can function effectively with those organizational forms, and because the forms tend to become institutionalized, the basic structure of the organization tends to remain relatively stable' (1965: 153).

[20] Similar arguments have been made for political institutions (Maier, 2012).

instructive because they experience the most extreme forms of compression. But we are *not* citing them as normative examples, nor do we regard economic growth as a singular measure of 'success', although it is certainly significant. Indeed, to the extent that they achieve high growth, compressed developers face novel and vexing problems which previous developers never had to face. These 'double burdens' and challenges are endemic to compressed development.

Finally, and relatedly, this is *not* a book on how to 'successfully' navigate the challenges and paradoxes of the compressed-development era, although we clearly identify policies and approaches which are more, and less, effective in such navigation. The book presents a framework or lens from which causal inferences follow, but not a theory of development per se. Nor are we proposing compressed development as an over-arching logic which imposes itself uniformly on countries. Development, as Dore (1966) once commented of modernization, is 'transitive', not 'intransitive'. It is by concrete means of institutional diffusion, overlapping business networks, and isomorphic innovation and technology adoption that similarities can be observed among compressed developers, ranging from the linked operations of multinational firms and global buyers in GVCs, adherence to international agreements (to varying degrees), technology licensing, and purchase of technology embodied in products and machines, to dispatching of students abroad, migration, market convergence, idea diffusion, and informal learning. There is a geopolitical and economic system shaped largely by dominant powers in which this takes place, but the way individual nations (and businesses) respond to the challenges and opportunities presented in the current era depends critically on their location, resources, institutional capabilities, politics, and legacies.

Focusing on compression and era sensitizes us to questions which are often passed over in studies of development and globalization, and it encourages us to see the familiar in a new light. What happens, for example, when a country undergoes a 'retail revolution' at the same time, or even in advance of, an 'industrial revolution', or financialization at the same time as industrialization? What happens when the most dynamic entrepreneurial businesses in a country are effectively 'born global', or when most advanced production facilities are owned and operated by foreign firms which turn out products invented elsewhere? Is 'thin industrialization' the result of policy failure, or is it systemic and unavoidable? Can it be unwound by neonationalists? What impact does this have on working and middle classes and social development? Looking forward, what are the implications of the 'digital economy' for developing countries? How does the state negotiate constricted policy space, scarce resources, and multilevel governance? How does the state address double burdens or challenges in health and education, and the paradoxes attending rapid growth in the compressed-development era? These, too, are some of the questions which will be taken up in this book.

Outline of the chapters

The book is divided into three parts: conceptualizing compressed development, experiencing compressed development, and navigating compressed development. We start in simple, broad-brush terms, and progressively build layers of complexity in successive chapters. We progress also from past to present, and from a primary focus on economic development to social development, policy, and politics.

The first chapter is concerned with time *compression*, and the collapse of what have commonly been considered stages of development into virtual simultaneity. Stage thinking has permeated approaches to economic development, from the terminology of primary, secondary, and tertiary economic sectors, predicated on predictable structural transformations in developing countries from agriculture to manufacturing to services, to stages of advancement within manufacturing. Along this path other changes have been expected to proceed in sequence, such as a shift from informal to formal employment. Models of transition and progression in development may have always been stylised, and normative, but today, we see patterns that are different enough to warrant systematic investigation and explanation. Critically, although industrialization has typically been seen as *the* path to economic development, in recent decades 'premature deindustrialization' (or 'simultaneous industrialization and deindustrialization') has rendered this problematic. Here we refer to 'thin industrialization' to denote a mode of industrialization that is something other than a (rapid) movement through ordered phases. Additionally, boundaries between sectors have become increasingly blurred, with the industrialization of agriculture, application of ICT to primary and secondary industries, and realization of scale economies in services through digitization. Financialization has permeated all sectors. Finally, we touch on compression in the social sphere and demographics, including the phenomenon of 'premature ageing'.

Chapters 2 and 3 add a historically grounded conceptual framework, and hence the basis for our concept of *eras*. At the heart of each chapter is a co-evolutionary dyad—states and markets, and organizations and technology, respectively. In Chapter 2 we argue that the evolution of the nation state and modern 'markets' are historically intertwined, and are further influenced by war. Their historical co-evolution within a global geopolitical system first constructed by Britain and later superseded by the United States provides the basis for our periodization of early development, early-late and late-late development, and then compressed development. The state is a key actor in economic development *throughout*, but in different ways in respective eras, which are influenced by the geopolitical system or context, as well as 'markets'. The concept of 'markets' is unpacked, at least partially, to draw attention to the multiple roles of finance, and financialization, including the latter's effects on the organization of production, as well as on the state.[21] We conclude Chapter 2 by introducing a different type of contemporary compression—that of policy space, and the challenges this poses for state building.

Chapter 3 focuses on the second, organization-technology dyad, and the interrelations between organization paradigms, management models, and technologies that underpin both product and organizational innovation. It presents a progression of techno-economic periods that layers onto, and integrates with, the periodization of development eras in Chapter 2, and extends the framework both spatially and institutionally. Organization paradigms, management models, and enabling technologies are especially reflected in the organization and spatial structure of key industries. From an evolutionary perspective, we particularly focus on the emergence of GVCs, new actors—including global buyers, tiers of global contract manufacturers, suppliers, and subcontractors—and new forms of organization in industries such as textiles, motor vehicles, and information and communication technology, which have changed the way emerging countries become integrated into the global economy. There have been some signs that the tide of globalization has begun to turn, if not after the 2008–2009 Global Financial Crisis, then perhaps from 2016 forward. At the same time 'fitting in' to GVCs and technology ecosystems has acquired a new meaning with the emergence of platform innovation in the digital economy.

Chapter 4 begins our examination of the experiences of compressed development. We restart the historical flow and add empirical cladding to our conceptual framework, beginning with a comparison between late-developer Japan and compressed-developer China's modern economic emergence. Historically China exerted great influence on Japan. Conversely, Japan was an influential model in China's post-1978 reforms, at least initially. Our comparison is thus based on certain commonalities, but it highlights contrasts. Japan created unique institutional solutions to the challenges and opportunities it faced, but these were recognizably products of the eras in which they were formed, particularly the postwar decades. The same applies to post-1978 China, particularly in the 1990s and 2000s. Critically, Japan's highly successful late-development innovations shaped its institutional responses to new challenges of the compressed-development era. These are illustrated in a focused comparison of education and skills, which concludes the chapter.

Chapter 5 explores in greater depth the ways in which less-developed countries experience and shape the era-related influences of compressed development, with a focus on various and often overlapping roles played in GVCs. Whereas Chapter 4 compared economically successful late and compressed

[21] Pressure exerted by finance on industry will be discussed further in Chapter 3. Financialization intensifies capitalism's 'creative destruction', with inherent benefits and problems. Problematically, it also shifts the balance of state-market relations (and affects the ability of the state to gather taxes, which is critical for the nation state), diverts resources to 'nonproductive' activities (admittedly a slippery concept: Mazzucato, 2018), creates periodic crises, and exacerbates inequality.

developers (i.e. Japan and China), countries with poor or mixed records of economic development also face the opportunities and constraints of compression, and many must do so with a set of institutions, policies, and industries which emerged under prior developmental conditions. Large-market countries such as China, Brazil, and India all have industrial histories and now face the era effects of compressed development with institutional, policy, and industrial legacies that are not necessarily suited to the challenges of the compressed-development era. Discontinuities and differences across sectors further complicate the role of the state in the era of compressed development.

Chapter 6 begins our analysis of the social dimensions of compressed development, at the core of which are employment relations. It has been commonly assumed that economic development will shrink the informal sector—and with it, informal employment—in favour of a growing formal sector and 'standard' employment. However, 'standard' employment is a product of specific historical circumstances, and it has come under intense pressure in industrialized countries. With 'thin industrialization' and financialization ascendant in compressed developers, not only does informal employment persist, but forms of 'nonstandard' employment as seen in developed countries have been growing as well. The muted scope of 'standard' employment has consequences for the emergence and stability of urban working and middle classes, equality, and the feedback loops between economic and social development. We apply this perspective to the 'middle-income-trap' debate.

Chapter 7 considers social policy, especially double challenges in health and education and how these are shaped—and intensified—by era influences. In health it means coping with noncommunicable diseases, including obesity, at the same time as fighting communicable diseases, and malnutrition. In education—the main focus of the chapter—double challenges include building a science-based innovation and graduate education system while also expanding basic education to achieve universal literacy. Earlier developers faced these sequentially. The challenges of time compression are shaped and intensified by era influences, including the global alignment of social policy, and in education, the rise of a global testing culture and policies premised on human capital theory. Policy entrepreneurs have been active in opening up education to multinational private sector participation. Actor proliferation and 'projectification' compound the challenges of achieving policy integration, which has become more important than ever.

Chapter 8 considers the state in the era of compressed development. Our premise is that a developmental state (broadly conceived) is still necessary for development, but that the state faces new challenges and must become more outward-facing and adaptive or flexible than in the postwar decades. Second, whereas the nation state has been the focus of late-development and developmental-state writing, other levels of governance have become increasingly important. Attention needs to be paid to these, multilevel governance, and the compression challenge of simultaneous centralization and decentralization. Here we look at China's 'local developmentalism', as well as the vogue of smart- and eco-cities in India. Third, developmental-state writing has tended to focus on state-business interaction. The business of the state and its embeddedness has always encompassed a broader set of civil society actors, but this has become more critical in addressing the challenges of compression, even as it has become more problematic.

The concluding chapter brings together threads from the preceding chapters to address current and emerging issues. The first section looks at the co-evolutionary effects of compressed development on industrialized countries, specifically the United States and Japan. Here we observe a Red Queen effect, in which developed countries are forced to run ever faster to stay in the same place. In some respects, this makes it possible to say, 'we are all compressed developers now'. Then, turning towards the future, we discuss the implications of the emerging digital economy, first for the geographic distribution of economic activity, and then in terms of 'rebalancing' and 're-embedding' through civil society and political movements. In the final section we further consider rebalancing of the state–market dyad, and changing geopolitics. We appear to be entering a period of turbulence between early and late compressed development, as happened with the respective eras of late development, with a reassertion of bellicose nationalism and rising populist authoritarianism. Overall, we propose that we are entering an age of three interlocking upheavals: the rise of the digital economy; reactions to excessive marketization, financialization, and inequality; and geopolitical tensions and shifts. Underneath these upheavals, we predict that many of the drivers of compression will persist as we enter a period of *late compressed development*.

In sum, this book is about compression, era effects, and their interaction in contemporary development. The compressed-development era is characterized by 'thin industrialization'—a different path of economic development from previous eras—and 'double burdens' or 'double challenges' in the social sphere, which need to be addressed by an 'adaptive' developmental state. The features and challenges unfold differently in high-growth and low-growth economies, and will persist and possibly accelerate in the digital economy. At the intersection of development and globalization studies, the analysis encompasses state-, society-, and company-level dynamics. While it focuses on middle-income countries, and geographically on East Asia, aspects of compression and era effects can be observed more widely; this provides fertile ground for future research.

PART 1

CONCEPTUALIZING COMPRESSED DEVELOPMENT

1

Time Compression

From Stages to Simultaneity

Introduction

September 1996, at a small die and mould factory on the outskirts of Taipei. In one room, a suite of late-model Swiss machining centres. In an adjacent room, an assortment of very basic locally-produced machine tools, none computer controlled. There are Taiwanese operators, Filipino operators, and two young English-speaking women in an office. The owner-manager:

> Well, we do the precision work with higher margins on the Swiss machines, and the less precise work on the local machines. If there's volume work, we do it in our factory in [mainland] China... Our biggest headache is staff turnover. We recruit young workers and within a year and a half they go off to do their military training. Only 10% come back. Fast food and the stock market – a parking boy in Taipei can earn more than we pay. In they come and out they go. There's an image problem. We're seen as a dirty, dangerous, and demanding industry, but it's not true. They say it's already like that around Beijing, but not in the Chinese countryside.[1]

Making sense of such scenes was a starting point for this book. They are common enough that one is tempted to pass them by without a second thought. Comparisons provoke second thoughts, however, and many questions. In the case of this factory, the late-model Swiss machines co-existed with very basic production technology. The same machines, or their Japanese equivalents, could also be seen in similar die and mould factories in South Tokyo, but the more basic machines had all but disappeared. In Birmingham, in the UK, the latter might only be found in a museum. In fact, there were not many die and mould makers left in Birmingham in the mid-1990s. Those in Tokyo were struggling; their major customers were moving overseas, and starting to place their orders elsewhere. The Taiwanese maker, however, was buoyant, gaining orders from as far afield as South America and Scandinavia, courtesy of a web presence and English speakers

[1] Paraphrased, from more than one source.

Compressed Development: Time and Timing in Economic and Social Development. D. Hugh Whittaker, Timothy J. Sturgeon, Toshie Okita, and Tianbiao Zhu, Oxford University Press (2020). © D. Hugh Whittaker, Timothy J. Sturgeon, Toshie Okita, and Tianbiao Zhu. DOI: 10.1093/oso/9780198744948.001.0001

in the office. Indeed, the company had already moved some production to China—not quite 'born global' (Welch and Luostarinen, 1988), but an extremely rapid internationalizer. This was partly in response to hiring difficulties in Taiwan. It seemed that half the factory was modern and half was traditional: half was caught up in industrialization, and half in deindustrialization, and increasingly engaged with global value chains (GVCs).

This chapter introduces the concept of time compression, the first of two key features of compressed development (the second being era effects). Focusing on time compression highlights some of the ways in which the experiences of later developers change relative to earlier developers. This was pointed out by Gerschenkron (1962) and others long before him, but their perspectives need to be updated. In the past half century many industrialized countries have experienced deindustrialization. Should developing countries 'leapfrog' directly into a service-oriented economy? Can they avoid it? What should they 'catch up' with? Or perhaps more compelling, is it possible to jump straight into the digital economy without prior experience of manufacturing-based industrialization? Are there dangers in attempting to do so? These are difficult questions, which we do not attempt to answer right away.

One way to approach time compression is through a consideration of stage theories, which are deeply engrained in the social sciences. They are engrained in the language we use, and in models which continue to exercise normative influence. Although stage theories fail to explain or predict what we see today, they can be a useful heuristic for highlighting compression.

The first section of this chapter considers industrialization—which in part entails the shift of resources (including people) from the primary to the secondary sector, particularly manufacturing—and subsequent deindustrialization (or post-industrial transition)—the shift of resources (including people) from secondary to tertiary industry, or services. In recent years, it seems that deindustrialization has been occurring at lower and lower levels of per capita GDP, with fewer workers absorbed in manufacturing. This has been called 'premature deindustrialization' by some, though it may be better characterized as simultaneous industrialization and deindustrialization (Whittaker et al., 2010).[2]

More encompassing, compression and era influences interact to produce what we call 'thin industrialization', featuring proportionately fewer workers absorbed in the modern manufacturing sector, even during high growth; a geographic separation of production and innovation, fewer domestic interindustry linkages, and a narrower span of manufacturing industries. Global value chains (GVCs), the adoption of advanced production technologies on the periphery, and 'out-of-sequence' service sector developments are contributing factors.

[2] In fact, many developing countries are nowadays *transforming* an *existing* manufacturing sector, rather than industrializing *ab initio*. This could be seen as 'reindustrialization'.

There are also stage models *within* manufacturing, relating to how the sector evolves, or is upgraded, over time. Again, these stage models offer the opportunity to examine both the components of development and what has changed in their progression. There is a strong tendency for scholars not only to relate the experiences of earlier developers to recent developers, but to *impose* their analytical frameworks derived from earlier experiences, thus missing the novelty of compressed development. An example we take up is the 'flying geese' model, influential in Japan, which is a stage model with an international component: older industries are allowed, or even encouraged, to migrate to less developed countries as a way to drive industrial upgrading at home. The model has its merits, but it can also obscure the presence and significance of 'out-of-sequence' phenomena (and indeed, the persistence of 'mature' sectors in Japan, such as textiles). At worst it tries to force round empirical pegs into square conceptual and normative holes.

Next, in the service sector we find 'out-of-sequence' developments as well, including, in recent developers, a 'retail revolution' unfolding in parallel to industrialization, featuring the rise of supermarkets and big box retailers. In fact, sectors are becoming increasingly blurred. Nearly all sectors now have technology- and innovation-intensive segments which generate increasing returns to scale, and, at the same time, many also have a very large informal or low-wage segment which, far from disappearing with economic growth, has tended to grow in recent years. In such respects, and others, the path of economic development for recent developers is very different from that of earlier developers. The growth of financial services and the 'financialization' of other sectors is also linked to this changing path. While undeniably crucial for economic development, as a driver rather than a servant, finance changes incentives and resource allocation in ways that are just as likely to intensify thin industrialization and labour market dualism.

Time-related compression is not restricted to economic development. In the final section we will consider demographic and social compression, which has implications not just for social sustainability, but also for economic development. Ironically, to the extent that economic development is prioritized, and aggressively pursued, the problematic social consequences of demographic and social compression and their feedback loops to economic development are likely to be even greater.

Industrialization

'Premature deindustrialization'?

For economists, development is fundamentally seen as the ability to shift resources from activities of low productivity to those of higher productivity (Kuznets, 1971). This was long equated with a shift of labour and capital from agriculture to manufacturing through industrialization, based on the example of Britain and subsequent industrializers. Lewis (1954) famously proposed a dual-sector model consisting of a traditional or subsistence sector and a modern, capitalist sector, commonly interpreted as agriculture and manufacturing, respectively.[3] The former harbours underutilized labour, which can be used cheaply in the capitalist sector, generating extra profits for investment until the underutilized labour is absorbed and wages rise in both sectors. This is known as the 'Lewis turning point' (LTP). Nations that cross it are on the road to development.

Similarly, Kaldor (1967) held that GDP growth is higher when manufacturing's share is rising because it produces increasing returns to scale. The faster the growth of the manufacturing sector, moreover, the more the productivity of nonmanufacturing is enhanced. This is because resources—especially labour—are shifted away from traditional sectors such as agriculture, and technology is applied to maintain (or increase) output. Furthermore, manufacturing growth typically enhances export growth, setting up additional positive feedback loops.[4] Kaldor (1966) feared that Britain was losing ground relative to later industrializers because it had matured earlier, and manufacturing had fewer surplus resources to absorb. Indeed, Britain began to face 'deindustrialization' from the late 1960s (Singh, 1977). Deindustrialization is typically defined as a declining share of manufacturing in total employment. There are both positive forms of deindustrialization, the former associated with rising productivity and continued competitiveness in manufacturing (in which manufacturing output may continue to expand even as employment shrinks), and negative forms arising from arrested productivity growth, declining competitiveness, and shrinking output; Britain had elements of both (Rowthorn and Wells, 1987). As the hearth of the industrial revolution, it began to lose its industrial lead in the late nineteenth century, although significant deindustrialization only took place from the late 1960s onward.

Britain has by no means been the only country to experience industrialization followed by deindustrialization (positive or negative). Other countries have followed, and significantly, they have followed with increasing rapidity. 'Late developers' of the nineteenth century began to deindustrialize from the 1980s. South Korea and Taiwan began to industrialize rapidly in the 1960s, and within three decades, were already deindustrializing. Rowthorn and Coutts (2004) called this 'premature deindustrialization'. In other words:

> In the United States, manufacturing constituted a share of employment comparable to its share in Korea throughout the latter half of the nineteenth century and

[3] Ranis and Fei (1961) interpreted the sectors as agriculture and non-agriculture, but Lewis allowed for the possibility of commercial agriculture's inclusion in the capitalist sector. For an assessment of the Lewis model and its contemporary relevance, see Gollin, 2014.

[4] For Kaldor, manufacturing is necessary for economic development, but does not guarantee it. Without complementary institutional innovations and changes its contributions are diminished.

> continued to expand its share of total employment throughout the middle of the twentieth century. In England manufacturing's heyday was even more prolonged, lasting almost 150 years. In Korea, manufacturing passed its peak within the span of 40 years. (Evans and Staveteig, 2008: 75–6)

This is not simply a matter of followers replicating the experience of pioneers more quickly, however. There are, in fact, two intertwined phenomena within this trend. First, deindustrialization is commencing at lower levels of per capita GDP. Second, manufacturing is absorbing a smaller share of the total workforce, even at its peak. Palma (2005) analyses a number of possible causes of this double trend, such as reclassification of certain manufacturing activities as services, demand-constraining monetarist, and neoliberal economic policies after the 1980s, rapid productivity catch-up in developing countries, and for natural resource producers, Dutch Disease effects.[5] He highlights the effects of policies, and the secondary effects of Dutch Disease in Brazil and the Southern Cone (Argentina, Uruguay, and Chile) countries. By Palma's calculation, the onset of deindustrialization dropped from $20,645 per capita GDP in 1980 to $9,805 in 1990 and $8691 in 1998 (all figures are in1985 international US$).

Rodrik (2015) highlights the effects of globalization. He finds cases of deindustrialization through technological progress (positive deindustrialization) mainly limited to developed countries and negative deindustrialization in developing countries, with some Asian exceptions. This is because globalization throws sand into the wheels of the Kaldorian industrial upgrading process.

> As developing countries opened up to trade, their manufacturing sectors were hit by a double whammy. Those without strong comparative advantage in manufacturing became net importers of manufacturing, reversing the process of import substitution. In addition, developing countries 'imported' deindustrialization from the advanced countries, because they became exposed to the relative price trends produced in the advanced economies. The decline in the relative price of manufacturing in the advanced countries put a squeeze on manufacturing everywhere, including the countries that may not have experienced much technological progress. This account is consistent with the strong reduction in both employment *and* output shares in developing countries.
>
> (Rodrik, 2015b: 4)

Importantly, Rodrik's 'decline in the relative price of manufacturing' has to do with the deployment of 'global frontier' production technologies and organizational methods (e.g., 'lean' production), which may happen, especially, as a

[5] Dutch disease refers to the negative impact on manufacturing of high revenues in another sector, such as oil or other natural resources, which raise exchange rates and input prices.

country's industries become engaged in GVCs. On the other hand, Haraguchi, Cheng, and Smeets (2017) find that the share of developing-country-manufacturing value added to global value added has, if anything, increased in the aggregate, but it has decreased on average because it has become concentrated in a smaller number of developing countries, notably including China. This has the apparent effect of prematurely deindustrializing the others. Finally, Felipe et al. (2014) note that manufacturing-*employment* share has declined more than output. This in itself is not surprising if labour productivity climbs rapidly towards the 'global frontier' (Rodrik, 2013). But it matters because, according to the models of Felipe et al., employment share is more strongly linked to economic growth than output share. They further show that today's high-income countries had manufacturing shares of at least 18–20 per cent at some point since the 1970s, and estimate that the ceiling for less developed countries today is about 13–15 per cent. This appears to apply, moreover, even to countries in which manufacturing has become concentrated.

Figure 1.1 shows the rise and decline of manufacturing-employment share with per capita GDP increase between 1950 and 2012 aggregated for forty-two countries, with thirteen high-income countries shown in black, twenty-six middle-income countries shown in dark grey, and the three less developed countries in the dataset in light grey. Each dot represents a country-year. We can easily see that manufacturing's share of employment in high-income countries has been higher than those of lower-income countries, but that this declines with increasing wealth, indicating deindustrialization. The dark-grey dots representing middle-income countries are concentrated in the 10–15 per cent manufacturing-employment-share range, suggesting the truncation of manufacturing employment relative to high-income counties. Only a few of the light-grey country-years exceed 5 per cent manufacturing employment, suggesting a failure to industrialize. Underneath, charts excluding the high- and low-income countries present the same data in decade intervals from 1950 to 2009. At first glance there does not appear to be a large difference between the charts, with most dots again concentrated in the 10–15 per cent manufacturing-employment-share band. However, the *number of countries* with dots above 15 per cent has declined significantly, from thirteen in the 1980s, to just seven in the 2000s. Not coincidentally, middle-income countries with higher manufacturing-employment shares are countries that have been deeply engaged with GVCs as export platforms: China, Costa Rica, South Korea, Mexico, Mauritius, Malaysia, and Thailand.[6]

China is a factor in this reduction, to be sure, and as the current 'workshop of the world', it has a huge manufacturing base, but even its manufacturing share of employment seems to have peaked at roughly 15 per cent. Compare this to the

[6] Only South Korea, Mauritius, and Malaysia have had more than a 20 per cent manufacturing-employment share at some point in the 2000s.

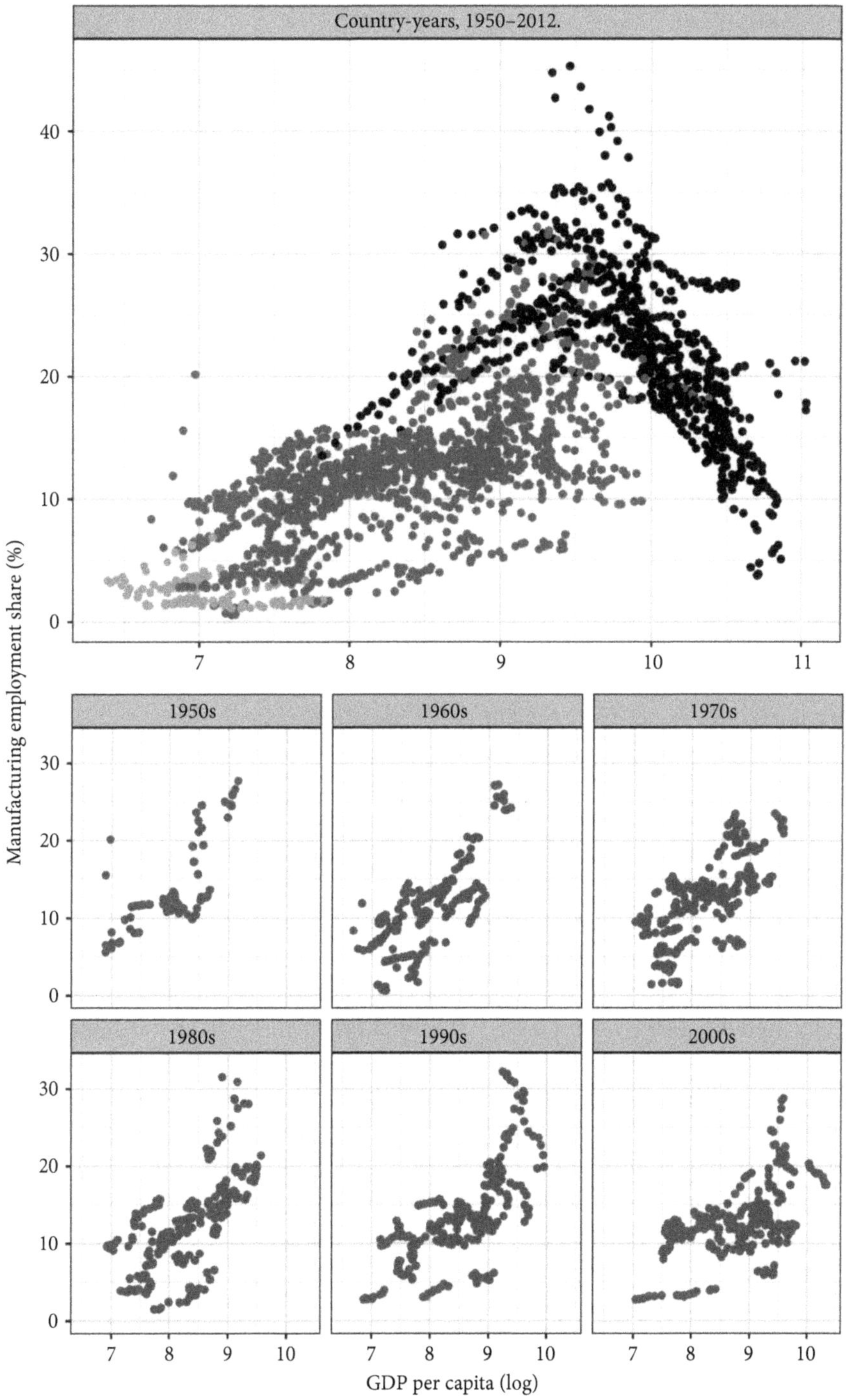

Figure 1.1 Manufacturing employment share with increasing wealth, 1950–2012, in 2011 US$

Sources: Groningen 10-Sector Database (Timmer, de Fries, and de Fries, 2015); Maddison Project Database 2019; World Bank Analytical Classifications (World Bank, 2013), compiled by Kazunori Fujimoto.

original workshop of the world—Britain—which exceeded 40 per cent for well over a century, and to the United States, which reached or exceeded 30 per cent for roughly sixty years. The growing gap between manufacturing output and employment share in China comes in part from production efficiencies in foreign-invested enterprises, and in part from restructuring of state-owned enterprises (SOEs).[7]

Figures 1.1 and 1.2 present a telling contrast from the perspective of compression. Figure 1.2 shows the average growth rates of selected countries across a middle-income zone (here taken as $2000 to $12,000 in 2011 US$), arranged according to the year that zone was entered. The thickness of the line indicates the average GDP growth rate, and the length, the time taken to cross the zone. At a glance, the graph suggests that the more recent the transition across the zone, the higher the growth rate and the shorter the time period, especially for those (mostly east Asian) countries crossing it in the 1960s or later. (Countries abutting the right hand line were still in transition in 2016: India, Vietnam, Indonesia, and the Philippines.)

Figure 1.2, by contrast, presents peak manufacturing-employment bands in the same countries, shown in the same order as Figure 1.1, this time with thickness of the lines showing peak manufacturing-employment shares, and line length, the duration of the peak. Here the line pattern is (mainly) reversed, with thicker and longer lines in earlier developers (nearer the bottom), and thinner, shorter lines in later developers (nearer the top). The pattern is complicated by higher manufacturing employment in several Asian countries, and lower peak employment rates and longer durations for India, Brazil, Mexico, and South Africa. Even with this variation, the chart suggests a changing experience of industrialization over time. Whether it also indicates a 'middle-income trap' for some of these countries is something we will consider in Chapter 6.

These trends may be linked to changes *within* manufacturing. Some studies have found an inverse-U pattern of specialization by income level (Imbs and Wacziarg, 2003). Simply put, with limited manufacturing capabilities, low-income countries measure high on production and export specialization. As they develop and expand their capabilities, countries tend to diversify, but at high-income levels, they respecialize in high-value-adding activities and products. This thesis is contested, however; there is always a diverse base of indigenous manufacturing, even at the outset of modern industrialization (or especially reindustrialization), and there are many factors behind diversification and specialization, some of them contradictory. While Romano and Traù (2017) support the inverse U-pattern

[7] China's manufacturing employment share dipped in the 1990s, then rose again, and levelled off in 2013–2014 at around 13.5 per cent (Hou, Gelb, and Calabrese, 2017, based on National Statistical Yearbook data). The share of *secondary industry*, which includes mining and construction, peaked in 2012 at about 31 per cent of the labour force (8), while the manufacturing share of *urban* employment also appears to have peaked in 2013–2014 at 20 per cent.

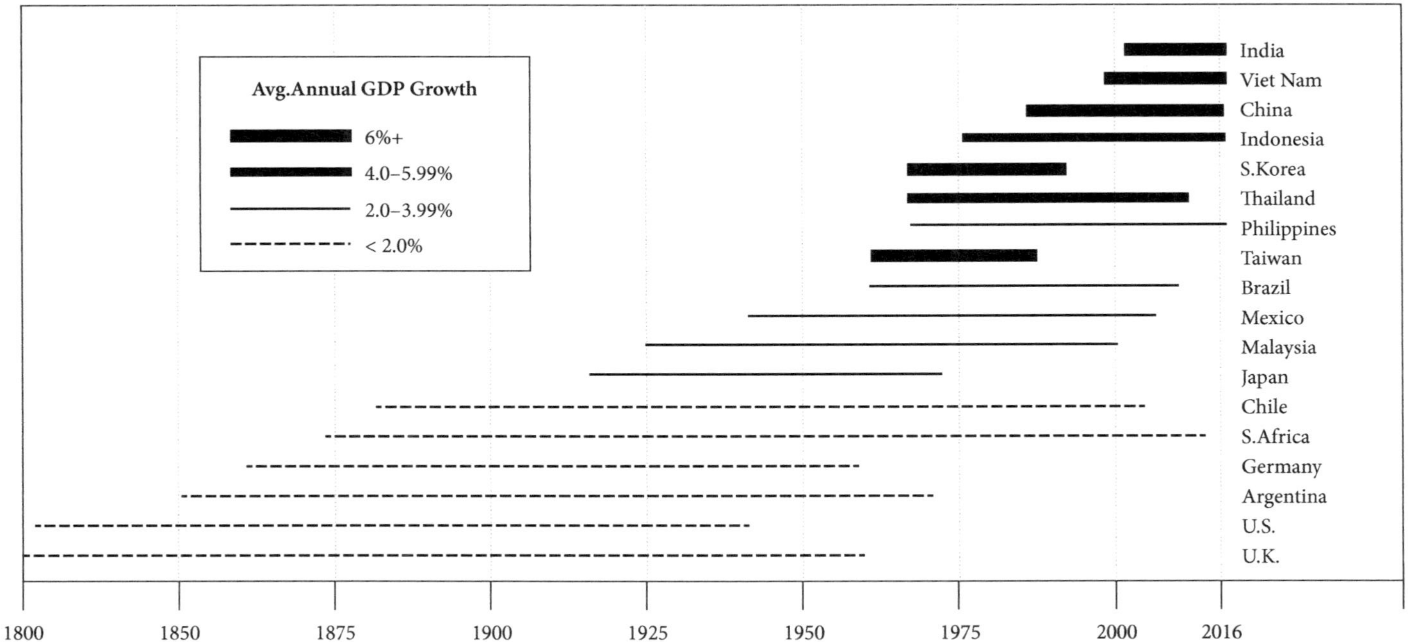

Figure 1.2 Accelerating average GDP growth during 'middle-income' transition

Notes: Lines depict time to transition from per capita GDP $2000 to $12,000 in 2011 US dollars, using cgdppc GDP time series. Countries with lines crossing 2016 have not reached high-income status.

Source: Maddison Project Database 2018.

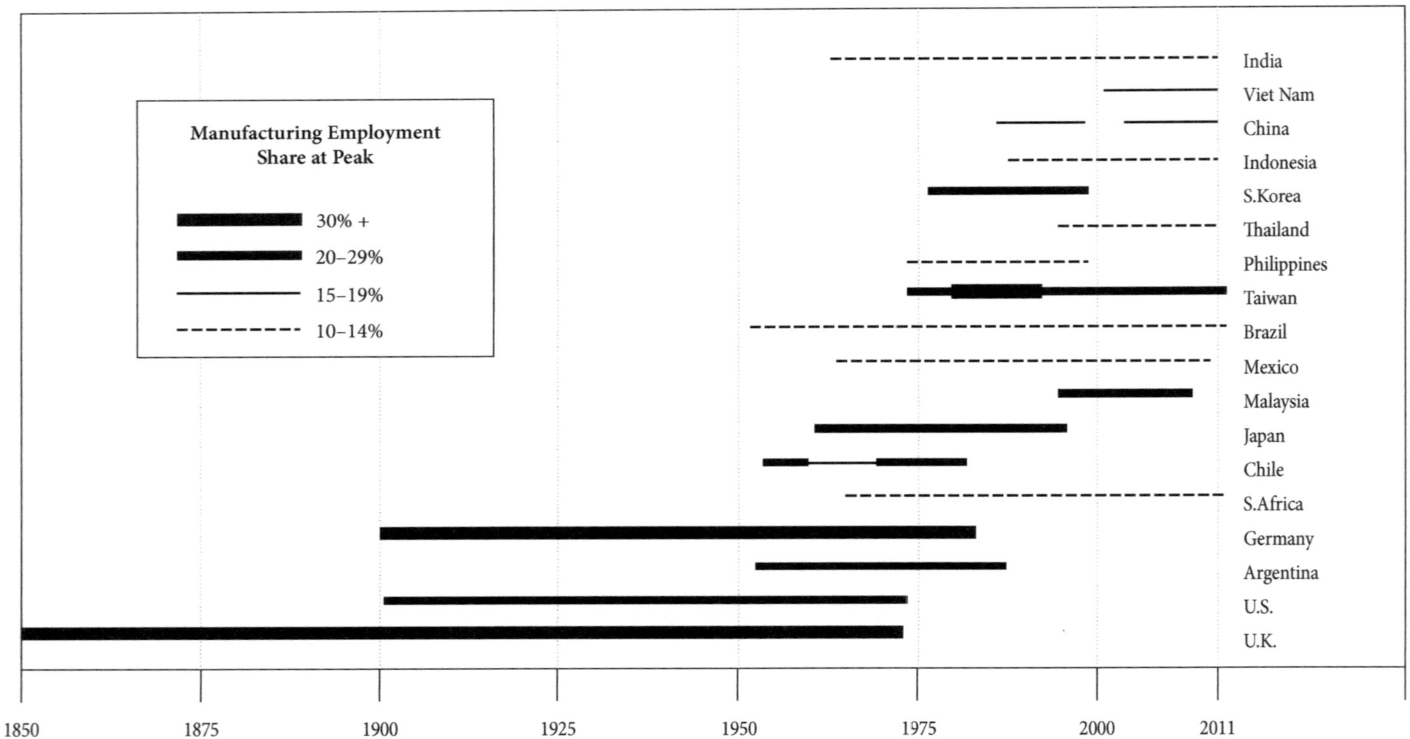

Figure 1.3 Shortening and thinning of peak manufacturing employment

Sources: Groningen 10-Sector Database (Timmer, de Vries, and de Fries, 2015) unless otherwise indicated: UK, pre 1950, Office for National Statistics (2013), 170 years of Industrial Change across England and Wales; post-1950 figures are for Great Britain. The United States pre 1950, Broadberry and Irwin (2005) and Johnston, (2012), both based on Johnston (2001). Germany, pre 1950, rough estimate based on a variety of sources; after 1991, The Conference Board (2013) International Comparisons of Annual Labour Force Statistics. Vietnam, ADB Data Library Viet Nam Key Indicators 2018 (note, the Vietnam figure reached 15 per cent in 2010 and 20 per cent in 2017).

thesis, they find that the transitions are now happening much more quickly. Analysing data from seventy-five countries between 1980 and 2011, they conclude that: 'The intensity and speed of this [specialization-diversification-specialization] change appears to have differed dramatically across countries, depending on to what extent they have become part of the global economy, and *in particular on the timing of the industrialization process*' (Romano and Traù, 2017: 35, emphasis added).

Finally, from a slightly different perspective, changes within manufacturing (indeed, within individual companies, as the quote at the beginning of the chapter suggests), as well as between sectors, suggest 'simultaneous industrialization and deindustrialization' in compressed development, rather than simply 'premature deindustrialization' (Whittaker et al., 2010). Yet even this qualification is inadequate, since countries such as China, South Africa, and Brazil industrialized earlier, and have in fact been *re*industrializing, or trying to, in a new era. Specifically, industrialization in the current era, especially in technology-intensive industries, requires some level of engagement with GVCs, which fragment industries across borders and result in industrialization that is partial in some way. A more adequate term, as we have suggested, and which we will return to, is '*thin industrialization*'.

Thin industrialization poses a number of challenges for policy makers, including whether to work with the processes contributing to thin industrialization by seeking out, or 'upgrading' to, higher-value business functions within GVCs (Humphrey and Schmitz, 2002), or to counter or complement these specializations with traditional industrial policies aimed at achieving 'thick' industrialization. We shall return to this dilemma in Chapter 5.

Stage compression within manufacturing

The idea that a country's manufacturing sector goes also through *qualitative* changes as it develops can be traced back at least to the 1930s. Hoffmann ([1931] 1958) theorized a shift in the relative weights of light consumer goods to heavy producer goods, based on a relative shift from labour to capital abundance. Further 'stages' have since been added based on a perceived shift to innovative or knowledge intensity. Such manufacturing upgrading is seen as central to economic development, reflecting the progressive mastery of technologies, skills, and managerial capabilities, along with capital accumulation. Indeed, it is often proposed normatively. However, this view has become increasingly difficult to sustain, and holding it creates blind spots.

The normative view of progressive upgrading is particularly strong in Japan, reflecting as it does Japan's own experience. The Japanese tradition started with the writings of Akamatsu, also in the 1930s, who proposed an industrial succession model of development using the metaphor of flying geese (Akamatsu, 1961; Kasahara, 2004). According to Akamatsu, products go through phases of import, domestic production (import substitution), and export back to the original and third countries. Over time there is both intraindustry diversification based on similar cycles, and a sectoral progression from consumer goods to capital goods. Manufacturing evolves towards greater sophistication as new products or technologies are mastered, and mature, simpler products are relinquished to later developers trying to catch up in the same way, creating a 'flying geese' formation.

Akamatsu's scheme was updated, and applied to the internationalization of Japanese industry in the 1970s. Kojima (1977) ventured that 'Japanese-type' FDI transferred mature products to following industrializers in a way which would 'harmoniously promote an upgrading of industrial structure on both sides and thus speed up the expansion of trade between the two countries' (14; Ozawa, 1979). The model, in fact, became a pillar of Japan's industry, trade, and development assistance policy in Asia from the mid-1980s.[8] It was also analogous to the 'product cycle' strategy of US multinationals as observed by Vernon, where production of older products was shifted to less-developed markets (1966; 1971).

The problem is that rigid adherence to stage models tends to shut out contrary evidence, which in the flying geese case has steadily accumulated. Ozawa (2008) ventures a five-stage industrial-development model—endowments driven, resource driven, assembly driven, R&D driven, and Internet based—to complement a five-stage model of infrastructure development (UNCTAD, 2008). Insisting that 'history repeats itself', he compares (1970s) Japanese and (recent) Chinese Stage 2 infrastructure development, which focuses on resource diplomacy and acquisition to feed voracious resource-driven growth.[9] Ozawa and UNCTAD both note that multinational corporations (MNCs) can 'time compress the catch-up process', resulting in simultaneous stage development, but only in passing. Ozawa further notes that India 'plunged first into the most advanced stage of growth' (7), but subsequently abandons the insight, and sees India as now 'bolstering heavy and chemical industries [Stage 2], and it will go through similar stage-delineated experiences as it moves up the ladder of economic development' (33).

One of the most thoughtful applications of the model is Suehiro's (2008) study of 'catch-up industrialization' in East Asia, particularly Thailand. Suehiro criticizes Gerschenkron for claiming that late developers can jump directly into leading sectors without having first built up the resources and capabilities. This is a common and valid criticism.[10] But Suehiro also recognizes 'compressed industrialization' and

[8] In the process, the logic for the geese-formation changed from 'bottom-up' catch-up to 'top-down' hand-me-down progression: Kasahara, 2004. See also Bernard and Ravenhill (1995) for a critique of the flying geese model.

[9] Among other things, this disregards China's prior history of industrialization.

[10] In Chapter 2 we introduce a more nuanced view of Ricardian exporting and Kaldorian industrialization of late developers, following Schwartz (2010). Soviet model late developers sought to truncate

indeed the possibility of stage skipping. And he rightly points out the role of local entrepreneurship in bringing this about, citing as an example Thailand's CP Group's rapid growth to become Asia's biggest agribusiness.

In fact, 'out-of-sequence' development has provoked indignation in China. Referring to Hoffman's scheme, Cai (2006) is highly critical of the 'self-glorifying obsession' of local governments in promoting capital-intensive industry whilst ignoring the fact that China is (or was) still in the stage in which labour is more abundant. The result of doing things out of order, he argues, is that far fewer jobs will be created, and there will be wealth polarization (i.e. thin industrialization). Indeed, taking Ozawa's five stages, there is ample evidence that China has been engaging in all of them simultaneously. At a time when a third of the population is still engaged in agriculture, the country spends over 2 per cent of its GDP on R&D, and rising.[11]

Cai may be right in asserting that fewer jobs will be created if stages are compressed into simultaneity than if stages are assiduously followed, but we venture that a rigid adherence to stages of industrialization and industrial succession is no longer possible because production systems in the current era have changed to such an extent as to preclude it. Manufacturing has become more footloose and extremely sensitive to rising wage costs, and production technology has become increasingly capital intensive. Yesterday's methods are rapidly superseded, at least in the formal economy, and in a globalized world, consumers are not satisfied with yesterday's models; they want to consume at the cutting edge. Foreign investment, for both export and domestic markets, is for mainly for current products and therefore requires current production technologies (Chapter 3). As a result, stagist upgrading strategies which may have worked in the past are increasingly elusive. If they *were* attainable, the dangers of developing countries becoming trapped into low-value-adding segments of global industries would probably be even greater than they already are.

There are risks for geese in breaking formation, but the risks in trying to stay in a formation appear greater. At a corporate level, there are increasing numbers of renegade geese—'emerging market multinationals' (Ramamurti, 2012) or 'dragon multinationals' (Mathews, 2002)—which grow as they internationalize and internationalize to grow, using their 'arrival as latecomers' on the global stage to capture advantages associated with being late, such as possibilities for linking to and leveraging the global knowledge, markets, and supply chains (Goldstein et al., 2006: 6).

this further, forcibly diverting resources from agriculture into heavy industrialization, while restricting the manufacture of consumer goods.

[11] Cf. http://www.xinhuanet.com/english/2019-09/07/c_138373248.htm

The service sector and 'out-of-sequence' sectoral shifts

> The transition from an agricultural to an industrial economy, which began in England and has been repeated in most of the Western world, has been characterized as a 'revolution'. The shift from industrial to service employment, which has advanced furthest in the United States but is evident in all developed economies, has proceeded more quietly, but it too has implications for society, and for economic analysis, of 'revolutionary' proportions.
>
> (Fuchs 1968: 2, cited in Schettkat and Yocarini, 2003: 3)

There have been many systems of classifying activities which cannot be called primary or secondary (Mazzucato, 2018). From the 1930s Fisher (1935), Clark (1940), Fourastié (1949), and others began to theorize about the 'tertiary' sector, with evolutionary schema based on growing sophistication of demand, hierarchies of needs, productivity differences, and technological progress. The theories do not concern us here, nor do further extensions into quaternary and quinary sectors, but in this section, we would like to broaden our scope to consider nonmanufacturing sectors and business functions, focusing on two phenomena that exhibit both the compression and era-related characteristics of compressed development. The first is 'out-of-sequence' sectoral shifts, specifically the implications of a 'retail revolution' occurring at the same time as industrialization rather than after it, and our initial consideration of how finance, or 'financialization', is changing the character of development. The second is sectoral blurring. Both the service sector and agriculture increasingly exhibit characteristics formerly attributed to manufacturing, and this has implications for how we conceive of economic development.

'Out-of-sequence' sectoral shifts

Supermarkets have spread rapidly in developing countries in the past two decades:

> Supermarkets spread quickly in the 1990s in Latin America and Central Europe and the first-wave countries of East Asia – much faster than the slow march of modern retail diffusion in the United States and Western Europe since the 1920s/1930s – but not close to how quickly modern retail has spread in Asia, especially in the third wave countries, in the 2000s. (Reardon, 2011: 18)

Their spread from large to small cities, upper- to middle- to poorer-class customers, processed to semi-processed to fresh and ready-to-eat goods, and indirect to direct sourcing, has accelerated, driven by both foreign direct investment and, increasingly, domestic capital. Governments have actively promoted the spread of supermarkets as agents of modernization. Nowhere has this been more evident than in China, where the number of supermarkets rose from 'initiation in a few metropolitan regions in 1990 to a $55 billion industry today – with 53,000 units in 2002 and 30% of the urban food retail market' (Hu et al., 2004: 557).[12]

The impact of supermarkets can be seen not just on consumption and retail, but in input sectors, as well, including agriculture and food processing, where modern procurement systems, bulk purchasing, and ICT-enabled supply chain–management practices have driven consolidation. A '"symbiosis" is emerging between medium/large food processing firms and supermarket chains, which seems to lead to "mutually reinforcing dual consolidation"', while 'land consolidation and rental market development seem to be underway... and are leading to a differentiated farm sector' (Reardon, 2011: 22–3). The retail revolution, in other words, is not only happening with extreme rapidity, but is having knock-on effects on other sectors through intersectoral linkages.

The retail revolution is also driving changes in manufacturing. In (late developer) Japan, large-scale retailers were *not* seen as agents of modernization and economic development—that was the role of manufacturing. Indeed, Japan's Large-Scale Retail Stores Law, condemned by US trade negotiators as a barrier to imports in the late 1980s and early 1990s, inhibited their spread. When they did eventually spread, however, they had a considerable impact on the profit levels of manufacturers. The tension (it would be difficult to describe it as symbiosis) was particularly marked in the case of electronics superstores. The early adoption of retail sector promotion, deregulation, and rationalization in developing countries thus may constitute a third 'whammy' for manufacturing in developing countries, in addition to Rodrik's double whammy of increased manufacturing imports and relative price decline, cited above.[13] It is likely to be a contributing factor to thin industrialization, and to add to dualism and informality.

If an 'out-of-sequence' retail revolution is affecting manufacturing by driving down prices and profits, it may also apply to other service sector activities as well. Financial services are an obvious example. Finance is not just another service activity, and the relationship between finance and industry is complex; here we will briefly consider finance and financialization in developing countries. That finance is crucial for development goes without saying. To accelerate economic development, international development finance was promoted in the postwar period. Reforms aimed at 'financial deepening', sometimes imposed through loan conditions by international financing institutions, were also subsequently justified on this basis. However, a growing number of studies have pointed to a 'vanishing

[12] China's Tenth Five Year Plan envisaged a fivefold expansion in the number of chain stores between 2000 and 2005. Director-general of the Department of Trade and Market Huang Hai said they must 'sharpen their competitive edge via re-organizations, acquisitions and mergers as soon as possible' (*China Daily*, 9 February 2002; also 19 November 2002).

[13] In fact, there is a fourth 'whammy', namely the lack of spillovers from FDI and export assembly.

effect' of financial deepening (Rousseau and Wachtel, 2011), or an inverted-U relationship between financial depth and economic growth (Arcand, Berkes, and Panizza, 2012) and stability of output growth (Easterly, Islam, and Stiglitz, 2000). Sahay et al. (2015), too, found a negative impact of financial deepening on total factor productivity growth beyond a certain point.[14]

It is a short step from financial 'deepening' to 'financialization'. Epstein (2005: 3) defines 'financialization' as 'the increasing role of financial motives, financial markets, financial actors and financial institutions in the operation of domestic and international economies', while Krippner (2005: 12) sees it as 'a pattern of accumulation in which profits accrue primarily through financial channels rather than through trade and commodity production'. Lapavitsas (2011) proposes three interrelated developments: large corporations acquiring their own financial capacities and orientations; banks shifting from traditional business lending to mediation in open financial markets, as well as transacting with households; and households becoming increasingly involved in financial markets through mortgage, investment account, and pension choices. He sees 'accelerated financialization' occurring in middle-income developing countries. In an increasingly liberalized global environment the process is accelerated by the entry of already financialized global banks and multinational corporations (MNCs), while the institutions supporting financialization become readily available to local businesses at a relatively early stage of development (Lapavitsas, 2009).

In his analysis of Argentina, Mexico, and Turkey, Demir (2007) makes a direct link between financialization and deindustrialization, arguing that it leads to savings being channelled 'to speculative short term investments instead of long-term investment projects and hence altering the pattern of capital accumulation in the real sectors of the economy' (351, 353).[15] In fact, the link between financialization and (de)industrialization is more complex than this suggests, as financialization is also a driver of (developed country) outsourcing and offshoring, which has *boosted* manufacturing in *some* countries, albeit in ways that create thin industrialization. We will return to this when we fully add 'era' effects to our picture of compressed development in Chapters 2 and 3.

Financialization can be measured in different ways. Figure 1.4 provides an indirect and perhaps simplistic indicator, showing the ratio of FIRE (finance, insurance, and real estate) plus business services to manufacturing value added in the same countries as Figures 1.2 and 1.3 (minus Germany and Vietnam, for which comparable data were unavailable) in 1980 and in 2010.[16] All countries

[14] The peak appears to be reached when private sector credit reaches 100 per cent of GDP.

[15] On financialization and deindustrialization in Latin America, see also Cibils and Allami (2013) and Levy-Orlik (2014).

[16] Unfortunately it is not possible to separate business services from FIRE employment, limiting the usefulness of the data for our discussion.

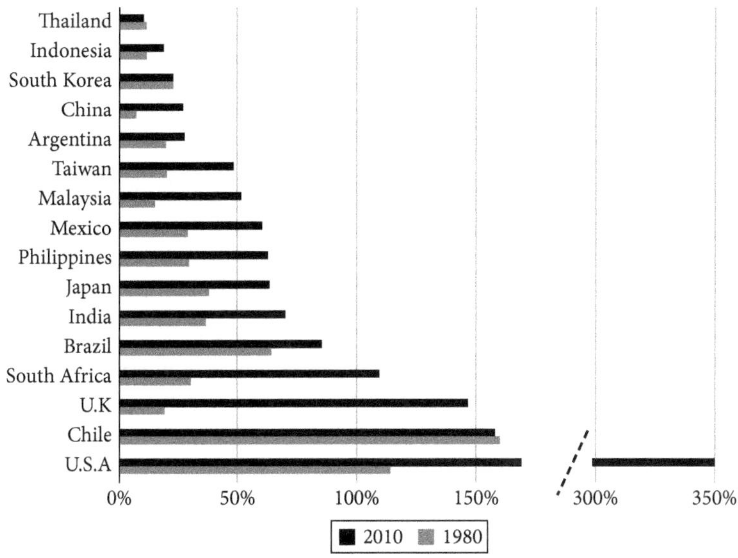

Figure 1.4 Ratio of FIRE + business services to manufacturing value added in selected countries, 1980 and 2010

Note: Finance = ISIC rev.3.1 codes J, K (finance, insurance, real estate, and business services); Manufacturing = ISIC rev.3.1 code D.

Source: Groningen 10-Sector Database (<https://www.rug.nl/ggdc/productivity/10-sector/>, accessed 14 October 2018; Timmer, de Vries, and de Vries, 2015).

except Thailand, South Korea and Chile experienced a shift in the ratio towards FIRE+BS–value added. The shift was most pronounced, however, in developed countries, and developing countries outside Asia. It was less pronounced in the Asian countries, and grew from a lower base. Financialization has been extreme in the UK, and especially the United States, and this has had an impact on developing countries through the globalization of big banks and also the involvement of international organizations such as the International Monetary Fund, through FDI, and through other means.[17] We will consider various aspects of financialization in more detail in Chapters 2 and 3.

[17] The UK FIRE+BS figure for 1980 may be anomalous. The US FIRE+BS figure for 2010 may also be anomalous, but even if the 2009 figure is used, the ratio is still around 300 per cent. US Bureau of Economic Analysis (BEA) data for the same year give a ratio of 256 per cent, up from 178 per cent in 1997 and rising to 285 per cent in 2017, with FIRE constituting nearly two-thirds of the combined category. Housing is the largest subcategory of FIRE; health care and computer services are the largest subcategories of Professional and Business Services. While accounting for only a small portion of US GDP, the category of 'funds, trusts, and other financial vehicles' had the fastest average annual growth from 1997 to 2017 (11 per cent). See: <https://apps.bea.gov/iTable/index_industry_gdpIndy.cfm>, accessed 26 October 2018.

Sectoral blurring and persisting (or resurgent) dualism

The rapid growth of services and the sector's rapidly evolving activity mix has generated a debate about whether Kaldorian dynamics are limited to manufacturing, or whether they can now be found in services (and potentially in technology-intensive agriculture as well). For Kaldor, an important reason for placing policy emphasis on manufacturing was from the disproportionate contribution it makes to a country's balance of payments through exports. Services, until recently, were considered to be 'untradable' (Sturgeon et al., 2006). However, Dasgupta and Singh (2005) suggest that this distinction may be becoming less important, as routine services became segmented and formalized in ICT–enabled GVCs after 2000.[18] The UN Statistics Division (2016: 13) explains these changes in this way:

> Almost all of the defining features of services, namely that they are non-tradable, non-storable, customized, delivered in-person, and insensitive to price competition, are changing in ways that enable and motivate international trade. Task fragmentation, codification, monitoring, and trade in services are burgeoning, both domestically and internationally. Services have become the focus of intense international competition and dynamic innovation, and are thus of growing interest to policy-makers.

Also citing these changes, Kharas and Kohli (2011: 285) contend that 'services have become a powerful engine of growth in many middle-income countries. In fact, service exports have become the fastest growing export sector globally and for many developing countries. Service productivity growth is outstripping industrial productivity growth in most developing and advanced economies.'

Szirmai (2009), amongst others, acknowledges that the *relative* capital intensity of manufacturing has declined over time—hence its advantage for capital accumulation—and that scale economies have become important in services industries which are ICT-based, but he still argues for the continued importance of manufacturing in economic development.[19] Others are more forthright; the Asia Development Bank (2013) argues that attempting to jump straight from agriculture into services leads directly to a middle-income trap.

Exportability, capital intensity and technological innovation can be found not just in manufacturing and services, but in agriculture as well. ICT, big data, and

[18] By comparing the Indian Government Ministry of Electronics and Information Technology's 2017 figures on IT–enabled services (ITES) exports (consisting of IT services, software, and business process outsourcing) to figures on India's total exports from the World Bank in the same year, the share of ITES in total exports can be calculated to be 26 per cent. Since most export growth has been in higher-value IT services, the share of software in total exports was only 6 per cent. The annual growth rate for ITES exports overall was nearly 11 per cent.

[19] Also Szirmai and Verspagen (2015); Haraguchi, Cheng, and Smeets (2017).

advanced robotics applications to 'precision agriculture', for example, are spreading rapidly. In fact, manufacturing, agriculture, and resource extraction are becoming increasingly deverticalized and permeated by services, blurring sectoral boundaries, even as consolidation takes place in specific business functions (see Lima-de-Oliveria and Sturgeon, 2017 for an example from the oil and gas industry). On the other hand, while all sectors now have 'modern', capital- and technology- intensive elements, they also have a large—and often growing—informal part. Largely jobless productivity growth drives the former, while the latter informal part, which dual-sector models predicted would disappear, has not simply persisted, but has expanded.

India provides an example. Dasgupta and Singh (2006) calculate that manufacturing-*employment* growth in India in the 1980s was around 1.23 per cent per annum. It then increased following the country's economic reforms in 1991 to 2.58 per cent, but this growth occurred almost entirely in the informal sector. Without employment growth, *formal* manufacturing-sector output nonetheless grew at over 7 per cent annually in the early 2000s, based on high rates of productivity growth. On the other hand, the informal sector was divided, with a large subsistence segment, and a more dynamic segment which 'does the important job of maintaining and increasing employment while increasing production' (14), albeit with low productivity growth. By Dasgupta and Singh's calculation, the informal sector accounted for 83 per cent of total employment in India's manufacturing.

This dualism is no coincidence. D'Costa (2014) sees 'compressed capitalism' in India and China as based on three integrated parts, which together create a very different model of accumulation than in earlier developers. The first is 'primitive accumulation', or dispossession of peasant land by the state; the second is a capital-intensive sector of rapidly increasing sophistication; and the third is petty commodity production. 'The state socializes costs for private accumulation, contributing to their maturity and competitiveness, while primitive accumulation and petty commodity producers keep labour costs low, which also reinforce capital accumulation' (D'Costa, 2011: 2). This 'low road' to capital accumulation, he ventures, may be part of a 'perverse convergence' whereby 'compressed capitalism's upward shift might intersect with the downward slide of the west's mature capitalism' (D'Costa, 2011: 2). Whether or not one agrees with this prognosis, it usefully points to different dynamics in these two giants relative to earlier developers, which are still relatively undertheorized.

Lewis turning point

Blurring of sectoral boundaries and persisting dualism predictably blur the LTP, at which 'surplus' subsistence-sector labour has been absorbed by the modern capitalist sector and wages start to meaningfully rise. Is there still an LTP? This has been the subject of considerable debate in China (e.g. Huang and Cai eds., 2014). Minami and Ma (2014) argue that while Japan clearly reached this point around 1960; Taiwan at the end of the 1960s; and South Korea in the early 1970s, mainland China was still under the threshold in the late 2000s. Urban unemployment had if anything increased—because of SOE restructuring—and, they estimated, there was still a large gap between agricultural and urban manufacturing wages (Minami and Ma, 2014). Knight, Deng, and Li (2010) reached similar conclusions.

Pointing to rising wages in both urban and rural China, on the other hand, Cai (2014a) argued that China reached the LTP around 2004. Wang (2014) also pointed to rising labour costs in agriculture since 2004. This is probably the majority view, but it would date the turning point very close to the onset of an overall *decline* in manufacturing employment. Significantly, Cai stresses not the expansion of the manufacturing sector as the primary cause of the LTP, but the fact that China has undergone an accelerated demographic transition.[20] We will look at this transition in the next section, but note here that the liveliness of the argument, and widely divergent conclusions, may signal the declining ability of such models to shed light on contemporary sectoral dynamics in developing and transition economies.

Demographics and social compression

Industrialization, economic development, and demographics have historically had a close and evolving relationship. In traditional or preindustrial societies, both birth rates and mortality rates tended to be high, with rates of population growth constrained by limited agricultural output. Through industrialization and increasing productivity in agriculture this constraint was attenuated. Mortality dropped. Eventually fertility rates fell, as well, until both birth and death rates were low.

'Demographic transition' theory, pioneered by Thompson (1929), envisaged a series of predictable demographic stages. In the first stage both mortality and fertility rates are high, but in the second stage (early transition, depending on the model), mortality rates fall as a result of improved nutrition, health, and sanitation, while fertility rates remain relatively unchanged. This creates a high proportion of children, where the effects of declining mortality rates are concentrated. However, in the next stage, the birth rate also falls—explanations

[20] Banister and Cook (2011), too, emphasize changing demographics in the rise of labour costs in China, as well as increases in human capital from rising education levels, rising productivity, and increased bargaining power of employees as a result of the 2008 Labour Contract Law. They note the unwillingness of many migrant workers laid off in the wake of the Global Financial Crisis to subsequently return from the countryside, and the rising reserve wage of new workers unwilling to tolerate harsh conditions and low wages.

include education of women, declining economic importance of children, rising education costs, urban lifestyles, etc.—and the previously dependent-child bulge moves into the working population age group. Combined with a relatively low proportion of elderly, this creates a 'demographic dividend' in which youthful workers vitalize industrial expansion. Savings rates rise, consumption rises, and the economy expands. Finally, a new equilibrium is created on the basis of low mortality and fertility.

Or not. From the 1960s a 'second demographic transition' appears to have gained momentum, associated with rising education and changing life-course aspirations of women in particular, and resulting in a further decline in fertility rates.[21] At the other end of the age spectrum, mortality rates of the elderly decline, and as the population bulge eventually exits working age, demographic ageing occurs. Without immigration, populations may even shrink.[22]

Accelerated demographic transition in East Asia

Demographic transition theory was based on the experiences of earlier developers. It has followed a different, accelerated path in some later developers, notably in East Asia, where economic growth has been particularly rapid and compressed.

As early as 1959, Dore noted that Japan appeared to be following the demographic experience of earlier industrializers, but in an accelerated fashion. The wartime pressure on women by the state to have more children gave way, in the early postwar years, to fears of mass starvation, and hence exhortations to limit childbirth. Companies made it clear to employees that their pay packets would go further with fewer children, and women's magazines avidly discussed birth control. Abortion controls were relaxed. The birth rate decreased, but Dore (1959: 111) asked: 'How can Japan find employment in the next decade for the vast increases in the labour force which the fertility rate of the recent past has already made certain?' The danger, he suggested, was not one of total unemployment, such as in England of the 1930s, but an exacerbation of the dichotomy between the modern, rationalized industrial sector and the traditional, small-scale sector, with

[21] In fact, fertility rates in a limited number of countries have rebounded, possibly because of the 'second half' of the gender revolution (Goldscheider, Bernhardt, and Lappegård, 2015), of men becoming more fully involved in family and home work, creating a 'household division of labour that is equitable' and in some cases egalitarian (Esping-Andersen and Billari, 2015: 25), whilst dependent on a supportive institutional environment.

[22] 'Epidemiologic transition' stage theories compliment this demographic picture, with an early, Malthusian stage giving way to a population- and life expectancy–increase stage as infectious diseases are brought under control, and finally a rise in noncommunicable diseases as the population ages. Siegel and Stuckler (2011: 54) critique these theories, showing that the risk factors for both types of disease are in fact interconnected.

its underemployment and badly paid labour force. It was the latter which would presumably have to absorb much of the increase.

History shows that Japan was on the cusp of its LTP and 'economic miracle' in 1959. The youth who left rural Japan by the trainload to seek employment in the factories of the urban industrial belts became the 'golden eggs' who supplied the labour for the country's unprecedented expansion in output. Japan was not the only beneficiary of a demographic dividend. It was followed by South Korea, Taiwan, and other emerging Asian economies.[23]

History also shows that Japan's accelerated transition was only the beginning of a trend, in which the demographic dividend window has often become much narrower. This brings us back to Cai and the LTP. China's demographic dividend is drying up, as the working-age population peaked around 2015. As in Japan, government policy has been a factor. However, Cai (2014b) notes that the fastest decline in the total fertility rate happened *before* strict implementation of the one-child policy. And although he believes China has reached the LTP, perversely, this may result in 'ageing before affluence'. In other words, labour shortages signal a shrinking workforce as much as a strong economy, and economic growth will soon be challenged by a rising (elderly) dependency ratio and associated tax burden and welfare costs.

'A transition in age structure that took the rich countries of the West more than a century is being played out in Asia over just a few decades' (Asian Development Bank, 2011: xvi). It is most noticeable in East Asia, in both developed and newly industrializing economies. Indeed, 'many developing countries in the region face the prospect of *ageing at low levels of income*', as Menon and Mendelez-Nakamura (2009:4, emphasis added) put it; they 'risk going over the hill before getting to the top'.[24] Echoing our earlier discussion of premature deindustrialization, Menon and Mendelez-Nakamura estimate that, in 1970, East Asian countries reached an old-age-dependency ratio (ratio of the 65+-year-old population to the 15–64-year-old population) of .15 at a per capita gross national product (GNP) level of $26,000 (high-income status), but by 2025, the level is expected to fall to just $3,800 (lower middle-income status)!

Far from reaping a 'demographic dividend' of young people to power industrialization, such countries thus face the prospect of accelerated demographic ageing without accumulating sufficient resources to construct sturdy public health and welfare systems for the elderly. Put alongside the more circumscribed contribution of manufacturing employment, it is a sobering prospect, and one not easily amenable to reversal by policy means.

Ochiai (2014) notes that a plateau between the first and second demographic transitions lasted about fifty years in Europe, and two decades in Japan, while

[23] Bloom et al. (2000) claim that demographic dividends accounted for up to a third of Asia's economic growth 'miracle' between 1965 and 1990.

[24] Or 'growing old before growing rich': World Bank (2015a: 2).

elsewhere in Asia, it went straight from the first into the second, with 'ultra-low' fertility rates below replacement level. She attributes this to 'compressed modernity'.

Social compression

Compression in the social sphere has been the theme of a group of Korean scholars led by K-S. Chang. According to Chang (1999, 2010a, 2010b), the breakneck speed of the South Korea's development(alism) created many vulnerabilities and pronounced social tensions. A series of building collapses, including a bridge over the Han River, underlined the vulnerabilities of what he calls South Korea's 'compressed modernity': 'There seems to be a sober awakening about their own miracle of achieving over a mere few decades what took Westerners two or three centuries. Such compressed modernity now turns out to be full of unexpected costs and risks that threaten the sheer sustainability, not to mention further development, of the current economic and social conditions' Chang (1999: 31). This passage was written in the wake of the Asian Financial Crisis in which, Chang argues, South Korean bureaucrats and corporate elites embraced neoliberalism to reassert control over challenges emerging 'from below' by workers and social groups.

Chang and Song (2010: 539) further note that families, and women, in particular, were expected to absorb many of the stresses of compressed modernity such that they became 'functionally overloaded and socially risk-ridden'. Rather than open revolt, women used their rising personal freedom to 'sabotage' social reproduction and embark on 'defamiliation' by controlling the scope and duration of family life. Ochiai (2011, 2014) contrasts this with Japan's 'semi-compressed modernity'. Although neither creates a sustainable social system, in Japan there was more time for the government to buttress the family and, indeed, to consolidate it as the cornerstone of the welfare system, while under full-blown compressed modernity, the market has been more influential:

> In its 'semi-compressed modernity' Japan managed to build a structure resembling the first modernity in Western countries, including a welfare state and a modern family, and solidified them in the familialist reforms of the 1980s. On the other hand, other East Asian societies joined the tide of globalization before constructing a welfare state and a modern family in their much more 'compressed modernity'. (Ochiai, 2014: 223)

'Compressed modernity' is sometimes compared to 'second modernity'.[25] Han and Shim (2010) argue that, in addition to the 'Western' focus on global risks as an

[25] Classical sociologists saw social changes accompanying industrialization as a unidirectional shift from 'traditional/community' (*Gemeinschaft*) relations to 'modern/individualized' (*Gesellschaft*)

unintended consequence of radicalizing modernity, compressed modernity entails a different category of risk brought about by 'deficiencies' as a result of the speed of modernization. They also cite Chinese sociologists' references to a 'triple mode' of risks—traditional, modern, and postmodern—'merging into a very complex constellation'.[26]

This constellation might include the combination of modern technology and traditional social attitudes, such as using ultrasound to act on preferences for male babies, resulting in 'missing girls'. The ratio of male-to-female births in China underwent a profound skew, from 108.5/100 in 1990 to 117/100 in 2000, as ultrasound technology moved from coastal to inland provinces.[27] Negative long-term effects include increased violence, trafficking and commercial sex, and a shortage of potential marriage partners for men (OWHORC/EDDC, 2006; Qui, Zhang, and Liu, 2019). The fact that a significant portion of China's population still lives in rural villages and engages in agriculture buoys the trend, but it is evident in cities, as well, and is related to traditional patterns of caring for the elderly (sons and their wives), which persist where state provision is weak. This imbalance is said to have fuelled property bubbles, as men have to prove their wealth credentials to increasingly choosy brides.[28]

The tone of compressed modernity analysis is quite pessimistic, in sharp contrast to the optimism of Rosling (2018), referred to in the introduction of this book. Although we deal with different aspects of social development and social policy, especially in Chapter 7, these too are sobering. There can be little doubt that many of the tensions accompanying compressed development are pushed into, and even magnified in, the social sphere.

Concluding comments

In this chapter we have taken an initial look at time compression through an extended exposition and critique of stage-based concepts. As our focus becomes more contemporary, the increasing simultaneity in processes which unfolded over extended periods of time in the past is highlighted. This changes the opportunities

relations. More recently, Beck and Beck-Gernsheim (2001) have proposed 'institutional individualization' as a key aspect of 'second modernity' (or reflexive modernity) from the 1980s.

[26] Zhang (2006); and Xue and Liu (2005). Separately, Chu et al. (2012) depict 'techno-social tension under compressed modernity' from overlapping industrialization and 'cyberization'.

[27] Hershatter (2007). The figures may be exaggerated to some extent by the nonregistration of some girls until they go to high school or get married, when registration is required, but even allowing for this, the gap is pronounced. The phenomenon is also widely reported in India.

[28] A study by Wei, Liu, and Zhang found that 'the ratios of home price to income and home price to rent are higher in areas where the sex ratios are more skewed. Strikingly, the sex-ratio imbalance explained between a third and a half of the increase in housing prices in 25 major cities from 2003 to 2009': *Nikkei Asian Review*, 17–23 April 2017, 17.

and challenges for recent developers in important ways, perhaps most notably in that industrialization has become 'thin'. Limited broadening of the industrial base, and specialization in 'thin' industrial segments with GVC engagement, is a part of the story that we will return to in detail in Chapters 3, 5, and 9. As a broad generalization, within those thin segments, from a relatively early stage of their industrialization, multinationals and local businesses have imported advanced labour-substituting technologies, which both limit wage growth and increase returns to the owners of those technologies. This is a factor in persistent, if not rising, inequality, contrary to the inverse-U curve proposed by Kuznets (1955) of rising inequality in early stages of industrialization followed by a decline (see Chapter 6).

In closing this chapter, we propose that the durability of some of the stage-based conceptual schemes may account for the scant attention compression has received, but also limited the usefulness of such schemes for understanding contemporary development challenges. For example, many contemporary developing and transition countries already have an industrial base of sorts, and hence are not industrializing *ab initio*. (We will consider some significant examples in Chapter 5.) The ambiguities of China's LTP are perhaps symptomatic of this. Finally, this initial sketch has not set out the drivers of compression, nor has it set out a conceptual framework in which to situate compression and compressed development. This requires a broader temporal and spatial perspective, which we provide in Chapters 2 and 3.

2

Eras

States and Markets

Introduction

The second key feature of compressed development, after time (and space) compression, is 'era' influences. These derive from the contemporary features of economic and geopolitical systems, which we explore in this chapter, as well as technology and organizations, which we take up in Chapter 3. We examine economic and geopolitical systems primarily through the co-evolving relationship between states and markets, which constitute the first of our two conceptual dyadic pairs, shown in Figure 2.1, which is similar to Figure 0.2 but with more detail. Recall that the arrows moving in opposite directions indicate that state developments feed into markets, and vice versa, indicating a co-evolutionary dynamic. The extra detail is an adaptation of Karl Polanyi's 'double movement' of 'disembedding' and 're-embedding' of markets, with corresponding liberalizing and regulating developments in states. In *The Great Transformation* (1944), Polanyi depicts the attempts of liberal reformers—through the state—to create a 'market society' by (more or less) 'disembedding' markets from social norms and legal and institutional constraints. The destabilizing process provokes a counter-reaction and attempts to re-embed the economy through legal and policy measures.[1]

There are limitations to this dyadic representation. It is not intended to depict a cyclical view of history. It does not show the role of wars in influencing the development of both states and markets. And critically, it depicts the national level and does not show the influence of the geopolitical systems created and projected by dominant powers—primarily Britain in the nineteenth century and the United States for much of the twentieth.[2] These systems changed over time, as each dominant power first consolidated its productive advantage, and then tried to extend (or maintain) it through an international trading and finance order backed by military power. In fact, the dynamics in the dyad are most fully

[1] As noted in the introduction, in adopting the terminology of disembedding and re-embedding, we recognize that markets are always institutionally and ideologically embedded (also Block, 2003; Fligstein, 2002). Similarly, liberalization takes place through regulation, not its absence (Vogel, 2018).

[2] Nor does it depict subnational levels, which have distinctive state–market dynamics; Chapter 8.

Compressed Development: Time and Timing in Economic and Social Development. D. Hugh Whittaker, Timothy J. Sturgeon, Toshie Okita, and Tianbiao Zhu, Oxford University Press (2020). © D. Hugh Whittaker, Timothy J. Sturgeon, Toshie Okita, and Tianbiao Zhu. DOI: 10.1093/oso/9780198744948.001.0001

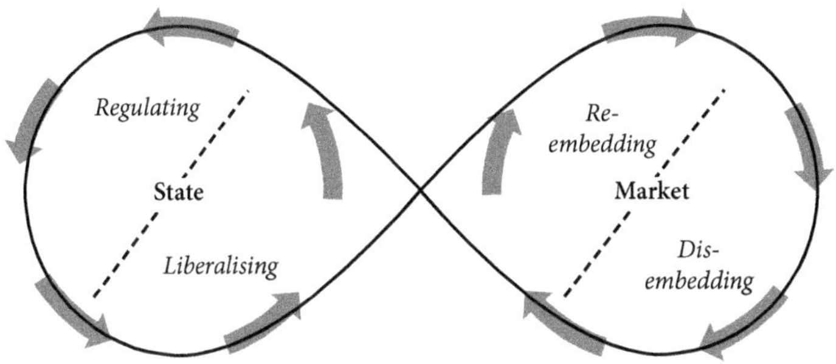

Figure 2.1 State–market co-evolution and Polanyian double movements

represented in the dominant power itself, and there may be substantial variations in countries caught up in its machinations.

'Markets' are influenced by states through macroeconomic, competition, trade, industrial, innovation, social, and other policies. The label 'markets' needs to be unpacked, however. In this chapter we pay particular attention to finance, which is a key—often considered *the* key—facilitator of development. However, finance can also be a destabilizer, as well as a political tool of the powerful. We insert this understanding into our historical discussion by looking at how the role of finance in economic systems has changed over time. In brief, not only did postwar 'embedded liberalism' give way to neoliberalism and marketization after the 1980s, but to financialization as well, with important consequences for developing countries.

Figure 2.1 is complemented by Table 2.1, summarizing how the dyadic pair evolves over time, highlighting the role of the dominant power, and providing a rough periodization. The periodization will be familiar to political and developmental economists, especially those acquainted with 'late-development' writing, and it is the basis of organization of the first section of this chapter. Some caveats are necessary, however. The labels in the individual cells are only indicative; elements of state mercantilism, for example, persisted beyond the era of early development; state 'planning' preceded the 1930s; and so on. The era dates are approximate, and they indicate a confluence of many of the row variables, with transition periods in between. The years between the 1920s and 1945, for example, were neither liberal nor representative of the 'embedded liberalism' postwar settlement. They also mark the decisive transition from British to US geopolitical dominance.[3] As well, the initial emergence of 'late developers' Germany and Japan was in the era of early late development, and their reconstruction from wartime devastation in the era of late-late development; institutionally, both eras were crucial. And the emergence of South Korea and especially Taiwan corresponds to

[3] There are some parallels in the Soviet bloc in the eras of late development, but states overwhelmed markets in this case. These are not our focus in this book.

Table 2.1 States and markets in historical eras

Historical Era	Early (1780s–1840s)	Early Late (1850s–1930s)	Late Late (1945–1980s)	Compressed (1990s–)
Dominant (Western) geopolitical power	Britain (1)	Britain (2)	United States (1)	United States (2)
Polanyian cycles and dominant power ideology	(Mercantilism)	Liberalism - marketization - financialization	Embedded liberalism	Neoliberalism - marketization - financialization
State (of new industrializers)	Mercantilist	Nationalist, imperialist	Planning	Adaptive, marketized
Movements and crises	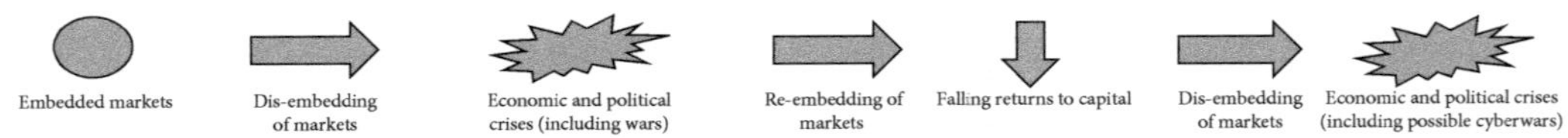			
Dominant organization paradigm (Chapter 3)	(Small factories and workshops, local)	Increasing scale, combination, professionally managed, unitary structure	Vertically integrated, Fordist, divisional structure, mass production	Ownership concentration, networks, outsourcing and offshoring in global value chains
Role of finance	Bifurcated (local, international)	Investment, universal banks, financialization	Diverse, national development banks, international development financing	Foreign direct investment, market-based, global, financialization
Policy space (for developers)	Open	Constrained, but forced to innovate	Relatively open	Constrained, need for adaptiveness

a transition between eras, reflected in their production systems and limited depth of institutional embedding from the late-late-development era. The chapter unpacks the rationale for the rows, columns, and individual cells, ultimately to highlight the characteristics of the era of compressed development, the right-hand column.

Chapter 3 will provide a complementary figure and table focused on the organization–technology dyad (i.e. the lower portion of Figure 0.2 shown in the book's introduction). While each set of dyadic pairs is to some extent functionally independent, and not expected to move or co-evolve in lockstep with the other, there are nevertheless broad trends that affect and create interdependencies across both pairs, not least the influence of the dominant power and role of finance and financialization, both of which are highlighted in this chapter. Together the dynamics and interactions between the two dyads shape 'eras' of development.

This chapter is structured as follows. The first section has a dual role. It provides a broad historical perspective on the state and economic development, subdivided into 'eras' which correspond to the columns of Table 2.1. This perspective assigns a key role to the state in the evolution of markets (and vice versa), as well as in industrialization, and it highlights how the economic and geopolitical systems of dominant powers—Britain and the United States, respectively—have influenced the character of development in emerging countries. The second section adds finance, showing that this, too, forms part of systemic-era influences on development. These two sections in turn frame the third, which looks at how policy space has become both constricted and altered—compressed—with implications for both states and markets in emerging countries.

The state and economic development in historical perspective

'Early' development (1780s–1840s)

A small island on the edge of a historically backward part of the world is an unlikely setting for the rise of an economic and state system which would radically change the world, as Britain did from the late eighteenth century. Some explanations have stressed cumulative domestic causes, while others have focused on external factors, and even backwardness and the role of chance.[4] The role of the state must be considered.

The state is by no means a fixed entity, and it has historically taken various forms. Tilly depicts the emergence of the modern nation state as the interplay of

[4] Anievas and Nisancioglu (2015), for example, invoke a wide range of factors, and draw on Trotsky's theory of uneven and combined development; Europe and Britain in particular reaped the benefits of their own backwardness.

'war making, extraction and capital accumulation' (1985: 172).[5] He contrasts 'capital-intensive' Italian city states such as Venice and 'coercion-intensive' states such as Russia. The most effective states—Britain, as well as France—developed a middle ground, combining capital and coercion (with standing armies), which made them highly effective competitors. As Weiss and Hobson (1995: 4) put it, the strongest or most effective states were not those which relied on (internal) violence to achieve their aims, but those 'which gradually sought more institutionalized, cooperative relations with civil society, enhanced their penetrative and extractive capacities, and hence their infrastructural power'.[6]

Britain thus successfully turned the tension between the polity and the economy—state and markets—into a co-evolutionary relationship (represented in Figure 2.1) that drove economic development. Business expansion increased the tax base and, hence, the ability to wage war, force open foreign markets, and grow an empire, enabling further business expansion... But the state went further than this. It actively engaged in 'industrial policy' from the fourteenth century, including the protection of wool cloth producers. Originally uncompetitive, wool production greatly expanded under Henry VII in the sixteenth century, and by the eighteenth century, it generated at least half of Britain's export earnings.[7] Similarly, initially uncompetitive but protected, cotton textile producers went on to become central in the industrial revolution. Technological and organizational advances in spinning and weaving in the late eighteenth century raised productivity dramatically. British cloth was still of inferior quality to that of Indian producers, but it found markets in the colonies in the Americas and Africa, the former contributing raw cotton for the trade, and the latter slaves to work on cotton plantations. India's labour-intensive industry eventually deindustrialized[8] as the country began to import British cloth—from 11 million yards in 1820 to 145 million in 1840. Hobsbawm (1988: 35) comments:

> This was not merely a gratifying extension of Lancashire's markets. It was a major landmark in world history. For since the dawn of time Europe had always imported more from the East than she had sold there... The cotton shirtings of the Industrial Revolution for the first time reversed this relationship, which had been hitherto kept in balance by a mixture of bullion exports and robbery.

[5] The war-making activities of the state themselves were a direct stimulus for the emergence of markets; as Tilly notes, standing armies were big business. Also Schoenberger, 2008.

[6] Weiss and Hobson are employing Mann's (1984) distinction between infrastructural power and despotic power, which is characteristic of *weak* states, and Hall's (1986) argument that state power is strengthened when working *with* social forces rather than against them.

[7] Chang, 2002a: 20–1, citing Defoe, 1728.

[8] Deindustrialization of India—or more broadly, the South—refers to the destruction of largely artisanal but often sophisticated capabilities.

It was not only a historical reversal, but the beginning of the 'great divergence' between the 'West' and the rest of the world (Pomeranz, 2000). It also marked major changes in the state, and the state's relations with emerging capitalism. State policies strongly influenced the emergence of capitalism and markets, and vice versa. These relations took on an ostensibly paradoxical form in Britain after the Napoleonic Wars—the espousal of liberalism on the one hand, and a massive expansion of state apparatus and legislative activity on the other. British liberalism had three basic tenets, according to Polanyi (1944: 141): 'that labour should find its price on the market; that the creation of money should be subject to an automatic mechanism; that goods should be free to flow from country to country without hindrance of preference; in short, for a labour market, a gold standard, and free trade'. Implementing this trinity required a new kind of state: 'The [eighteen] thirties and forties saw not only an outburst of legislation repealing restrictive regulations, but also an enormous increase in the administrative functions of the state, which was now being endowed with a central bureaucracy able to fulfil the tasks set by the adherents of liberalism' (Polanyi, 1944: 145). The 'self-regulating market' required constant intervention, and where necessary, state-sanctioned violence, at home and abroad.

A growing national state bureaucracy was not just a British phenomenon. The French Revolution and Napoleonic Wars spurred centralized government and bureaucratic expansion on continental Europe as well. Also, paradoxically, given the role of war in state formation, this brought about a *relative* decline in military expenditure, civilianization of governments, and specialization of the military.[9] Indeed, states began to create national systems of education with national languages and symbols, and systems of welfare which went well beyond care for war veterans. Maier (2012) depicts this as the emergence of 'Leviathan 2.0'. Late developers, which were simultaneously engaging in nation (state)-building and industrialization, were often quicker than Britain to adopt these measures, and to extend the franchise.

Early late development (1850s–1930s)

By Gerschenkron's (1962) logic, Britain was the first and only *early* industrializer. All others were latecomers because they were confronted with an emerging dual economic and geopolitical 'system', backed by distance-shrinking technologies such as steam power, rail, iron and steel ships . . . to which they had to respond. With its combined industrial revolution, financial supremacy, and aggressive empire building, Britain imposed developmental imperatives on its neighbours

[9] This is the fourth stage of Tilly's (1990) warfare and state transformation (patrimonialism, brokerage, nationalization, and specialization).

that brought about new roles for the nation states that were in many cases in the process of being built or consolidated and thus acquired the imprint of late development.

Employing von Thünen (1826) and Krugman's (1991a, 1991b) models, Schwartz (2010) maps the challenge posed to such late developers as a series of concentric rings emanating from the British core. States in these rings faced the challenge of industrializing or becoming peripheralized as food or raw material suppliers to the core. Countries near the core responded first, but they were faced with a dilemma: they needed technology and finance from Britain to create their own railways and infrastructure. They adopted 'Ricardian' strategies of exporting agricultural and labour-intensive products to finance this borrowing, but risked becoming locked into a relationship of technological dependence. To avoid dependence they had to shift away from their comparative advantages and to build up capabilities similar to Britain through investment in the manufacturing technologies of the day, or 'Kaldorian' industrialization'.[10]

This posed another dilemma, however, namely how hard to squeeze agriculture to gain resources for industrialization while still being dependent on agriculture for export earnings. Eventually these dilemmas also created unintended consequences, such as overproduction, as many European countries attempted to export similar products at the same time, and responded to falling prices by expanding output and exports further. The resulting depression of 1873 pushed millions into poverty or migration.

Moreover late developers joined the global economy when supplies of gold were not expanding, stoking the deflation. Designed to insulate economies from politics, the gold standard ironically led to new roles for the state such as the creation of central banks that could cushion monetary pressures and shocks. As Polanyi (1944: 223) puts it:

> The free trade and gold standard system was not wantonly wrecked by selfish tariff mongers and soft-hearted legislators; on the contrary, the coming of the gold standard itself hastened the spreading of these protectionist institutions... From this time onwards tariffs, factory laws, and an active colonial policy were prerequisites of a stable external currency. (Great Britain with her vast industrial superiority was the exception which proved the rule).[11]

In other words, the institutions and pressures from British liberalism generated a 'double movement', with new roles for the state, which were necessary to preserve

[10] Schwartz (2010) rightly notes that such Ricardian and Kaldorian strategies were complementary, and they evolved over time.

[11] In the United States, with its vast land and increasing labour, there was no commitment to fixed exchange rates until the turn of the century, and high tariffs were maintained up until the close of World War II.

markets themselves. 'If money now avowedly ruled the world, that money was stamped with a national die' (Polanyi, 1944: 211).

These developments were not confined to Europe. In the Far East, having seen at close hand the Opium War and carving up of China, and having been forced to end its (partial) isolation and sign its own unequal treaties, Japan underwent a political transformation in the Meiji Restoration of 1868. This brought about administrative centralization and state building, as well as a concerted effort to promote industrialization. By the time Japan was incorporated into the global economy in the 1880s, it was already well on its way to becoming a modern, centralized state, as we shall see in Chapter 4.[12]

Gerschenkron (1962) proposed not only systematic differences between Britain and later developers, but differences among the later developers themselves, depending on their degree of 'backwardness'. In moderately backward Germany, with a well-developed business culture, universal banks which combined investment and retail functions were created under private capital to promote rapid industrialization. More backward Russia had less capital available and low levels of trust needed for long-term banking. Here the state had to play a more direct role in financing and initiating industrialization, starting with construction of the railroads in the 1880s. But the differences between the two countries also had political significance. Germany forged an alliance between 'rye and iron'—Junker *landowners* of the east and *industrialists* of the west—but as Trotsky (1906) astutely observed, in Russia there was a potential for a revolutionary alliance between *peasants* and *workers*. This materialized in the severity of World War I.

Social tensions in Europe in the aftermath of World War I were extreme and were exacerbated by ultimately futile attempts to restore the gold standard, often at prewar parity (and in Germany's case, by punitive reparations). As Britain's liberal world (dis)order crumbled, states' involvement in economies and social life increased everywhere, from Britain's own 'very gingerly and sensitive corporatism' (Fox, 1985: 343) through to fascist regimes in Germany, Italy, and Spain.[13] The United States, which emerged from World War I with most of the world's gold (Ahamed, 2009), had resources and had acquired technological advantages, but when the Wall Street bubble burst, it too plunged into depression, eventually ushering in a new era of Keynesian state–market co-evolution that demanded a much larger role for the state.

[12] Iriye (1989: 749). To the contrary, Japan saw that becoming modern and winning the respect of the 'great powers' meant having an expansionist foreign policy as well.

[13] Polanyi comments: 'The stubborness with which economic liberals, for a critical decade, had, in the service of deflationary policies, supported authoritarian interventionism, merely resulted in a decisive weakening of the democratic forces which might otherwise have averted the fascist catastrophe' (1944: 242). We will explore echoes with the 2010s subsequently.

Late-late development (1945–1980)

Government direction of national economies through planning and resource allocation survived World War II. The new US–led international order was not a liberal order, as such, but a calibrated attempt to avoid the recent dislocations which had led to war and depression, through reindustrialization and the creation of a stable, regulated trading system. Ruggie called it 'embedded liberalism':

> The task of post-war institutional reconstruction . . . was to manoeuvre between these two extremes [of liberal orthodoxy and its rejection] and to devise a framework which would safeguard and even aid the quest for domestic stability without, at the same time, triggering the mutually destructive external consequences that had plagued the interwar period. This was the essence of the embedded liberalism compromise: unlike the economic nationalism of the thirties, it would be multilateral in character; unlike the liberalism of the gold standard and free trade, its multilateralism would be predicated upon domestic interventionism. (1982: 393)

In an effort to balance openness with domestic stability, the multilateral trading system was to be maintained for manufactured goods while agricultural products would be protected from global market forces. The system would be supported by multilateral institutions, which were worked out at Bretton Woods in 1944. Although the dollar became the de facto international standard, and was convertible to gold, the demands of New York bankers to resurrect the old liberal world order under the dollar were overridden (Ruggie, 1982).

Imbalances between supply and demand, both domestic and international, also needed to be addressed. Large productivity increases in the United States in the 1920s from the early adoption of new organizational forms and high-volume process technologies (as detailed in Chapter 3) had both stoked the domestic stock market and created overcapacity, threatening industry in Europe. By 1945 the productivity gap was even greater, and war-torn European economies needed to be rebuilt through aid, procurements, technology transfer, and opening of US markets to avoid the post–World War I debacle, as well as, from the US perspective, to build markets for US products and create a network of strategic allies for the Cold War.

Wall Street was now expected to serve the main street (or, the 'real' economy). Full employment, full production, and stable prices were to be achieved through planning (and the judicious use of monetary and fiscal policy), and domestic peace through class compromise in a social contract between capital and labour. With institutional variations, the formula was repeated across the Western world.[14] The

[14] 'The structure of the postwar settlement between labour and capital was fundamentally the same across the otherwise widely different countries where democratic capitalism arose. It included an

role of the state had thus changed again, quantitatively and qualitatively, although this was not always recognized or appreciated in the context of the Cold War, as Galbraith (1967) noted in his book *The New Industrial State*.[15] Planning required a technocracy in both government and corporate management. The spirit of managerial or organized capitalism 'operated in an era when the driving force was large national firms pursuing endogenous growth' with a 'national system of "industrial relations" under state auspices' (Boltanski and Ciapello, 2007: 500).[16]

Yet there was sufficient policy space for national variations. In Asia, Japan's 'developmental state' was replicated, broadly speaking, by Korea and Taiwan (Cumings, 1984; Wade, 1990). Latin American 'developmental states' also promoted industrialization (Ocampo and Ros, 2012), but with an emphasis on import substitution and domestic consumption. As Hirschman (1971) noted, 'late-late industrialization' in Latin America focused on consumer goods rather than producer goods.[17] Many postcolonial nations, another set of 'late-late developers' (Kohli, 2004), also adopted this orientation, albeit with fewer resources and state building limited by the legacy of artificially imposed borders (amongst other things) that undermined the cohesiveness of postcolonial states.

Yet there was an underlying tension between liberalism and its embedding, especially in the United States and the UK, a tension which became more acute over time. By the late 1960s productivity gains were slowing and inflationary pressures were increasing. For the United States, trade deficits and overseas investments were both mounting. Dollars held abroad came to exceed gold reserves. In 1971, the United States went off the old standard, devalued the dollar by 10 per cent, and raised tariffs by 10 per cent (the so-called 'Nixon shocks'). Two years later the Arab–Israeli War triggered the (first) 'oil shock'. The ensuing stagflationary pressures drew divergent political reactions; neo-corporatism on the one hand, and neoliberalism on the other. For Amsden (2007) this turbulence marked the transition to the 'Second American Empire', a geopolitical context much less benign for developing countries.

expanding welfare state, the right of workers to free collective bargaining, and a political guarantee of full employment, underwritten by governments making extensive use of the Keynesian economic toolkit' (Streeck, 2016: 78).

[15] 'The services of the Federal, state and local governments now account for between a fifth and a quarter of all economic activity. In 1929 it was about eight percent. This far exceeds the government share in such an avowedly socialist state as India . . . and is not wholly incommensurate with the share in Poland' Galbraith, 1967: 14).

[16] Boltanski and Ciapello's three 'spirits' of capitalism correspond with our early, late-, and compressed- development eras.

[17] Hirschman attributed this to 'the fact that it has become possible for industrialization to penetrate into Latin America and elsewhere among the late-latecomers without requiring the fundamental social and political changes which it wrought among the pioneer industrial countries and also among the earlier group of latecomers' (1971: 123).

Compressed development and neoliberalism (1990–)

The post-1970s swing to neoliberalism, and the changing role of the state this brought, unfolded in a series of steps summarized by Streeck (2016) as follows. Governments attempted to accommodate conflicts arising from embedded liberalism by allowing inflation, but the inevitable backlash from the owners of capital intensified after 1979. This ushered in a period of falling inflation, but rising unemployment and rising public debt which could no longer be masked by inflation. To stop interest rates from rising, financial markets were deregulated, but debt servicing remained a political problem. Financial markets exerted pressure to cut public debt and reduce taxes, leading to cuts in social spending, privatization, and, simultaneously, to a massive increase of private debt through credit expansion. The rich moved their money into the financial sector (and often into offshore financial centres) and made huge profits, while subprime mortgages were offered to the less well-off.

The effects spread far beyond the United States. For highly indebted countries, the straitjacket of Washington Consensus policy orthodoxy and loan conditionalities became even tighter than that of the gold standard. To hedge the risks of open capital accounts, many countries were forced to stockpile scarce financial resources and invest them in the United States at low interest rates. US investors in turn used the money for foreign direct investment (FDI) or portfolio investment overseas, earning on average 2 per cent more in a form of arbitrage similar to that of the UK in the nineteenth century (Schwartz, 2010).

The transformation of the United States—our main point of reference here—was not simply economic. Block and Somers (2014) argue that tensions from the Vietnam War catalysed a *social* transition as well. On one hand a (well-funded) counter to the anti–Vietnam War movement, school integration, affirmative action, and abortion began to take shape. On the other, slowing economic growth and fiscal pressures sapped business support for (New Deal) domestic social programmes and internationalism. Block and Somers find strong parallels between the attack on the Poor Laws and Speenhamland by Malthus and his supporters in early nineteenth century Britain, and the conservative movement against welfare and 'Big Government' in the United States under Reagan in the 1980s. The former led to British liberalism, the latter to US neoliberalism. The result in both cases was an ideological fusion of social conservatism and economic liberalism.

As with the earlier British case, moreover, the 'liberalization' of markets in the 1980s and 1990s was produced by concerted state action, not state withdrawal (Vogel, 2018). For opponents of postwar embedded liberalism, it was ideologically convenient to portray a battle between 'Big Government' and a benevolent market which would self-adjust through market signals and maximise overall welfare, if only governments would get out of the way. As Crouch (2011) points out, however, there existed in the United States a strong historical distrust of 'Big Business', as well as 'Big Government', exemplified by antitrust legislation in the late nineteenth and early twentieth centuries. By the 1970s and 1980s, such concerns had largely fallen away, and only mistrust of 'Big Government' remained. Antitrust legislation was relaxed, and competition policy became focused on maximizing (theoretical) consumer welfare and market 'efficiency' rather than (actual) market structure and behaviour. Concentration accelerated under powerful global corporations which not only wielded strong market power, but also political power. Automation and import competition were allowed to drive deindustrialization in the name of lower consumer prices. Developing countries adopted similar, lax competition policies (Davis, Kaplinsky, and Morris, 2018).

In brief, the US–led international geopolitical and economic 'system' in the era of compressed development became dramatically different from that of the post-war decades, particularly following the collapse of the Soviet Union. Legal changes and market concentration, moreover, were accompanied by financialization, which we will now consider, and global value chains, which we will discuss in Chapter 3.

Markets, finance, and financialization

Big business is not the only presence lurking in the conceptual box labelled 'markets'. Its companion is finance, whose concentration has similarly been enabled by regulatory relaxation, especially in the United States and UK. This has altered the balance between states and markets, restructured manufacturing in developed countries, contributed to the growth of global value chains, and shaped 'thin industrialization' in the compressed-development era. Finance is thus an important shaper of development, and development eras, and is a link between our two dyads.

Gerschenkron (1962) had a view of how finance and financial institutions differ between early and late developers, but it was based on an unproblematic view of finance as an enabler of development. However, finance can also be a destabilizer, a political tool of the powerful, and a global industry that can alter the landscape for aspiring developers. Here we consider how its role has changed over the eras we have set out above. Liberalism, we shall see, is not just related to the growth of markets and marketization, but to financialization as well (Dore, 2008), which is in part the product of a dominant power's attempt to extend or maintain its economic and geopolitical power.

Historically, financial innovations (new financial instruments, institutions, and markets) have played a central role in launching trade, commerce, and industrialization, as Rousseau (2002) sets out for the Dutch Republic (1600–1794), Britain

(1700–1850), the United States (1790–1850), and Japan (1880–1913). In their study of eighty countries between 1960 and 1989, King and Levine (1993: 719) find 'an important link between financial development and long-run growth as suggested by Schumpeter 80 years ago'. But as Minsky (1988: 3) further points out: 'Those who finance a Schumpeterian innovator always have novel problems in structuring the financing. Two new sets of combinations, in production and in finance, drive the evolution of the economy.' And the relationship between production and finance can be problematic, as well as beneficial.

At a broad level, Britain is a case in point; its capitalism was powered by the expansion of credit after the Glorious Revolution in 1688, but it was divided between the industrial heartland and the City of London.[18] It may have been the 'workshop of the world', but it was also the world's financial clearing house (Ingham, 1984).[19] Where interests clashed, the state tended to favour those of finance. Cain and Hopkins's (1980) 'gentlemanly capitalism' represented an alliance between the state, the City of London, southern English investors, and landed interests.[20]

Observing the United States, Minsky (1992) described four models of structured relations between finance and business dominant in successive eras. These closely match the eras we described in the previous section and in Table 2.1. Specifically, *commercial capitalism* (our early development era) involved the financing of goods that were traded or processed. The main instrument was the bill of exchange, and it corresponded to the structure of finance when the scale of production was relatively small. With *finance capitalism* (early late development) nonlabour costs—plant and machinery—became more important and the corporation emerged as a dominant form of ownership. Here markets for stock and bond flotations were created under the organization of investment bankers (in Germany universal banks played this role), some of whom, like J.P. Morgan in the United States, became extremely influential, both politically and in orchestrating industrial concentration.[21] *Managerial capitalism* (late-late development)

[18] The settlement between William III and London financiers saw the creation of the Bank of England, which enabled not only the king to finance his war with France but also a significant expansion of domestic credit (Ingham, 2004: 127–8).

[19] London consolidated its position as the centre of *haute finance* following the Napoleonic Wars, based on the credibility of its gold standard, and ideologically buttressed by liberalism. Rothschild's London house issued over half the sovereign bonds issued by banks in London between 1815 and 1859, but it also sold French, Prussian, Austrian, Neapolitan, and Brazilian bonds, and virtually monopolized bond issues by the Belgian government after 1830 (Ferguson, 2008: 86). Industry's financing needs, by contrast, were met by local and regional banks, which only gradually became integrated into the financial activities—and financial pressures—of the City of London.

[20] '(T)he gentlemen of the City were well placed, by virtue of social and physical proximity, to carry their interests into the corridors of power in London, unlike British industry, which suffered from being heterogeneous, small scale and provincial' (Cain and Hopkins, 1993: 87). Britain was a case of 'capitalism divided' (Ingham, 1984).

[21] In Germany, Hilferding ([1910] 1981: 370, 301) analysed how finance capitalism concentrated 'economic and political power in the hands of the capitalist oligarchy' as it sought to create a 'centralized and privilege-dispensing state'. The context was intensifying competition and declining profits.

emerged through the Wall Street crash of 1929, the Depression, New Deal, and World War II. The government's expanded role came to include supporting mortgages and the institutions which finance them as part of maintaining aggregate demand. This ensured a level of profits which enabled companies to finance their needs from internal cash flows, enhancing managerial autonomy. Finally, *money manager capitalism* (compressed-development era) emerged from the 1970s as the financial sector became unshackled from industry and capital gains-oriented blocks of managed money became a major independent influence. Minsky viewed this development with deep concern:

> Today's narrowly-focused financiers do not conform to Schumpeter's vision of bankers as the *ephors* of capitalism who assure that finance serves progress. Today's financial structure is more akin to Keynes' characterization of the financial arrangements of advanced capitalism as a casino. (1992: 113)[22]

Minsky's second and fourth periods, in which finance and financial innovation become the driving force for economic change rather than its enabler, are periods of instability. Drawing on Keynes, as well as Schumpeter, Minsky argued that instability is *endogenous* to finance.[23] There has been an upsurge of interest in Minsky's views, and the downside of financial innovations, as financial crises have proliferated since the 1980s (Leathers and Raines, 2004).

Financialization

A parallel upsurge of interest in 'financialization' has prompted comparisons with the 'first financialization' of the late nineteenth century (Vercelli, 2014), including its impact on industry, as well as on the state. For industry, 'financialization' refers to the rise of financial officers to the top of large corporations and the concomitant valorizing of dept over equity, applied over basic research, variable over fixed assets, and the interests of capital over labour—all justified by the installation of maximization of shareholder value as the ultimate corporate objective.

In the United States, corporate managers came under increasing pressure from the 1980s to prioritize shareholder interests in the face of declining profits (Useem, 1996). They were disciplined by 'markets for corporate control' and

[22] Ephors were elected leaders or magistrates of Sparta who shared power with and checked the activities of the Spartan kings. Schumpeter (1934) saw bankers as 'ephors' of the exchange economy.

[23] Minsky identified three investment profiles—hedge, speculative, and Ponzi. Periods of stability and expansion breed euphoria and speculative bubbles which move profiles in the Ponzi direction. When the bubbles are eventually popped as credit is tightened, casualties move in reverse, engulfing firms with even sound profiles. See, for example, Bernanke's (2015) account of how the US subprime mortgage crisis morphed into a full-blown financial crisis, and then an economic crisis. The length of 'Minskian cycles' is contentious; Davis et al. (2019) make a case for long waves. Speculative cycles also form around new technologies, as we shall see in Chapter 3.

incentivized by stock options, orienting them towards financial markets, to which they increasingly went when they needed finance. They restructured their organizations, slashed their workforces, and sought flexibility from those left. Lazonick (2015) characterizes this as a shift from 'retain and reinvest' to 'downsize and distribute', a shift that we link with a shift from the Fordist to the Network organizational paradigm in Chapter 3.

Within the finance sector, banks shifted from using household deposits for loans, which they kept on their books until maturity: 'originate-to-hold', to trading a range of products funded by a range of sources: 'originate-to-distribute' (Bord and Santos, 2012; Lazonick and O'Sullivan, 2000). This stimulated a massive growth in the syndicated loan market, the secondary loan market, and in collateralized loan obligations organized by nonbank financial intermediaries—the so-called shadow banking system.[24] Banks also turned to households and individuals with new financial products. Household borrowing surged, as did ownership of financial assets through money market accounts, retirement accounts, pensions, and insurance plans. Indeed, in many cases, home ownership, too, shifted from a fixed, real asset to a shorter-term financial asset.

Financialization progressed further in economies which were historically more market based, notably the US and UK economies, nonetheless it advanced broadly in developed countries, including continental European and Nordic countries.[25] New technologies have been combined with financial innovations to restructure capital markets and exchanges, whose governance and high-speed, algorithm-based trading has allowed privileged insiders to accrue massive profits at the expense of small businesses and ordinary investors (Mattli, 2019). Financial concentration has been accompanied by increasing political power among the financial elite, as it did a century earlier. Indeed, Wray (2009) proposes that financialization has created a 'predator state', which is 'Big Government operating in the interests of money managers under cover of laissez faire marketing' (815; Galbraith, 2008).

Finance and financialization in developing countries

Postwar 'international development' as exemplified by the International Monetary Fund (IMF) and World Bank was originally based on the simple, optimistic

[24] The scale of these markets rose from \$339 billion in 1988 to \$2.7 trillion in 2007; \$8 billion in 1991 to \$176 billion in 2005; and under \$20 billion before 2003 to \$180 billion in 2007, respectively (Bord and Santos, 2012: 21–2). Pozsar et al. (2010: 9) estimated gross liabilities of the US shadow banking system in June 2007 at \$22 trillion, compared with \$14 trillion for banks.

[25] Zalewski and Whalen (2010). Financialization takes different forms in different countries. Lapavitsas (2019: 41), for example, describes the distinctiveness of German financialization as 'the maintenance of a strong industrial base in spite of weak aggregate investment' through wage suppression and exchange rate manipulation, benefiting from the creation of a European 'peripheral south'.

expectation that providing finance to developing countries would be sufficient to bring about development, given their abundance of labour. A finance-enabled 'big push' would set them on the path to self-sustaining development. After a dip in the 1960s, inflows of finance increased sharply in the 1970s with the recycling of petro-dollars, but the unfixing of exchange rates, and the hike in interest rates in the United States in 1979 led to a sharp reversal, and the emergence of financial crises and devaluations, starting with Mexico in 1982. Consequently '(t)he conventional wisdom that emerged emphasized getting a country's fiscal house in order, and letting markets do the rest' (UNCTAD, 2015: 41). Private capital inflows in the 1990s proved highly volatile, however, sparking the Tequila Crisis in 1994, the Asian Financial Crisis in 1997, the Russian Default in 1998, the Brazilian exchange rate crisis in 1999, and termination of the Argentine Convertibility Law in 2000–2001. Kregel (2004) interprets these crises through a Minskian lens, with developing countries facing heightened uncertainty because of exchange rate movements and variable repayment schedules.

Moreover, developing countries have experienced their own financialization, as noted in Chapter 1. The financial sectors of developing countries have also moved towards market-based systems, the expansion of stock markets, nontraditional roles for banks, and increasing influence of institutional investors. Nonfinancial firms have become increasingly involved in financial activities, as have households. Even development banks have become financialized.[26] Foreign banks 'are often key agencies in transmitting "financialized" practices, that is, they obtain high profits through activities unrelated to lending, such as trading, as well as through fees and commissions and aggressive household lending' (Bonizzi, 2014: 91).

Equity flows to developing countries have been seen as more stable than debt, and direct investment as more stable than portfolio investment. This is because FDI is often seen as a long-term commitment which can bring with it much-needed technology, expertise, and network connections, and can stimulate local suppliers to raise their game (Romer, 1993; Lall, 1993). FDI to developing countries has surged in recent years. But even—or *especially*—here, the impact of financialization can be seen. Some 30 per cent of cross-border corporate investments are now estimated to be routed through 'offshore hubs', largely—but not exclusively—because of 'tax planning'. This not only reduces tax revenues in the country of origin, but in recipient countries as well.[27] Companies have increasingly incorporated in low tax jurisdictions, and manipulated different tax regimes

[26] Bonizzi (2014) cites the case of Cagmas in Malaysia, 'a state-led financial institution set up to facilitate the availability of affordable housing, which slowly turned into the biggest securitization provider in the country'. He might also have cited the infamous 1MDB, set up in 2009 to make Kuala Lumpur a financial centre, but which became embroiled in scandal in 2016; or the changing role of the Development Bank of Singapore (Lai and Daniels, 2015).

[27] UNCTAD (2015: xiii) estimates that MNC foreign affiliates contribute $730 billion in taxes to developing countries annually, but an additional $100 billion is thought to be lost through 'tax planning' and offshore hubs.

and the valuation of intangible assets to minimize tax payments. A study by Damgaard et al. (2019) found that nearly 40 per cent of all FDI was comprised of such 'phantom investment' in 2017.

While we chart the growth of global *value* chains in Chapter 3, Seabrooke and Wigan (2014, 2017) draw attention to the parallel growth of global *wealth* chains. It is not easy to trace the flow of intermediate and final goods in cross-border value-added chains, but the flow of profits is even less visible. A sample of multinational enterprises (MNEs) from twenty-five developed countries booked almost double the profits in Bermuda than they did in China in 2014, and these profits were almost eight times the gross domestic product (GDP) of Bermuda itself (UNCTAD, 2016: 21). Relatedly, UNCTAD (2016) estimates that 40 per cent of foreign affiliates worldwide have 'multiple passports' that enable them to pick and choose tax jurisdictions. In fact, the top one hundred MNEs on UNCTAD's Transnationality Index have:

> ...on average more than 500 affiliates each, across 50 countries. They have 7 hierarchical levels in their ownership structure (i.e. ownership links to affiliates could potentially cross 6 borders), they have about 20 holding companies owning affiliates across multiple jurisdictions, and they have almost 70 entities in offshore investment hubs.[28]

These structures are very difficult for tax authorities to understand, and they allow MNEs to obfuscate tax liability and pick and choose tax jurisdictions. Critically, businesses from less developed economies increasingly use them as well. The British Virgin Islands (BVI) are the seventh largest source of FDI into China, but also the 'second largest destination for Chinese investment abroad, attracting more than 10 times Chinese FDI as the USA' (Sharman, 2012: 504–5, citing Vlcek, 2008). More companies are opened in the BVI for Chinese investors than for all other countries combined.[29]

In brief, financialization now pervades international flows of finance, and increasingly, business practices in developing countries. When we recall the importance of taxation for nation state and economy building (cited earlier in this chapter), the implications are stark. Initiatives such as Base Erosion and Profit Shifting' (BEPS, started in 2012 by the G20 and OECD) and the Common

[28] UNCTAD (2016: xiii). Defenders of such structures claim they are necessary to handle complex investment and taxation issues—to avoid double taxation, for instance—and to provide stability in a complex and uncertain world (*Financial Times*, 7 April 2016: 'Tax Havens are a Cog in Global Economy, Say Defenders').

[29] These statistics suggest significant 'round tripping'. Similarly, Mauritius is the largest source of FDI to India (Sharman, 2010). Sharman emphasizes the 'calculated ambiguity' of offshore financial products, catering to attempts to evade regulatory constraints and tax liabilities.

Reporting Standard have been launched to stem the tide, and have become all the more important in the age of the digital economy.

Financialization has an impact on the relations between states and markets. In fact, states themselves have become facilitators of marketization and financialization. If a key institutional feature of the postwar developmental or planning state was a 'pilot agency' (such as MITI in Japan, or the Economic Planning Board in Korea), its counterpart in the financialized state, or 'competition state' (Cerny, 2010), is an independent central bank preoccupied with inflation targeting.[30] In developing and transition countries in particular, dependence on foreign capital and integration into global financial markets has often meant adopting these structures and policies, thereby prioritizing the interests of international investors and shareholders. The same applies to preferential trade agreements, which are often more about protecting investments in GVC industries than reciprocal trade per se (Manger, 2014).

In conclusion, increasing engagement with global finance, and the adoption of its tools in developing countries, is one of the clearest differentiators between late and compressed development. It is also one of the drivers of narrowing, or compressed policy space, which we will now consider.

State building and policy space compression

States and markets co-evolve, but not in isolation from larger geopolitical, economic, and institutional contexts. In the era of compressed development, these contexts have become even more influential, and often more constraining. Chang (2002a) refers to the habit of developed countries to impose constraints on less developed countries, which they themselves did not face at a similar stage of development, as 'kicking away the ladder', after List (1841). The phenomenon is not new, and not all of it is bad by any means, but it has intensified, creating what we might call 'policy compression' in developing countries.

At the broadest level, international norms against territorial aggrandizement strengthened after World War I, and especially after World War II, foreclosing the military path to nation state building that European countries had previously followed. These norms, while laudable, have 'made it more difficult for Southern states to forge strong, synergistic states whose security concerns are externally- rather than internally-oriented' (Dannreuther, 2007: 317). As a result, the security concerns of state elites have sometimes been turned inwards, making them more

[30] Inflation targeting and related policies 'are designed to create . . . a central bank that is consistent with an economy with a small government role, privatized industries, liberalized financial markets, and flexible labor markets. These central bank proposals include adopting central bank "independence", and in developing countries, adopting currency boards, and/or substituting a foreign currency—most commonly the dollar—as domestic legal tender' (Epstein, 2005: 3).

concerned with internal rather than external threats, sometimes causing citizens to fear the predations of their own states rather than those of their neighbours. Thus, Dannreuther argues, we see 'state fragility, the tendency towards weak civil societies; and the difficulties of integration into global economic processes' (318).

But more immediate, and institutional influences have intensified as well, particularly from the 1980s. Wade (2003: 621–2) puts it bluntly:

> Developing countries today, as a group, are being ever more tightly constrained in their national development strategies by proliferating regulations formulated and enforced by international organizations. These regulations are not about limiting *companies*' options, as 'regulation' normally connotes; rather, they are about limiting the options of developing country governments to constrain the options of companies operating or hoping to operate within their borders.[31]

In particular, the United States and the UK 'have come together to legitimize a level of intrusion into the economies and polities of developing countries hitherto frowned on by the international community, framing the intrusion in the shape of international agreements' such as TRIPS, TRIMS and GATS (Wade, 2003: 622). Under the standard of 'good governance' and 'getting the institutions right', (which developed countries themselves had not achieved at similar levels of per capita GDP: Chang, 2002a; Rodrik, 2016) the scope has been expanded to include (electoral) democracy, protection of property rights, financialized corporate governance, openness to global financial institutions, and aspects of social welfare.

With the emergence of the WTO, Babb and Chorev (2016) note, developing countries were required to accept all the obligations of a given round of trade negotiations. This made it more difficult to create and implement industrial policy favouring—and suited to—local firms, and more difficult to impose restrictions on foreign investment. Indeed, one of the strongest aspects of the WTO was the mandate to create a 'level playing field' for multinational firms. Babb and Chorev (2016) distinguish between the 'loosely coupled' development regime from 1945 until the end of the 1970s, and the 'tightly coupled' regime from the outbreak of the Third World debt crisis in the early 1980s, which brought an 'unprecedented tightening of the linkages between rules, resources and ideas' (83).

The results can be perverse. Pritchett, Woolcock, and Andrews (2010) assess 'accelerated modernization via transplanted best practices' as creating persistent 'techniques of failure' and 'state capability traps'. Such transplantation, they argue, encourages the adoption of institutional forms without any meaningful adaptation to local conditions, hence without accompanying functionality. The subsequent

[31] An often-cited example is investor-state dispute settlement provisions. Also UNCTAD, 2002, 2006. Countries with structural weaknesses and high dependence on foreign capital are particularly constrained, and less willing and able to use what policy space they have (Akyüz, 2009).

failure, which can undermine even existing capabilities, results in a search for new solutions, and a new cycle of failure.

Using different terminology, Eriksen (2017) argues that the creation of effective states requires the creation of state-centred societies which cannot be brought about by external actors. External actors may encourage a 'politics of pretending', which reinforces networks of patronage, weakening rather than strengthening the state. Or as Wimmer (2018: 2) puts it, 'public goods need to be provided by local governments, rather than foreigners, if the goal is to foster the political cohesion of struggling nations. Furthermore... building nations cannot be done within the time span of an American presidency or two. It is a matter of generations rather than years.' It is easy to see how time compression, and the extreme pressures of the current era, can work to undermine such long-term nation-building projects.

Evans (1995) famously proposed that a requirement for successful developmental states is 'embedded autonomy', in which 'autonomy' refers to the ability of a rationalized bureaucracy to devise and implement policies without excessive interference from rent-seeking interest groups, and 'embedded' refers to networks with dominant *domestic* social and economic groups to help set up the necessary information and feedback loops between states and markets, preventing state elites from becoming rent seeking themselves. However, we propose that an *outward-facing* embedded autonomy is also necessary, in which the state is embedded in relevant external networks, but also has the autonomy to make policy most relevant for its developmental needs, and to create the conditions for domestic coalitions to enable this. Such embeddedness is not necessarily detrimental in itself, a point we shall return to.

Policy compression does not simply refer to external constraints on autonomous policy making, but to the proliferation of new actors, as well, such as nongovernmental organization (NGOs), private development financing with a public mission, donors, and increasing BRIC/G20 influence. Navigating this increasingly complex terrain, and avoiding policy fragmentation and contradiction, has become an increasingly important state requirement in the era of compressed development (Chapters 7 and 8).

Concluding comments

We close this chapter with some comments comparing our historical approach with that of Gerschenkron. At a very general level, we concur that institutions by necessity differ across eras, as earlier developers change the conditions for those coming after. We have presented this in the form of economic and geopolitical systems more explicitly, however, and treated states and markets not as fixed reference points, but as co-evolutionary. And while Gerschenkron appears to have accepted a liberal view of the British state, we have argued that the state plays a crucial role in economic development in *all* eras, including that of early development. That role increased in the era of late developers, but it increased in the UK as well.

The relationship between finance and industry, on the one hand, and states on the other, also evolves. Finance is not just an enabler of innovation or industrialization, but also a potential destabilizer, and a tool of the powerful, who can bend markets and states to their ambitions.

Concretely, in early developer Britain, divided finance was behind a divided capitalism, with provincial banks supplying industry, and the city playing an international finance role. Provincial banks and industry were also present in (early) late developers like Germany prior to the 1850s—and subsequently (Herrigel, 1996)—but new technologies and the growing scale of industry required a new kind of financial institution: universal or investment banks. These were not entirely beneficial, however, as they played an increasingly powerful role in 'finance capitalism', or the 'first financialization', and its speculative overextension, which was largely ignored by Gerschenkron.

In the era of post–World War II late-late development, the extended roles of the state which redressed these distortions were maintained, and finance was constrained. Liberalism was not abandoned, but was 'embedded'. The tensions between liberalism and its embedding resurfaced in the 1970s, and subsequently, finance was not only freed from its shackles, but financial innovations created a shadow banking system which accelerated a new financialization. Attacked as being a threat to the market, the (United States) state was increasingly influenced by finance (Galbraith, 2008). Even then, or perhaps through this, the ideology of the self-regulating market came with increasing state intervention and regulation (Vogel, 2018). These developments, and arguably the new production systems linked to the organization–technology dyad which we will explore in Chapter 3, would not have been anticipated by Gerschenkron's framework.

Perhaps the bottom line for compressed developers, though, is something Gerschenkron *would* have predicted: that externally imposed institutions are no substitute for state building, and without state building, there can be no sustainable long-term development. This is a key challenge for compressed developers, which, as we shall see, some have navigated with considerable creativity.

3

Eras

Organizations and Technology

Introduction

In the book's introduction we wrote that compressed development has two main features: 'compression,' and 'era' effects. '*Time* compression' (Chapter 1) refers to the tendency for economic growth—to the extent it happens—to take place faster than in earlier developers as a result of catch-up learning, leapfrogging, and other shortcuts (Gerschenkron, 1962). This feature of development also interconnects and compresses *space*, juxtaposing the old and new spatially, as well as temporally, disembedding connected places, especially large 'global cities', from their own hinterlands and histories (Sassen, 1990, 2002; Massey, 1994).

The second feature, which can feed into and accentuate time and space compression, has to do with the 'era' in which a country's integration into the global economy takes place. Compression arises not only from faster development as later (successful) developers learn from what has come before, but also from the stamp placed on development processes by the historically specific characteristics of the contemporaneous era. In Chapter 2 we explored the how the co-evolution of states and markets (including finance), in conjunction with the geopolitical and economic systems projected by dominant powers, have shaped development eras. We further pointed to the narrowing of policy space as a characteristic of the current compressed-development era.

In this chapter we bring in the second of our era-shaping dyads, organizations and technology, to document how historically situated organizational paradigms and management models and their co-travellers (i.e. the ascendant, transversal, general-purpose technologies of the day) shape development experiences and accentuate compression. Specifically, we examine 'revolutionizing' and 'balancing' cycles in dominant organizational models, typically exemplified by an era's most important enterprises based in dominant powers. They are loosely coupled to disrupting and generalizing cycles in technology, as depicted in Figure 3.1.

The cycles in organizations and technologies mimic the Polanyian double movements described for states and markets in Chapter 2 in that new technologies open up both new markets and possibilities for reconfiguring existing organizations and industries. Both technological and organizational change tend to

Compressed Development: Time and Timing in Economic and Social Development. D. Hugh Whittaker, Timothy J. Sturgeon, Toshie Okita, and Tianbiao Zhu, Oxford University Press (2020). © D. Hugh Whittaker, Timothy J. Sturgeon, Toshie Okita, and Tianbiao Zhu. DOI: 10.1093/oso/9780198744948.001.0001

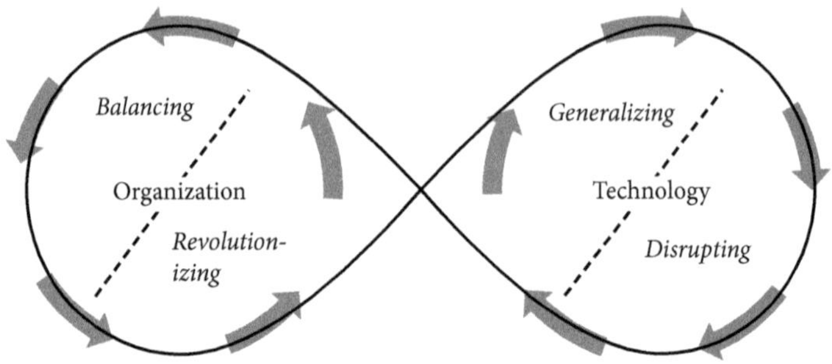

Figure 3.1 Organization-technology co-evolution and cycles

provoke predictable counter-reactions. After the rush of possibilities from new, technology-enabled management models, which are typically embodied at first in a few highly successful companies, soon stimulate their widespread imitation both at home and abroad, and organizations seek to balance and consolidate their gains while offsetting negative consequences.[1] Similarly, technologies tend to become more standardized as they become generalized across firms and industries, often by necessity, via a variety of transmission mechanisms (Ponte and Sturgeon, 2013; Dallas et al., 2019). As between states and markets, the two cycles do not move in lockstep, but co-evolve in ways that are as likely to be sequential or dissonant as simultaneous, complementary, or coordinated. Despite this complexity and unevenness, it is worth characterizing these organizational and technological era effects on development in a general way, at least as a starting point for our subsequent discussion.

The chapter is organized as follows. To set the organizational and technological era characteristics of compressed development in context, we present a stylized framework for the evolution of *organizational paradigms* and their accompanying management models within historically situated *techno-economic periods*, following Bodrožić and Adler (2017). This framework draws primarily on the US experience, which has been particularly influential in the periods under review. In the second section, we briefly trace the shift from the *corporate*, or *Fordist organizational paradigm* of the latter half of the twentieth century, to what has become known as the *network organizational paradigm*, a set of strategies and business practices that rose to prominence in the 1990s and 2000s, strongly influenced by financialization.

[1] Of course, the question of who benefits from these balancing efforts is a contested one. Consequences might be negative for one set of actors but positive for others. For example, the generalization and standardization of management models and technologies can have the effects of lowering barriers to entry, lowering the profits and technological dominance of incumbents, but opening up possibilities for newer entrants.

A spatial corollary of the network organizational form can be found in global value chains (GVCs), where production processes are fragmented and spread across multiple countries, and innovation and market-facing activities are commonly separated from production and routine services. The implications for developing countries are profound. Like financialization, GVCs work to compress policy space because they disembed fragments of economic activity from domestic institutions. The separation of production and innovation and constrained domestic inter-industry linkages engendered by GVCs are therefore key factors in thin industrialization.

To this sequence, we add the *platform* organizational paradigm, which has been creating a set of new industries and revolutionizing many established ones while the techno-economic period of the *digital economy* unfolded in the 2010s. The chapter is closely linked to Chapter 5, which provides evidence of how era effects intersect with industrial policy by drawing on specific developing country-industry examples. In Chapter 9 we include some possible scenarios related to the emergent techno-economic era, the *digital economy*. Although primarily focused on the US experience, this chapter enables us to understand how production systems have changed, and the impact of this on developing countries in the era of compressed development.

Techno-economic periods and organizational paradigms

While most easily recognized and characterized *ex post*, ideas about 'best practices' in management and industrial organization tend to build and coalesce over time to eventually become conventional wisdom, if only temporarily. A fitting place to start our discussion of organizational paradigms is with the technologies and management innovations of the Industrial Revolution, whose profound impact rippled out from Britain, transforming the way people live and work, by dramatically raising productivity, and producing a 'great divergence' between northwest Europe and other countries, including China and East Asia (Pomeranz, 2000). It was not a one-off revolution. Successive bursts of technological, work organization, and business model innovations produced further upheavals whose impact spread as more countries began to industrialize. Such 'waves' or 'cycles' of innovation are spatially and temporally irregular, and incompletely deployed, but they nevertheless provide a useful heuristic.

A sequence of techno-economic periods

The notion of waves of economic and social change based on a sequence of underlying techno-economic periods or 'Kondratiev cycles' caught the attention of Joseph Schumpeter, who saw economic development as driven by innovation funded by credit money (Schumpeter, 1934). Others have taken Schumpeter's ideas and refined and updated them. In Perez's (2002) schematic, a new techno-economic period begins with 'installation' following an 'irruption' of a new, invasive technology. Investors are attracted, and a split occurs between parts of the 'old' economy and parts of the new. As the latter gains momentum, investors pile in. Speculation mounts, and financial capital comes to dominate, both in the decline of the old and the emergence of the new. When speculation reaches an unsustainable level, a turning point is reached—often in the form of a crash—at which point the government regulators step in, laying the grounds for a 'development' phase, starting with a golden age of 'synergy', followed by maturity and eventually stagnation.

Perez describes five such periods or cycles occurring since the late eighteenth century. Her schematic, in turn, has been refined and elaborated by others, most recently by Bodrožić and Adler (2017), who significantly, for our purposes, link each new period of technological innovation to a corresponding wave of change in dominant *organizational paradigms and their associated management models*. The rise of each new wave overlaps with the previous one since incubation and exhaustion periods can be long. Still, new technologies and their attendant management models are spawned and incubated, codified and installed, promoted and deployed, and often contested within an identifiable constellation of managers, consultants, and 'management gurus' from both within and outside of the academy. They tend to be pioneered within one or a small set of firms and industries, and are associated with clusters of radically new products, processes, and business practices, which eventually diffuse across wider swathes of the economy, not least because the technologies underlying each wave tend to be general-purpose and transversal. Developing and commercializing products and processes based on new technologies often requires changes within firms, as well as in supporting institutions (e.g. finance and education), and critically, to the quantity, location, and content of jobs.[2] Thus the structure of firms, industries, and employment may face significant upheavals, especially in the earlier phases of each period.

Bodrožić and Adler further note that each organizational paradigm can be conceived as evolving through subphases and that what are often taken as competing management models at the time are better understood, with hindsight, as dialectical cycles. First comes a *revolutionizing cycle*, when rapid adoption of new technologies and business practices are pursued mainly for the sake of efficiency, with decisions often taken with little consideration of the consequences for labour or the politics of organizations. This provokes disputes and disruptions

[2] Here Bodrožić and Adler build on Chandler's (e.g. 1977) pioneering work to show how organizational forms shift to match the strategies enabled by new waves of technological innovation.

for both management and labour, which are then ameliorated—though not necessarily resolved—by a second, *balancing cycle*, during which management attempts to harness the social and psychological inputs from labour rather than purging them. The techno-economic periods, organizational paradigms, and management models identified by Bodrožić and Adler, along with four corresponding dialectical pairs, are summarized in the *unshaded* section of Table 3.1.[3]

In the revolutionizing and balancing cycles of first three organization paradigms, the line and staff model gave way to industrial betterment in the professionally managed firm; scientific management gave way to human relations in the 'factory'; and strategy and structure gave way to quality management in the Fordist Corporation. It is the subsequent techno-economic period of computers and telecom and the associated network paradigm these technologies have enabled that capture our attention because of the revolutionary and balancing management models that emerged during that period—with linking and rationalizing giving way to knowledge management—that have been influential in the era of compressed development.[4]

The techno-economic periods in Table 3.1 broadly overlap with the historical development eras of Chapter 2.[5] This raises interesting questions about causation, and relations between the dyads. Causal relations are complex and may be temporally separated or delayed, especially across space (Vernon, 1966). Clearly, however, a dominant power—or other country—may fail to fully exploit new technologies, even ones which it has pioneered, because of difficulties in moving on from previously successful organization paradigms. This may contribute to its waning influence, and, conversely, successful adoption may contribute to the rise of a new power, and (historical/developmental) era. Britain in the late nineteenth century is a well-known example which failed to fully utilize the emerging technologies and organization forms of the late nineteenth century (Chandler, 1990; Chapter 2). Similarly, the successes of Japan in implementing key organizational and management innovations in the late- and late-late-development eras—innovations that helped to define and diffuse the balancing

[3] Bodrožić and Adler omit the first of their five techno-economic periods—water-power and iron (1750s–1840s)—as it was centred in Britain, and was not associated with a clear management model. The table, to repeat, is based on the United States.

[4] Bodrožić and Adler propose that the arena for change is progressively widened in each revolutionizing phase, from the professionalization of managers, to rationalizing work stations and factories, to adapting the structure of corporations to match increased geographic and market scope of the multidivisional and multinational enterprise, and finally, to re-engineering the firm through outsourcing and specialization in the network paradigm. The secondary, balancing cycles also expand from individual managers and workers, to teams, and to external 'communities of practice'. This has involved a broadening cast of characters, as well, from owners to key managers and academics, to a wide array of specialized service providers and targeted results-oriented policy-makers.

[5] We should note, however, that the periodization of Table 3.1 is not our own, and transitions are marked by overlaps rather than gaps, as in Table 2.1. Our development eras are depicted at the bottom of Table 3.1, without dates.

Table 3.1 Compression of techno-economic eras, organizational paradigms, management models, and concepts, 1860s to present

Techno-economic period	Steam power and rail		Steel and electricity		Autos and oil		Computers and telecom		Digital economy	
Organizational paradigm	The professionally managed firm: rationalized management of a geographically dispersed enterprise 1861–1913		The factory: enterprise with a unitary, centralized organizational structure 1896–1945		The [Fordist] corporation: mass production in strategically integrated yet autonomous divisions 1955–1992		The network: linking and rationalizing processes across internal and external boundaries 1991–2005		The platform: platform ownership augmented by complementors in nested ecosystems 2008–present	
Phas	Revolutionizing cycle	Balancing cycle	Revolutionizing cycle	Balancing cycle	Revolutionizing cycle	Balancing cycle	Revolutionizing cycle	Balancing cycle	Revolutionizing cycle	Balancing cycle (speculative)
Dominant management model and key elements	Line and staff: specialized management, unrelated to owners, responsibly manage firm	Industrial betterment: Social function added to management to improve living and working conditions	Scientific management: Time and motion study, incentive wages and workflow analysis to accelerate production	Human relations: Line managers and staff specialists become responsible for mitigating alienation induced by rationalization	Strategy and structure: Differentiating internal structure to match differentiated products	Quality management: Deploying a management system to involve personnel at all levels in continuously improving product and process quality	Linking and rationalizing: Redesign of business processes up and down the value chain, redrawing and bridging internal and external boundaries	Knowledge management: Cultivation of communities of practice to regain, retain, or improve the innovation capacity of dispersed employees	Platform innovation: Leveraging user data and platform complementors for continuous integration and deployment, and automated decision-making	Data democracy/ meritocracy Data subjects provided default control over personal data and platform complementors tagged and duly compensated for contributions to technology ecosystem?
Key concepts/ search terms	• Line and staff • Organization chart	• Industrial betterment • Employee benefit • Welfare work • Welfare secretary	• Scientific management • Taylorism • Standards and methods	• Human relations • Group dynamics • Personnel counselling	• Profit centre • Operations research • Corporate strategy • Multidivisional • Matrix structure • Management by objective	• Lean production • Job enrichment • Quality circle • Organizational learning • Total quality management • Continuous improvement	• Outsourcing • Business process redesign/re-engineering • Core competencies • Horizontal organization • Process improvement • Business model • Interfirm network • Supply-chain management	• Offshoring • Knowledge management • Knowledge repository • Intellectual capital • Communities of practice • Agile • Scrum	• Cloud computing • Crowdsourcing • Internet of things • Technology ecosystems • Network effects • Two-sided markets • Social media • Big data analytics • Automated testing • Open innovation • Predictive maintenance	• Data privacy, • General Data • Privacy Regulation, right to be forgotten, privacy by design? • Data protection officer? • Block chain? • Guaranteed income? • Organizing contingent workers?
Time periods	1861–1895 34 years	1895–1913 18years	1896–1929 33 years	1929–1945 16 years	1955–1972 7 years	1972–1992 20 years	1991–1996 5 years	1996–2005 9 years	2008–2018? 10 years	2018–? ? years
	52 years		49 years		37 years		14 years		? years	
Organizational form	Unitary				Multidivisional and multinational		Networked and globally integrated			
Vertical structure	Integrated, with geographically proximate suppliers				Internal network, captive supply bases		External network, shared supply base		Two-sided markets, platform complementors	
Geographic scope	National				Multinational		Global value chain			
Development era	(Early) late development				(late)		(Early) compressed development (late?)			

Source: Adapted from Bodrožić and Adler (2017: 7–8). Shaded cells added by the authors. Search terms for key managerial concepts were dated by Bodrožić and Adler according to the first year in which the frequency of the term accelerates in the literature as found in bibliographic data sets including ABI/Inform complete, Hoovers Company profiles, ProQuest Historical Annual Reports, American Periodicals, and ProQuest Historical Newspapers collection.

cycle of Fordism—made it difficult for many of Japan's flagship industrial firms to adapt to the network model which took hold in the late 1990s and 2000s (Sturgeon, 2007, and Chapter 9).

Linking techno-economic periods to industry and spatial organization

We have added our own rows in the shaded lower portion of Table 3.1 to characterize and temporally situate firm-level organizational forms, vertical structures, geographic scopes, and associated development eras roughly within Bodrožić and Adler's techno-organizational periodization. At the firm level, organizational forms have evolved from the *unitary form*, carried over from the family firm of the earliest period of industrialization (not shown in Table 3.1) but adapted to the increased scale allowed by mechanization and formalized management in the first two periods, to the *multidivisional and multinational forms*, which rose to prominence in the postwar (Fordist) period, to the *network and globally integrated forms* emblematic of the network and (apparently) digital periods.

Changes in the vertical structure of firms and industries mirrored these shifts. In the first two periods, firms were likely to be embedded in clusters or *vertically integrated* in instances where scale and geographic coverage required it (e.g. railroads), and technology and product standardization allowed it. With the rise in both scale and scope in higher throughput factories, the critical nature of inputs led Fordist enterprises to either internalize supply chains or secure inputs through captive linkages with suppliers (Chandler, 1962). In the network era, weaker modular ties and growing supplier capabilities allowed flexibility and global expansion of buyer-supplier relationships, leading to an externalized, shared, yet globally integrated supply base (Sturgeon, 2002; Sturgeon and Lester, 2004; Gereffi et al., 2005), as we shall see. In the platform organizational paradigm, suppliers often come in the form of platform complementors, adding value to the larger network via even looser ties.[6] These shifts are broadly associated with a simultaneous increase in geographic scope and improvement in spatial integration, moving from national, to multinational, to GVCs, where vertical functions, including the supply of physical and intangible inputs, can be spread across multiple locations before final products and services make their way to end users.

Finally, as indicated by the bottom row on Table 3.1, techno-economic periods, organizational paradigms, and prevailing management models can be loosely

[6] Platform complementors arise at multiple levels in nested platform ecosystems, both as contributors to the basic functioning of the platform or as providers of final goods and services discovered and delivered to end users via the platform (Thun and Sturgeon, 2019; UNCTAD, 2017).

associated with development eras, shifting from organic development processes to more explicit developmental processes over time, where industrialization, growth, and technological learning are specifically targeted by large firms, entrepreneurs, financial actors, and the developmental institutions of the state. This row links Table 3.1 to Table 2.1, without suggesting unidirectional causation (or technological determinism). We time the early phase of compressed development with the latter stages of the balancing cycle of Fordism, when quality movements in advanced economies began to put pressure on developing country suppliers to meet higher requirements, at first in the foreign affiliates of multinational firms, and later, during the core compressed-development period, in the extended and externalized supply bases prominent in GVCs.

This broad and highly stylized narrative warrants a number of caveats. First, technology alone does not 'unleash revolutions', since it is the heterogeneous technology-based strategies of firms and the diverse institutional and societal responses to these strategies that create revolutionizing and balancing cycles and shape specific outcomes. Second, there is nothing purely mechanical or performance-based about shifts to new organizational paradigms and management models. 'Best practices' are rarely based entirely on objective, long-term performance measures, and are commonly driven by ideology (e.g. management fads) or competitive isomorphism (Christensen and Raynor, 2003). Although the shift from one organizational paradigm to another is signalled by the rise of a few highly competitive firms emblematic of the new model, it is always less than clear—and almost certainly untrue—that any new model is 'best' for all firms or under all circumstances. Third, management models can be seen as distinct from practice because paradigms are grossly altered and adapted as they are translated into specific action across divisions such as industry, geography, or firm size (Barley and Kunda, 1992). In fact, rather than bringing convergence towards a norm, the diffusion of management models tends to trigger diversity as they are adopted and adapted across industries and institutional *milieus* far from their points of origin (Sturgeon, 2007).[7]

Still, there are several additional insights to be gleaned from this extended historical framework in regard to development models, and specifically for time compression. The first has to do with timing and duration. Bodrožić and Adler do not foreground the obvious shortening of techno-economic periods, but nevertheless have timed the onset of organizational paradigms, and their double cycles, by identifying the first year in which the appearance of key management concepts accelerate in a corpus of bibliographic datasets (see Figure 3.2).[8] This approach

[7] Observing, characterizing, and explaining these variations has become a cottage industry of sorts, under the rubric of 'varieties of capitalism', business systems, and other institutionalist approaches.

[8] The onset of the digital era was timed by identifying the acceleration of key phrases—'cloud computing' and 'crowdsourcing'—in Google's N-gram corpus of scanned books, a data set that currently ends in 2008 (see Figure 3.2).

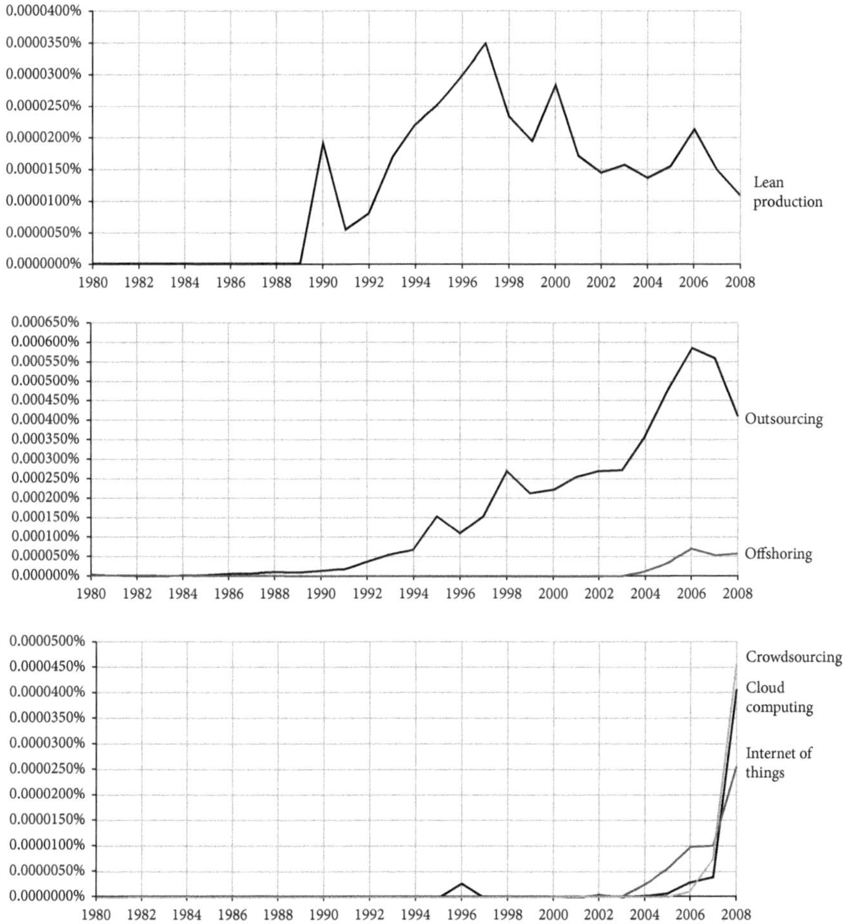

Figure 3.2 Bibliographic timing of key concepts from the network and platform organizational paradigms (appearance Google N-gram corpus, per cent of books)

Notes: Google's N-gram viewer shows the occurrence of words or word phrases in books published through 2008 as a percentage of all books in the corpus, a body of scanned volumes which contains about 5 million books. In this case the corpus includes all scanned books written in English. The data are normalized by the number of books published in each year, and only matches found in at least forty books are included in the data set. As of 2008, 'lean production' appeared in the title of 125 books, with the phrase appearing in 433 volumes. The concept was stretched to adapt to the network era with modifiers such as 'lean extended enterprise' and 'lean supplier development' which focused on relationships with suppliers. 'Outsourcing' appeared in about 480 book titles through 2008, and 'offshoring' in about 223. Similarly, the phrase 'Internet of things' appeared in 233 book titles published between 2003 and 2008; 'cloud computing' in 403 titles between 2004 and 2008; and 'crowdsourcing' in 122 titles between 2005 and 2008.

Source: Google N-gram viewer: https://books.google.com/ngrams.

accounts for instances when key concepts gain currency long after they are first introduced in the literature. By summarizing the time periods associated with each organizational paradigm, a clear pattern of compression can be detected: the overall period for the past four techno-economic periods has shrunk from fifty-two years for the professionally managed firm to just fourteen for the network paradigm. As intriguing, the relative periodicity of the revolutionizing and balancing cycles appears to have reversed, with longer revolutionizing cycles and shorter balancing cycles in earlier eras, and shorter revolutionizing cycles and longer balancing cycles in later eras. These figures are not based on any exact science, but rather the possibility that it has become easier to quickly upset the status quo with new technologies and organizational paradigms and more difficult for society at large to adapt to them is intuitively appealing.

The crisis of Fordism and the rise of the network model

As Table 3.1 suggests, the dominant organizational paradigm for most of the twentieth century was the large, professionally managed, vertically integrated, and (eventually) multidivisional and multinational 'modern' or 'Fordist' corporation. Vertical integration and the seemingly inexorable increase of firm size was noted and debated by scholars early on (e.g. Chamberlin, 1933; Schumpeter, 1942; Chandler, 1962) and explained (or justified) along several lines, from realizing the potential scale efficiencies offered by mechanized production equipment by internally controlling the flow of both inputs (suppliers) and outputs (distribution channels) (Chandler, 1977), to blocking suppliers of inputs from acquiring excessive power (Williamson, 1981), to accumulating the resources and scope to engage in science-led innovation and attract public sources of R&D funding (Gibbons et al., 1994).[9]

The crisis of Fordism came in several forms and engendered several responses. First was the rise of successful competitors to American and European flagship firms, mainly from Japan, and the notion that the crisis had to do specifically with the Western form of Fordism. If the Japanese model could be understood, codified, and adopted in the West, competitiveness could be restored (Dertouzos et al., 1989; Womack et al., 1990; Florida and Kenney, 1991, 1993). Indeed, the tenets of 'lean production'[10] were eventually codified and rolled out

[9] Alongside these organizational characteristics was the approach to managerial control over labour, which evolved from coercion in the premodern era, to efficiency- and self-interest-seeking (Taylorist, or rational) to an appeal for emotional (normative) buy-in by deepening ranks of middle managers (Barley and Kunda, 1992).

[10] These include low work-in-progress inventory via a 'pull', or 'kanban', system that exerted tight control over suppliers and ordered parts components only as needed, team-based multitasking and job rotation in 'cellular' nodes rather than long assembly lines, and worker involvement and quality circles to engender a culture of 'continuous improvement'.

from sector to sector, giving rise to a huge consulting industry which continues to thrive. With the adoption of lean production, quality went up and design cycle time down in Western firms.[11] However, despite objections from most 'gurus' of lean production, lean practices can and often were applied piecemeal, with reduced in-process inventory and increased monitoring raising productivity and quality without the employer commitments to job security—required to motivate buy-in from workers—that was a central feature of the model in Japan. The result, especially when sales remained the same, was downsizing, as workers were eliminated in the warehouse, for example, while on production lines work was intensified (deTreville and Antonakis, 2006). So, the adaptation of US industry to pressure from the Japanese model laid the groundwork for a shift towards vertical dis-integration and the rise of the network organizational paradigm. By the late 1990s, even the Japanese version of Fordism had come under pressure, forcing Japanese flagships to restructure and adapt (see Chapters 4 and 9).

Outsourcing

The 1990s were a time of widespread downsizing, computerization, and outsourcing in large organizations in the United States. While Japanese firms initially relied more on external sources of supply than Western firms did in the Fordist period, outsourcing in Japan was 'quasi-hierarchical', with closer ties maintained to long-term suppliers than what emerged in the 'new American model' (Nishiguchi, 1994; Humphrey and Schmitz, 2002; Sturgeon, 2002), albeit with variations by industry. With new, more powerful enterprise computing systems and information technology (IT) systems for tracking material flows and work processes, business processes were rationalized in the United States, sometimes brutally so. Such corporate 're-engineering' and its ugly twin, 'downsizing', were technologically enabled, but driven by *finance*, not engineering or R&D departments. In the revolutionary phase of the network cycle and beyond, financialization led institutional investors to demand that manufacturing companies in the United States (and later, Europe) to shift their balance sheets away from fixed expenses (owned plant and equipment) towards variable expenses (purchased inputs, manufacturing, and other business services). The equity residing in fixed

[11] A data-driven corollary of lean production in the United States was 'Six Sigma', a statistical approach to quality control in manufacturing that gained currency in the late 1980s through the 1990s. Six Sigma was so-called because it aimed to reduce defect rates to only 3.4 per million process steps: a 99.99966 per cent yield rate. Like lean production, Six Sigma was rooted in the teachings of US statistician W. Edwards Deming, who consulted with Japanese companies in the 1950s, and later with US companies, such as with Ford, General Motors, and eventually Motorola, where his ideas were formalized as Six Sigma in the mid-1980s. And like lean production, it eventually grew into a consultancy-driven management fad that pushed it into business functions, such as sales and marketing, where its applications are dubious (Staley, 2019).

assets such as factories could be extracted and distributed to top management and investors, while purchasing could be financed with debt. As a result, large manufacturing firms were rewarded by financial markets for selling off manufacturing plants and component divisions to contract manufacturers and parts suppliers from which they could buy services and inputs on an as-needed basis (Sturgeon, 2002).

One argument for these changes was that the network paradigm provided a nimbler and more innovative alternative to the giant firm (Fine, 1998). Using changes in the computer industry as a model (see Figure 3.3) Grove ([1996] 1999) argued that the [Fordist] vertically integrated enterprise had become too sprawling and slow to react to accelerated technological changes, and that more focused firms could better adapt to and advance rapid technological change. There was hope among some observers that the 'crisis of Fordism' (Lipietz, 1987) would mean less concentration, smaller firms, more responsiveness to local institutions, and more egalitarian management and labour relationships (Sabel, 1989). This was based in part on the re-emergence (or at least durable competitiveness of) Italian 'industrial districts'.[12] This view was generalized by Piore and Sabel (1984) and their followers as 'flexible specialization', characterized by spatially concentrated and socially embedded networks of specialized and interdependent small firms and spreading to the affiliates of large firms as well.

Critics were quick to point out that there was no empirical evidence of large firm decline, no necessity for them to become more spatially embedded, and no incompatibility between small firm networks in industrial districts or technology clusters, and horizontal integration and consolidation (Harrison, 1994). Indeed, large scale yields important competitive and survival advantages for firms, and was retained even as scope was attenuated with industry fragmentation in the 'new American' network model. The focus on 'core competencies' on one hand and 'strategic outsourcing' on the other hand came with 'horizontal integration' and consolidation across nearly all value-chain segments (Prahalad and Hamel, 1990; Quinn and Hilmer, 1994; Sturgeon, 2002; Jacobides, 2006). Harrison (1994: 8) referred to this as 'concentration without centralization'.

Concentration was especially notable in *middle* segments of the value-added chain that had previously been populated by locally embedded small and medium-sized firms. In addition to large firms at the head (e.g. car and computer companies) and tail (materials like steel) of the value chain, specialized large firms emerged across a range of products and business functions, from intermediate goods such as car parts and semiconductors, to machinery, retail, and business services (e.g. software, accounting, mortgage banking, consulting, and finance). The shift from vertical to horizontal integration, along with increasing scale and

[12] Brusco (1986); Becattini (1978); and ultimately Marshall ([1890] 1961), who had noted that specific industries tended to be concentrated in specific cities—often referred to today as 'clusters'.

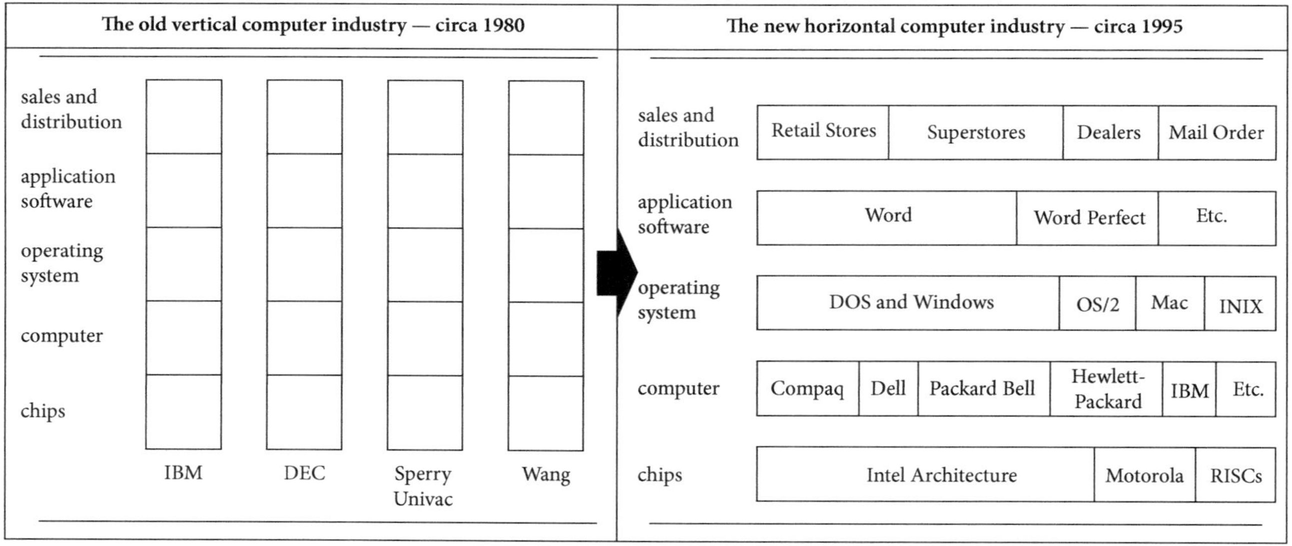

Figure 3.3 From vertical to horizontal industry organization, the case of computers

Source, Grove ([1996] 1999: 42), not to scale.

scope in the largest suppliers, added new external economies derived from inter-firm networks to the traditional scale advantages of large firms (Sturgeon and Lester, 2004).

The industry structures of the network organizational paradigm were not novel, but the economies of scope enabled by the rising capabilities and plummeting costs of computers and telecom supercharged the model. And crucially, as business processes were computerized and modularized (compartmentalized and standardized), higher levels of complexity in business systems could be supported without internalization in the giant firm. The result was aggregation of both scale and scope in horizontal slices of industries, and where business functions transcend industry-centric application, such as IT services, call centres, and manufacturing services. It also increased both in the flexibility and the scale of production in what has been referred to as 'mass customization' (Pine and Davis, 1999) supported by 'value-chain modularity' (Gereffi et al., 2005).

Finally, along with the shift in industry organization was a shift in ideology about the nature of competition and employment. Vertically fragmented industries enabled innovation in open architectures, based on either *de facto* or *de jure* standards, to ensure interoperability and the design and integration of larger systems (Principe et al., 2003).[13] Technology, especially computerization, accelerated the pace of change. Companies were told to follow the 'HP way', and jettison deep management hierarchies in favour of flat organizational structures to speed communication (Packard, 2006). Workers were exhorted to 'be the CEOs of their own careers', and engage in lifelong skill development (Grove, [1996] 1999). Independent contracting, rather than long-term regular employment, began its long march towards the mainstream.

Offshoring and the rise of global value chains

The spatial corollary to outsourcing in the network model was 'offshoring'. As Williamson (1981) observed, the modern corporation in its multidivisional form was well suited for internationalization. Divisions in multinational firms were

[13] Open product architectures are common today, but their use in technology-intensive industries can be traced to IBM's introduction of its 360 series computers in the mid-1960s, for which connections were standardized and requirements were published, allowing third-party firms to produce complementary equipment such as printers and data storage. This was considered a revolutionary step at the time, but it was eventually seen to be responsible for increasing IBM's market reach, improving functionality based on innovations by complementors, and reducing costs through competition in areas IBM was less focused on. As such, the (modest, at first) opening of its product architecture to others was a precursor to the outsourcing wave of the 1990s, but once the network model was established, open, modular product architectures and standards for interfaces that facilitate the interconnection devices into larger, more complex systems became a necessity.

semi-autonomous and set up to serve markets in countries with large potential markets and regulatory barriers to imports. Management hierarchies were duplicated in each geographic division, and when necessary, products were developed or at least adapted to suit local markets. As Vernon (1966) noted, obsolete manufacturing equipment was often physically transported to less-developed economies following a 'product-cycle' logic.[14] While outmoded and inflexible, such Fordist-era production equipment tended be fully amortized and, therefore, highly profitable. The ability of multinational corporations (MNCs) to succeed in developing country markets, especially in technologically intensive goods such as automobiles and computers, was seen to stem from a series of firm-specific advantages that offset any 'liability of foreignness' emerging from cultural, economic, institutional, or geographic distance (Buckley and Casson, 1976; Dunning, 1988).

Many important manufacturing industries took on a new character with the rise of the network model. In labour-intensive industries such as household goods, garments, footwear, and agro-foods, a highly influential set of 'global buyers' from the United States had been gaining greater scale and influence since the 1970s (Hamilton and Kau, 2018). This included discount retailers such as J. C. Penny, Kmart, and Wal-Mart, companies that placed huge orders with suppliers around the world without establishing any factories of their own (Gereffi, 1994). Often, intermediaries (for example, trading companies such as Hong Kong's Li & Fung) were used to link buyers to producers, first on mainland China and eventually in multiple countries. The market focus of global buyers, at least initially, was to undercut domestic competition at home, and their success at doing so demonstrated that low-cost products could be supplied and even seasonally replenished through international outsourcing, especially to East Asia (but also, for U.S. markets, Mexico).

Focusing on the emergence of Taiwan, Hamilton and Kao (2017) provide a detailed account of how the rise of discount merchandisers in the United States led to increased sourcing from 'the Orient' and how this in turn helped to create a set of 'demand responsive' economies in East Asia that based their development on contract production for export. What looked like export success by East Asian economies was often driven by large-scale purchases from Western buyers and (MNC) affiliates (Feenstra and Hamilton, 2006). Eventually, retailers and branded

[14] Cf. also the 'flying geese' model (Chapter 1). This practice was common in industries with high fixed-capital requirements, such as textiles and automobiles. For example, production equipment for the original 1959 Ford Falcon was moved to Argentina in 1962, where the model remained in production with only minor modifications until 1991, by which time 490,000 units had been produced (Sturgeon and Florida, 2004). As we shall see (Chapters 5 and 9), the willingness of consumers and companies in less-developed countries to accept 'hand-me-down' products and production technology has diminished rapidly in the era of compressed development.

merchandisers in Europe (Tesco and Schwarz Gruppe) and even Japan (Uniqlo) followed suit.

The broadening of the network model accelerated in the 1990s when technologically intensive industries fully embraced the entwined strategies of outsourcing and offshoring, creating vertically and spatially fragmented production systems that came to resemble the sourcing networks in labour-intensive industries, but with a need for tighter coordination given the more complex nature of the products. This was enabled by the ongoing shift to horizontal organizational structures, which allowed narrow, labour-intensive and otherwise cost-sensitive slices of the value chain to be more easily located in places with 'low operating costs'—a term that encompasses not only low labour rates but poor worker safety and environmental protections.[15]

These changes caught the attention of a few scholars early on, who discerned the emergence of something other than the replication of MNC's home operations abroad: a 'new international division of labour' (Fröbel et al., 1980), where export-oriented, cost-cutting 'maquiladora' plants and 'global factories' (Grunwald and Flamm, 1985) concentrated labour-intensive segments of the value chain in places, including export-processing zones, with low operating costs, such as Mexico, North Africa, and East and South-East Asia. When large countries Brazil, India, and China opened to large-scale investment with the establishment of the World Trade Organization in 1995, the field for globalization suddenly and vastly increased. Freeman (2005) refers to this as the 'Great Doubling' of the available global labour force.

In addition to the cost-cutting motivation for globalization of the network model, the market-seeking motives of multinational firms and newly ascendant (and increasingly factoryless) global brands were also keen. Faced with often anaemic growth at home, large enterprises rushed to build brand recognition and market share in rapidly expanding and newly opening consumer markets in large countries such as Brazil, India, and China. For industries with shorter, regional supply lines, such as motor vehicles, the countries of Central and East Europe joined traditional export-processing locations such as Mexico and North Africa.[16] GVCs thus came to consist of a set of complex, fragmented, nested, and overlapping regional- and global-scale production networks that were at once cost-cutting and market-seeking in purpose.

[15] It was no accident that the firms that pioneered the use of 'export-processing zones' came from the semiconductor, consumer electronics, and high-volume computer industries (e.g. disk drives), where labour-intensive processes commonly involved the use of caustic or otherwise toxic chemicals (Smith et al., 2006). Similarly, in the garment industry, textile production often used and produced toxic chemicals, while the garment-assembly part of the value chain relied on heavily exploited, low-cost labour.

[16] Harvey's (1990) theory of uneven development refers to such regions as 'integrated peripheries'.

Developing countries and global suppliers

In in an attempt to capture the gains from GVCs, host governments imposed increasingly stringent local content requirements to generate employment and create opportunities for local suppliers (Lall, 1993). This set up a tension, as multinational firms often felt obliged to vertically integrate more than they would at home because suitable inputs were often unavailable from local firms, or because local supplier development was considered cumbersome. Critically, pressure to source locally was coming during the revolutionary cycle of the network model, when suppliers were not only absorbing more work, but also the tenets and practices of lean production, and were adopting modern IT systems compatible with lead firms. Thus, the requirements for suppliers were increasing by leaps and bounds just as multinational lead firms were under rising pressure to meet local content requirements in multiple jurisdictions.

A common solution was to outsource to a select group of suppliers, based mostly in advanced economies but also in more recently industrialized countries such as Taiwan and South Korea. Suppliers received great quantities of new work and pressure to follow their customers to offshore locations (Humphrey, 2000), and otherwise shift existing production to lower-cost locations, especially China (Kawakami, 2011). By the end of the 1990s, what previously had to be done within the confines of multinational affiliates could be externally sourced from newly competent 'global suppliers' and service providers with multiple offices, technical centres, and factories around the world (Sturgeon and Lester, 2004).

As a result, the character of MNCs changed. It is no longer accurate to conceptualize MNCs only as large brand-carrying enterprises, such as IBM, Nokia, or Toyota. Suppliers, vendors, and service providers such as Flextronics, Foxconn, Denso, Robert Bosch, Valeo, and Pao Chen have dozens, and sometimes hundreds, of production locations around the globe, as do distributors, equipment maintenance providers, logistics providers, and consultants of various stripes. This is straightforward enough for the enterprises involved—branded 'lead' firms sought to simplify and centralize their supplier relationships as they globalized by asking their largest suppliers to provide services in multiple locations. But this in turn compressed the space for industrial policy in developing countries. With global suppliers the preferred and in some cases only option for key inputs, the space for industrial policies to foment backward linkages to domestic suppliers in developing countries shrank dramatically. Local content requirements that had been established in part to provide opportunities for domestic suppliers instead had the effect of populating domestic industries with a new layer of MNCs.[17]

[17] This also shrank the organizational distance between lead firms and suppliers, allowing better monitoring and control at the first tier, including labour and environmental conditions. In lower tiers, however, pressure to conform to these standards has tended to be weaker, while pressure to lower costs

The crisis of the network model and its rebalancing

Outsourcing and offshoring was perceived as increasing flexibility and reducing costs and risks for lead firms. Competitive outcomes were not always positive, however, as some lost control over key intellectual assets related to production and the design of key parts and components, and others found vertical specialization and spatial fragmentation at odds with the technological and organizational interdependencies in the work being performed.[18] Moreover, the sustainability of the network model was called into question. Because they were being asked to contribute to lead firm design and engineering activities, underwrite warranties, and finance upstream component purchasing and inventory-carrying costs without adequate compensation (all a boon to newly financialized lead firms), the profit margins for global suppliers were razor thin or turned negative.

The bursting of the 'tech bubble' in 2001 tipped the network model into its balancing cycle. In some cases, especially in the automotive and commercial aircraft industries, supplier bankruptcies were rampant (Sturgeon, Van Biesebroeck, and Gereffi, 2008). With the global financial crisis in 2007–2008, some previously spun-off parts divisions had to be reabsorbed by their former parents, especially when it was clear that poor performance rendered them unable to meet pension liabilities (Sturgeon and Van Biesebroeck, 2010). In other cases, the balancing cycle was characterized by the selective addition of key knowledge-intensive components and functions, as with Apple's move to design its own central processing units for mobile handsets in 2016. More generally, it was signalled by heightened awareness of what could be lost through outsourcing, and the risks of relying on external parties for critical inputs. Companies turned to concepts such as 'knowledge management' (Alavi and Leidner, 2001), and began to worry about 'modularity traps': the loss of product distinctiveness from overreliance on suppliers for critical knowledge inputs (Chesbrough and Kusunoki, 2001).

'Sustainability' was thus to be achieved through a 'rightsizing' process (Wilkinson, 2005); the task was not to focus on a narrow set of competencies and outsource everything else, or to move all manufacturing to China or software development to India, but to dynamically curate a cohesive set of internal capabilities linked to external partners in ways that could ensure an enduring, profitable position within networked business ecosystems. Deciding what to

and meet faster delivery cycles continue to be transmitted, via the first tier, often worsening working and environmental conditions (Ponte, 2019). 'While lead firms exercise control over some aspects of complex supply chains— such as design and materials—other demands tend to fall by the wayside as network distance increases' (Bartley et al., 2019: 6).

[18] Colfer and Baldwin (2016) review the normative research on industry-, firm-, and project-level experiences under the network model.

outsource and what to retain or develop internally became a central preoccupation for senior managers, as did methods for better integrated spatially distributed teams.

A 'new' digital economy?

We have further extended the schematic set out by Bodrožić and Adler in the shaded righthand columns of Table 3.1 to accommodate what many perceive as a 'new' techno-economic period—the *digital economy*, characterized by the *platform organizational paradigm*, with a revolutionizing cycle driven by *platform innovation*.[19] Using the same bibliographic technique, we date the onset of the digital economy to about 2008 (see Figure 3.2). The digital economy can be described as a platform-based ecosystem of ICT-based products and services. The underlying theme, as in the network paradigm, is that of horizontal integration, shared supply bases, and global reach. The differences reside in the growing importance a handful of key technologies, the extreme scale and complexity of the external economies required, and the speed in which these mainly software-based products and systems can achieve global scale. The specific technologies include (1) new sources of data from mobile and ubiquitous Internet connectivity (sometimes referred to as the Internet of Things [IoT]), (2) cloud computing, (3) big data analytics, and (4) artificial intelligence (AI). The broad structure of the digital economy is evolving rapidly as larger and larger volumes of data flow from sensor-laden factory automation and business IT systems as well as Internet-connected user devices, most obviously smart phones, but including a growing list of Internet-connected products, from home appliances to automobiles. This is generating 'big data' pools that, because they reside in the 'cloud', can be aggregated and analysed, or 'mined', for patterns and correlations that remain hidden when data is more fragmented. Data can also be analysed by AI systems where machine learning and automated decision-making can suggest solutions for users, including upgrades to system elements or even entire systems.

The technological advances of the digital economy have come with a set of business models and industry organization characteristics that are meant to dynamically cope with growing system complexity. There is no way any one individual or organization can fully understand or control the underlying technology of the digital economy or the specific domains where it operates. Therefore, systems must be designed to dynamically cope with growing complexity without breaking, most generally by: (1) relying on platforms to connect users to third parties offering complementary products and services, (2) drawing on

[19] 'New' is presented here in scare quotes because of strong forces of continuity across techno-economic periods.

outside and even communally held sources of knowledge and technology,[20] and (3) partitioning systems into self-contained, manageable, affordable, yet interoperable modular segments. In other words, the digital economy is based on platforms, open innovation, and modularity. Platform innovation refers to the use and combination of these three strategic approaches.[21]

In Chapter 1 we introduced the concept of time compression as a general condition of development, but the shortening of what previously were more distinct 'stages'—to the point of simultaneity—is also a characteristic of technology adoption. The network and platform organizational paradigms, and the role of modularity in supporting organizational and geographical flexibility and scalability (in terms of both markets and geographic reach), have been in part enabled by Moore's Law, a rule of thumb used to explain the steady rise in capabilities and fall in costs in the information and communication technologies.[22] This has enabled a continual stream of new applications based on more powerful, lower-cost, smaller, and less-power-hungry electronic devices, which fosters a secular shortening of technology-adoption (and -replacement) cycles.

Table 3.2 shows the number of years it took for various technology applications to reach 50 million home users. Technology applications with great usefulness and consumer appeal have always, in a relative sense, spread 'like wildfire'. During the 'radio craze' of the 1920s, sales of in-home radio receivers in the United States grew from 5000 units in 1920 to 25 million units in 1924 (Howeth, 1963). And when population growth is taken into consideration, the acceleration of technology adoption appears much less dramatic, since 50 million users today represents a much smaller share of the population than in the past. Nonetheless, the general trend of faster technology adoption is still very apparent, especially with the digital and mainly software-based applications of the digital economy.[23]

There is no shortage of evangelists, promoters, and hand-wringers prognosticating about the promise and perils of the digital economy (e.g. Rose, 2016). Institutions such as the World Economic Forum have taken up the call under the banner of a 'Fourth Industrial Revolution' (Schwab, 2015, 2016), as have giant

[20] The complexity and multiplication of technology domains in the digital economy have led industry players to make heavy use of 'open innovation' (Chesbrough et al., 2006) to create the resources needed to develop and ensure the interoperability of a range of subsystem elements, from network infrastructure, to operating systems, to AI test datasets and algorithms. Open innovation refers to the strategy of relying on external, often shared and sometimes crowd-sourced resources as an integral part of a company's innovation process.

[21] See Parker et al. (2016) and UNCTAD (2017) for fuller discussions.

[22] Since the invention of the integrated circuit in 1959, improvements in semiconductor design and fabrication processes have progressed at an exponential, or log-linear rate, allowing the doubling of circuit density per square inch every sixteen months. This so-far inexorable path of improvement is often referred to as Moore's Law, as it was first expressed by Gordon Moore, co-founder of Fairchild Semiconductor and Intel.

[23] The mobile augmented reality game Pokémon Go crossed the 50-million-user threshold in only nineteen days and generated $207 million in revenue in its first month (Iqbal, 2019).

Table 3.2 Number of years for analogue and digital technology applications to reach 50 million home users

			Number of years to 50 million home users		
Technology basis	Applications	Year introduced for home use	Nominal	US population adjusted (2010)	World population adjusted (2010)
Analogue and mainly hardware-based	Telephone	1876	75.0	11.2	15.3
	Radio	1920	38.0	13.0	9.9
	Television	1928	13.0	5.0	3.7
Digital and manly software-based	Internet	1991	4.0	3.3	3.1
	Facebook	2004	2.0	1.9	1.9
	YouTube	2005	0.8	0.8	0.8
	Twitter	2006	0.8	0.7	0.7
	Instagram	2010	1.6	1.6	1.6

Sources: Years to 50 million users: Interactive Schools. US population: US Census Bureau, Statistical Abstract of the United States, 2011. World population: Worldometers.

firms seeking to position their technology solutions as dominant platforms in various realms of life and work.[24] In reality the development of the digital economy is likely to be contested along many fronts. Social and technical factors, such as data security risks or a backlash across various digital divides, could slow or even derail the development of the digital economy.[25] And rates of technology and business model adoption always vary widely across geographies.

This raises the question of a possible balancing cycle. Many of today's most highly valued (in terms of market capitalization) and fastest-growing companies (e.g. Facebook, Amazon, Apple, Uber, and WeChat) have platform innovation as their dominant business model. One could argue that this is the most intricate, interdependent, and globally integrated business model yet, with armies of platform complementors (e.g. Uber drivers, Airbnb hosts, Apple and Android app makers, etc.) both enabling its revolutionary cycle and perhaps helping to rapidly precipitate its balancing cycle as complementors push for better compensation

[24] Readers may be more familiar with the swirl of platform-based competition and regulatory controversy around social media services, but there are many counterparts on the industrial side, such as General Electric's Predix and Siemens' Mindsphere platforms, which offer centralized data storage and analytics and a host of third-party applications for use in manufacturing and other industrial settings.

[25] Nevertheless, as stressed by McAfee and Brynjolfsson (2016), the impact of any revolutionary technology is often over-estimated in the short term and under-estimated over the long term.

and more control over personal data.[26] We return to the question of a possible balancing cycle in the digital economy in Chapter 9.

Concluding comments

Consensus about how best to innovate, produce, and compete in vertically integrated 'Fordist' enterprises built to a peak in the 1970s (Hymer, 1976) but gradually swung towards fragmentation and specialization as the network organizational paradigm entered its deployment phase during the 1990s (Powell, 1987, 1990; Fine, 1998; Adler, 2001). While network organizational forms (including GVCs) were resilient in labour-intensive industries such as apparel, footwear, and household goods, the 'new' paradigm was loudly trumpeted in fast-moving, technology-intensive sectors such as computers and communications hardware and software. This interest was motivated at least in part by the spectacular growth of personal computer and computer networking firms (e.g. Intel, Apple, Microsoft, 3Com, Cisco, and Oracle) in US technology clusters such as Silicon Valley and Seattle (Storper and Scott, 1988; Davidow, 1992; Saxenian, 1994), but also by the rapid expansion of the global suppliers that grew along with them (Sturgeon and Lester, 2004). The network organizational paradigm was spearheaded by a specific set of corporate managers, management consultants, and academics (Bodrožić and Adler, 2017). It was deployed, with mixed results, in a range of important global industries, prominently including electronics, automobiles, and commercial aircraft, which joined the ranks of less technologically demanding industries that had begun to fragment and disperse in GVCs earlier (Fröbel et al., 1980).

Today, the network model is in full deployment across a broadening range of industries (e.g. oil and gas, services, tourism, etc.), and it involves a range of strategies beyond outsourcing and offshoring, including supplier monitoring programs and corporate code of conduct initiatives, and selective reintegration

[26] There does seem to be a Durkheimian trend towards organizational paradigms with an increasingly fine-grained division of labour, or 'roundaboutness', and increasing interdependence among actors. As Leamer and Storper (2001: 662) put it, 'Roundaboutness refers to number of intermediate steps required to generate a final output. A modern economy fragments production into an ever-increasing number of different specialized business units and separate sectors, such that a final product emerges in a "roundabout" way through the combination of intermediate products via transactions between these units and sectors. Roundaboutness is measured, in modern terms, through input-output analysis. The more roundabout the organization of production, the more complex the upstream division of labour or input-output system at hand.' Young (1929) introduced the concept of roundaboutness as a secular trend. While this is an intuitively appealing idea, the rationalizing possibilities of new technologies are often deployed to reduce complexity and increase flexibility in cases where roundaboutness may have become excessive or overly rigid. Moreover, the vision of small scale that it suggests can be offset by consolidation and global-scale market penetration by firms dominating specific GVC segments.

and reshoring to adapt to new production technologies and walk back some overreach in regard to offshoring and outsourcing. However, the necessity, and even possibility, of codification in electronics and software was not as evident in following sectors such as automobiles and commercial aircraft, and this, along with overvaluing of technology start-ups during the dot-com bubble, drove the network model to a crisis and into its balancing phase around 2001. Labour-intensive industries have also seen some balancing pressures related to labour and environmental conditions at anonymous contract manufacturers and smallholder farms (Barrientos, 2013).

The network and platform organizational paradigms have a strong influence on compressed development. The notion that globalization of production and markets, especially when combined with modern air travel and communications, 'shrinks' or compresses space, brings us to well-trod if contested ground (Berman, 1982; Harvey, 1989; Castells, 1996; Friedman, 2005), but when placed in context of the network model, a signature feature of GVCs comes to the fore: the geographic separation of innovation from production. More than anything else, perhaps, it is this disjuncture that characterizes the era-related effects of compressed development. Others include financialized valorization of variable over fixed assets and capital over labour, deindustrialization, the casualization of work, and rising inequality in industrialized countries; and low-value-added traps, thin industrialization, weakening state control over key economic agents, and the intrusion of global norms in social policy-making in developing economies. We will explore the development and policy implications of compressed development's era effects in more depth in Chapters 5–8.

Successive historical eras can be understood as the institutional and ideological stage upon which development processes are played out. In prior historical eras, compression was driven by later developers learning from earlier developers, not only in regard to technology but also in the institutional and financial models deployed for the establishment and operation of large-scale mass production. Today, in a historical period where the complex patterns of outsourcing, offshoring, and computerization of the network model are being overlain with the nested and interoperable platform ecosystems of the *digital economy*, it is easy enough to see how business models have been driving compression more intensely than ever before.

PART 2

EXPERIENCES OF COMPRESSED DEVELOPMENT

4
China's and Japan's Divergent Institutions

Introduction

When China embarked on its post-1978 reforms, Japan was riding high economically. Its late-development growth model was naturally of great interest to China's leaders as they set about opening up the economy and overhauling a wide range of institutions. Despite some parallels, however, China has not followed Japan's developmental path. The reasons relate to profound changes in technologies and the organization of production discussed in Chapter 3, as well as changes in the geopolitical and economic systems associated with the era of compressed development discussed in Chapter 2, particularly from the 1990s, when China's reforms deepened and growth accelerated, and after World Trade Organization accession in 2001. Conversely, Japan struggled with these same changes, diminishing its lustre as a model.[1]

In Chapters 2 and 3 we proposed that the 'era' in which a country becomes integrated into the global economy has a profound influence on institutional and economic development. We also developed some conceptual building blocks which helped to create a framework for comparisons of economic development. In this chapter we apply them to a country comparison of China and Japan. The comparison is made on the basis of both commonalities and contrasts. At various points over the last millennium and a half, ideas, technologies, and institutional blueprints flowed from China to Japan—either directly or through Korea—creating a cultural sphere underpinned by the use of written Chinese characters and classical writing. This culture arguably created a strong base for subsequent importation and mastery of Western technologies, at least for Japan, with its tradition of borrowing from abroad. Other similarities can be discerned, as well, including a basic attitudinal approach to development, sometimes labelled as 'techno-nationalist'. In fact, the Meiji Japan slogan which expresses this orientation, 'rich nation, strong army', derived from China's warring states period.

[1] With organizational and institutional similarities inherited from its time as a Japanese colony, South Korea has provided an updated, simplified, and accelerated version of Japanese-style late development. For this reason, it is South Korea, rather than Japan, that has provided a model for more recent developers such as Vietnam.

Compressed Development: Time and Timing in Economic and Social Development. D. Hugh Whittaker, Timothy J. Sturgeon, Toshie Okita, and Tianbiao Zhu, Oxford University Press (2020). © D. Hugh Whittaker, Timothy J. Sturgeon, Toshie Okita, and Tianbiao Zhu. DOI: 10.1093/oso/9780198744948.001.0001

Yet there are contrasts as well. Some derive from the two countries' different histories, resource endowments, and sizes, but time and timing have also been important. Japan's response to the Western challenge in the nineteenth century ushered in a period of remarkable institutional transformation and industrialization which catapulted Japan into the imperialist club, at China's expense. Its second emergence from wartime defeat in 1945 brought further institutional change, close alignment with the United States, and spectacular technological advances. Japan was Asia's first successful late developer, in two movements. But its success made subsequent change difficult, a point we return to in Chapter 9.

China, on the other hand, struggled to meet the same challenge from the West in the nineteenth century. While Japan rose to the challenge of creating a modern, centralized state, China faced an extra challenge—to 'build down' an imperial system with ancient roots, as well as to 'build up' a largely local and provincial system into a nation state (Zhang, 2001). That China's whole civilization had been so widely admired and influential also made it hard to change. But it was shaken to the core, leading to a gradual collapse of the Qing dynasty, domestic chaos, civil war, and losing a war with Japan, which curtailed nascent industrialization. Post-1949 central planning—essentially a socialist version of late development—led to 'over-industrialization' with 'under-urbanization' (Naughton, 2007).[2] China's post-1978 transformation, however, has been spectacular. And after initial attraction to Japan's late development model, it has followed a different path as Asia's pre-eminent compressed developer.

These major East Asian economies epitomize the differences between late development and compressed development, respectively. Differences include a comprehensive, 'full-set' industrialization (Seki, 2004) of Japan over one hundred years, and the recent 'thin'—or 'thinning'—(re-)industrialization of China, even as it became an export dynamo and the new 'workshop of the world'. Japan's relational, productionist industrial culture persists, while China embraced networks, global value chains (GVCs), and financialization more quickly. A central difference is the nature of integration into the global economy, including relatively insignificant inward foreign direct investment (FDI) in Japan versus massive inward FDI in China. Indicative is the ratio of outward to inward FDI between 1970 and 2014; it was a massive 1178 per cent for Japan, compared to 68 per cent for China (including Hong Kong). China was also the second largest recipient of inward FDI during the same period, after the United States.[3]

The chapter first considers Japan as a late developer, showing that while it developed unique institutional solutions to the challenges and opportunities it

[2] State–market relations were obviously distinctive in the Soviet or socialist model, but there are similarities in the state's attempt to promote rapid (heavy in this case) industrialization, and in the use of Factory and Fordist organization paradigms, indicative of the strength of late-development era influences.

[3] UNCTAD, DIAE FDI statistics database, accessed 21 February 2019.

faced, these were recognizably products of the eras in which they were formed, namely early-late and late-late development. The influence of these institutions remains in the era of compressed development. Next, we apply the same basic approach to China, focusing on the post-1978 period, and particularly on the 1990s and 2000s.[4] China too developed unique institutional solutions to its challenges and opportunities, and these are recognizably products of the era of compressed development. In some ways, its strengths and weaknesses are a mirror image of those of Japan. The final part of the chapter complements this bird's-eye historical-institutional comparison with a specific contrast of era, global integration and compression. Its focus is on education and skills, which are crucial for economic development. As the chapter concludes we will begin our consideration of employment, social development, and social policy, taken up in Chapters 6 and 7.

Before we begin, some caveats and comments on institutional change and national histories are in order. The first concerns Streeck's (2009: 6) lament about the 'comparative statics' of recent institutional analysis cited in the introduction, and his call for a dynamic, historical perspective focusing on the social and institutional formation of modern capitalism. Streeck and Thelen (2005: 1) stress incremental changes arising from ambiguities and 'gaps' which 'may become key sites of political contestation over the forms, functions, and salience of specific institutions whose outcome may be an important engine of institutional change' (17–18).[5] This makes sense at a theoretical level. There is, however, an *empirical* question of whether institutional change is endogenous and incremental or exogenously induced and far-reaching. And relatedly, institutions which are formed after a punctuation, and which tend to take a particular form which reflects the era of formation, may subsequently become resistant to change. We need to be sensitive to both types of change.

Second, we also need to avoid 'methodological nationalism', which is 'found in every corner of the contemporary social scientific landscape', although no one wants to admit it (Chernilo, 2011: 100).[6] It is evident in institutional writing, including 'varieties of capitalism' and 'business systems', which tend to pay little regard to the international geopolitical and economic systems described in Chapters 2 and 3 or, for that matter, to subnational systems. As a counter, Beck and Sznaider (2006: 3) propose 'methodological cosmopolitanism', which recognizes that 'the dualities of the global and the local, the national and the international, us and them, have dissolved and merged together in new forms that require conceptual and empirical analysis'. Again, there is an empirical issue, of

[4] We will unpack aspects of China's emergence more fully in the chapters which follow.

[5] Also Blyth, 2002.

[6] Chernilo (2011: 99) defines methodological nationalism as 'the equation between the idea of society as social theory's key conceptual reference and the historical processes of modern nation-state formation'. See also Wimmer and Glick Shiller (2002).

the more nationally self-contained production system of post–World War II Japan (and even more so postrevolution China) and the more internationally integrated system(s) of postreform China. The difference is also striking in the realm of education, as we shall see.

Finally, we must acknowledge the inherent dangers of brief, stylized accounts of history.[7] Our aim, however, is not historical analysis per se, but to highlight certain contrasts between Japan and China as a way to situate the countries more clearly in the conceptual framework we have developed so far.

Japan as a late developer

As Asia's first 'successful' late developer, Japan's influence on Asia's subsequent development cannot be overestimated. We look at its experience here not just for its own sake, but to provide a reference point in how different the development path has become in the era of compressed development, with China as an emblematic example. There were two 'movements' to Japan's modern economic development, occurring in the years of early- and late-late development, respectively. Japan's institutions bear the influence—stamped with a national die—of the respective eras.

In the mid-nineteenth century, Japan's leaders and would-be reformers were acutely aware of the turmoil in China from the Opium Wars and their aftermath, and Japan was itself forced to sign open port and extraterritoriality treaties in 1857. With the country divided over how to respond, a group of midranking samurai from western Japan, cloaking themselves in the timeless authority of the (hitherto largely unknown) emperor, took power in the Meiji Restoration in 1868. One who had witnessed the shelling of Kagoshima by British ships in 1865, and understood the links between military and economic power, characterized Japan's goals as building a 'rich nation and strong army' (*fukoku kyōhei*) by nurturing domestic industry (*shokusan kōgyō*). Ōkubo Toshimichi established and headed a new Home Ministry 'through which every variety of industrial policy (save the impossible protective tariff) could be implemented' (Samuels, 2003: 82). The policies were inspired by Germany, and by *Britain* prior to its advocacy of liberalism. Ōkubo reasoned:

[7] To give just one example, the significance of the Meiji Restoration for Japan's economic development is highly contested. Economic historians have shown that for at least the first four post-Meiji decades, economic growth was concentrated in the countryside, and it can be seen as a continuation of a pre-Meiji trajectory. In this view, the Meiji Restoration was not the decisive turning point it is often claimed to be, and Japan did not in fact skip a stage and plunge straight into capital-intensive industrialization. Even more radically, Konishi (2013) brings to light early Russian observers who saw the Meiji Restoration as a modern revolution, but one which introduced cooperative practices of Japanese commoners to the world rather than Western material civilization to Japan. Ideas, he shows, flowed in both directions. And Ambaras (2018) sees the Meiji Restoration as a reopening of Japan to China as much as to the West.

> Britain prevented the inflow of foreign goods and promoted the development of local industries. It was not until local industries developed and until their capacity exceeded local consumption that Britain abolished its protectionist trade policy and allowed liberal free trade. This is why Britain emerged as a great power today. (Samuels, 2003: 82)

The problem for Japan was that the unequal treaties limited its ability to impose tariffs on manufacturing imports to a mere 5 per cent, which was much lower than most other countries, including the United States (40–50 per cent in 1875), and indeed the UK early in the nineteenth century (45–55 per cent: Kasza, 2018). For better or worse, the treaties forced Japan to mobilize along the lines of its comparative advantages, at least initially (Bergsten, Ito, and Noland, 2001). Japan's new leaders might have *wanted* to build a strong military, and to industrialize quickly, but they had limited resources to bring this about. As Kasza notes, from late-1867 to mid-1875, paying off the previous regime's debts, suppressing domestic civil war, and meeting financial obligations to former samurai absorbed half the new regime's modest budget.

Building an industrial economy requires significant financial innovation (Rousseau, 2002, cited in Chapter 2). In Japan's case, Rousseau cites the commutation of rice payments (taxes) to the domain lords through the issue of long-term government bonds which, reminiscent of Alexander Hamilton in the United States, could then be used for banking capital. Japan established its national currency in 1871, the Bank of Japan in 1872, and the Tokyo Stock Exchange in 1878. New banks were created, including the Yokohama Specie Bank to service growing foreign trade. After adopting the silver standard in 1885, Japan switched to the gold standard in 1898, to enhance exchange rate stability and to obtain lower transaction and borrowing costs (Mitchener, Shizume, and Weidenmeir, 2010). It was helped by reparations from the first Sino-Japanese War (1894–1895).

The government did set up a number of model factories, but these were typically loss making and were eventually sold off. In fact, as critics of Gerschenkron point out, small-scale private rural industry played a key role in the first decades. Up until the end of the Meiji period in 1912, around three quarters of gross domestic expenditure was in personal consumption, mainly of products produced by small firms. In some industries small-scale industry proved highly adaptable, displacing production in capital-intensive factories with state-of-the-art imported machinery (Whittaker, 1997).

Nonetheless, Japan rapidly absorbed new technologies and organization forms, spurred by the First Sino-Japanese War, the Russo-Japanese War (1904–1905),[8]

[8] Some have called the Russo-Japanese War 'World War Zero'. In terms of technologies, organization, and financing the Russo-Japanese War resembled World War I more than any nineteenth-century war: Steinberg (2008).

and then World War I. As Tsutsui (1998: 18) notes, 'when accounts of the Taylor System first began to appear in Japan in 1911 – the same year as the publication of [Taylor's] *The Principles of Scientific Management* – a receptive audience already existed'.[9] And similarly to the United States, the necessity of coordinating operations across distance meant that railway companies were 'pacesetters in the introduction of modern administrative practices' (Ericson, 1989: 182; Table 3.1).

The decade after World War I was a very difficult one, however, marked by a deterioration of conditions in the small-scale industry sector, and hardship in the countryside from depressed prices with the global glut of agricultural goods. Preparations to return Japan to the gold standard at prewar parity created deflation, and the Great Kanto Earthquake of 1923 caused enormous damage to the capital Tokyo. Crucially, accelerating industrialization brought new problems, namely growing labour unrest and friction; and tensions between finance (and financialization) and industry.

The industrial boom of the 1910s, and growing urbanization, brought with it a growing labour movement and industrial unrest, which were taken very seriously in the wake of the Russian Revolution in 1917. Following the creation of the International Labour Organization in 1919, an 'Industrial Harmony Association' and movement were established to ameliorate the tensions (Kinzley, 1991), although in practice the labour movement was increasingly suppressed, and its flame all but extinguished by the 1930s.

Tensions between finance (and financialization) and industry intensified into a struggle for the soul of emerging Japanese capitalism. In the words of one spinning company manager:

> In Japan, there are capitalists who buy up stock for speculative reasons and attempt...to raise the market value of stock, then sell their shares of stock to make big profits.... Such avaricious capitalists keep the employees in a miserable state and endanger the basis of the existence of the company.[10]

Opposed to 'avaricious capitalists' were industrialists like Ōkochi Masatoshi, founder of Riken in 1917,[11] who advocated 'scientific industry'.[12] Banking

[9] The receptiveness was facilitated by advances in the education system, whose literate graduates staffed the growing ranks of professional managers. This is a key aspect of Dore's version of late development: 'Education seems to have become the major mechanism of social selection at an earlier stage of industrialization in Japan than in Western countries. Learning was the royal road not only to the professions, but also to business success as well—as the very high proportion of university graduates among Japanese business-men suggests. Undoubtedly one explanation of this fact is that Japan was a late developer, catching up by learning, and hence having more practical use for already systematized knowledge' (Dore, 1963: 293).

[10] Cited in Morikawa (1989: 42).

[11] Riken—Institute of Physical and Chemical Research—and its founder incubated roughly sixty companies employing 40,000 workers (in addition to 1800 of its own) by 1940 across a range of emerging industries. Some, such as Ricoh, became independent and prospered after 1945.

[12] Cusumano (1989). Ōkochi's views echoed Veblen, who saw 'technology' in very broad terms which included the 'joint stock of knowledge and experience of the community' of the 'industrial

scandals and failures were not uncommon, and 'avaricious capitalists' came to be identified with the established *zaibatsu* conglomerates, which absorbed many ailing businesses, and whose banks were accused of betting against the yen—and Japan—in the brief gold standard restoration in 1930.[13]

The Showa Financial Crisis (1927), Wall Street Crash (1929), and gold standard debacle (1930–1931) fundamentally changed state–market relations, and the direction of Japan's development. The financial sector was restructured, and industry was increasingly aligned with the military through reflationary government spending. The infamous 'Manchurian Incident' staged by the Japanese army in Mukden (Shenyang) in September 1931 dealt a decisive blow to liberal capitalism, and saw increasing government control over the economy and a build-up of heavy industry and munitions which were deployed when the Second Sino-Japanese War started in 1937.

The transformation during Japan's first 'movement' was enormous. In the half century between 1888 and 1938, the share of agriculture in Japan's gross domestic product (GDP) decreased from 42 per cent to 16 per cent, while the share of manufacturing, mining, and public utilities rose from 12 per cent to 52 per cent. The share of chemical and heavy industries within manufacturing rose from 14 per cent to 51 per cent. Between 1913 and 1938, Japan's real growth rate averaged 3.9 per cent; at least double that of most of the major powers (Minami et al., 1995: 3–4; Nakamura, 1988: 453). Crucially, many of Japan's distinctive institutional features began to take shape in this period. They were, however, reshaped after 1945.[14]

Japan's surrender in 1945 amidst massive devastation marked a further turning point in the country's late-development trajectory. It is true, as many observers have pointed out, there were continuities with Japan's wartime-controlled economy.[15] But the Occupation reforms included, *inter alia*, a new Constitution, land reform, a (partial) dissolution of the *zaibatsu*, legalization of labour unions and collective bargaining, and education reform. These reflected US New Deal thinking, maintaining a significant role for government and government planning. Japan's increasingly strong alliance with the United States, moreover, enabled it to concentrate on domestic economic reconstruction with far less attention to wider strategic or military considerations. Thus, the conditions were set for the flowering of Japan's 'plan rational' 'developmental

system', which was threatened by the short-term profit orientations of 'captains of finance' and industry (Veblen, 1919: 33–4).

[13] Colpan and Hikino attribute the persistence of *zaibatsu* in Japan to a late-development effect. 'In most of the economies, spearheaded by Japan, that experienced late industrialization, large business groups appeared in the early phase of industrial development, and those very groups have collectively and individually remained the prime and leading business organizations in the relevant economies up to the twenty-first century' (2010: 51).

[14] Johnson (1982); Gordon (1985); Hazama (1960).

[15] E.g. Okazaki and Okuno-Fujiwara (1999); Noguchi (1998).

state', with powerful bureaucracies that both cooperated and competed with each other, and were relatively insulated from pork barrel politics (Johnson, 1982; Kim et al., 1995).

In a much-condensed rerun of its first industrialization, light industry underwent a revival, but investments were soon ploughed into energy and heavy industries such as shipbuilding, steel, and the machine industries.[16] US management and organization models (spanning the 'Factory' and 'Fordist Corporation' paradigms of Table 3.1) were eagerly studied. US procurement for the Korean War entailed demanding product specifications, and Japanese manufacturers 'learned the fundamentals of standardized parts manufacture, testing standards and quality control' (Samuels, 1994: 14). Deming's quality message found a more receptive audience in Japan than in the United States. The productivity movement both raised productivity and helped to quell labour militancy, giving workers a (limited) voice on the shop floor. The fruits were diffused through co-ordinated wage bargaining—the Spring Wage Offensive—and a positive feedback loop was established between economic and technological upgrading on the one hand, and 'social upgrading' on the other, which has become more tenuous in compressed developers, as we shall see in Chapter 6.

Japan 'reindustrialized' towards civilian and export industries, and its capitalism was 'reformed'. Finance was regulated to serve industry. Tiered government and private institutions provided long-term and short-term finance to large and small firms, while access to foreign capital was strictly limited. Industrial groups reformed as bank-centred 'horizontal *keiretsu*', creating a distinctive form of 'patient capital'. Relationships between large-firm assemblers and their subcontractor suppliers were stabilized, as were industrial relations. New human resource management practices came to form the core of 'Japanese-style management', including the nurturing of technical skills in-house under conditions of long-term but competitive employment (Koike, 1981). 'Community firms' featured substantial welfare provision for both blue-collar and white-collar workers.[17]

Japan created a 'full-set' industrial structure (Seki, 2004) which in manufacturing employed over 30 per cent of the workforce until the late 1970s, and over 20 per cent until 2004. Furthermore, it was a 'national system', in some ways unique, but also with recognizable features of postwar 'embedded liberalism', capital-labour compromise, and the Fordist organizational paradigm.[18] It helped to bring inflation under control quickly in the 1970s, and fostered the price

[16] Between 1955 and 1970, the primary sector share of GDP dropped from 17 per cent to 6 per cent, while mining, manufacturing, and public utilities rose from 29 per cent to 48 per cent, of which the share of heavy and chemical industries (including machinery) surged from 39 per cent to 60 per cent, all the while with high overall growth (Minami et al., 1995: 4).

[17] Dore (1973); Inagami and Whittaker (2005); Miura (2012).

[18] The newly formed Keizai Dōyūkai (Japan Committee for Economic Development) in 1947 called for a 'reformed capitalism' in which companies should be seen as a community comprising capital, management, and labour, each entitled to a voice and a fair share of profits.

competitiveness of Japanese machine tools, electronic goods, and vehicles. By 1980, government panels were declaring that Japan had finally achieved 'catch-up'. A blue-ribbon council set up under then Prime Minister Ōhira declared:

> In order to 'catch up' as speedily as possible with the advanced nations of the West, Japan has proactively pushed forward with modernization, industrialization and westernization since the Meiji Restoration. As a result, Japan succeeded in reaching the stage of a mature, highly industrial society, and everyone has come to enjoy freedom and equality, progress and prosperity, economic wealth and the convenience of modern life, high education and high welfare standards, as well as advanced scientific technology. These are all qualities we can be proud of in the world.
>
> (Age of Culture Research Group, 1980: 2, cited in Kariya, forthcoming)

Henceforth, the council argued, Japan would have to find its own path. This proved to be difficult, however. Japan came under increasing pressure from the United States to curb its trade surpluses, open its markets, and appreciate its currency. The pressure intensified in the late 1980s, when the United States sought major changes to Japan's capitalism itself, through the Structural Impediments Initiative. Some attribute Japan's subsequent problems to abandonment of its postwar model; others to its continued adherence to it in a changing world. As we shall see in Chapter 9, elements of both views apply.

China as a compressed developer

Japan's rise was rapid relative to earlier industrializers, but China's ascent has been truly remarkable. China maintained an average real GDP growth rate of 9.5 per cent between 1979 and 2018, doubling the size of the economy every eight years.[19] Over the same time period the proportion of the population living in urban areas jumped from less than 20 per cent to 60 per cent.[20] Comparing China and Japan, Tasker (2015) comments that 'China's dizzying ascent has been so fast, complex and uneven that no single comparison can do it justice', and that it overlays several distinct time periods of Japan's own ascent, from the 1930s to the present day.

China's ascent has occurred in a different era from that of Japan, however, and its institutional innovations bear the imprints of the compressed-development era. While China's leaders have also followed a 'rich nation strong army' and 'techno-

[19] <https://fas.org/sgp/crs/row/RL33534.pdf>, accessed 20 September 2019.

[20] According to Dadao Lu's calculation, it took 22 years for China's urban population share to rise from 17.9 per cent to 39.1 per cent (1978–2000), while the same shift took Britain 120 years, the United States 80 years, and Japan more than 30 years: <https://en.wikipedia.org/wiki/Urbanization_in_China>, accessed 20 September 2019.

nationalist' vision (Cheung, 2014) by attempting to nurture national champions along the lines of Japan and South Korea, its actual paths to high-growth emergence have been quite different. We say 'paths' because several can be observed, reflecting China's immense size and complexity. Distance from the 'centre' (Beijing, literally and metaphorically) has produced regional variations, as well as different modes of engagement with the global economy. In general, however, China has relied much more on foreign direct investment (FDI) and acting as a sourcing location for global brands and retailers, while inward FDI to Japan was (and remains) minimal. Technological 'borrowing' in Japan relied to a large extent on book learning, technology acquisition and licensing, and study visits rather than learning by doing in the context of business partnerships and GVCs.[21] As a result, China's (re-)industrialization bears the hallmarks of compressed development.

China's transition was bound to be more tortuous than that of Japan's in the nineteenth century. It faced a double challenge, as we noted earlier—to 'build down' an imperial system with ancient roots, as well as to 'build up' a largely local and provincial system into a (European-style) nation state (Zhang, 2001). Its external tributary system was eroded as countries on its borders were absorbed into other empires. Its imperial institutions were eroded from within as well, and ideologically, were dealt a fatal blow by the Sino-Japanese War of 1894–1895. The final rejection of the old order can be dated to the nationalist, anti-imperialist, and antitraditionalist 1919 May Fourth Movement (Mitter, 2004), but building a new one was fraught.

Although we treat China as a compressed developer, it was before that a (socialist) late developer. Following the Second Sino-Japanese War (1937–1945), civil war, and the Communist triumph in 1949, China (not inevitably) ended up on the Soviet side of the Cold War after its revolution. The Soviet economic model (with Fordist elements) it adopted eliminated both landowners and private business owners, and promoted state-led industrialization through central planning and vertically integrated state-owned enterprises. 'China has a long history of state domination over society and the economy; however, with the central planning system, this domination became extreme' (Zhu, 2015: 8).[22]

The primary sector's share of national income dropped from around 58 per cent in 1952 to 36 per cent in 1980, while secondary industry's share rose from 23 per cent and 54 per cent over the same period (Minami, 1994: 10). China became

[21] As transitional cases emerging on the global scene in the 1980s and 1990s, South Korea leaned in the direction of limited FDI and arms-length technology acquisition (reverse engineering and book learning) even as it became an 'OEM' source for Western brands, while Taiwan more purely became a compressed developer after it abandoned early attempts and developing flagship global brands and embraced its rising role as a hub for contract manufacturing (Feenstra and Hamilton, 2006; Hamilton and Kao, 2017).

[22] Zhu (2015) argues that China's external environment played a big part in fostering China's late developer—as well as its subsequent compressed developer—characteristics.

'overindustrialized'—oriented towards heavy, and often inefficient, industry—and 'under-urbanized' (Naughton, 2007), with less than 20 per cent of the population living in urban areas in 1978. Services and consumption were under-developed. Its planned economy was, however, more decentralized than that of the Soviet Union, and this facilitated the sort of local experimentation that blossomed in the compressed-development era (Qian and Xu, 1993).

The rift between China and the Soviet Union in the 1960s, US awareness in the 1970s of the possibility of drawing China into the US-led global economy (Cumings, 1989), and the post-Cultural Revolution plan to 'leap forward by foreign means' ultimately paved the way for China's open-door policy.[23] This reorientation had a massive impact on China's institutional evolution. The initial phase was cautious—'crossing the river by feeling for the stones' as Chen Yun and Deng Xiaoping famously put it—initiated in the countryside and in special economic zones (SEZs) that were at first distant from Beijing (see Chapter 5), as well as close to Hong Kong and the Chinese diaspora. The gathering momentum of economic change led to a sharp fall in the share of state revenue to GDP, as well as rising inflation and growing social unrest, culminating in the June Fourth/Tiananmen Square crisis.

China's reforms were paused, but not abandoned. Ambivalence towards entrepreneurship and private enterprise was relinquished following Deng's 'Southern Tour' in 1992, which included the burgeoning special economic zones (SEZs) around the Pearl River Delta near Hong Kong, and was seen as tacit approval of the embrace of FDI-driven industrialization. This opened a new period, marked by legal and regulatory reform, reform of the tax and banking systems, and a significant overhaul of and greater willingness to shrink the state-owned enterprise (SOE) sector. By 'grasping the large and letting go of the small', the overhaul aimed to create one thousand SOE champions. As Nolan (2001) observed, however, attempts to create this 'national team' in key sectors largely failed, since the powerful global firms they were intended to compete with proved to be too far ahead (and some subsequently became directly imbricated with China's economy through FDI). This prompted fierce debates about the merits of national industrial policy, as well as WTO accession, with advocates of the latter arguing that joining the WTO would promote faster change and help to combat corruption (Nolan, 2001).

Debate about WTO accession also concerned opening the finance sector to foreign investment. Although under heavy pressure from the US government and financial institutions to do so, the Chinese government was very cautious, taking the Asian Financial Crisis as a cautionary tale of rapid liberalization, and acknowledging finance as a source of power, to be monitored and controlled (Williams,

[23] US President Nixon's visit to China in February 1972 was followed later that year by normalization of Sino-Japanese relations, also crucial for China's reorientation.

2019). Reflecting the global tide of corporate governance reform originating in the United States and UK, as well as this caution, SOE reform became refocused on governance and accountability, with the creation of the State-owned Asset Supervision and Administration Commission in 2003 (Wang, 2015).[24] In short, China's reforms increasingly reflected era contexts and influences as the late development model it was pursuing slipped away, given the overarching drive for accelerated growth through openness. It also reflected the (central) state's determination to navigate this opening on its own terms, by maintaining firm control of the financial sector.

In the 1990s SOEs began to face domestic competitors unencumbered with the substantial welfare costs related to maintaining long-term employment, known as the 'iron rice bowl'. Pre-reform organizations fused the economic, social, and political in the work unit (*danwei*). In Chan's (1997) assessment, the 'state-oriented system' with centrally planned employment, remuneration and placement systems began to shift towards a (Japanese-style) 'organization orientation', in core industries, while other parts of the economy became more market-oriented and United States–like: 'What appears to be happening now is a gradual readjustment of the ratio of core-versus-peripheral labour force within state industry so as to attain nationwide labour flexibility' (Chan, 1997: 94–5).[25] Employment in the state sector declined by as much as half in the decade after 1994 (Naughton, 2007), however, and employment became less secure for many who remained.

The 1990s also saw a massive increase in FDI as the network organizational paradigm (Table 3.1) took hold, and the legal protections that SEZs provided foreign investors, especially in the electronics industry, with the confidence to invest in massive factories. The role of local companies was, and often still is, largely limited to standardized parts manufacturing (e.g. batteries and power supplies) and final assembly. As a result, the share of electronic goods in China's exports rose from 5.9 per cent in 1992 to 22.8 per cent in 2002, with much of this accounted for by foreign-invested enterprises (Wang, 2006: 387; Chapter 5).

Privately owned enterprises faced many regulatory and institutional headwinds well into the 1990s, in fact until at least 2004. The headwinds 'compelled and motivated entrepreneurs to build their own networks of suppliers and distributors, and below the radar of the state to develop competitive advantage in self-organized clusters of producers, suppliers and distributors' (Nee and Opper, 2012: 9). These clusters and networks embodied and encouraged the diffusion of cooperative

[24] Wang refers to this as the 'shareholder state'. President Jiang Zemin commented in 2006: 'The shareholding system is an efficient way of organizing capital. Capitalism uses it. Socialists can use it too' (Wang, 2015: 611).

[25] See Chapter 6. Chan was using Dore's (1987) typology of organization versus market orientation. In fact, Japanese employment relations were themselves moving in the same direction in the 1990s, with a marked rise in the proportion of non-regular workers.

norms, allowing entrepreneurs to survive outside the state-owned manufacturing system. Nee and Opper depict such 'bottom-up' entrepreneurship as 'capitalism from below'. However, because in some sectors the ultimate customer for many parts, components, and services were often foreign investors and global buyers, with control over product design and marketing and established relationships with vendors of advanced technology, China's burgeoning industrial base was concentrated in low value-added segments of global value chains, leading to extremely fast growth, but also to 'thin industrialization'.[26] Products made for the local market entirely by local firms tended to be easily copied by others, leading to hyper-competition and a failure of companies to grow to scale.

As a symptom of this, and a lack of support from the central government, private enterprises have often struggled for access to capital. Favoured SOEs, on the other hand, have been slow to engage in long-term technological upgrading. Success stories often have 'untypical' corporate governance which combines state ownership and private entrepreneurship (Tylecote, Cai, and Liu, 2010). Fuller (2015), too, sees 'hybrid' firms established by ethnic Chinese (some with transnational business ties, including returnees) whose sources of finance lie primarily outside China, as contributing most to China's economic upgrading. By accessing foreign capital, such 'hidden dragons' have avoided the 'heavy hand of the state', and have compartmentalized and to a degree self-selected their institutional environment—some domestic and some external. Such financing, corporate governance, and management is very different from that of postwar Japan.

In this context, state–market relations in China have evolved in distinctive ways. The relaxation of centralized command and control led to a tiered hierarchy, in which SOEs are directly supervised by the central government, and progressively larger numbers of enterprises are more loosely supervised by lower tiers of government, including collectively owned enterprises, privately owned enterprises (POEs), and foreign-invested enterprises (FIEs) (Tan, Li, and Xia, 2007). Furthermore, there are many regional variations within China linked to local policy and institutional configurations.[27] As a generalization, POEs have been prevalent in the Yangtse River Delta (especially in Zhejiang Province), SOEs in inland provinces, and FIEs in the Pearl River Delta (especially in Guangdong Province).[28]

We close this part of the chapter with some statistics which are indicative of China's rapid internationalization and growing presence in the global economy in the era of compressed development, in comparison with Japan. In May 2017,

[26] Exceptions such as telecom giant Huawei and drone-maker DJI have systematically internalized key components, built internal R&D capabilities, and fiercely policed their hard-won intellectual property (IP), often in foreign jurisdictions where IP protections are more robust than in China.

[27] Thun (2006); Segal (2003); Oi (1992); Chapter 8.

[28] By activity, many POEs are in downstream, consumer-facing sectors; SOEs in domestically oriented upstream sectors; and FIEs in export-oriented intermediate and final goods sectors.

some eighty-three Chinese companies were listed on NASDAQ, compared with just two Japanese companies; forty Chinese companies were listed on the New York Stock Exchange compared with twelve Japanese companies.[29] In 2007 Chinese cross-border mergers and acquisitions accounted for just 1 per cent of the global total; by 2016, this had risen to 14 per cent, second only to the United States (19 per cent), and well above Japan (9 per cent).[30] More generally, of Forbes' Global 2000 companies in 2016, 540 were from the United States; 249 from China; and 219 from Japan.[31] And of the thirty highest-valued 'unicorns' in 2017, thirteen were from the United States; ten from China; and none from Japan.[32] These statistics point to a very different type of international orientation and engagement than that of Japan in the postwar era, differences that persist today, and which can also be seen in education and skills, which we now turn to.

Education and skills

The contrast between compressed-developer China and late-developer Japan is not limited to economic and technological development. Parallel contrasts are evident in social development, and this section of the chapter highlights them in the realm of education and skills. In this section we seek to broaden the discussion to underline the thoroughgoing nature of compressed development, and to preface our analysis of employment, social development, and social policy, which we take up in Chapters 6 and 7. Here we discuss how prewar Japanese education was focused on nation-building and the indigenization of knowledge, how postwar reforms were spectacularly successful in widening access and producing highly literate and numerate blue-collar workers, and how this very success has handicapped Japan's quest to promote internationalization in the compressed-development era. China's post-1978 reforms, by contrast, facilitated internationalization, and the country has provided a major market for the globalization of education as an industry with still basic shortcomings in domestic general and vocational education, a concise reflection of the compressed-development era.[33]

[29] From the NASDAQ website, accessed 20 May 2017. Emblematic is Alibaba, whose $25 billion NYSE listing in 2014 was the largest ever initial public offering (IPO). The shares were actually for a Cayman Islands–registered company to avoid conflicting with China's foreign ownership laws (Alibaba Group Wikipedia page, accessed 2 August 2016).

[30] White and Case (2017). R&D has also been rapidly internationalized; as of 2005, as many as 750 R&D centres had been established outside China (Sun, Zedtwitz, and Simon, 2007).

[31] https://en.wikipedia.org/wiki/Forbes_Global_2000. The ranking combines four metrics: sales, profits, assets, and market value.

[32] *Nikkei Asia Review*, 24–30 April 2017, 10–11. A 'unicorn' is a high-growth, recent business valued at US $1 billion or more.

[33] Again, era effects are lasting. Kawakami contrasts Japanese and Taiwanese executive education engagements with Stanford University's Centre for Biodesign. The Japanese contingent took courses in

By way of introduction, education and human resources development are a fundamental requirement for economic, social, political, and cultural development.[34] Max Weber, who drew attention to the role of rationalization and bureaucracy in modernization, also highlighted the roles of professional training and placement based on performance in competitive examinations, validated by a *Bildungspatent* or diploma. It is no accident that late-developer Germany most clearly demonstrated these connections for Weber. They were institutionalized much earlier in the process of nation-building and industrialization in Germany than in early developer Britain, where they were slow to take hold.

It is no accident that Japan learned these lessons quickly from Germany. Citing Japan, Dore (1976) noted that later developers access the technologies needed for rapid catch-up through formal, written means rather than informal training, an argument also made by Amsden (1989) for Korea. Technical progress in late-developing countries was based on what Amsden called 'imitation' (the copying of foreign technology through tactics such as reverse engineering) and 'apprenticeship' (the acquisition of foreign technology through licensing and technical-assistance programmes). As well, late developers such as Japan and South Korea tended to create large, bureaucratic organizations with specialized personnel departments relatively quickly, and to rely on the formal education and credential systems to filter worthy job applicants into the modern sector, which offered workers superior prestige, pay, and job security. In South Korea salaried managers, not entrepreneurs, were the key players in implementing foreign technology on the shop floor.

There were downsides, however, namely that diplomas would become a substitute for genuine learning—the 'diploma disease'—and that even if they were part of a meritocratic system, diplomas would soon become a passport for the children of the privileged (Dore, 1976). These tendencies have intensified in the compressed-development era, as education has become a global industry, the ranking of universities and diplomas have expanded from a national to global scale, and students have flocked to tertiary education, once reserved for the elite. Merit has given way extremely quickly to privilege, as wealthy parents not only send their children to the best universities abroad, but to the secondary schools which have the best record as feeders to those universities. This can be seen particularly in the case of China.

California, and then translated the curriculum for use in Japan, while the Taiwanese contingent focused on *in situ* learning and network building in Silicon Valley and the Bay Area, where many stayed to launch 'born global' start-ups (Kawakami, personal communication).

[34] Conversely, education reflects wider political, economic, and social concerns. Ever since compulsory education became part of nation-building efforts in the nineteenth century, social concerns have become 'educationalized', whether to foster habits of obedience, thrift, and hygiene, or more recently, to solve economic growth and adjustment problems (Smeyers and Depaepe, 2008).

Japan: education for catch-up

Literacy rates were already high in Japan in the mid-nineteenth century, and in its nation-building and modernization efforts, the Meiji government introduced compulsory education in 1872, just four years after the Meiji Restoration, and two years after the first English Education Act. By 1900 most Japanese children were receiving primary education. But catching up with the great powers and creating a 'rich nation and strong army' required more than primary education; it required the rapid absorption of advanced knowledge from overseas, initially through the medium of foreign languages. A two-pronged strategy was adopted; promising youth were sent abroad for education, and foreign specialists were brought to Japan to help establish institutions of higher education. One of these was a young Scottish engineer, who claimed to establish Britain's first modern engineering college—in Japan.[35]

Such elite institutions, which used foreign languages for instruction, were eventually brought together as the Imperial University (renamed Tokyo Imperial University when other Imperial Universities were created). To enter, however, foreign languages had to be mastered, and for this purpose preparatory schools were established, with another tier under them to form a bridge with primary schools. The ladder thus established was a very narrow one, however, and demand for advanced learning by the emerging middle classes far outstripped capacity. Private institutions were authorized, creating a 'collateral' system of specialist schools, while traditional schools that taught Chinese classics withered (Amano, 2011).

Sending students abroad and hiring foreigners to teach was extremely expensive for a poor country. Within two decades most of the foreigners had been replaced, and although foreign languages remained important, students were able to study most subjects in Japanese (unlike in colonized countries which later retained the metropolitan language for elite education, even after independence). While use of the vernacular at all levels helped to open access to education, there was an ironic downside. Learning foreign languages became confined to passing examinations, and the resulting spoken language 'regression' ultimately proved a major handicap when Japan tried to internationalize its education in the 1990s. What had originally helped Japan access knowledge from around the world ultimately created a barrier (Kariya, forthcoming).

The US–led occupation after World War II brought an overhaul of the school system in the US image. Compulsory education was extended to nine years, and access to post-compulsory (upper secondary and tertiary) education was widened. In 1950 half of fifteen year olds continued to upper secondary school and more

[35] McCormick (2000). The German *Technische Hochschule* was also an influential model for Japan, needless to say.

than 10 per cent of eighteen year olds to a university or junior college; by 1980, the figures were 95 per cent and 37 per cent respectively (Amano, 2011: 192). Japan's education system became much more egalitarian, and was particularly successful in providing literacy and numeracy skills for the country's rapidly upgrading productionist-oriented economy.[36]

Access to the upper levels of Japan's education system was through highly competitive examinations, in what was dubbed 'examination hell', which was criticized by the teacher's union, which described it as the 'root of all educational evils' (Kariya, forthcoming). By the 1980s the government had come around to this view, as well, and associated the disease with Japan's catch-up modernization. It sought to create a 'post-catch-up' education system which nurtured creativity and reduced pressure throughout the system. In this it has encountered many problems. Universities, too, struggled from the 1990s to produce the 'global human resources' now required by outward investing businesses, and to become more internationalized themselves (Kariya, 2018).

China's compression in education

Literacy rates, or at least school enrolment rates, were quite high in pre-reform China, as well, although the Cultural Revolution created considerable disarray in the country's education system, and the institutions linking education and the economy were not efficient, generating low returns to education (Naughton, 2007). During the 1990s and 2000s, however, China underwent changes paralleling those in Japan, but in a much more condensed form, and in ways that reflect era influences.

The shift to a meritocratic education-based placement system was signalled by the reintroduction of the now (in)famous university entrance exam (*gao kao*) system in 1977, but sorting in China starts well before university entrance. Only half of those taking the post–compulsory education exam for admission to general high schools pass. Those who fail face a number of choices, but many find themselves in vocational high schools, which are lower in prestige and offer inferior prospects to graduates (Hansen and Woronov, 2013). Despite efforts to improve vocational education and training, the jobs at the end of them are often 'precarious, possibly short-term, likely dead-end. These new service-sector jobs link them to the new global precariat, which in turn helps define some of the characteristics of China's new urban working class' (Woronov, 2016: 115; Chapter 6). Japan, too, had—and still has—a range of vocational institutions typically of lower prestige than general education schools, but some of these had

[36] Whittaker (1990) found significant numeracy differences between Japanese and British machine tool operators, for example.

strong local reputations and links with employers from the prewar period, making 'regular' secure employment, particularly in manufacturing, a real possibility. Such jobs have become increasingly scarce in China (and Japan), and are likely to be taken by graduates with 'superior' qualifications.

Those who are fortunate enough to be registered in areas with good schools, or have parents with financial resources, enjoy enhanced chances of passing the high school entrance exam, and especially the university entrance exam, as high schools are not necessarily free. Therefore, while the system does open access to high-ranking education institutions for talented but poor students from rural China, and a path to a prestigious job in the future, it has become a system that favours privilege. Indeed, while there was a considerable time gap in postwar Japan for the transition of university entrance exams as a mechanism for upward mobility to one of reproducing social advantage (Kariya, forthcoming), this shift has been time compressed in China (Liu, 2016).

There are aspects of education and its placement functions in contemporary China which were largely missing in postwar Japan, including the option of overseas education. In the early 1980s, the Chinese government began sending students overseas, mostly on postgraduate or short courses to acquire advanced technological knowledge, as the Japanese government did during the Meiji period. Returnees were to play an important role in China's subsequent transformation. Numbers were limited, however, and wavered around the time of the July Fourth/Tiananmen Square protests. Numbers increased in the 1990s, however, with funding from overseas scholarships or families. At the beginning of the 2000s, there was a huge increase in students going overseas, now mostly family funded as incomes and wealth rose—to undertake undergraduate or language courses rather than advanced degrees. In 1998 11,000 self- (or family-) funded students went abroad; by 2002, this number had surged to 117,000 (Xiang and Shen, 2009: 516). By the late 2000s, overseas education of Chinese students was contributing some $4 billion to the 'exports' of favoured destination countries like the United States and UK.[37]

China was at the same time undergoing a domestic transition to mass higher education. Admission to universities within China doubled between 1998 and 2001, and doubled again over the next five years (Chapter 7). The opening of mass higher education predictably led to a finely gradated domestic ranking system as well. The top public universities continued to attract the top students, who might then pursue a foreign postgraduate degree, funded by scholarship, to further enhance their credentials. Those failing to gain access to top universities, but whose families had the means to support them, might go directly overseas,

[37] The growth was coming not just from leading universities in these countries, but from a range of secondary and feeder institutions, such as preparatory schools, and high schools with an established route to the top universities.

whereas in Japan, the alternative had been to go to a domestic private university. As Xiang and Shen (2009: 516) put it, the 'frantic investment in international education' was stimulated not just by the potential benefits—'pull' factors—but also pushed by fears over the future, and rapid social stratification and growing inequality. And with (mostly) a single child, the stakes for families were high.

The rapid internationalization of Chinese higher education is undoubtedly linked to the rapid internationalization of (parts of) the Chinese economy, which we discussed earlier in the chapter. Conversely, difficulties in internationalization on the part of Japanese companies are often linked to the more domestic orientation of Japanese education. The education system worked very well for Japan as a late developer, but it has proved difficult to change, despite government policies designed to promote 'global human resources'.

Concluding comments

Time and timing matter for economic and social development. Institutions are shaped by the context in which they emerge, and they may subsequently prove difficult to change, even if the environment changes. The comparison between China and Japan highlights this.

Japan was a very successful late developer; China has (re-)emerged dramatically in the era of compressed development. At the firm level, reflecting the dominant production system of vertical integration in line with the Fordist model, Japanese firms have emphasized the mastery of technologies through internal capability development. The 'productionist system' was supported by 'patient capital' (main bank system, silent shareholders), 'relational contracting' between firms, 'Japanese-style employment' (lifetime employment buttressed by the wage and industrial relations systems, obviously more fully realized in large firms than small ones), and stakeholder corporate governance. At the policy level, this was supported by macroeconomic stability, industrial and innovation policies, and proemployment labour market policy. Although this system has moved in the direction of marketization, and to some extent financialization, Japan's national champions have proved resilient, and the system is marked by adaptation rather than upheaval.

There are significant variations within China, but since the 1990s, FDI has played a much larger role, as have hybrid forms of governance, where the state interacts with private industry at multiple levels. Reflecting changes in production systems, engagement with GVCs has been crucial, and not just in FIEs. This engagement has allowed firms with limited capabilities to establish specialized niches, which then are leveraged in various ways to achieve growth. Significantly, the means of doing this has resulted in greater emphasis on strategic choice—with whom to engage, in what niches, and how to manoeuvre to obtain new opportunities to develop rapidly—and less emphasis on internal capability building. In a sense, the institutional weaknesses of both countries are mirror images of each other—China's extremely rapid growth has been achieved despite institutional gaps and ambiguities, while the solidity of Japan's institutions, stabilized in the postwar decades, has limited options for change.[38]

The education systems of both countries also reflect compression, and changes in era. The Japanese basic education system was particularly effective in supplying numerate and literate graduates for rapidly upgrading manufacturing companies, and this supported stable jobs and company-based welfare. Mass higher education in the 1960s supplied the human resources for expanding white-collar jobs. The modernization of China's education system has occurred with extreme rapidity, and has been part of the internationalization of the Chinese economy. At the same time, it has accentuated inequality, which also expanded extremely rapidly. Here the structure of labour markets and regulation of work are also significant, and we will turn to these in Chapter 6.

It is worth remembering that China was itself a (socialist) late developer in the postwar period. It might have developed very differently had Mao's initial overtures to the United States borne fruit. As it was, it adopted Soviet-style central planning in which the state stifled 'markets'. Three decades later, after rapprochement with the United States, it embarked on a series of reforms to rebalance the state–market relationship. It became a compressed developer, still with a strong state, but critically influenced by the contemporary features afoot in the (US-dominant) global economy into which it was integrating. Japan, on the other hand, aligned with its former enemy the United States after World War II and successfully adopted—or created—institutions enabling a more dynamic relationship between state and 'markets'. As a (late-) late developer with a developmental state, Japan's development was imprinted by the features of the postwar era as it (re)integrated with the global economy. Subsequent institutional change in the compressed-development era proved more difficult, and incremental. Both countries are faced with difficult choices in the context of geopolitical tensions, growing protectionism and nationalism. These may well signal a further shift—potentially to a late-compressed-development era—which we will consider in Chapter 9.

[38] Japanese companies in recent years have also begun to position themselves more strategically, not at the expense of their former internal capability building practices, but in combination with them; cf. Whittaker, Sturgeon and Song, 2016.

5
Varieties of Compressed Development

Introduction

Time compression and contemporary-era-related influences—which prominently include global value chains (GVCs)—have combined to significantly alter the path of development, most notably from the 1990s onward. With time compression, the tendency is for processes which were previously experienced sequentially to be compressed, to the point where they layer over one another, creating new development experiences, opportunities, and challenges for state and society. But time compression is not the only thing altering development. Era-related features introduce new production systems, technologies, and actors. The more direct inclusion of global actors in development creates new vectors for learning and the exertion of power. All of this creates pressure for institutional responses. The combination of time compression and contemporary-era effects is altering the playing field for development profoundly, and in the broadest terms. However, actual development experiences vary widely.

In this chapter, we use the lens of GVCs and industrial policy to explore the variety of country experiences in the compressed-development era. These experiences are conditioned not only by compression and era influences in a general sense, but more specifically by the policy and regulatory choices made at the national and often subnational levels. In some cases, industrial policymakers have failed to recognize the new realities of compressed development and have instead attempted to re-create the experiences of successful late developers (most notably last-in South Korea), with generally poor results. In other cases, states have attempted to engage with GVCs to help promote development (often following early compressed developers Singapore or Taiwan and more recently mainland China), with mixed or still-unknown results. Developing global specializations and upgrading from lower to higher-value-added business functions in GVCs (Gereffi and Sturgeon, 2013) have proven difficult, and may in fact be historically contingent options that are now closing for latecomers. More typically, however, the approach is ad hoc. Industrial policymakers set out to follow a late-development path, only to find the pressures of compressed development altering their strategy until it evolves into something entirely different. Support for national champions can give way to engagement with MNCs, for example, and pushes for indigenous technology development can give way to engagement with global technology

Compressed Development: Time and Timing in Economic and Social Development. D. Hugh Whittaker, Timothy J. Sturgeon, Toshie Okita, and Tianbiao Zhu, Oxford University Press (2020). © D. Hugh Whittaker, Timothy J. Sturgeon, Toshie Okita, and Tianbiao Zhu. DOI: 10.1093/oso/9780198744948.001.0001

ecosystems. Difficulties with GVC upgrading may also lead policymakers in the reverse direction, away from global engagement. Because industrial policies are, almost by definition, *sectoral* policies, the result is often a muddle, with high variation across industries. To illustrate this, we contrast the experience of China with that of Brazil, India and several other countries. Before we delve too deeply into the experiences of specific countries, however, we provide a more general characterization of the different roles various countries have come to play in GVCs.

Country roles in GVCs

Countries play various and sometimes multiple roles in GVCs. Some of the variation has to do with natural endowments and geography. Most obviously, countries with rich mineral resources or high levels of agricultural production tend to export primary products or resource-based manufactures. Ricardian comparative advantage and specialization in exports is nothing new, but in the context of fine-sliced GVCs, specializations can be very narrow and industry-, business function–, and even task-specific. (Grossman and Rossi-Hansberg, 2008). The digital economy appears to be providing more opportunities for this sort of spatial fragmentation of work, a dynamic that comes with both risks and opportunities for developing places (Sturgeon, 2019). The result is that segments of specific national economies, often the most dynamic and technologically advanced, can become specialized on a global basis, with the spatial separation of innovation from production discussed in Chapter 3 a central feature. Places with low labour and operating costs and adequate export infrastructure, for example, have received investments in labour-intensive slices of goods-producing value chains, sometimes concentrated in export-processing zones (EPZs), which provide specific infrastructure, tax, and legal advantages for investors. Production in GVCs can also be inward facing, with foreign investors focused on producing for domestic markets. Other places specialize in exporting finely sliced services, such as software coding or customer service. This section of the chapter associates countries with several of these patterns with an eye to highlighting the scale and complexity of GVCs in the compressed-development era.

Backward and forward GVC participation

Prior to the emergence of GVCs, it was safe enough to assume that most if not all of the value of an exported product or service was added in the exporting country by domestic industries and enterprises. This lent gross export statistics a great deal of analytic power and policy relevance because industrial capabilities could be judged by the scale and technological content of exports (for example, see Lall,

2000; Staritz and Whitfield, 2019). GVCs undermine such assumptions and complicate the formation of trade and industrial policies, not least because reliance on imported inputs (e.g. parts, components, and software) increases the level of foreign value in a country's exports (i.e. the import content of exports). When imported inputs are technologically sophisticated, *gross* export statistics overstate the value of exports, but also lose their usefulness as a development yardstick since in-country value added may be small and processes simple, even for technologically sophisticated products and services.

To measure the *net* value of exports, a series of ambitious projects emerged in the late 2000s that brought together statisticians and economists from the fields of national accounting and trade to produce a series *international (global and regional) input-output* (IIO) datasets that gave researchers an ability to decompose the value of imported intermediates and domestic value added in exports.[1] In such datasets, 'backward participation' refers to the share of imported intermediate goods and services embodied in exports, while 'forward participation' refers to the share of export value incorporated in the products and services exported from receiving (importing) countries. In short, countries with high backward GVC–participation rates tend to rely on imported content to produce and export final products (playing an export-processing role in GVCs), while countries with high forward participation rates tend to be producers and exporters of that 'intermediate' content (playing a role in exporting parts and components in GVCs).

In the context of regional integration, especially in Europe and North America, countries with lower operating costs on the 'periphery' of large existing markets are, as a group, the most reliant on export assembly. This is reflected in the left-hand chart in Figure 5.1, which ranks the top-twenty-five economies according to their 'backward' participation in GVCs, as measured by the 2011 share of imported intermediates in the value of exports. Again, high rankings in backward GVC participation suggest an export-processing role, where parts and components are imported, further processed and assembled, and then exported as either higher-level intermediates or finished products.

Eight of the top-twenty-five economies are in Central-East Europe (including the top three: Hungary and the Slovak and Czech Republics), reflecting the surge of investment for export processing that came with the dissolution of the Soviet Union in 1989 and the formation of the European Union in 1992, timing which dovetailed exactly with the rise of the network organizational paradigm (Hoekman and Djankov, 1997; Krätke, 1999). Tunisia (ranked nineteenth), in North Africa, assembles cars and apparel for Western Europe, and in the context

[1] These projects include the Asian International Input Output (AIIO) Table created by Japan External Trade Research Organization's Institute of Developing Economies (IDE-JETRO), initially released in 2006; the EORA dataset, developed by KMG Associates (spun off from the University of Sydney), and Purdue University's Global Trade Analysis Project (GTAP); and the World Input-Output Database (WIOD), a large-scale EU project centred at the University of Groningen in the Netherlands.

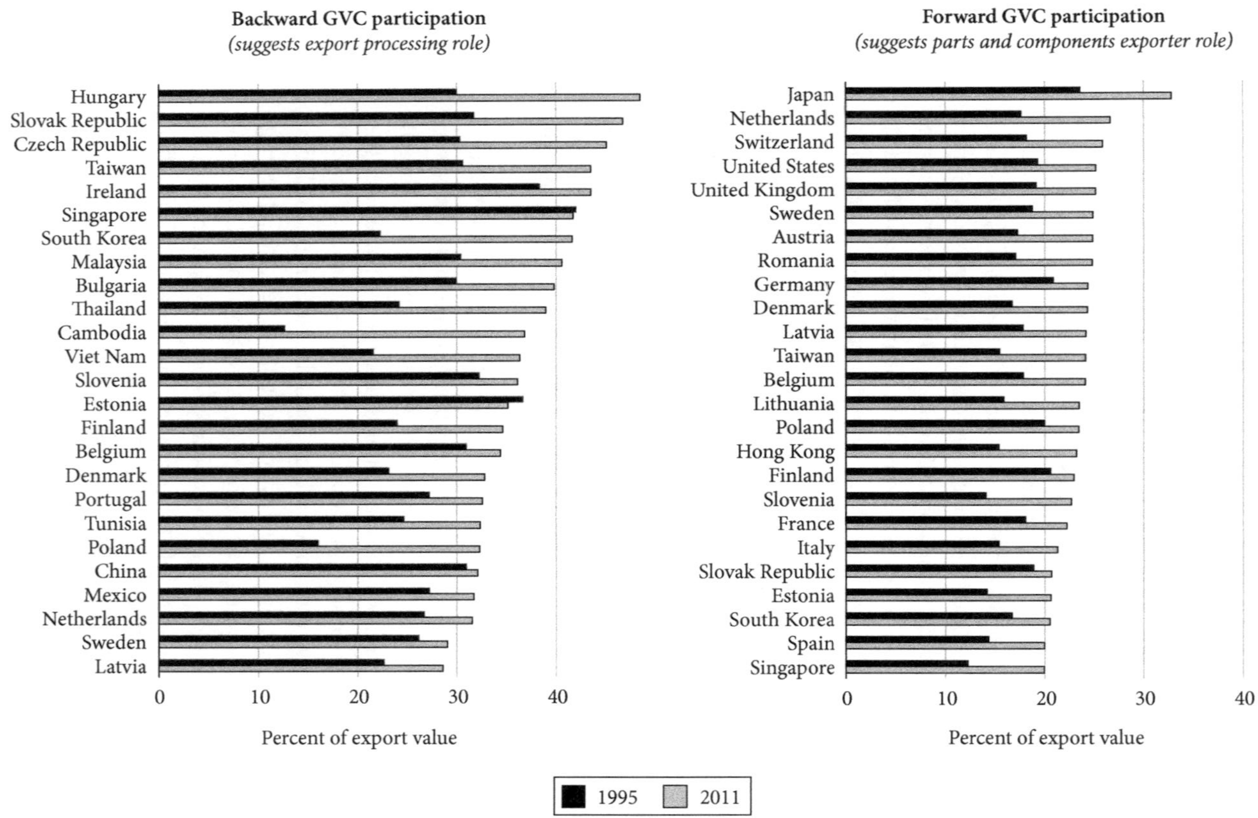

Figure 5.1 Forward and backward participation in global value chains, 1995 and 2011 (top-twenty-five economies as ranked in 2011)

Notes:
- Backward global-value-chain (GVC) participation is the share of imported intermediates embodied in the value of exports (suggests an export-processing role in GVCs).
- Forward GVC participation is the share of export value embodied in the exports of trading partners (suggests an intermediate parts and component exporter role in GVCs).
- Forward ranking excludes countries with 49 per cent or more of 2011 exports in primary commodities (consisting of ISIC industries 0, 1, 2, 3, 4, and 68). Excluded countries are Brunei Darussalam, Saudi Arabia, Norway, Russia, Peru, Chile, Indonesia, Colombia, Australia, the Philippines, Iceland, Brazil, and South Africa.

Sources: • GVC participation: OECD/WTO Trade in Value-added Indicators—https://stats.oecd.org/, compiled by Matthew Kidder.
• Commodity share of exports: UNCTAD—https://unctadstat.unctad.org

of production networks in North America, Mexico (ranked twenty-second) plays a similar role for cars, electronics, home appliances, apparel, and many other products, including aircraft parts and avionic software.

East Asian late-late and compressed developers are also prominent on the list, including those that increased their contemporary linkages with the global economy across the transition from late-late to compressed development (Singapore and South Korea, Taiwan, and mainland China), along with Southeast Asian nations which have either been export platforms for decades (Malaysia and Thailand), or have more recently become so with their membership in Association of Southeast Asian Nations (Cambodia and Vietnam).[2]

Rounding out the backward participation ranking on the left-hand side of Figure 5.1 are several small European countries (Ireland, Finland, Belgium, Denmark, Portugal, the Netherlands, and Sweden) that have production systems that cross borders with neighbouring countries more as a practical matter than as a signal of any specific role as an export assembler, although they may indeed play such roles.

It is striking that backward GVC–participation rates are estimated to have increased sharply in the period 1995 to 2011 for twenty-four of the twenty-five countries listed, revealing a strong secular trend towards GVC participation in the global economy. The lone exception, tiny Singapore, has remained steady at a high rate, with about 42 per cent of its export value accounted for by imported intermediates—a result of the country's aggressive targeting of investment for hard disk drive assembly from the mid-1980s onward (Gourevitch et al., 2000). The largest increase has been for Cambodia (from 13 to 37 per cent), which has become an export assembler for apparel only recently, and unlike other major apparel exporters such as China, Vietnam, Bangladesh, Sri Lanka, and India, the growth in apparel sewing has not been accompanied by large-scale local production of textiles.

As this discussion suggests, the countries listed on the left side of Figure 5.1 are not the largest exporters, just the most dependent on exports with high import content. China is by far the most important export assembler, but the size and diversity of its economy and its growing role as a producer (and exporter) of intermediate goods places it twenty-first among the top twenty-five in regard to backward GVC participation. Not coincidentally, the 'outlier' countries in the bottom Figure 1.1 with a manufacturing employment share of more than 15 per cent—China, Costa Rica, South Korea, Mexico, Mauritius, Malaysia, and Thailand—all make an appearance on the left side of Figure 5.1 (except for Costa Rica, which ranks twenty-sixth, and Mauritius, which is not included in the TiVA dataset). This is because backward GVC participation tends to drive investment in manufacturing to higher-than-average levels for less-developed

[2] Indonesia is also an important export platform in GVCs but does not appear because economies that are heavily reliant on primary commodity exports (e.g. oil) are excluded from Figure 5.1.

countries. Industrialization occurs but is 'thin' because it is only weakly linked to domestic institutions and innovation systems. This increases a country's vulnerability to middle-income traps.

The right-hand chart in Figure 5.1 ranks economies that are likely to be at the 'front end' of GVCs, exporting parts, components, and other intermediate inputs to export assemblers. Japan has the highest ranking, with about a third of its export value accounted for by intermediates which are then embodied in the exports of its trading partners. Again, the high ranking of small countries in Western Europe (i.e. the Netherlands, Switzerland, Sweden, Austria, Denmark, Belgium, and Finland) should be partially discounted. These countries are certainly exporters of high-value intermediates, but they are also deeply integrated with neighbouring states and so play multiple roles in regional GVCs. After these countries, the most important exporters of high-value intermediates in GVCs make an appearance: the United States (ranked number five), the UK (six), Germany (nine), France (nineteen), Italy (twenty), and Spain (twenty-four). Like the left-hand chart, there is a clear secular trend towards greater participation and specialization in GVC–related trade from 1995 to 2011, with each of the top-twenty-five countries increasing their forward participation over that period.

The appearance of several countries in Central-East Europe (Romania, Latvia, Lithuania, Poland, Slovenia, and Estonia) on the forward participation list, and the appearance of compressed developers in East Asia (South Korea, Taiwan, and mainland China) in both charts reveals the growing complexity of GVCs, where countries can simultaneously be important importers and exporters of intermediates. Taiwan, in particular, shifted its role after China's accession to the World Trade Organization (WTO) from an original design manufacturer supplier of intermediates and finished goods, as ordered by firms in West, to a major investor and supply chain orchestrator in mainland China.[3]

The economies listed in Figure 5.1 are only indicative of a larger and more complex set of interlocking trends in the geography of global production. Economies excluded for high reliance on primary commodities may also be major players in GVCs (e.g. Canada in autos and Indonesia in electronics and apparel). Important countries in terms of GVC engagement may have backward participation rates too low to be included in Figure 5.1 because of the size and diversity of their exports (e.g. India). As already suggested, local production of intermediate inputs can also lower a country's position in regard to backward GVC participation, even though it may be a major export assembler.[4]

[3] In this context, the term 'ODM' refers to contract manufacturers that provide design inputs in addition to manufacturing services for their customers (Sturgeon and Lee, 2005).

[4] This is especially common in the apparel sector, where 'yarn forward' rules of origin are often a requirement for exports to be included in preferential trade agreements, even though the design, supply chain orchestration, and sales of products like footwear and apparel might be closely managed by global brands such as Nike and Gap (Locke et al., 2009; Sturgeon and Memedovic, 2010).

Further, the statistics underlying Figure 5.1 are best at estimating the geography of value added in goods production, and leave out many of the 'intangible' contributions to GVCs such as supply chain finance and orchestration. Similarly, GVCs can also serve up 'ICT–enabled' services (ICT-ESs) such as computer help desks, 'back office' functions like credit card and claims processing, and customer service, and this type of trade is poorly measured (UNCTAD, 2015). Customer-facing ICT-ESs are commonly exported from call centres located in places were communications infrastructure is adequate and labour has the right skills (e.g. language, computer programming) such as India, the Philippines, Russia, Ukraine, Costa Rica, and Egypt, none of which appear in Figure 5.1. Indeed, policymakers have come to see ICT-ES exports as a path to upgrading in knowledge-intensive segments of GVCs (Chipidzaa and Leidnerb, 2019). Finally, with only twenty-five of the sixty-four economies in the OECD's TiVA dataset included, Figure 5.1 can be considered restrictive. Some countries outside the top twenty-five are key exporters of technology-intensive intermediates, such as Israel for electronic components and software, or important exporters into regional GVCs, such as Turkey for automotive parts and engineering services.

Inward and outward foreign direct investment

Trade is one indicator of GVC involvement, especially when the import content of exports is taken into consideration. Another is foreign direct investment (FDI), which signals the establishment or expansion of MNCs. Figure 5.2 shows inward FDI flows on an annual basis for the period 1970–2018 for the top-twenty FDI recipients during the period.[5] The importance of the United States and other developed economies is evident, but also the steadily rising share in key developers, especially China, can be seen.

Figure 5.3 maps the headquarters and subsidiary locations of MNCs in 2011. The data only include 'vertical linkages' where subsidiaries supply inputs to parents; the cases most obviously representing GVCs.[6] The size of the circles indicates the total number of parent companies headquartered in that country. The thickness of the lines represents the number of bilateral vertical subsidiaries between each parent country and a corresponding host country. The figure shows that MNC parents with vertical subsidiaries are heavily concentrated in developed countries, and the largest portion of these subsidiaries are located in other developed economies. European integration and the dense bilateral relationship between the United States and UK are evident. However, Mexico and middle-income countries in East Asia, especially China, show a high density of

[5] Cumulative figures are used, rather than 'FDI stock' figures that adjust for investments that are sold or otherwise withdrawn, to highlight the countries that have been the most important recipients of FDI in the forty-eight-year period.

[6] The data exclude both 'horizontal linkages' where parents and subsidiaries produce the same products, and 'complex linkages' where parents and subsidiaries produce both inputs and finished products.

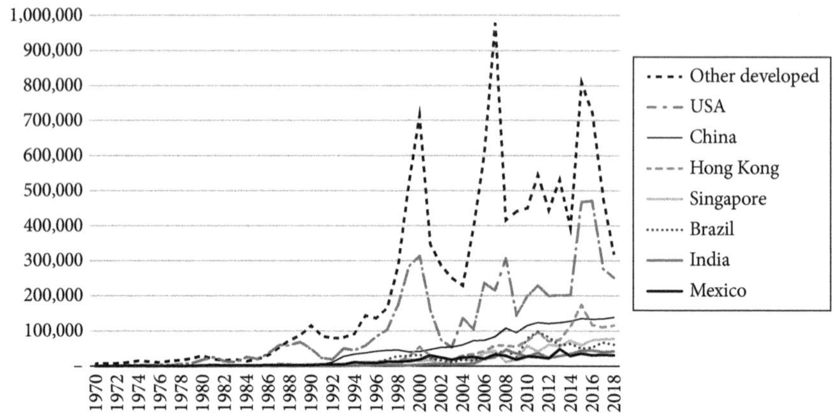

Figure 5.2 Inward foreign direct investment flows, top–twenty economies 1970–2018

Notes: US$ millions (current prices). Excludes offshore financial centres in the Caribbean. 'Other developed' includes the UK, the Netherlands, Belgium, Canada, Germany, France, Spain, Australia, Ireland, Italy, Switzerland, and Sweden.

subsidiaries, while their representation in terms of headquarters is generally low, suggesting a largely subservient, export processing role in GVCs. Latin America and Africa show fewer subsidiaries *and* few parent headquarters, suggesting their marginal role in GVCs as both sources and recipients of FDI. The dark lines linking parents in Hong Kong to subsidiaries in China, and parents in the United States to subsidiaries in Canada, reflect the especially high number of parent–subsidiary relationships in those cases.

The complex patterns of trade and investment here reflect the multiple, overlapping, and co-evolving roles countries play in GVCs, such as export assembler, importer of knowledge-intensive intermediates, exporter of intermediates, outward investor, recipient of investment, and so on. The precise patterns observed in a given economy reflect the (often-overlapping) strategies for cost-cutting, market access, and access to location-specific skills and infrastructure by 'lead' firms in GVCs; the trade, investment, and industrial policies of states; and the broader historical-institutional conditions—both national and international—that have set the rules and provided context for the emergence of GVCs. Despite this complexity, broad patterns exist, especially the still-dominant position of MNCs from developed countries, particularly the United States, and the rising importance of recent developers, especially China.

China's emergence as the world's most successful compressed developer

In Chapter 4 we discussed the compressed development of China in a general way, comparing it with late-developer Japan. Here we take a closer look at China's

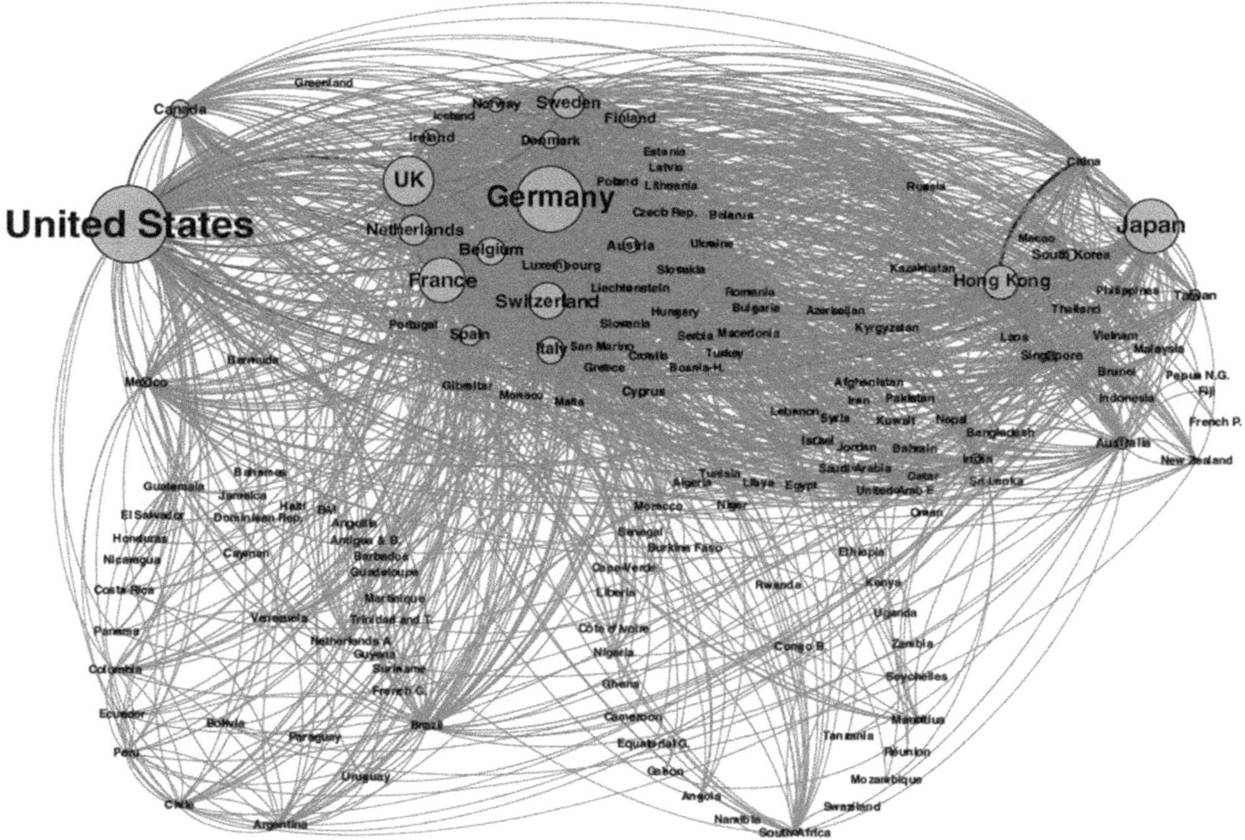

Figure 5.3 Vertically linked foreign subsidiaries and their parents, 2011

Source: Blyde (2014), using calculations based on data from Dun & Bradstreet.

engagement with GVCs, and its attempts to navigate the challenges of economic and industrial upgrading in the compressed-development era.

In 1980, China's National Congress approved the Regulations on Special Economic Zones for Shenzhen, Zhuhai, and Shantou in Guangdong Province, and the city of Xiamen in Fujian Province. The regulations were meant to accelerate and concentrate foreign investment by assuring investors that their interests would be protected, and to funnel investment funds to local administrators assigned with responsibility for site and infrastructure development. The programmes were spectacularly successful, especially in the southern Province of Guangdong, a former backwater located across the border from Hong Kong.[7]

China's accession to the WTO in 2001 accelerated the flow of investment by providing additional protections for multinational firms operating in China. It also came in the same year as the bursting of the 'technology bubble' in the United States, which refocused US firms on cost-cutting, as well as on the pursuit of growth strategies in 'big emerging markets' (Garten, 1997). What began as a set of modest strategic moves in the late 1980s and early 1990s by a relatively small set firms under extreme pressure to cut costs and avoid environmental and labour regulations at home became a full-fledged part of the network model, with financial markets and venture capital investors insisting that companies, even technology start-ups, craft and execute a 'global strategy', and often, more specifically, a 'China strategy' (Tse, 2010).

The success of the first special economic zone (SEZ) led the central government to approve dozens of additional zones, notably in the midcoast Yangtze River region, including Wuxi and Suzhou and adjacent Shanghai, in and around Beijing, including the coastal city of Tianjin, and in many inland cities as well, as overcrowding and rising wages in coastal cities motivated the state to try to direct investment inland.

China's leadership in electronic hardware exports

China's increasingly dominant role in electronic hardware production and export is worth highlighting. China surpassed the United States in the export of electronic intermediate goods (i.e. parts and components) in 2002 and final goods in 2004. By 2008, the sector was China's largest manufacturing sector, accounting for 8.6 per cent of all urban manufacturing employment (Banister and Cook, 2011). In cities such as Shenzhen, Dongguan, Guangzhou, and Suzhou, factory

[7] Export production of toys and household goods was first carried out in urban factories within British Hong Kong and later shifted across the border by Hong Kong producers and trading companies, the most important being Li & Fung. Today, according to the company's website, Li & Fung orchestrates production for global buyers in more than 8000 factories, located primarily in China (73 per cent of factories), Vietnam, Bangladesh, India, and Indonesia.

Table 5.1 China's dominant role in electronic hardware GVCs—exports and imports by value-chain stage, in thousands of US dollars

	1988	2011	2015
Exports by value-chain stage			
World electronic hardware final goods exports	$41,151,832	$1,291,191,048	$1,263,240,042
China's exports	$294,281	$453,316,448	$520,192,992
China's global share	1%	35%	41%
World electronic hardware intermediate goods exports	$28,213,566	$1,195,654,609	$1,162,084,718
China's exports	$16,625	$315,589,536	$331,651,712
China's global share	0%	26%	29%
Imports by value-chain stage			
World electronic hardware final goods imports	$86,866,215	$1,207,667,328	$1,184,154,591
China's imports	$1,621,470	$89,607,104	$64,121,784
China's global share	2%	7%	5%
World electronic hardware intermediate goods imports	$43,467,296	$1,051,138,505	$1,015,291,169
China's imports	$680,097	$229,371,808	$245,368,576
China's global share	2%	22%	24%

Source: World Bank MC-GVC database, which includes balanced panel of 175 countries representing 93 per cent of world trade for final and intermediates in three 'GVC industries': electronics, automotive, and apparel and footwear.

complexes run by global contract manufactures such as Foxconn (Taiwan) and Flextronics (the United States) employ and house thousands, and even hundreds of thousands of workers at a time. These factory complexes are served by a world-class logistics infrastructure that can deliver products almost anywhere in the world in a matter of only a few days.

As Table 5.1 shows, China's trade position in the electronic hardware grew from only 1 per cent of global final goods exports in 1988 (and zero per cent of intermediate goods exports and 2 per cent of intermediate goods imports), to 35 per cent of global final goods exports in 2011 (along with 26 per cent of intermediate goods exports, and 22 per cent of intermediate goods imports). After the global financial crisis, China consolidated its position as an export producer of electronic hardware further, even as the pace of trade growth slowed worldwide, with final product exports rising to an astonishing 41 per cent of the world total by 2015. The importance of electronic intermediates (components) imports (24 per cent of world imports in 2015) reflects both the complex nature of the electronics GVC—where partially completed components and subassemblies (i.e. intermediates) sometimes cross borders multiple times as before being incorporated into final goods—and the gravitation of intermediate goods production to China to fuel its burgeoning final goods assembly sector. Table 5.1 also shows that China's imports of *final* electronic goods has been modest throughout, despite its rise as one of the world's largest markets for consumer electronics such as phone handsets and television sets. In this we see the dual role of China in GVCs as an export platform and a magnet for production intended for the domestic market.

The case of mobile phones: escaping low-value-added traps?

Countries and regions that are deeply connected to GVCs as export platforms can fall into 'low-value-added traps' (Sturgeon and Kawakami, 2011; Xing, 2019). This idea was first articulated (from direct experience) by Stan Shih, the former CEO of Taiwan personal computer maker Acer, as the 'Smiling Curve' which depicts value addition and capture (profits) as being higher at the beginning (high value components) and end (retail) of the value chain and less value added—or at least profit—in the middle (product assembly). This was demonstrated empirically by the research of Linden et al. (2009) with the case of the 30 GB Apple iPod, which estimated that assembly in China contributed only $3.70 of the iPod's $144 factory gate (preshipping wholesale) price, and that the contract manufacturer (Taiwan's Foxconn, operating in Guangdong Province) captured only 11 cents of the estimated $33.37 of gross profit earned by companies contributing to iPod's bill of [physical] materials (BOM). The value added for Foxconn's contract assembly services (component insertion, final assembly, and test) was far below higher-value items in the BOM, such as the central processing chip set (52.5 per cent) and the miniature hard drive made by Japan's Toshiba (26.5 per cent).[8] So, in the case of the Apple iPod, at least, value added in China was low—and profits even lower—relative to imported inputs produced by firms in the United States, Europe, Japan, and South Korea.

To see if Chinese value added for Apple was increasing over time, Sturgeon and Thun (2018) compared data from an OECD study of the 2011 iPhone 4 with data from IHS Markit for a 2017 iPhone7 and found the breakdown of value added for the assembly portion of value added is nearly identical at about 1 per cent of retail.[9]

Still, two important caveats are in order. First, even though assembly is carried out by foreign-invested enterprises, and profit margins are thin, massive production and export volumes can create significant foreign-exchange for China's

[8] Additional product-level GVC research by Linden and his colleagues (Dedrick et al., 2010), and others Ali-Yrkkö, 2011; OECD, 2011) found similar results in similar products (various editions of the Apple iPhone and other mobile phone handsets).

[9] Note that because of the popularity of the iPhone and the proprietary nature of its application ecosystems (iTunes and the App Store), Apple is able to charge a very significant premium for its handsets, driving up profit margins to an estimated 45 per cent for the iPhone 4. Other smartphone makers, based on the free Google Android operating system, earn far lower or even negative margins.

central and city governments in the form of industrial taxes and other fees. Second, the physical value (material and assembly costs) of a mobile phone handset is not only comprised of assembly and high-value components. About 10–12 per cent if the phone's retail price is accounted for by relatively simple and in some cases generic components such as bare circuit boards, plastic and metal cases, miniature precision screws, sockets, capacitor, resistors, and the like. We can assume that a high and growing proportion of this business is going to Chinese firms producing not only for Apple, but for the many products made in China. Thus, the giant contract manufacturers in the region are surrounded by thousands of domestic suppliers, large and small, along with many smaller branded firms (*shanzhai*) that sell an ever-changing array of low-cost products to the domestic market. This has helped to nurture a unique, highly efficient, and effective 'fast-manufacturing' and 'maker' ecosystem in Southern China that supports production in high volumes, with great responsiveness and product variety, for both export and domestic markets (Lindtner et al., 2015).

China's policy response to thin industrialization: intensified techno-nationalism

China's policymakers have been acutely aware of the high share of foreign value added in technology-intensive products such as mobile phone handsets in both exports and production for the local market, and have embarked on a strong import substitution push to increase local content, notably with the Made in China 2025 policy, which includes a goal of increasing the domestically produced portion of intermediate inputs to 70 per cent. State support for the construction of new LCD display factories, mainly for televisions, has already resulted in the capture of 80 per cent of the large format LCD market in China (CSOT, 2017). The state is also spearheading a US $115 billion surge of investment in semiconductor fabrication factories using a three-pronged financing strategy of central government funding ($21 billion), city-level funding ($41 billion), and state-backed private investment funds ($53 billion) (SEMI, 2017). The goal is to move from consuming two-thirds of the world's semiconductors but producing only 12 per cent (Semiconductor Industry Association, 2015), to satisfying 70 per cent of domestic consumption by 2025, with full self-sufficiency in all areas of the integrated circuit (IC) supply chain by 2030 (Tayal, 2016).

These goals may be unrealistic. At the proposed rate of investment, China would account for 100 per cent of expected the world's incremental increase in semiconductor foundry capacity through 2025 (Thomas, 2015). And the industry-dominant players in semiconductor equipment from the United States and Japan that outfit new foundries currently have no viable substitutes. However, there is no doubt that China's huge market, growing pool of engineering talent, and (controversial) requirements that foreign companies selling technology-intensive goods and services in the domestic market establish engineering and R&D centres, are driving a larger share of global R&D to China.[10]

The results of China's upgrading push remain uncertain, but given the scale and breadth of the effort, it is likely to yield progress. China's policy response to the challenge of improving its position in GVCs (including its innovation gap) runs the gamut. It includes massive investments in basic science, university research and education, and domestic production of higher-value components, as just discussed. Domestic companies have been encouraged to engage in technology-seeking foreign acquisitions (Henderson and Hooper, 2019). Important policy goals such as reduction of urban air pollution have been tied to industrial policies such as the development of domestic electric vehicle producers (Hao et al., 2014). To foster creative start-up companies and a culture of innovation, hundreds of incubators, accelerators, and 'maker spaces' have been created.[11]

These strategies are not mutually exclusive, and both will almost certainly be pursued simultaneously in the coming decades (Fu et al., 2016). Motivation for greater technological independence has increased markedly with the US–China trade conflict and China's confidence is well-founded with its vast market size and huge foreign-exchange reserves earned during its successful export push. However, its strategy poses risks as well. An excessive focus on 'made in China' *for* China could lead to over-investment, falling prices, and isolation from the frontiers of technology, especially if the current putative retreat from global trade is short-lived.[12] Specifically, lack of access to key technology inputs could stall the rising potential for innovation in China and diminish domestic Chinese companies' international competitiveness.

On the other hand, there may be a good—but fleeting—opportunity for China to upgrade its position in the global economy, with signals of retreat from political leadership and global economic engagement by some of China's important trading partners. A new class of innovative and globally competitive lead firms could use this opportunity to capture greater value in GVCs and step into a more innovative role in the world economy. By emphasizing branding, global exports, and integration with global ecosystems—while leveraging the country's strengths in manufacturing and rapid product development—China could distance itself

[10] This is reflected in the example of Samsung's global R&D footprint, which in addition to core R&D in Korea; two long-standing advanced research centres in the United States; a major software and technology development centre in Bangalore, India; a smaller research facility focused on wireless, displays, and batteries, in Japan; and several others, includes five large technical centres in China.

[11] In an author's interview on 31 March 2017 with Shenzhen City officials, it was indicated that more than 200 such 'maker spaces' had been established in the city.

[12] In particular, the very high current and planned levels of public spending for electric vehicles and higher-value ICT intermediates (semiconductors and flat panels) create the risk of overcapacity, market fragmentation, poor technology choices, and a glut of current-generation production that will soon become older-generation.

from the bottom of the Shih smiling curve (Nahm and Steinfeld, 2014). The most innovative Chinese firms have already done this.[13] An outwardly engaged China—characterized by innovative domestic Chinese firms with their own intellectual property, strong bilateral trade in technology-intensive intermediates, exports, and outward FDI that fully engages host-country skill development, inputs, product markets, and institutions—could place China at a long-term advantage and contribute to a prosperous, peaceful world economic system.

Other country experiences with compressed development

Engagement with GVCs (opening to massive foreign investment, especially for export assembly) became central to China's development project in the 1990s and 2000s. Because it dovetailed with outsourcing and offshoring strategies of global firms seeking to cut costs for export and access China's huge domestic market at the same time, the strategy was enormously successful for China and for foreign investors and their suppliers. But this is not the only experience of compressed development, even if it is arguably the most notable. In fact, the era effects of compressed development, in addition to feeding back into *developed* economies (see Chapter 9), have altered the context for development—in regard to investment, finance, employment, job content and skill requirements, technological learning, and industrial policy—in high-growth, lower-growth, and stalled economies across the globe. Next, we provide three cases (with selective detail) that provide useful contrast with mainland China in regard to the form and effects of GVC engagement: Brazil, Taiwan, and India.

Thin industrialization, Brazilian style

Brazil's development path has been different than China's, with different outcomes, but the era effects of compressed development have nevertheless had an impact. Simply put, Brazil faces thin-industrialization challenges similar to those faced by China, but it has weaker tools to address them. The most striking difference relates to Brazil's integration with the global economy. Brazil has an inward focus which contrasts markedly with the export orientation of successful developers in East Asia. This is not to say that multinational firms are unimportant or that Brazil is unengaged with GVCs. In certain sectors, such as motor

[13] For example, Shenzhen-based Dajiang Innovation Technology Co. (DJI) has become the world's leading producer of consumer drones, combining its own technology—which it protects internationally—with powerful, low-cost ICT components readily available in Shenzhen, and global sourcing: the Swiss chip design company U-blox supplies the main GPS positioning chip for DJI's popular Phantom series drones.

vehicles, electronics and telecommunications equipment, industrial machinery (including electricity generation equipment), and home appliances, multinationals dominate. The difference is that these firms, along with their global suppliers, operate mainly to serve the protected Brazilian market.

Drawing on dependency theory (Prebisch, 1950; Cardoso and Faletto, [1969] 1979), Brazilian policymakers have worked to substitute imports since the 1950s. Explanations for Brazil's inward focus include a reliance on consumption, rather than production; an absence of existential threats that seem to have driven developmentalism in East Asia; and land reform patterns that left power in the hands of large landowners rather than industrialists (Kay, 2002; Anglade and Fortin, 1990). We concur, but from 1990 onward, Brazil's import-substitution policies have necessarily co-evolved with the GVC investment boom linked to the network organizational paradigm (i.e. outsourcing and offshoring, vertical specialization in production and trade, concentration in the middle of the value chain and the emergence of global suppliers, and so on). Specifically, GVCs have changed the calculus for Brazil in four important ways.

First, high costs and low productivity in Brazil have obviated any significant role for Brazil as an export platform. While Brazil's domestic market has been large enough to attract market-seeking investments, the high cost of products made in Brazil has inhibited the sort of export-oriented investments that generated the vast foreign-exchange reserves that China is now using to invest in indigenous innovation and import substitution. In the context of a fragmented political system that has created a weak state, high costs come from series of labour bargains and political patronage that have raised wages and instilled labour market rigidities in the formal sector well above those of less-developed countries in East Asia (and Mexico and Africa). This—combined with an ineffective education system, high taxes and tax compliance costs, high interest rates, poor trade and transport infrastructure, and high costs of imported business services, including advanced software and IT services—is ubiquitous and well-known enough to have earned its own moniker: the *Custo Brasil* (Brazil Cost). Given higher costs in Brazil than in successful exporters in East Asia, as well as a lack of geographic propinquity that has created export-processing roles for countries such as Mexico, Central-East Europe, Turkey, and North Africa, exports from Brazil must be based on quality and high productivity rather than price. Both have proven to be elusive to achieve in Brazil (Dutz, 2018).

Second, for the technology-intensive industries Brazil has targeted for import substitution, local content rules have been both comprehensive and very detailed.[14] Adaptive, GVC-oriented industrial policies that target a set of narrow

[14] The primary mechanisms to promote import substitution in Brazil are high import tariffs and the imposition of an industrial production tax (IPI). Companies, including domestic firms and foreign multinationals, that comply with these requirements are awarded 'tax breaks' that reduce or eliminate

but globally competitive specializations have not been pursued (Gereffi and Sturgeon, 2013). The imposition of import and domestic-content-dependent production taxes encouraged many MNCs to invest for production for the local market, but items with very high investment costs and minimum scale requirements such as semiconductors, electric turbines, oil drilling equipment, and automotive electronics continue to be imported in large numbers. In the face of this, companies producing in Brazil often continue to import high-value machinery, parts, and components, and pay penalties for doing so.[15] Domestic firms (e.g. the Brazilian personal computer brand Positivo) are also subject to the same regulations, and must also pay high taxes for imported components.[16] Reliance on high-cost imports both inhibits exports and raises costs for consumers in Brazil. According to Lima de Oliveria and Zylberberg (2019), the motivation for companies to seek relief from these high costs depends on their ability to pass them on to customers. In oil and gas, where prices are set on world markets and have plummeted after 2014, companies (including the state oil and gas company Petrobras) have been able to obtain some relief, while in consumer electronics and automobiles, consumers either pay higher prices or receive inferior products.

Third, supply chain consolidation in GVCs means that local content requirements, when they are complied with, are often met by global, not local suppliers. A main purpose of import-substitution policies, historically, has been to stimulate the development and upgrading of domestic suppliers. However, when global suppliers fill these niches, import substitution stimulates investment and employment, but does little in terms of developing the domestic industrial base.

IPI. In electronics, the Informatics Law stipulates that companies can attain 'basic productive process' (PPB) certifications for their products by committing to purchasing or producing a certain percentage of each product's components in Brazil. For example, computer manufacturers (or more likely their contract manufacturers in Brazil) are required to procure a certain percentage of motherboards, hard disk drives, memory chips, and plastic parts domestically to receive tax credits for IPI and relief on other state and federal taxes. In the automotive industry, the Inovar Auto policy (relaunched as Rota 2030 in 2017) stipulates the number of steps in the manufacturing process (e.g. large metal stamping, body welding, body undercoating, and painting) that must be completed in Brazil in order to qualify for a reduction or elimination of an additional 30 per cent IPI imposed by the program. In the oil and gas industry, the policy from the Brazilian National Agency of Petroleum, Natural Gas and Biofuels (ANP) sets local content requirements for oilfield development equipment down to the component level such as pumps, tubing, etc.) (Zylberberg, 2016; Lima de Oliveira, 2017; Sturgeon et al., 2017).

[15] Tellingly, the aeronautics sector has not been subject to high import tariffs or other local content rules for intermediate inputs. Because of this, Embraer, Brazil's national champion, has been able to achieve a high level of success in international markets for small (regional) commercial jets by combining its capabilities in system design, development, integration, and assembly with imported components sourced from the global supply base such as aviation design software, jet engines, landing gear, avionic control systems, and many others (Sturgeon et al., 2013).

[16] Indeed, the main difference with past policies was the level playing field provided for MNCs and domestic firms, which was a requirement for Brazil's accession to the WTO in 1995.

Fourth, because core technology and product development tend to remain in the home countries of multinational firms (lead firms and suppliers), including lead firm–supplier collaboration on new product development in core technology districts, investment for the local market brings little in the way of technological learning. Simply put, Brazil's protected market provides relatively little incentive to for companies to invest in innovation. The result is a low value-added trap without the benefit of exports to generate tax revenues. Industrialization takes place, but is unbalanced and thin, and because it is scaled only for the domestic market, costs are higher and productivity is lower than when imported inputs flow more freely and production is scaled for export.[17]

The Brazilian government has sought to overcome these challenges by incentivizing greater R&D spending and encouraging more meaningful relationships between MNCs and various actors in the Brazilian innovation system, such as universities and government-supported contract research and technology providers (Reynolds et al., 2019). However, because R&D spending requirements (ranging from .5 to 4 per cent of annual revenues depending on the industry) are layered on existing industrial policies, and formulated in similar ways, they produce similar results. For example, incentivized R&D is broad-based and fragmented rather than targeted in a way that plays to Brazil's strengths and might lead to scale and globally competitive specializations. Agents charged with overseeing these R&D policies lack the capacity for effective monitoring and evaluation, as is evidenced by the multiyear backlog of projects to be evaluated for meeting the government's vague definitions of what constitutes R&D. Because the Brazilian market may represent a small slice of global sales and thus be a lesser priority, R&D spending is often on superficial activities (Zylberberg, 2017). If judged in terms of the creation of internationally competitive products suitable for export, innovation remains weak in Brazil in all but a few sectors.[18] As a result, Brazil does not have a robust set of internationally competitive, efficient, or innovative domestic firms at any level of the value chain, although there are exceptions.[19]

[17] Import-substitution and investment-attraction policies are not without merit. In Brazil, they have likely led to greater levels of industrialization and greater nonagricultural employment than would have otherwise been possible. According to the Brazilian electric and electronics industry association (ABINEE), the electronics industry employed 230,000 to sell $37 billion worth of electronic devices in 2017. The automotive industry employs 500,000 people and produces more than two million motor vehicles a year (Sturgeon et al., 2017).

[18] Sturgeon et al. (2017) find that the effect of the automotive industrial policy, *Inovar Auto*, on output, labour productivity, and R&D expenditures has been limited. Similarly, Zylberberg (2017) finds that although the Informatics Law has led to increased production and R&D spending in Brazil, especially by MNCs, it has not enabled Brazilian firms to carve out a high-valued added role in either global production or knowledge networks.

[19] In addition to Petrobras for deep water oil and gas development and Embraer's success in regional jets, a list of globally competitive Brazilian firms might include WEG (industrial equipment), Welle Laser (industrial lasers), Stefanini (ICT services), Embraco (compressors for buses), Marco Polo (buses), and young ICT firms such as Tempest (cybersecurity software).

India's varied roles in GVCs

The roles India plays in GVCs vary according to the sector. In electronics and motor vehicles, India's long-standing policies have been similar to Brazil's: attracting FDI to substitute for imports, including a few joint ventures (such as Maruti-Suzuki). Ford, General Motors, Kia, Isuzu, Mercedes-Benz, and other global brands have assembly plants in India aimed mainly at the domestic market, plants that are supported by major investments by global suppliers. The situation is similar in electronics.

On the other hand, India is an export platform for apparel, with a large domestic textile sector that feeds both local and export markets. Like neighbouring Bangladesh, Sri Lanka, and Pakistan, export assembly is mainly for global brands. Global buyers are also important in the agricultural sector, especially tea (Neilson and Pritchard, 2009). India's IT services sector constitutes one of the main GVC success stories of the 2000s. It consists of a mix of large domestic contractors and foreign affiliates performing 'back office' and customer services functions for their parents. Although the offshoring of basic software coding began in earnest in 1998 with the run up to Y2K, offshore call centres began to grow rapidly after 2000 with plummeting international telecommunications rates. Prominent examples included banks such as Citicorp, HSBC, and JP Morgan, as well as technology firms such as Accenture, Dell, Hewlett-Packard, and IBM. The largest US-based IT services firms, including IBM Global Services and Electronic Data Services, established large operations in India, and Indian contractors, including HCL, Infosys, Satyam, TCS, and Wipro, all reported extremely rapid growth (Dossani and Kenney, 2003). Since then, Indian IT services firms have continued to grow, and some have established global operations, in addition to robust programmes to send (or 'bodyshop') Indian engineers to work on site at their customers, mainly in developed countries and especially in the United States under the H1-B visa programme. Most recently, however, AI and other forms of digital automation have apparently begun to cut into India's export IT-ES sector (Bhattacharya, 2017), and in the United States the H1-B visa programme has been dramatically curtailed from a peak of 644,000 visas issues in 2015 to just 363,000 in 2018 (D'Souza, 2019).

In the face of this, the government of India has taken some inspiration from China to accelerate export-oriented FDI in formerly protected manufacturing sectors under the banner of 'Make in India', launched in 2015. The policy proposes a series of investment-attraction measures and regulatory reforms, including streamlining of construction permits, guarantees for the provision of electricity (within seven to fourteen days), looser logistics and import/export regulations, tax compliance, bankruptcy law, and contract enforcement reforms more favourable to foreign invetors. These policies make explicit reference to showing improvement to India's ranking on related measures in the World Bank's *Doing Business Report*.

The emergence of India's ICT-ES sector was almost entirely due to firm strategies (both MNC and domestic) based on the new possibilities from low-cost international voice and data communications, and the quality and size of India's English-speaking workforce. It remains to be seen if India can follow China's lead and become a large-scale export platform in GVCs for manufactured goods (autos and electronics are the first two 'superstar' sectors identified in policy documents). Given that China's export boom co-evolved with the outsourcing and offshoring wave linked to the network organizational paradigm in the 1990s and 2000s, a window that may be closing, it is difficult to imagine India having a similar experience in the coming years.

Taiwan, the first true compressed developer

Finally, we include a comment on Taiwan, arguably the first true compressed developer. After a brief period in the 1970s and 1980s, when Taiwan was host to significant FDI, mainly by US and Japanese multinationals seeking low-cost production in the central city of Kaohsiung, late-development-style policies were put in place to try to develop a full set of national champions (Wade, 1990). When this largely failed, Taiwan eventually embraced its supplier role in GVCs, providing components and product-level contract design and manufacturing services from afar, mainly to brands in the United States (Dedrick and Kraemer, 1998; Sturgeon and Lee, 2005; Kawakami, 2011; Hamilton and Kau, 2018).

The role of Taiwan in GVCs had a major impact on the mainland, especially in the electronics sector. In the period 2001–2006, Taiwan-based contract manufacturers moved nearly all of their high-volume manufacturing from Taiwan to mainland China, largely at the behest of their global customers, who were demanding lower costs. For example, as notebook PCs expanded rapidly at the end of the 1990s, surpassing desktop units in the early 2000s, production in Taiwan, mainly for Western brands such as IBM and Dell, soared from 2.3 million units in 1995 to a peak of 14.3 million in 2002. After 2002, however, notebook PC production in Taiwan dropped just as rapidly, even as Taiwanese firms produced a larger share of the world's output, reaching 92 per cent in 2008. This migration was driven by customer demands, especially by IBM, to produce a personal computer that could be sold in the United States for less than US$1000. This shift contributed to the dramatic expansion of electronics manufacturing clusters on the mainland, especially in the Pearl River Delta for the assembly of desktop PCs, PC main boards, and peripheral products, and in the Yangtze River Delta near Shanghai, focused on the final assembly of notebook PCs. Smaller Taiwan-based contract manufacturers and component suppliers were not able to make this move, leading to a dramatic consolidation—the number of Taiwan-headquartered contract manufacturers specializing in notebook PC assembly fell from forty-five in 1993 to only twenty-one in 2006, with market share shifting dramatically in favour of the largest five producers—Foxconn, Quanta, Compal, Wistron, and Inventec (Sturgeon and Kawakami, 2011, 131–32).

As important, the world's largest contract producers of logic semiconductors—Taiwan Semiconductor Manufacturing Corp. and United Manufacturing Corp.—emerged on the island to provide services to the world's burgeoning population of 'fabless' semiconductor design companies. Taiwan-based contractors emerged in other sectors as well. In footwear, Pao Chen produces for Nike and many other brands in Taiwan, China, Vietnam, Indonesia, Bangladesh, Cambodia, Myanmar, and Nicaragua. In fact, contractors from Taiwan have emerged as some of the world's most important foreign investors, importers, and exporters, even if they make no products under their own brand names. In 2012, Foxconn's eleven mainland subsidiaries accounted for 17.3 per cent (US $79.3 billion) of the aggregate (gross) export value of China's top-200 exporters (Grimes, 2015). More recently, Jacobs (2018) reported that Foxconn employed 1.4 million workers in mainland China, including 350,000 in one factory complex in Zhengzhou that produced 500,000 iPhones per day, or about half of world output.

Many of Taiwan's contract manufacturers still operate near the bottom of the smiling curve. The development of Taiwan companies' marketing and branding skills are weak, resulting in a thin-industrialization profile. Nevertheless, for this small island of only 20 million people, Taiwan's contractor role in GVCs has allowed for the development of a rich set of design and technology development capabilities, mainly linked to its production role (e.g. in the realm of IC design; Imai and Shiu, 2011), and the orchestration of its global network of subsidiaries. This has been more than enough to cement and expand its Taiwan's high-income status even as it has 'hollowed out' much of its manufacturing and become the world's seventh-largest source of outward FDI.[20]

Implications for industrial policy

As GVCs have been identified as an important feature of the global economy, policymakers and entrepreneurs in many countries have sought to harness them to foster development (World Bank, 2015b). It is no surprise that these policies have been most successful in countries with the market size necessary to attract

[20] This ranking is based on Taiwan's cumulative FDI outflows from 1970–2018 in US$ millions (current prices). Like Figure 5.2, the ranking excludes offshore financial centres in the Caribbean. Data are from UNCTAD data centre (https://unctadstat.unctad.org/wds/).

investment on the basis of domestic demand (especially the BRIC countries, Brazil, Russia, India, and China, although the inclusion of Russia in the group has become increasingly questionable). Host-country governments have been able to exact concessions from MNCs eager to gain access to, and establish brand loyalty with, new, upwardly mobile customers in large emerging markets. It is tempting to frame Brazil and India's domestic-market-focused investments as something other than GVCs. However, under the network organizational paradigm, not only did the roster of multinationals change as first-tier suppliers set up global operations, but large-scale export assembly was added to the long-standing motivation of serving domestic markets. Many of the same firms, supply chains, and technologies were brought to bear in both instances, especially as less-developed country consumers began to demand, and be offered, more up-to-date products, allowing the same factories to produce for domestic and export markets. Similarly, the regional production networks that place Mexico and Eastern European countries on the backward GVC–participation list in Figure 5.2 are populated by a similar roster of global firms. Thus, like so many features of the compressed-development era, there are a multiplicity of structures operating simultaneously: import substituting and export-oriented production are not pursued separately or in sequence, or mainly by domestic actors, but by multinationals pursuing both strategies at the same time within a geographically nested set of domestic, regional, and global production networks. In China, for example, it was often difficult to say if a given multinational's medium-term interest was in producing for export or for the domestic market.

Strategic external fit and adaptive industrial policy

Although the acquisition and assimilation of foreign technology once facilitated the creation of vertically integrated industries in countries which previously lacked them, the fragmentation of production in the network organizational paradigm has made this an increasingly difficult proposition. Notwithstanding this fact, the lure of traditional industrial policies which seek to replicate entire value chains remains strong, as can be seen in the cases outlined above, all of which took the late development model as their starting point. All have sought to fill gaps in value chains, identify segments where they are dependent on imports, and create policies aimed at substituting those imports with domestically produced components. Mainland China (in combination with Taiwan) has been at the epicentre of GVCs since the closing years of the late-development era, but the growth of China as an export-production platform was not only driven by industrial policy, but also by the sourcing and investment strategies stemming from global firms' embrace of the network model. This a classic case of what Kimura (2007) refers to as 'dynamic external fit', where the strategies of developers align with strategies and paradigms emanating from already developed economies. The experiences late- and late-late East Asian developers Japan and South Korea were, and still are, much more insular.

This is the key insight provided by our discussion of GVCs. Less-developed countries cannot simply 'catch up' with industrialized economies; they must do so by 'fitting in' with GVCs by identifying and flexibly navigating an upgrading path within global industries. In Brazil and India, especially, many technology-intensive industries are protected yet largely captured by multinational lead firms and now, by global suppliers as well. This raises the question of what purpose industrial policy is meant to serve. The industrial policy challenges posed by GVCs means that if funds exist, as they do in China, the temptation is to double down on techno-nationalist policies that aim to gain leadership in innovation in every segment of the value chain, and to spend vast sums on state-led investments in manufacturing to move up to the high-value-added 'edges' of the smiling curve, at the risk of poor returns, over-production, and obsolescence.

Taiwan's example and mainland China's most promising growth path would suggest a gradual and perhaps subtle shift to an innovation role in GVCs rather a clean break where 'indigenous innovation' in self-sufficient domestic industries propels development. For this to take place, however, techno-nationalist tendencies need to be held in check by the public and private sector actors who have profited by leveraging GVCs and the global technology ecosystems that underpin them. This task has recently been made much harder by geopolitics.

Concluding comments

As we noted in the book's introduction, because of era-related effects, it matters critically *when* a country develops, since supporting institutions co-evolve with high-growth industries (the 'Stinchcombe effect'). Specifically, a country's economic institutions, including innovation systems, business culture, corporate governance, industrial organization, industrial policies, and regulatory responses to development, can be expected to reflect era effects. In the context of GVCs, we see important high-growth and technology-intensive industries being implanted in less-developed countries by direct investment from MNCs or driven less directly when global buyers oversee supply chains from afar, or use intermediate actors to coordinate production and trade on their behalf (Gereffi, 1999; Humphrey and Schmitz, 2002; Kaplinsky, 2005). In these cases, there can be a disjuncture between the inward- and outward-facing segments of an economy, since important parts of the supporting environment of each global industry will remain embedded in that industry's heartlands. But over time, such 'global' institutions and routines can become important elements of a host country's business system.[21] Thus, GVCs may begin as 'enclave' economies (Warr, 1989; Gallagher and Zarsky, 2007), operating independently within EPZs, but over time they can generate spillovers that help to shape institutions and industries within host economies (Farole and Gokhan, 2011).

This argument, like stagist theories of development—based either on economic or demographic factors, as discussed in Chapter 1—can implicitly or explicitly frame GVC engagement as beginning at a nonindustrialized (i.e. agricultural or premodern) starting point, a condition faced by very few of today's less-developed nations. As the cases of China, Brazil, and India show us, the co-evolution of domestic industries and institutions with GVCs is a complex story. Successful late-late developers often had existing industries that had to be transitioned out of or upgraded to accommodate the development and state-building processes, as discussed in Chapter 2, and compressed developers have their own legacies to contend with. For many countries today it is not precise to say that the goal of development is to industrialize. Rather, it is often to *re*-industrialize, since the initial phases of industrialization may well have taken place many decades in the past. Countries might be 'less developed' than their peers, but hardly be 'developing' in the classic sense implied by stage theories, and any characterization of them as 'emerging' is aspirational, or at best an empirical question. In such cases, older industrial sectors, which may or may not have included a role for foreign capital, today must operate in the context of industries that have often been transformed by the network paradigm: consolidated in global firms at every level of the value chain, organizationally fragmented and geographically integrated in GVCs, and increasingly mediated by the emergent tools and markets of the digital economy. And, unlike fully domestic firms, these globally engaged firms are motivated by, and operate within, an elaborate and overlapping set of multilateral and bilateral trade agreements that can specify, sometimes in great detail, what 'optimal' international sourcing strategies might entail.

Despite the poor record of less-developed countries following Japan and South Korea into higher bands of income, the lure of copying their 'late-development' policy approaches remain strong, not least because the policy approaches followed by compressed developers are hard to disentangle from the external business systems and institutions that have been ascendant during the compressed-development era. Still, for less-developed countries, the trade, investment, and knowledge flows that underpin global sourcing arrangements can provide attractive mechanisms for rapid learning, innovation, and industrial upgrading (Lall,

[21] For example, with the rise of bulletin boards the early Internet engineers in Silicon Valley and other core technology centres developed a practice of posting questions to technical problems for other engineers to answer, as well as posting solutions to common problems. This approach to innovation and technical support has now been disseminated worldwide (usually under the banner of 'open innovation') and has become common, if not fully accepted practice for engineers in both developed and less-developed countries.

1993). GVCs have clearly helped to stimulate investments in new productive capacity and massive infrastructure improvements. While little if any of this business or technological competency is likely to be fully or even mostly indigenous to 'host' countries, it seems clear enough that economic globalization has boosted manufacturing output and employment (to a point), enabled global engagement through vertical specialization and larger scale production, driven more efficient geographical allocation of industrial activities, and increased the availability of intermediate goods and advanced technologies available in the developing world. Engagement with GVCs can provide better access to information, open up new markets, and create opportunities for fast technological learning and skill acquisition, as has been the case in Taiwan. Because transactions and investments linked to global sourcing and MNEs typically come with quality-control systems and prevailing global business standards that exceed those in less-developed countries, enterprises and individuals can be 'pushed' to acquire new competencies and skills (Humphrey and Schmitz, 2002). GVCs can bring local firms into closer contact with 'open-innovation' systems, where firms draw on and contribute to freely available technologies and standards (Chesbrough and Kusunoki, 2001). Local firms can also take advantage of specialized knowledge garnered through participation in GVCs, or by providing goods and services to MNE affiliates. The open and modular character of GVCs in some industries (electronics, software, and ICT-enabled services, and the technology and tools of the digital economy come to mind) even make it possible for smaller and local firms to 'move to the head' of GVCs; leveraging global resources (inputs and services) to develop novel products aimed at local, regional, and even global markets (Sturgeon, 2019). As a result, GVC-linked industrialization can compress the development experience in a positive sense, making nonlinear catch up possible (Breznitz and Murphree, 2011).

What then, are the net outcomes for development? In a study of the long-run effects of GVC participation for 58 countries between 1970 and 2008, Pahl and Timmer (2019) found that exporting via GVCs accelerated productivity growth in the formal manufacturing sector, especially when a country's distance from the global productivity frontier was large, but because GVC engagement tends to be concentrated in a small number of well-integrated firms (including affiliates of MNCs), it has little or no positive effect on employment generation. They refer to this as the 'mixed-blessing hypothesis' of GVC participation (p, 2), and we have argued that it is a feature of 'thin industrialization'.

When considering how to jump-start or restart economic development through engagement with the global economy, industrial policymakers must recognize, characterize, and seek to adapt to the era effects of compressed development. Such 'adaptive industrial policy' entails, in part, understanding, leveraging, and seeking to avoid the pitfalls of engagement with GVCs. This is a lot to ask of policymakers, especially in small and remote countries without the market size or funds to play in the investment attraction game. In addition, for policy-makers with responsibility for specific jurisdictions, GVCs create a dilemma of control, since many of the key resources in the networks will be located outside of the jurisdiction. This dilemma forms an undercurrent to industrial policy the era of compressed development, which can become a source of confusion or new thinking, contradictory policy or policy innovation.

6
Employment, Skills, and Upgrading

Introduction

Employment and skills are at the heart of economic development. Capital is undoubtedly important, but how labour is secured, trained, and deployed is also a crucial enabling factor, especially in the organization of production and for productivity growth. Labour relations—the terms and conditions under which labour is secured, and rights and entitlements recognized—matter a great deal for social development as well, and for social and political stability. The postwar years were 'golden' for many countries because economic and social development were brought together in a complementary relationship, supported by national institutions and regulations under embedded liberalism. 'Standard' employment was at its core.[1] In the last quarter of the twentieth century, however, key elements of these bargains were revised or undermined in many countries. This happened in two steps, which relate to implementation of the network and platform organizational paradigms (as described in Chapter 3).

First, 'nonstandard' or 'atypical' work increased amidst deindustrialization, outsourcing, and growth of the service sector. At the company level the rise of shareholder primacy, financialization of company objectives, and outsourcing and offshoring of noncore activities, had a profound influence on how, when, and where labour is employed. Weil (2014) characterizes the result as the 'fissured' workplace. Employment has become less direct, and frequently obscure. 'Even the lawyers who handle our business transactions and the consultants who work for well-known accounting companies may now have an arms-length relationship with those by whom we think they are employed' (4). Labour-market deregulation and marketization of employment relations, and managements' quest for flexibility, have all produced these fissures in the middle class, creating a new dualism and rising inequality (Milanovic, 2016).

Second, and related to the platform organizational paradigm, a new breed of Internet-enabled 'platform' companies (Parker et al., 2016) such as Uber and

[1] In the United States the 'Treaty of Detroit' was negotiated in 1950 after a series of major strikes by Walter Reuther, President of the United Auto Workers, and the US 'Big Three' automakers (General Motors, Ford, and Chrysler). This pact not only raised wages, but won pensions and health care coverage for workers, setting the terms of labour agreements in the United States for decades (Barnard, 1983), and fostering the growth of the middle class, home ownership, and suburban development that characterized US postwar economic and social development (Walker, 1974).

Compressed Development: Time and Timing in Economic and Social Development. D. Hugh Whittaker, Timothy J. Sturgeon, Toshie Okita, and Tianbiao Zhu, Oxford University Press (2020). © D. Hugh Whittaker, Timothy J. Sturgeon, Toshie Okita, and Tianbiao Zhu. DOI: 10.1093/oso/9780198744948.001.0001

Airbnb widened these fissures in two ways. First, they amplified the disjuncture between successful innovation and large-scale employment. Airbnb, for example, was founded in 2008 and reached a market valuation of $21 billion in 2015 with only 3,000 direct employees.[2] By contrast the hotel chain Marriot, founded in 1927, with a 2015 market value of $19 billion, had 200,000 direct employees (Van Alstyne, 2016). Second, their 'two-sided' platforms (linking producers and service providers to end users) have provided large-scale work for quasi-independent contractors in the 'gig' economy, whose working conditions, while likely more flexible, are far more precarious than those of the handful of direct employees.

These developments have had an impact on the evolution of employment relations in less-developed and transition countries as well. In developing countries, 'standard' jobs have traditionally been concentrated in manufacturing and the public sector. 'Thin industrialization', however, has truncated manufacturing's share of employment, while pressure from international institutions has worked to dampen direct public sector employment. Multinational corporations (MNCs) bring their human resource management (HRM) models with them—sometimes relying on nonstandard employment in their own operations and, more importantly, putting pressure on suppliers through global value chains (GVCs) to reduce costs, leading to labour exploitation, precarity, and poor working conditions. Financialized business models and associated HRM practices have been adopted by entrepreneurs and domestic firms in less-developed countries as well. Finally, many platform companies (e.g. Uber and Airbnb) now have global reach, and they have, either directly or through the local competitors they have inspired, fostered the growth of gig work.

While the erosion of standard employment in developed countries has attracted considerable academic and press attention, less-developed countries often have substantial informal sectors to start with—traditionally associated with underdevelopment. Stagist development models assumed the informal sector would disappear as economic development advanced, but rather than vanishing, this 'old dualism' not only persists, but is overlain by a 'new dualism' (of 'nonstandard' or 'atypical' employment), with a thin layer of 'standard' employment between. This sandwich represents a compression of employment relations that is characteristic of thin industrialization,

The implications are significant. If 'standard' employment was central to the industrialization experience of earlier developers, what happens when many new jobs—nonstandard, precarious, and arising from the gig economy—interrupt the positive feedback between economic (and technological) development and social development? The assumption that economic and technological development naturally brings about social development, which seemed to be borne out by

[2] These figures do not include the thousands of Airbnb 'hosts' which supply the actual lodging for Airbnb users.

empirical observation in the postwar period, may well be breaking down. Whereas futurologists, consultants, and marketers have waxed lyrical about the rise of the middle class and their spending power in countries like China and India[3]—and in reality, the growth of middle-income earners in those countries has been remarkable—appearances, at least, belie a very different and more brittle prosperity than what was seen in the postwar late-late development era.

We summarize the shift pictorially in Figure 6.1, the upper half of which depicts the mutually reinforcing links between national (and corporate) economic development and technological advancement on the one hand, and social development—notably stable middle-class formation—under class compromise and embedded liberalism on the other. The lower half depicts the breakdown of this relationship, as class compromise and associated welfare systems have been repudiated, profits have increasingly accrued to capital, and middle classes have become fragmented and insecure as nonstandard and gig work has increased.

We unpack this argument in the sections that follow. First we briefly introduce some of the debates around middle-income transition, primarily to highlight assumptions that economic and technological development will naturally bring about social development, and the absence of employment considerations in the debates. This may be related to 'standard' employment being taken for granted in the context of stagist development models. As we show in the next section, however, 'standard' employment is embedded in a complex set of era-based institutions which emerged in the late-nineteenth and twentieth centuries, shaped by social, economic, and political forces. These institutions have been under pressure for decades, supressing standard employment and creating new forms of social cleavage, insecurity, and inequality. The next section considers informal and nonstandard employment in less-developed countries, the layering of 'old dualism' and 'new dualism', and what we refer to as the 'organized informality' of gig work in the digital economy. The situation in China is discussed, as is employment in GVCs. Then we briefly consider the politics of dualism and upgrading, and political reasons why it is difficult to create new sustained virtuous feedback loops between economic and social upgrading in the compressed development era. We conclude with some comments on inequality.

In summary, we argue that a key challenge in the era of compressed development is not so much technological catch-up and upgrading per se, although this is difficult enough. Rather, it is to establish a virtuous loop between economic or technological development on the one hand, and equitable, inclusive growth and social development on the other. Employment and skills are at the core of this challenge.

[3] To give just two examples: 'The Biggest Story of Our Time: The Rise of China's Middle Class', (Helen Wang in *Forbes*, 21 December 2011; *The 'Bird of Gold': The Rise of India's Consumer Market* (McKinsey and Company, May 2007) <https://www.mckinsey.com/featured-insights/asia-pacific/the-bird-of-gold>, accessed 29 January 2020.

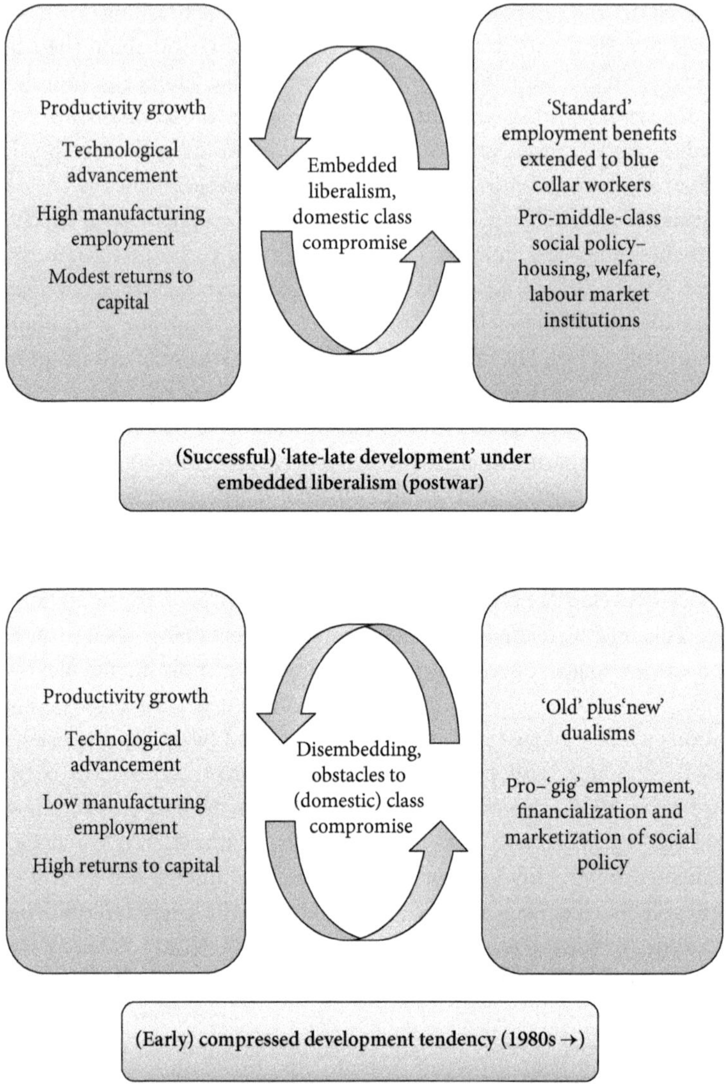

Figure 6.1 Economic and social development coupling (postwar) and decoupling (1980s →)

The 'middle-income-trap' debate

Kuznets (1971:1) defined economic growth as a long-term rise in a country's capacity to supply increasingly diverse economic goods to its population based on advancing technology and the institutional and ideological adjustments it demands. This is a complex and challenging formula. In recent years increasing attention has been paid to a group of countries which have experienced economic growth sufficient to propel them into the ranks of middle-income countries, but whose growth thereafter appears to have slowed, if not stalled. Gill and Kharas (2007: 5) comment: 'The idea that middle-income countries have to do something different if they are to prosper is consistent with the finding that middle-income countries have grown less rapidly than either rich or poor countries.'

Building on this observation, Kharas and Kohli (2011: 282) see countries as getting caught in a middle-income trap (MIT) when they are 'unable to compete with low-income, low-wage economies in manufactured exports and unable to compete with advanced economies in high-skill innovations.... Put another way, such countries cannot make a timely transition from resource-driven growth, with low-cost labour and capital, to productivity-driven growth.' Contrasting Latin American and East Asian countries from the late 1970s to the early 2000s, they argue that Latin American countries became mired in a MIT because they failed to shift from resource-based strategies, which helped them to grow when incomes were low, to technology- and market-based strategies.

Kharas and Kohli see growth in low-income countries as being driven by *supply*-side organization, of both factor inputs and enabling policies and institutions, whereas growth in middle-income countries is—or should be—driven by a combination of changing supply-side inputs (increased capital and skill-intensity with a rising contribution of services), and increased *demand*. 'Middle-income countries that successfully sustain growth develop sizable middle-class populations that are prepared to pay more for quality, differentiated products. That extra profit margin, in turn, spurs firms to invest in marketing, branding, and new product development, which are the ingredients of innovation and further growth' (286).[4]

Malaysia is an example of a country seen to be susceptible to a MIT. Despite a per capita GDP annual growth rate of over 3.6 per cent since 1980—over twice the growth rates of the UK and United States in comparable periods (Flaaen, Ghani, and Mishra, 2013)—it had not made the transition to high-income status three decades later, unlike South Korea and Taiwan. Other countries in Southeast Asia seen to be in a similar situation include Thailand (Phongpaichit and Benyaapikul, 2012), and Vietnam (Ohno, 2009). Implicitly using a late-development/developmental-state perspective, Ohno argues that Vietnam must 'acquire capability to embrace an appropriate industrial vision and implement effective measures towards it', including skill and technology upgrading (2009: 29). In China, the post–Global Financial Crisis slowdown fuelled a growing awareness of the magnitude of rebalancing necessary for future sustainable growth and sparked a lively

[4] In other words, a low consumption share of GDP (and an undervalued exchange rate) increases the chances of a middle-income slowdown: Eichengreen, Park, and Shin (2012: 83).

debate about a MIT danger.[5] The IMF warned China (among others) about the spectre of a MIT behind (infrastructure) investment-led growth, a danger that increases when real wage growth outpaces productivity growth (Aiyar et al., 2013; Zhuang, 2012).[6]

The notion of the MIT has been dismissed by some as a myth, or at least an ill-defined concept. Pritchett and Summers (2014a) argue that slowdowns after high growth should be seen as reversion to a mean; the higher the growth spurt, the greater the likelihood of a subsequent slowdown. Seeking to sustain high growth can make matters worse, and the MIT narrative risks doing just that. It invites, they suggest, unhelpful policy interventions. Sustaining growth depends on 'creative destruction'; the first word is popular with policymakers, the second word is not. MIT proponents would hardly disagree, nor would they disagree that growth at every stage requires 'the constant renewal of good policy along with good luck' (Pritchett and Summers, 2014b).

The debate has usefully drawn attention to evolving challenges that confront middle-income countries, of moving away from sources of past growth, and attending to qualitative aspects of productivity growth at the level of firms and industries. But while countries are urged to transition to innovation, challenges associated with the separation of innovation from production that we discussed in Chapter 5 have received little attention. Moreover, both proponents and critics focus on economic or industrial policies. The implicit assumption is that labour-market changes which ultimately underpin middle-class formation naturally follow technological and economic upgrading. This assumption, however, is suspect.

Employment relations and 'standard employment'

A brief account of the rise of 'standard' employment, and its subsequent erosion, will help to put into perspective what is at stake for economic and social development, and show how employment relations link to the development eras and organizational paradigms of Chapters 2 and 3. There are differences by country, needless to say, which highlight the importance of timing, as well as institutional legacies and politics (including geopolitics). Terms such as 'nonstandard' and

[5] E.g. Juzhong Zhang, Deputy Chief Economist, ADB ('How China Can Avoid the Middle-income Trap') in *South China Morning Post*, 12 November 2012; Danny Quah ('Decoding the Middle-income Trap') on *china.org.cn*, 20 July 2013; 'Reaching for the Summit: What China Has to Do to Break Out of the Middle-Income Trap and Reach Developed Country Status', *China Daily*, 19 August 2013. Much of Asia (Aiyar et al., 2013) and the BRICs ('BRIC Powerhouses Risk Middle-income Growth Trap' CNBC.com, 3 June 2013) are seen to be at risk. Quah notes that 400,000 Google references to 'middle-income trap' in January 2013 had jumped to 1.3 million just six months later (<http://www.economonitor.com/blog/category/monitors/asia-monitor/>. Accessed 21 August 2013).

[6] There were optimists as well. The World Bank (2013: 361, 11) opined that, with appropriate reforms '(t)he next twenty years will radically differ from the previous twenty years as China moves towards a successful transition to high-income status'. See also Fu et al. (2016).

'atypical' employment, 'bad jobs', 'destandardization', and the 'degradation of employment' suggest a normative view of employment which is full time, contractually defined, and a cornerstone of social security and welfare institutions. But it is increasingly apparent that there is nothing inevitable or necessary about this model under capitalism.

The rise of 'standard' employment

Standard employment in Britain was the product of a long and tortuous evolution, intertwined with the emergence of capitalism and the market economy, starting in the aftermath of the mid-fourteenth-century Black Death, and eventually taking its 'standard' shape in the late-nineteenth century and first half of the twentieth century (Deakin and Wilkinson, 2005; Deakin, 2005).[7] The repeal of the Statute of Artificers in 1813 and the draconian Poor Law Amendment Act of 1834, which featured so prominently in Polanyi's (1944) portrayal of 'free' labour markets in nineteenth-century Britain, were stepping stones in this evolution. Employment contracts of sorts did emerge for white collar workers, but manual workers were employed under the Master and Servant Acts until the last one was repealed in 1875. Even then, 'not just the terminology of master and servant but also many of the old assumptions of unmediated control were still being applied by the courts as they developed the common law of employment' (Deakin, 2005: 7). The contractualization of employment relations took place against this background, with the growth of the labour movement and the emergence of collective bargaining. The transition, however, and the transition from poor laws to social security, was not complete until the mid-twentieth century: 'The term "employee" is truly a very recent innovation in British labour law' (Deakin, 2005: 8).

Significantly, industrialization in Britain happened *before* the emergence of many of these social and legal institutions, and before mid-nineteenth-century legislation enabled the formation of large, capital-intensive enterprises. Small-scale, owner-managed Victorian businesses relied on internal contracting and Master-Servant laws, which ensured managerial prerogative in lieu of managerial capacity. As Gospel (1992) notes, this pattern persisted well into the twentieth century in many industries.[8] Salaried management and the internalization of employment relations was correspondingly slow to spread.

Labour law in continental Europe evolved somewhat differently, influenced by timing and legacy. In France the concept of *contrat de travail* was used by employers from the mid-1880s to foster a sense of duty and obedience in workers,

[7] The following comments on Britain and continental Europe draw on these two sources, particularly the latter, unless otherwise stated.

[8] We have referred to this as the 'Stinchcombe effect'.

and was subsequently used to as a cornerstone for collective bargaining and social protection institutions; subordination in return for companies' assumption of social risk. In Germany, the Civil Code of 1896 saw the duty of loyalty balanced by reciprocity on the part of the employer, embodied in the notion of the firm as community. Both employers and employees had mutual responsibilities tied to the interests of the enterprise. This 'owed much to the concentration of industry and the emergence of vertically integrated and bureaucratically-organized enterprises during the same period, a process which... began earlier and was more complete in the continent than in Britain' (Deakin, 2005: 11).[9] In other words, the evolution of employment relations on the continent was influenced by its late development.

In the United States, 'at-will' employment was still widespread at the end of the nineteenth century. The 'will' was that of the foreman, who implemented the 'drive system' of 'close supervision, abuse, profanity, and threats' (Jacoby, [1985] 2004: 15). Labour turnover and dissatisfaction were very high. When large enterprises began to task professional engineers with systematizing production, however, they began to implement paternalistic techniques to make workers 'more sedulous, sober, and loyal' (Jacoby, [1985] 2004: 29). Personnel departments were established during World War I, and as employers sought to stabilize their workforces, paternalism was employed to foster loyalty and ward off unionization. This did not survive the Great Depression, however. Under Roosevelt's New Deal, a new legal framework for employment relations was created—in the face of employer opposition—leading to explicit, legalistic collective agreements and employment contracts, which combined very effectively with job standardization and mass production technology in postwar manufacturing.

Japanese employment evolved somewhat similarly, with the important caveat that employer paternalism survived the Depression, and was enhanced rather than undermined by growing government intervention in the economy (Moriguchi, 2000; Gordon, 1985). Postwar, paternalism was replaced by negotiation, and both employment and employee welfare were largely internalized in the large 'community firm', supported by government policy (Dore, 1973; Inagami and Whittaker, 2005). Standard employment in Japan provided the base for, and was buttressed by, state-backed (and often provided) welfare measures, including unemployment insurance and active labour-market (retraining) schemes, health insurance, and pensions. Japan became the fourth country in the world to achieve universal health insurance coverage in the early 1960s, although much of it was provided by employers (Neary, 2019; Miura, 2012). Economic development and social welfare, mediated by employment, created the positive feedback loops, as shown in the top half of Figure 6.1.

[9] It also began earlier, and was more complete in Japan: Chapter 4.

The deterioration of 'standard' employment

To sum up the preceding section, 'standard' employment became established in the process of mass-production-oriented industrialization, and more specifically, with attempts to mould employment relations around the needs of integrated production systems—the Factory and [Fordist] Corporation organizational paradigms as summarized in Table 3.1. Employment relations differed by country, dependent in part on timing of development, and on the interplay between employers, the labour movement, and the state.[10] They reflected the growth of organization scale, and the dual priorities of efficient coordination of increasingly complex production processes on the one hand, and risk allocation and social welfare on the other.[11] 'Standard' employment came to be taken for granted by social scientists. However, it came under increasing strain from the 1970s on, as managers were forced or incentivized to prioritize shareholder interests, again, with differences across countries. Focusing on 'core' activities, especially in the United States, managers slashed direct workforces and sought flexibility from those who were left. The labour share of value added declined, and wages began to stagnate (Weil, 2014: 4). Economic concentration in employment-light 'superstar' firms has been an important factor (Autor et al., 2017).

New forms of 'nonstandard' employment began to proliferate, especially in contractor companies which took on both outsourced work and the risk and fixed costs of plant and equipment. While jobs at contract manufacturing and supplier firms are not necessarily contingent, they are more likely to be non-union, and empirical studies show systematic differences between unionized, non-union in-house, and outsourced jobs, with the latter 'scoring the lowest on virtually all dimensions of job quality, including substantially lower pay, benefits, and discretion at work; they also show greater use of electronic monitoring and part-time and contingent work', not to mention inferior health and safety protection (Bernhardt et al., 2016: 20). 'Servicization' also led to an increase in such work, enabled by deregulation. Jobs were more often filled by staffing agencies, which became major players in labour markets, shaping hiring and job tenure norms, setting normative pay rates for different skills, benefits, and protections (or lack of them). As staffing firms such as Manpower and Adecco grew to become the world's largest employers, and set up global operations, they expanded from the low end of the skills spectrum to the high end, from the periphery of workforces to

[10] In Mexico, Brazil, and Argentina, the growing labour movement was incorporated directly into 'state corporatism' between the 1910s and 1940s, drawing selectively on European models, and giving rise to a distinctive variant of employment relations and job rights (e.g. Cardoso, 2004). Peasant organizations were also incorporated in Mexico.

[11] The centrality of the employment relationship in industrialization, and industrial relations in shaping this relationship, were highlighted in Kerr et al.'s (1960) *Industrialism and Industrial Man: The Problems of Labour and Management in Economic Growth.*

the very core. In addition businesses began to probe the grey zones between employment, contracting, and self-employment, zones that have expanded dramatically with the gig economy.

Work in the gig economy defies simple categorization, but the ILO cites two broad types: 'crowdwork', in which workers operate online through platforms connecting workers to large numbers of clients, organizations, and businesses, often ICT-enabled and across borders; and 'work-on-demand-via-apps', which tend to be more place-based and geographically limited because they advertise for in-person services (ILO, 2019). Together these gig-work platforms enable management's quest for outsourced, just-in-time inputs. Gig work offers flexibility and 'independence', but has been shorn of the employment and social security which were central features of standard employment. It fits well with the neoliberal ideology of each individual taking control of their own destiny—everyone is an entrepreneur, especially in the variant offered in network organizational paradigm as envisioned by Intel's Andrew Grove (mentioned in Chapter 3). But in reality, most gig workers are not entrepreneurs at all, and the scalability of digital gig-work platforms means that this type of precarious work has been growing rapidly on a worldwide basis.[12] It has been estimated that around a third of US workers did some form of gig work in 2017 (ILO, 2019). Overall, nonstandard employment has grown to constitute 30 per cent or more of total employment in many developed countries, although there are wide variations (Vanek et al., 2014; Fernández-Macaís and Hurley, 2008).[13]

Informal and nonregular employment in the era of compressed development

Deakin (2005) draws a parallel between the fluidity and diversity of employment relations at the beginning of the twentieth century and those a century later. Then, as now, there were concerns about entrenchment of inequality, the effects of technological change and globalization. But 'standard' employment was still in the process of formation in the early twentieth century, with a growing labour movement accompanying the formation of vertically integrated production

[12] After five years of operation in Brazil, a country with persistently high rates of un- and under-employment, Uber's ride-hailing platform had 600,000 registered drivers and had logged 2.6 billion trips by mid-2019 (Rio Times, 2019).

[13] The ILO (2015, 2016) categorizes 'nonstandard forms of employment' (NSE) into temporary employment; temporary-agency work and other contractual arrangements involving multiple parties; ambiguous employment relationships; and part-time employment. Training-cum-employment (e.g. internships) and 'clandestine employment' (undeclared work; family work; work done by foreigners without work permits, and work in micro-enterprises beyond the reach of inspectors) are growing categories, the latter being 'informal' rather than nonstandard (Córdova, 1986). On different political economies of nonstandard work, see Thelen (2014).

systems in new industries, while in more recent years labour unions have often been in retreat, and production systems have been dis-integrated and dispersed geographically in GVCs. In today's developing countries, the situation is even more complex, as 'nonstandard' employment is layered onto existing labour-market informality.[14]

Postwar development economists assumed that economic growth would shift labour from the informal or subsistence sector into the modern, capitalist sector, and hence into 'standard' employment.[15] Even until the 1990s and 2000s, development experts believed that economic development 'would shrink the informal sector in the same way that it shrinks the agriculture sector in the Lewis model' (Freeman, 2014: 111). There were exceptions. Singer (1970) , for example, believed that the importation of capital-intensive technology, particularly in MNCs, would create fewer jobs in developing countries than required by population growth, and new types of duality would result. This was a prescient view. Far from disappearing, informal employment has grown in developing countries in recent decades, to the extent that the 'informal has become normal' (Jütting and De Laiglesia, 2009). 'Even in environments that have benefited from sustained growth, informal employment is often rising faster than formal employment', according to Huitfeldt, Sida, and Jütting (2009: 97), who cite India and China as examples. In India, despite robust economic growth, the formal sector actually shrank between 1999–2000 and 2004–2005.[16] We shall look at China shortly.

Quantification of informal employment is difficult, and problematically, categories of informal and contractual nonstandard employment (NSE) often overlap.[17] Vanek et al. (2014) estimate that informal employment constitutes more than half of total nonagricultural employment in most of the global South—82 per cent in South Asia, 66 per cent in Sub-Saharan Africa, 65 per cent in East and Southeast Asia, 51 per cent in Latin America, and 45 per cent in the Middle East and North Africa. Avirgan, Bivens, and Gammage's (2005) study of five countries in 1998–2003 produced estimates of informal employment ranging from 14.4 per

[14] Informality is not limited to a specific sector or sectors, and increasingly 'informal economy' and 'informal employment' are used. The International Conference of Labour Statisticians sees the informal sector as the production and employment that takes place in unincorporated small or unregistered businesses, and informal employment as employment without legal and social protection. The informal economy encompasses both (Chen, 2012).

[15] As Chen (2012: 2) puts it: 'It was widely assumed during the 1950s and 1960s that, with the right mix of economic policies and resources, low-income economies could be transformed into dynamic modern economies. In the process, the traditional sector comprised of petty trade, small scale production, and a range of casual jobs would be absorbed into the modern capitalist – or formal – economy and, thereby, disappear.'

[16] Corbridge, Harriss, and Jeffrey (2014: 159–60); also Gooptu (2007).

[17] Developing country statistics are oriented towards informal employment, and developed country statistics towards nonstandard employment. In principle, informal employment is without legal protection, while NSE may be without *social* protection, but it exists within a *legal* framework.

cent in Russia and 22.5 per cent in South Africa, to 40.1 per cent in Egypt, 69.1 per cent in El Salvador, and 92.1 per cent in India.

Within these figures, however, many people actually work in the formal sector, and many have contracts. Only the contracts are not necessarily with the company they are working for because they are employed by agencies or brokers. In India's case these intermediaries act as a buffer, instituting a range of measures to ensure worker docility for their clients, including threats, blacklisting, and the preferential hiring of (in-country) migrants, who want to save money and return home.[18] Actual workplace relations are informalized under the employers' unilateral control (Mishra, forthcoming). In her study of private security guards in India—'servile sentinels of the city'—Gooptu (2013), too, depicts a regime of 'organized informality' in which recruitment and training are formalized, while employment relations remain informal and insecure. Such informality extends beyond employment itself to encompass dormitories, courts, local politicians, and bureaucrats, in a wider system of 'urban informality' (van Dijk, Bhide, and Shivtare, 2016), in which regulations are contravened and/or not enforced. This is one of the three legs of India's 'compressed capitalism' (D'Costa, 2014) which we referred to in the Chapter 1 (along with 'primitive accumulation' through dispossession and petty commodity production). It is not a passing aberration, but a systemic feature of many developing countries' economic growth and integration into the global economy.

Other aspects of that integration include 'body shops' and 'body shopping'—networks of agencies which recruit, train, and place IT trainees in companies abroad, also dealing with personnel and disciplinary matters in those locations (Biao, 2006), and 'virtual migration', placing such workers in Western companies within India (Aneesh, 2006).[19] Finally, up to a quarter of the world's gig workers may be in India, a country which sees almost three times as many school leavers and graduates entering the job market as job openings.[20] Many now end up in the gig economy where, far from being upskilled with economic development, their skills often atrophy. Suraj (2018) refers to this situation as a 'skills trap', and as a form of deindustrialization, with workers moving out of semi-skilled production to low-skill services because of a lack of better alternatives. Here he is specifically referring to Indonesia, the home of Go-Jek, whose green helmeted motorbike

[18] In the many places where foreign 'guest' workers are prevalent, such as the Gulf States, Malaysia, developed countries, and at sea, intermediaries are also common, with practices (e.g. physical abuse, debt bondage, and holding of passports) that border on or include human trafficking and modern slavery. See Mortensen (2019) for an example from Malaysia, and Stringer et al. (2016) for abuses on fishing boats in New Zealand waters.

[19] These phenomena are not confined to India. Migration has grown markedly in recent decades, and alongside legal migration, illegal migration and human trafficking has risen sharply, creating an underclass very vulnerable to abuse and exploitation.

[20] FICCI, NASSCOM, and EY (2017), citing Kässi and Lehdonvirta (2016) for the gig-worker proportion. The latter statistic recalls the 'diploma disease', discussed in Chapter 4.

drivers are now prominent across Southeast Asia, but his observation could also apply to India.[21]

In sum, the employment side of economic growth for compressed developers has been vastly different from that of early and late developers. The informal economy has grown rather than shrunk, and NSE forms have been imported, adapted, and layered onto informal employment, sandwiching an intermediate layer or 'stage' of standard formal employment in between.

Nonstandard employment in China

'Standard' employment is not standard in many developing countries. It is not standard in China.[22] In pre-reform China, state-owned-enterprise (SOE) employees had job security and welfare benefits, but there were various forms of precariousness, such as temporary employment (Feng, 2018). In the reform period the forms of precariousness have changed, and they have become more prevalent. Feng describes it as a shift from SOE-temporary worker dualism to contract employee-agency worker dualism, on top of urban-rural, and male-female labour-market dualisms. The government moved to introduce labour contracts in 1986, and after the Labour Law of 1994, fixed-term contracts became the new norm. However, standard employment 'had a very short life' (Xu, 2016: 146). It was cut short in China and Asia more broadly by the Asian Financial Crisis, which marked a turning point in labour-market development in the region (ILO, 2016: 66). Specifically, there was a sharp move from direct employment to use of workers hired and dispatched by staffing agencies.

China's Ministry of Human Resources and Social Security put the number of workers dispatched by staffing agencies at 27 million in 2011, while the All-China Federation of Trade Unions put it at 60 million, and some estimates put it higher still, at 75 million (Liu, 2014). A survey in Shanghai in 2011 found that almost three-quarters of enterprises used staffing-agency workers, which accounted for over a third of their workforces on average (Feng, 2018). Government labour bureaux were the first entrants into this industry in the 1980s, but private agencies were allowed in the early 1990s. The state sector became both a major supplier of

[21] Go-Jek was founded in 2010 and was Indonesia's first 'unicorn' company. Its platform has expanded rapidly to include over twenty apps.

[22] Again, distinguishing between informal employment and NSE is difficult. Huang (2009) calculated that roughly 60 per cent of China's urban workforce in the late 2000s were in the informal economy (168 million out of 283 million). Just over two-thirds were 'peasant workers', and the rest were regular urban residents, many previously employed by SOEs or collective enterprises. Roughly 70 million were officially registered, and of these, 30 million were self-employed, while 40 million were employed in small or micro businesses, which increased rapidly from the early 1990s. The other 100 million were unregistered. Another 80 million peasant workers were employed informally outside urban centres.

agency workers and a major customer. In some local governments and SOEs, in fact, dispatched workers constitute a majority of the workforce.

Global staffing agencies are active in China, too, and operate at strategic and policy levels. FESCO (Beijing Foreign Human Resources Service Company), the first Chinese agency authorized in 1979 to provide staffing to foreign companies, teamed up in 2009 with Adecco, headquartered in Switzerland, to provide a comprehensive suite of HRM services for employers. In 2005 ManpowerGroup entered into an agreement with China's Bureau of Labour and Social Security to 'develop human resources strategies and infrastructure aimed at supporting the country's continued economic growth'.[23] It is worth noting, too, that staffing agencies have become active in brokering the transition from education to work, while in the vocational education sector, schools themselves have become active participants, brokering, monitoring, and enforcing the terms of 'internships' which ostensibly round out theory with practice, but in reality, often serve as a way to funnel labour into positions outside the framework of the Labour Contract Law. In companies like Foxconn, such 'interns' have constituted up to 15 per cent of the workforce (Smith and Chan, 2015).

The Labour Contract Law, implemented in 2008, was supposed to usher in a new era for labour-market policy in China, from deregulation to reregulation, and protection of workers. It required employers to provide open-ended contracts for workers with ten years or more of continuous service, or after two fixed terms. Contrary to the intention of the law, however, many employees with long-term service were promptly shifted to short, fixed-term contracts. The law attempted to restrict dispatched work, and to provide equal rights for agency workers (Liu, 2014), but employers found loopholes. Attempts to close these in 2014 were met with further avoidance strategies.

Gig working has also boomed in China, although estimates of its extent vary widely. According to one estimate, up to 33 million workers who left first and second-tier industrial firms between 2015 and 2017 may have started to work in the gig economy (Shen, 2019). In 2019 the Beijing municipal government began to introduce new regulations to protect gig workers amid growing social unrest, starting with delivery companies and ride-hailing companies like Didi Chuxing.

This is a very different type of labour market and employment evolution than that of early and late developers, which we depicted in the preceding section. It has its attractions to policy makers in terms of shifting workers quickly to sectors of the economy expected to grow without creating unemployment, but there is likely to be a significant long-term cost. In mainstream employment, too, the picture is

[23] As part of the agreement, 'Manpower and its subsidiaries provide consulting expertise to help establish local government-sponsored employment offices in some of China's largest cities' (Manpower Inc. press release, 24 May 2005). Feng (2009: 459) notes that the linkage between staffing agencies, 'talents', and clients is presented as making a major contribution to 'China's move toward a knowledge-based economy'.

mixed, with wide variations by region and industry. Lüthje, Luo, and Zhang (2013) identify five 'production regimes' in China, each with distinctive ways of dealing with management prerogatives, employment relations and conflict.[24] Case studies from the Pearl River Delta, in particular, are often grim (e.g. Choi and Peng, 2015), depicting upskilling for a small minority of workers, while consigning the majority to low-skilled, often dangerous, and badly paid precarious jobs 'more pronounced and sharper in many aspects than in most capitalist countries' (Lüthje, Luo, and Zhang, 2013: 229). The division of the workforce between highly skilled professionals and low-skilled and cheap migrant workers, Butollo (2014) observes, reflects 'global norms of technology and production' which have emerged internationally in commodity mass manufacturing in recent decades in the quest for competitive advantage vis-à-vis other emerging countries, triggered by constant pressure from lead firms and global buyers for suppliers to reduce costs. The picture is not entirely grim, however. On the positive side, employer provision of labour contracts has increased sharply, and renewal rates have risen, as have employer social insurance contributions. And in Lee, Brown, and Wen's view, collective bargaining in Guangdong and has gained some traction, while in Jiangsu the piece-rate wage system is being modified in what may prove to be a step towards internal labour markets (2014: 16).

Skills upgrading in GVCs?

GVCs are implicated in the observations of Lüthje, Luo, and Zhang, and Butollo, as just mentioned. Barrientos, Gereffi, and Rossi (2010) identify conflicting pressures within GVCs—to raise quality *and* lower costs (to which we might add increase speed and flexibility). These pressures can be addressed through a variety of strategies, some leading to social upgrading, and some to downgrading.[25]

Nike, a leading global buyer of footwear and apparel produced according to its ever-shifting designs, appears to have achieved both economic and social upgrading in its worldwide suppliers, albeit unevenly. In a study of 300 Nike suppliers across eleven developing countries, Distelhorst, Hainmueller, and Locke (2015) found that the adoption of lean production methods, aimed at improving

[24] The five regimes are: 'state bureaucratic', common in SOEs, particularly in steel and petrochemicals; a 'corporate bureaucratic' model in MNCs and joint ventures in the auto industry; 'corporate high performance' in some multinational electronics firms and newer Chinese multinationals (such as Huawei); 'flexibilized mass production' elsewhere in electronics, especially in contract manufacturers (such as Foxconn); and both this and a 'low wage classic' model in textiles and garments. Friedman and Kuruvilla (2015) similarly list a range of managerial strategies, including paternalism.

[25] Barrientos, Gereffi, and Rossi propose four types of economic upgrading: process, product, functional (higher-value-added or new tasks), and value (moving to more technologically advanced value chains), and they define social upgrading, based on Sen (1999a, 2000) and linked to the ILO (1999) Decent Work framework, as 'the process of improvement in the rights and entitlements of workers as social actors, and enhancing the quality of their employment' (7).

management and increasing productivity, was also associated with improved terms of employment, such as wages and benefits, but with much more modest benefits for health, safety, and environmental compliance. They also found differences by country: the introduction of lean methods raised labour compliance in India and Southeast Asian countries, but factories in China showed no improvement on this count.

Such 'upgrading' depends on the type of GVC. Corresponding to Gereffi, Humphrey, and Sturgeon's (2005) five governance models of GVCs, Lakhani, Kuruvilla, and Avgar (2013) propose that employment relations in supplier firms differ systematically. In hierarchically governed GVCs (i.e. within multinational firms), lead firm norms and influence are high, and skill upgrading and employment stability are also likely. At the other extreme, where governance is market-based and lead firm influence on employment relations is weak, skill upgrading is limited and not systematic, and employment stability is low. Within a single GVC, multiple types of employment relations may exist. In the apparel and footwear sector, for example, where disasters such as the Rana Plaza collapse in Bangladesh in 2013 were widely reported on, the industry is characterized by relational links between lead firms and intermediaries, but market links between intermediaries and individual factories, obscuring the fact that lead firms' 'fast fashion' demands are creating poor working conditions. In some industries, too, labour may be employed through 'labour chains', with a 'cascade' of labour intermediaries which go beyond simple third-party triangular employment relationships, and which increase the scope for the worst kinds of exploitation, including child labour (often in the home) and debt bondage (Barrientos, 2013). Barrientos, Gereffi, and Rossi (2010: 14) conclude that '(t)here is no clear evidence proving that economic upgrading necessarily leads to social upgrading' in GVCs, although pressure is mounting on lead firms to demonstrate such a link.

Such pressure comes in several forms. In addition to government regulation ('public governance' at levels ranging from international to local), Gereffi and Lee (2016) note that 'social governance' (civil society pressure on business from labour organizations and nongovernmental organizations (NGOs)) and 'private governance' (corporate codes of conduct and monitoring) have become increasingly important in the wake of deadly workplace disasters such as Rana Plaza. This requires more active corporate-social-responsibility strategies. These strategies, however, may be defensive, in the sense of attempting to pre-empt public and social governance.

Politics of dualism and upgrading

The layering of old and new dualisms, and polarizing pressures in regular employment, have implications for economic and social development, and their interactions. The mutually reinforcing interactions of economic and technological development on the one hand, and social development on the other, which were evident in successful late developers such as Japan under embedded liberalism, have loosened (see Figure 6.1, top and bottom). There are multiple factors at play, but the bottom line is that the assumption that economic upgrading and skills upgrading are tightly coupled can no longer be taken for granted. Far from dissolving, dualisms have become multilayered, and in many cases the 'standard' layer has become thinner. The path for skill development in the informal or nonregular layers is navigated by individuals, very often without social protection beyond family or kin at best.

As a result, the middle class has become more fragile and fragmented between those with secure formal jobs and those without, those with access to higher education and those without, and those with access to finance and benefiting from escalating real estate prices, and those—an increasing number—who 'are neither extremely poor nor, in all likelihood, secure from the risk of experiencing future poverty' (Sumner, 2012: 11). 'Precarious prosperity' (Budowski et al., 2010) characterizes significant portions of the middle class. Yet as Kharas and Kohli (2011) note, middle-income countries require increased and sophisticated domestic demand to avoid becoming ensnared in a MIT, and for this they need a sizable middle class. While some emerging middle-income countries appear to have created a burgeoning middle class and upgrading dynamic, the reality for many citizens is one of fragility rather than security.

Pressure from international organizations to target poverty in the 1990s may have contributed to the fragility. Deacon and Cohen (2011: 236) criticize World Bank and IMF economists who 'knew nothing about the political economy of inclusive welfare state building within which the middle class were central' for their 'direct assault on embryonic welfare states' in their belief that welfare programmes benefit middle classes without helping the poor. An increasing number of developing countries *have* subsequently attempted to introduce pro-middle-class policies, such as China's 'harmonious society' welfare and employment reforms. But there are conflicting goals, as well, which compromise states' commitment to such policies. As Freeman (2014: 110) says: 'It is difficult to imagine that China could have increased productivity as rapidly and reallocated workers among sectors as successfully as it did without a market driven labour system with high turnover.' This system brought about new dualisms as China attempted to bring about economic transformation quickly. The same motive has seen high levels of foreign direct investment (FDI), engagement in GVCs, and the importation of advanced technologies, which raise productivity quickly, but displace labour, or render it precarious.

As important, informality makes it harder for nonelites to organize politically as a class to secure binding commitments from elites (Rodrik, 2015a). Doner and Schneider (2016) link informality and high levels of inequality to the absence of strong upgrading coalitions because of fragmentation—'societal disarticulation'—and link this in turn to the politics of clientelism and populism, segmented strategies, and tolerance of informal economy practices. 'The general point is that several different strategies can incorporate informal workers into electoral politics with promises of benefits not connected to upgrading and in ways that divide formal and informal workers' (626). It is not just labour that is divided, but business, as well, especially between domestic businesses, which might have a mutual interest in developmental policies and politics, and foreign-invested companies and multinationals. The latter might see the costs of developmental policies as outweighing the benefits. It is not coincidental that some of the bleaker studies of labour conditions in China cited above were from the south of the country, where there have been high levels of FDI. For Doner and Schneider, the fragmentation of social groups, and the absence of strong upgrading coalitions, have created the MIT. For us, this is overlain with the era aspects of compressed development, which include the adoption of new technologies, business models, and employment practices flowing from engagement with GVCs and in some cases, accelerated by financialization pressures transmitted from lead firms into their global supply chains.

Concluding comments

Labour markets and employment relations have undergone major changes in recent decades. Compressed developers face a double challenge in this regard, deriving from 'old' and 'new' dualisms. On the one hand the informal economy has persisted, even with economic growth. It has become 'organized informality', supported by multiple stakeholders in growth coalitions, rather than a problem to be solved through modernization. At the same time, 'nonstandard' employment has expanded in both developed and developing countries, through growth of the service sector, new business and production models, the disembedding of capital and employers from the institutions of class compromise, and employment-light technologies, often related to the emergence of the digital economy. Thin industrialization and curtailment of public sector employment are contributors, as manufacturing and the public sector have been traditional bastions of 'standard' employment.

The implications of this double challenge are not widely appreciated. Based on historical experience, it has been optimistically assumed that economic development and upgrading would naturally bring about social development and upgrading. The 'middle-income-trap' debate has highlighted economic and technological transition challenges, but maintained this assumption. But even amidst economic growth, 'standard' employment has been in retreat. This has created a rupture between economic and social development, undermining the formation of stable middle classes. Politically, the class and social coalitions necessary to couple economic and social development have been weakened. This, we venture might be the real heart of the MIT. Put differently, compressed developers are only likely to be successful in the long run if they recouple economic and social development.

We close this chapter with some comments about inequality, about which much has been written over the past twenty-five years, and which is lurking in the background of any discussion of dualism, old, new, or layered. Evidence of the pernicious effects of inequality has steadily mounted (Aghion et al.,1999). Using harmonized data covering OECD countries over thirty years, a 2014 OECD report affirmed that 'income inequality has a negative and statistically significant impact on subsequent growth' (Cingano, 2014: 6). Inequality has also been linked to many social and medical ills (Wilkinson and Pickett, 2009), creating a threat to both economic and social development that is especially severe for developing countries.

Historically, inequality in industrialized countries peaked after World War I, and then began a long downturn until the 1970s, when it began to grow again. Milanovic (2016) links the post–World War I decline to both 'benign' and 'malign' mechanisms. The former include rising education levels, growth of the labour movement, increased demands for redistribution, and decreasing returns to capital, while malign mechanisms include revolutions and wars, themselves strongly influenced by inequalities.[26] The decline corresponded to the transition to, and duration of, embedded liberalism of late-late development.

Behind the rise of inequality from the 1970s are numerous, inter-linked causes. The OECD report referred to a widening gap between poor and lower middle-income households—the 'bottom 40 percent'—and the rest of the economy, brought about by a lack of education opportunities, which lowers social mobility and hampers skill development. Milanovic attributes it to 'TOP': the information *technology* revolution, increased *openness* and globalization, and pro-rich policies and *politics*., Aghion et al. (1999) also linked growing (income) inequality to trade liberalization, technical change and the emergence of new organizational forms (the network organizational paradigm). And Piketty (2014) attributes the post-1970s upturn in *wealth* inequality to a return to low growth rates, and the tendency for returns on capital to exceed those rates. In slowly growing economies past wealth becomes disproportionately important.[27]

Borrowing Milanovic's 'TOP', *technological innovation* has been implemented in many countries in ways that intensify labour-market polarization and generate

[26] 'Rising inequality indeed sets in motion forces, often of a destructive nature, that ultimately lead to its decrease, but in the process destroy much else, including millions of lives and huge amounts of wealth' (Milanovic, 2016: 98).

[27] Cf. also Berg and Ostry (2011).

high returns to capital.[28] The effects are especially consequential in developing countries, and in leading growth sectors.[29] *Openness* and globalization have massively expanded the available labour force—Freeman (2006) refers to the opening of China, Russia, and India after 1989 as a 'great doubling' of the workforce available to global firms—and through GVCs (and labour chains), have given employers increased leverage over employees and their unions, thereby putting downward pressure on wages and conditions, not to mention increasing the options for tax avoidance and sheltering wealth from national tax authorities. Yet *politics* matters. Acemoglu and Robinson (2002) speculate that inequality will eventually provoke a political reaction towards a more redistributive system. They subsequently become more ambivalent, however, and argue that the more entrenched inequality becomes, the more difficult it is to bring about sustained development, since those with wealth also possess the political power to shape the economy for their own benefit (Acemoglu and Robinson, 2012; Flechtner and Panther, 2013).

This brings us back to Kuznets. Based largely on intuition, and partly on US and comparative data, Kuznets (1955) proposed that industrialization, urbanization, and economic development are initially accompanied by rising inequality followed by a decline. Kuznets's inverse U curve has been subjected to many statistical tests, with mixed results. Even if he was correct for his time, there is a distinct danger that compressed developers will experience initially rising inequality…but no subsequent downturn—a Kuznetian 'wobble' rather than a U-shaped curve.

Even in Asia, where 'miracle' late developers achieved growth with increasing equality (World Bank, 1993), there has been a sharp reversal since the 1990s (Jain-Chandra et al., 2016), nowhere more apparent than in China, to the extent that Islam (2015) opines that an 'inequality trap' could entrench a MIT. China has in fact achieved stunning economic growth with growing labour-market polarization and growing inequality, but in the long run, economic and social development may only be recoupled if inequality is addressed, not least that deriving from employment and skills, as well as education, to which we now turn.

[28] Acemodglu and Autor (2010); Karabarbounis and Neiman (2013); McAfee, Brynjolfsson, and Spence (2014). From his literature review Autor finds that 'computerization is strongly associated with employment polarization at the level of industries, localities and national markets' (2015: 139).

[29] Technological change was cited as an underlying cause of layoffs in Bangalore's software sector in 2017. 'As IT companies start working on newer technologies such as cloud computing, they are fast moving from a people-led model, which means they need fewer employees. Meanwhile, many of the IT companies have embraced automation tools to perform the mundane, repeatable tasks that were performed by an army of engineers earlier' *Live Mint,* 12 May 2017 ('Top 7 IT Firms Including Infosys, Wipro to Lay Off at Least 56,000 Employees This Year').

7

Social Policy

Education as a New Frontier of Compression

Introduction

Chapter 1 examined time compression mainly in economic development, and only briefly in the social sphere. It is often in the social sphere, though, that compression and the interaction of compression and era influences are most visible. A key objective of this chapter is to highlight this, especially in education and education policy, as well as to further consider the changing relationship between social and economic development. We argued in Chapter 6 that economic and social development are closely interlinked. That recognition, according to Mkandawire (2004: 15), was integral to the experience of late development. '(I) mplicit in late industrialization was social policy that served not only to ensure national cohesion (as is often asserted of Bismarck's innovative welfare legislation) but also to produce the social pacts and the human capital that facilitated industrialization.'

This recognition was also part of the East Asian late-development experience (H-J Chang, 2002b; Jomo, 2003). Sen's (1999a, 1999b) East Asian model is characterized by: (1) an emphasis on basic education from the beginning of the modern development process, if not before; (2) wide dissemination of economic entitlements through education and training, land reform, and credit availability; and (3) a deliberate combination of state action and the market. Enabled by basic education and health care, human development 'make(s) it possible for the bulk of the people to participate directly in the process of economic expansion' (Sen, 1999b: 5).

By the end of the late-development era, however, and especially in the era of compressed development, states were skimping on social expenditure, espousing growth first and distribution later (if at all). K-S Chang (2019) argues that successive South Korean governments did this through a combination of 'private developmentalism' and repression. This imbalance intensified after the Asian Financial Crisis, but did not start with it. Chang refers to this stance as 'developmental liberalism'.[1] We also saw this imbalance in Chapter 6, in which layered

[1] See also Goodman et al. (1998) on East Asian 'developmental welfare systems', featuring relatively low state expenditure and weak guarantees of welfare as a social right.

Compressed Development: Time and Timing in Economic and Social Development. D. Hugh Whittaker, Timothy J. Sturgeon, Toshie Okita, and Tianbiao Zhu, Oxford University Press (2020). DOI: 10.1093/oso/9780198744948.001.0001

dualism had either been incorporated into the growth model, or tacitly accepted, making it more difficult to link economic and social development.

Indeed, in many respects, social development and social policy during the eras of late development and compressed development are a world apart. Late developers engaged in institutional borrowing when they built their own health and education systems, but adapted them to their own nation-building and economic-development goals. Where there was a mix of public and private providers, the overall framework and key institutions were part of national public policy, which took shape alongside industrialization. In the era of compressed development, by contrast, the conception, design, and implementation of social policy has changed dramatically, influenced by powerful international organizations, transnational networks, and private sector actors. Education, which is the main subject of this chapter, has become a greater focus with the rise of the 'knowledge economy', and is tasked with solving an increasing range of socioeconomic problems, while at the same time it has been reshaped by several constellations of factors.

First, human capital theory has penetrated the discourses and goals of education. In essence, education has widely come to be seen as the process of preparing individuals to participate and compete in a global knowledge (and increasingly digital) economy. Second, policies designed to accomplish this must be 'evidence-based', a slogan privileging 'hard', numerical data which can be tabulated and compared across contexts. A 'global testing culture' is one visible expression of this. Third, this positivist approach to educational attainment has opened the door to a host of new actors—policy entrepreneurs, big data analysts and consultants, public–private partnerships in education (ePPPs), charter school advocates, for-profit schools and universities, textbook and software publishers, computer and tablet producers, test preparation services, and so on. The social has thus become a new frontier for business and social entrepreneurs to influence, penetrate, bypass, and at times subvert national-level social policies in ways that were unimagined even two decades ago.

These changes all intensify compression. Recent developers now face simultaneous challenges in social development which early and late developers confronted sequentially. At a basic level, these can be characterized as 'double burdens' (as they have been called in the area of public health) or 'double challenges', which states confront with limited resources. In public health, they include addressing the traditional health issues of less-developed countries such as under-nutrition and communicable diseases even as noncommunicable diseases such as obesity become urgent problems. In education it means constructing a higher education and research system at virtually the same time as universalizing basic education (even in countries where literacy rates may be relatively high), as education becomes an arena tasked with solving increasingly complex social and economic problems.[2]

[2] In fact, era-related factors can create *triple* challenges; for example, add building in the testing and assessment culture at all levels of education.

Double challenges can be seen in other areas, as well, such as 'old' and 'new' food policy, noted at the end of this chapter. The inevitable result is *policy stretch*, where resources are stretched across challenges that were faced by earlier developers over time, challenges that interact and may have contradictory or controversial solutions that make policy integration difficult. Strains on state capacities increase the attractiveness of international and multisector participation and solutions, intensifying compression and the challenges of policy integration. Navigating these challenges requires new state-society relations, and a very adaptive state, as we shall see in Chapter 8.

The chapter is organized as follows. First key challenges related to compression in the areas of health and education are introduced. Then education is examined in more detail by adding 'era' influences to the picture, first exploring the global alignment of social policy in basic and advanced education, and then the rise of the global testing culture and discourses premised on human capital theory. Next the proliferation of actors, decentralization, and projectification, which together create 'centrifugal forces' acting on the state's policy formation processes are explored. The following section considers how era-related factors have played out in education in China, where the state has sought to mute some influences of compression, and has transformed others. The final section briefly sketches the challenges of policy stretch and policy integration.

Double challenges in health and education

There is a dynamic relationship between economic development and human and social development. The United Nations Millennium Development Goals (MDGs) and Sustainable Development Goals (SDGs) recognize this, and have a particularly strong focus on health, as well as poverty reduction and education. The relationship is complex, however, and it harbours many tensions. Some are common to developers in all eras, but some are new, or intensified, in compressed developers. Here we look at double challenges in the areas of health and education, which earlier developers faced sequentially, but recent developers face simultaneously. Given pronounced compression in China, examples will be taken mainly from that country. The basic concepts are shown in Figure 7.1.

Double burden of disease

A country's health system is a fundamental part of development. With compressed development, however, the interval between establishing a system to combat under-nutrition and communicable diseases, and the onset of over-nutrition and noncommunicable diseases, has effectively disappeared. The onset

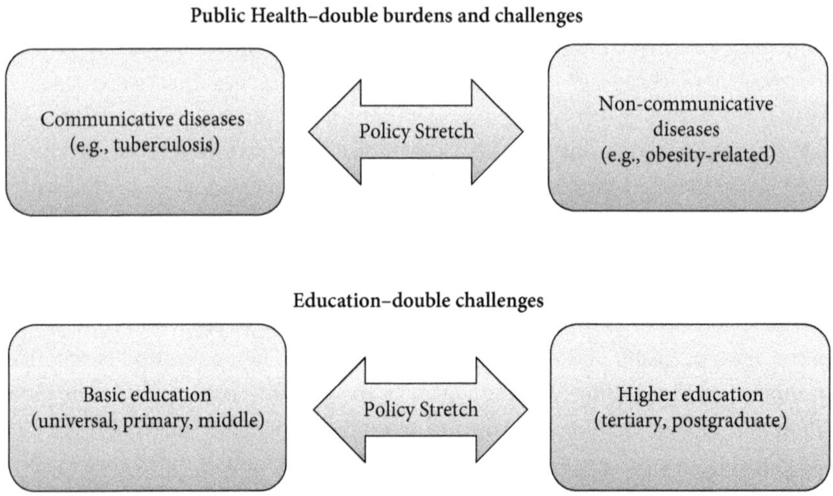

Figure 7.1 Double burdens and challenges in public health and education

of over-nutrition and noncommunicable diseases has been happening at lower income levels, so much so that they can co-exist with under-nutrition and communicable diseases, not only in the same generation, but even in the same household! The World Health Organization (2006) refers to the 'double burden' of disease in which:

> Preventable, communicative diseases, which are common in low-income countries remain a significant cause of death, particularly among children. In addition to this, driven by socio-economic and demographic transitions, chronic non-communicable diseases, which are common in high-income countries, have become increasingly prevalent. (OWHORC/SDDC, 2006: 11)

While high-profile alliances such as the Global Fund to Fight AIDS, Malaria and Tuberculosis, and the Global Alliance for Vaccines and Immunizations have been formed to fight the former, as Ollila (2005) and Stuckler and Basu (2011) note, much less attention has been given to noncommunicable diseases in developing countries, despite their rapid spread, high costs, and difficulty to fight, and despite the projection that four out of five deaths from chronic diseases in 2030 will occur in low- and middle-income countries.

Although the number of cases has been declining, in 2015, there were an estimated one million new cases of tuberculosis in China, which, together with India and Indonesia, comprised 45 per cent of the world's total cases. Some 16 per cent of all new cases and relapses were reported in China in 2012, where over 100 people die daily from the disease. China and India are on the WHO's high burden list for tuberculosis, tuberculosis-HIV, and multidrug-resistant tuberculosis.[3] At the same time, China has an even higher proportion of the world's *obese* population—around one-fifth of the total—and the problem is becoming more serious (Popkin 2002; Prentice, 2006). By 2014 China was second only to the United States in the number of obese people, with a surge in the number of obese children (Li et al., 2016). The rapid growth of obesity is attributed to urbanization and accompanying lifestyle change, including rising consumption of fast and processed food. There are cultural factors as well. As a Chinese Vice Minister for Health once noted: 'Parents and grandparents often feed their offspring excessively to make up for being fed inadequately themselves.'[4] Grandparents take their grandchildren to Western fast food restaurants—symbols of modernity (and cleanliness)—as a special treat.[5]

Further factors intensify the problem in less-developed countries, where consumers are exposed to fast food earlier in their development than in now-developed countries,[6] and may be exposed to antibiotics fed to animals as their meat intake increases. They are exposed to sophisticated marketing techniques earlier, as well, as the discipline of marketing itself has evolved immensely over the past fifty years, including marketing directly to children.[7] This problem is compounded when less-developed countries do not have the consumer protection and advertising guidelines in place that developed countries have implemented. Combining many of these factors, the Internet exposes children and youth to online advertising and 'advergames' which often breach even minimal standards of regulation. Organizations such as the International Obesity Task Force called for an international code in 2006 (Rydell and Bremberg, 2006; Carlson, 2005), but the results have been patchy.

The spread of Internet use among children and youth results in a reduction of exercise, which contributes to obesity, as it does in developed countries. But there is an additional risk in developing countries, which is a distinctive compression phenomenon. If a baby has suffered from metabolic problems in infancy, which is more likely in a developing country, the risk of obesity increases when he or she is

[3] WHO *World Tuberculosis Report*, 2013, 2016. It is estimated that roughly a third of children in India, Indonesia, and the Philippines suffer from stunted growth through malnutrition: (see 'Chronic Malnutrition Stunts Asia's Rising-star Economies ', *Nikkei Asian Review*, 29 April 2019).

[4] BBC News, 12 October 2004.

[5] A McDonald's executive commented: 'We do extensive focus group studies of Chinese consumers, and one of the things that Chinese consumers say over and over again is that "we come to you because you are a Western brand, and if we want rice or congee we can eat at home; we want to sample the Western brand"' (quoted in *China Daily*, 8 September 2008). The early spread of supermarkets also exposes consumers to nontraditional, processed food.

[6] Late developers like Japan and South Korea had more time to mobilize efforts to preserve the healthful elements of their traditional diets (Lee et al., 2002).

[7] Ironically these sophisticated marketing techniques emerged from research originally aimed to protect children (John, 1999).

exposed to new diets and lifestyles later in life (Hofman et al., cited in Popkin, 2002). From this and other causes:

> Before they were born, their bodies were at much greater risk of becoming ill, 'pre-polluted' by toxic exposures in the womb. By the time they become adolescents, their blood pressure will be too high, their arteries calcified with plaque and fatty streaks, and their chance of developing 'adult-onset diabetes' will be significantly elevated. (Stuckler and Basu, 2011: vi)

It is not surprising, then, that in countries like China there is a positive correlation between socioeconomic status and obesity, rather than a negative relationship, as in developed countries. The problem is very hard to tackle, but it must be done at the same time as the ongoing fight against communicative diseases.

Double challenge of education

Education is also fundamental for human development and citizenship, as well as economic development. Countries which grew strongly in the second half of the twentieth century had all achieved almost universal levels of literacy first (Hallak, 1990). But recent developers have an extra challenge, somewhat analogous to double burdens in health. In this case, they face a 'basic' education challenge normally associated with early industrialization alongside an 'advanced' education challenge normally associated with advanced or knowledge economy development. The former concerns the (actual) implementation of universal basic education and literacy goals, and the latter concerns the expansion of higher education to produce the knowledge and skills needed for upgrading modern production systems, global-value-chain engagement, and knowledge-based innovation (which is difficult in a context of thin industrialization and the separation of innovation and production). As UNESCO researchers Varghese et al. (2014: 15) put it: 'Many governments see universities as centres of research that will yield positive economic returns to the country. University research is typically done at the graduate level (Master's and doctoral). Hence, expanding graduate education is viewed as a means of increasing the economic competitiveness of the country.'[8]

China is a good example of a compressed developer committed to both challenges simultaneously. The Chinese government expended considerable effort to expand school education from the 1950s, but there was much unevenness and confusion about educational content in the wake of the Cultural Revolution.

[8] Such expansion can be accelerated by inviting foreign higher education institutions to set up satellite campuses and other arrangements.

By 1980, an estimated *enrolment* rate of 90 per cent had been reached in rural China,[9] but enrolment is not the same as completion, or even attendance. There were still large gaps, and widespread illiteracy, and in 1986, a number of education laws were passed, including the Law of Compulsory Education, which envisaged the progressive introduction of compulsory nine-year education throughout China over a ten-year period, effecting a 'simultaneous correction of the disproportionate investment in higher education (too high proportionately) and in basic schooling (too little), in line with development needs' (Rong and Shi, 2001: 112–13).

Accomplishing the 'two basics' (promoting and consolidating compulsory nine-year education, especially in rural areas, and eradicating illiteracy, especially among middle-aged people) has been difficult, however, in spite of China ostensibly, by 2006, reaching the second Millennium Development Goal of universal primary enrolment, a five-year retention rate of 99 per cent, and a gross enrolment ratio in junior high school approaching 100 per cent, albeit with regional variations. Achieving literacy targets has also been difficult.

At the same time as the goal of compulsory nine-year education was introduced, higher education reform was begun, with the aim of creating more opportunities for advanced learning (Mok, 2003; Chapter 5). Higher education sector expansion was pushed by both the ambitions of the state to participate and compete in the global economy and the needs of youth for higher qualifications to improve their prospects in rapidly changing labour markets. The proportion of high school graduates going on to tertiary education in China jumped from just 4 per cent of the 18–22-year-old cohort in 1990 to 21 per cent in 2005, and 43 per cent a decade later. Master's and PhD enrolments, and female participation, have had even sharper growth rates.[10]

China's massive expansion of higher education has taken place at almost the same time as the consolidation of basic education. Japan's expansion of higher education took place in the 1960s and 1970s, after lower levels of education had been consolidated. But China has also been developing its postgraduate education system since the early 1990s, *at the same time as Japan*.[11] As we saw in Chapter 4, moreover, the internationalization of China's education has been similarly dramatic, and much more so than in Japan.

The sum of these points brings the double challenges of improving basic and advanced education simultaneously into focus. As with health, the simultaneity of the double challenge in education creates *policy stretch*. At a relatively early stage,

9 Fan et al. (2002), cited in Zhang and Kanbur (2005).

10 OECD/MoE (2007: 15; 17); Gallagher et al. (2009); UNESCO (2016): <http://uis.unesco.org/en/country/cn?theme=education-and-literacy>, accessed 29 August 2017.

11 Postgraduate participation in Japan almost tripled between 1990 and 2005, with the proportion of graduates advancing to master's degrees increasing from roughly 6 per cent to 17 per cent (OECD/MEXT, 2006: 136–7).

and with limited resources, the state is faced with simultaneously developing health and education capabilities which earlier developers were able to develop over a longer period of time, and sequentially.

'Era' influences: global alignment of education policy and global testing culture

As has been implied by the examples used in the previous section, double burdens or challenges from compression are shaped by 'era' influences. Relevant here are those relating to international development organizations and the way they influence policy space, which we discussed in Chapter 2. Here we explore these influences in the area of education policy. Whether or not there is 'global social policy' per se, there is broad agreement that social policy across the globe has become strongly influenced by international organizations, resulting in increasing alignment across countries.[12] National policymaking and implementation in many developing countries was constrained under structural adjustment programmes of the 1980s and early 1990s, and in the context of strong criticism of these programmes, and to recover lost legitimacy, the World Bank in particular led a policy shift focusing on poverty alleviation through targeted measures. Major international summits played strong symbolic, galvanizing, agenda- and target-setting roles. Tarabini (2007: 24) notes:

> Since the beginning of the 1990s, the struggle against poverty has served as the central pillar of the international development agenda, occupying a key place in the discourses and action priorities of both governments and international organizations. The international development summits (Copenhagen, 1995 and Geneva, 2000) and the Millennium Development Goals (approved in 2000 by the largest gathering of heads of state in history) have played a key role in shaping this agenda and setting out specific commitments, objectives and goals that would enable the progress and advances made by different countries to be assessed.

Three of the MDGs concerned health, but education was also elevated, as it was seen to be a key to developing the productive capabilities of the poor. World Education Summits (in Jomtien in 1990 and Dakar in 2000) shaped this expectation, as did several influential reports by the World Bank. These were not simply

[12] Deacon, Hulse, and Stubbs (1997) and Deacon (2005) argue that global social policy in the sense of global redistribution, regulation, and rights is now a reality, while in education, Dale (2000), argues there is a 'globally structured education agenda'. See also Mundy et al. (2016). This alignment is similar to isomorphic tendencies in regard to organizational paradigms and management models discussed in Chapter 3.

opinion-shaping exercises. Action agendas with targets, milestones, and monitoring were set, and the World Bank, through its International Development Association and other means, provided funding for projects and companies in less-developed countries. For these, numerous statistics and indicators were deployed. UNESCO, historically the main provider of education statistics, came under increasing criticism in the 1980s for its reluctance to present them in comparable tabular form, as it emphasized diversity in contexts of different national systems. The World Bank, OECD, and other organizations began collecting, analysing, and publishing their own education statistics in the 1990s, in line with the new strategic importance attached to education. A review of UNESCO's statistical services followed which stressed new statistical needs, new technologies, new human capital needs, and the presence of new international actors, including those of the private sector. The services were subsequently restructured and moved from Paris to Montreal, and greater alignment with the OECD was implemented (Cusso, 2006).[13]

Statistics were used not just for simple comparison—now available in homogeneous and hierarchical tables—but to explore reasons for differences, including the relative efficiency of inputs to outputs, and political decisions influencing these. These were then compared with targets and milestones. 'Best policies' and 'best practice' were established. Again, citing Tarabini (2007: 25):

> The current education policy agenda thus not only indicates what education is expected to achieve, but also sets forth how to achieve it, including a strong normative component that contributes to numerous countries adopting the agenda. It should also be borne in mind that the process of globalization reinforces the importance placed on investment in education as a strategy to foster development and competitiveness.

At the same time, the overall education policy agenda was narrowed through subsector targeting, for example, a focus on primary education (King, McGrath, and Rose, 2007). The rationale was efficient use of scarce resources. As a result of its modelling, the World Bank estimated that for poor countries to reach their MDG of universal primary education by 2015, 50 per cent of their public education budgets should be allocated to primary education, and other levels should be reduced in relative if not absolute terms (Cusso and Amico, 2005: 211). The World Bank's model even set out optimum teachers' salaries, recommended levels of private sector education, and the most efficient pupil/teacher ratio.

Selective studies were cited in support, such as Lockheed et al. (1980), which suggested that four years of basic primary education for rural children raises

[13] Cusso and Amico (2005) characterize the changes in the design and use of the statistics as a shift from 'development to globalization'.

agricultural productivity by ten per cent. Without the study's qualifying contextual caveats, and research which showed that education by itself does not reduce poverty or spur development, this became a justification for targeting of basic education in Africa (King et al., 2005; Bonal, 2007). Another study by World Bank researcher Thobani (1984) claimed that school fees were not only effective in raising educational levels in Malawi, but also equitable, as savings could be reinvested, and would lead to rising enrolments.[14] This and other studies contributed to the 'rupture of the free primary education consensus' (Tomasevski, 2003) in the 1980s.

Yet another set of studies pointed to high rates of private return in education, justifying private provision, and while directing the savings to improve primary schooling was also advocated, the logic of targeting and private provision was strengthened, with little evidence that savings (profits) were actually invested back into primary education (Klees, 2008: 314).[15] Those who could not afford to pay were to receive scholarships or exemptions—another form of targeting—but the associated administrative costs are high, and capabilities needed to administer such schemes may simply not exist (Mkandawire, 2004).[16]

There was a powerful movement towards global alignment and measurement in basic education policy, therefore, and in the way questions are framed, statistics collected, and studies cited. This involved processes of decontextualization, numericization, and targeting. The underlying ethos has been characterized as 'four Es'—economics, effectiveness, efficiency, and evidence—which became 'the new battle cries for the development community' (Ollila, 2005: 3). The fourth E—evidence—moved as 'evidence-based policy' from finance, through the medical field, into the broader social policy sphere in the 1990s (O'Dwyer, 2003; Thomas et al., 2010; UNICEF, 2008, 2009). The evidence-based policy movement emerged as a means of improving the basis of political decisions, but in practice, political decisions are often bolstered by 'politically based evidence making' (Nilsson et al., 2008; Radaelli, 2004).[17]

[14] Without citing Thobani, World Bank researcher Kattan (2006) later pointed out that when school fees in Malawi were *abolished* in 1994, a decade after they were introduced, gross enrolment rates rose by 49 per cent.

[15] Psacharopulos (1985); Mingat and Tan (1985); Mingat (1998). Both the primary education focus and user-pays concepts were incorporated into the 1986 World Bank policy paper 'Financing Education in Developing Countries' (Tan et al., 1986), which marked a tide change for the widespread enforcement of loans conditional on restructuring of public provision, user charges, privatization, and diversification (Hinchcliffe, 1993).

[16] Mkandawire notes that many policies were taken from developed countries, where they were embedded in different policy sets, including universal programmes. Severed from these contexts, they could not produce similar results. Targeting also means devoting fewer resources to non-favoured areas which may in fact influence those areas favoured. Completing primary school, for example, may be dependent on the availability and affordability of middle schools and high schools.

[17] McCarthy and Rose (2010) suggest that 'evidence-based' should be relabelled 'value-based'.

A related development has been the emergence and rapid spread of a 'global testing culture' (Smith, 2015) from the late 1990s. As the SDGs replaced the MDGs in 2015, the emphasis in education shifted from access to 'quality', and with a new emphasis on secondary education, this trend became even more pronounced. The plethora of testing acronyms includes EGRA (early grade reading assessment), EGMA (early grade mathematics assessment) from the United States, OECD's PISA (programme for international student assessment—'PISA for Development' was launched in 2018), IEA's Progress In International Reading Literacy study, TIMMS (trends in international mathematics and science study), and many others. Some are standardized international tests; some are regional, and some national. Testing as a policy tool:

> ... has been legitimized within international educational development to measure education quality in the vast majority of countries worldwide. The assumed, taken-for-granted, nature of testing can be described as the global testing culture and permeates all aspects of education, from financing, to parental involvement, to teacher and student beliefs and practices. The reinforcing nature of the global testing culture leads to an environment where testing becomes synonymous with accountability, which becomes synonymous with education quality.
>
> (Smith, 2015: 7)

As the testing culture spread to developing countries, it consumed proportionately more resources. Linked to 'high-stake' outcomes (Smith, 2016)—budgets, salaries, and reputations—teachers were increasingly pressured to teach to these tests. Preparing students to participate as individuals in the global knowledge economy, less scope was left for the more humanistic and social goals of education.[18] The 'diploma disease' (Chapter 4) was thus strengthened.

Higher education and lifelong learning for the global knowledge economy

Higher education has also been the subject of powerful era influences, captured in the mantra 'lifelong learning for the global knowledge economy'. Both 'lifelong learning' and 'knowledge economy' have undergone considerable conceptual evolution, both independently and together. In the 1960s lifelong *education* was associated with radical thinking or disillusionment with formal schooling. In the 1970s and 1980s, it became a concept for tackling unemployment through retraining, and by the end of the century, it was recast as lifelong *learning*,

[18] On the globalization and growth of testing, see also Kamens and McNeely (2010).

something for individuals to strive towards rather than something to be provided (Preece, 2005).

The idea of a 'knowledge (-based) economy', also originated in the 1960s (Machlup, 1962), and it was resurrected by the OECD in the mid-1990s (Godin, 2006). Expenditure on R&D, education and software was recast as 'investment in knowledge'. The concept was then combined with globalization to create the 'global knowledge economy' (Roberts, 2009). After recasting itself as the 'Knowledge Bank' in 1996, the education policy practitioners in the World Bank began to promote the concept, and brought it together with lifelong learning in its 2003 report 'Lifelong Learning for the Global Knowledge Economy: Challenges for Developing Countries', a report that included input from a range of academics and professionals from other international organizations such as the OECD, ILO, and German Institute for International Educational Research. It was subsequently elaborated, with varying emphases, by these and other international organizations.[19] This union powerfully influenced the global alignment of higher education policies in developing (and developed) countries.

It is difficult to object to the concept of lifelong learning itself, especially when presented in terms of inclusiveness: 'skills upgrading for all'. Its conceptual vagueness may be part of its attraction. It takes problems such as unemployment, which may be structural, and deftly transforms them into a problem of skills that is for individuals and project stakeholders to solve (Borg and Mayo, 2005). The 'global knowledge economy' was somewhat more contentious, but the vigour with which it was promoted to some extent created its own reality.[20] The 'knowledge economy' is a postindustrial one, in which universities and corporate laboratories have replaced factories as powerhouses of economic development.

The use of indicators, numericization, and hierarchical tables are evident here as well, most prominently in university ranking tables. The three most commonly used ones—Times Higher Education's World University Rankings, QS World University Rankings, and Shanghai Jiao Tong's Academic Ranking of World Universities—employ different methodologies, and although these have been subject to extensive criticism, they nonetheless exert a strong influence on national higher education policies, university planning, academics' time allocation, and student choices.

For example, Malaysia experienced a fourfold increase in graduate enrolments between 2000 and 2010. The government's aim was to increase indigenous research capabilities, and to produce an educated workforce, evidence of which

[19] While the World Bank's version was informed by market individualism, and advocated private financing (Palacios, 2003; McMahon, 2003), the OECD's version was somewhat more institutional, and that of the ILO was more social democratic (Jakobi, 2009; Robertson, 2005).

[20] Alternative versions of lifelong learning were proposed in criticism of globalization and the 'knowledge economy', especially in Latin America (Robertson, 2005). These feature concepts such as ecology of learning, transformative practice, and sustainability in education.

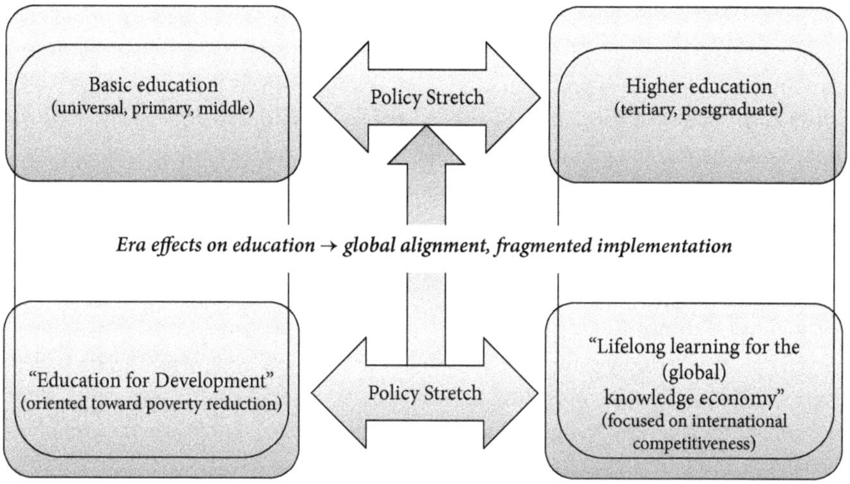

Figure 7.2 Double challenges in education, with 'era' effects up to the early 2000s

would in turn attract international investment, thereby accelerating economic development (Chapman and Chien, 2014: 40). This meant, however, scoring well on international rankings, and lecturers publishing in international (predominantly US and European) top-tier journals. To accelerate this, Malaysia's central bank inked a deal in 2015 with the Massachusetts Institute of Technology's business school (the Sloan School) to create a new Asia School of Business (ASB) to offer MBA degrees and executive education courses taught by a combination of Sloan and ASB faculty using field-research-based 'action learning' (i.e. company visits, especially to multinationals in the region).

The influences of such 'era' factors on the double challenges of education, up to the early 2000s are sketched in Figure 7.2. In brief, there has been considerable alignment in themes and agendas (bottom row), around which the 'double challenges' of compressed development (upper row) have been recast. The themes and agendas have been created or adapted to appeal to a wide range of actors. As in health, and in social development more broadly, what is depicted in Figure 7.2 is a layering of challenges in education that compounds policy stretch.

Actor proliferation and centrifugal forces

Two of the three constellations of era-related influences mentioned in the introduction of this chapter have already been discussed—the recasting of education as human capital development which can be measured, managed, and improved by appropriate tools; and 'evidence-based policy', the hallmarks of which are measurement, tabulation, comparison, and targeting of resources, and the discarding or relegation of contextual data. The third constellation is the agency which has transformed education, for better or worse depending on one's viewpoint, into a dynamic frontier of development, and compression. In this section we look at the rapid entry of new actors into education, enabled by and in turn transforming the first two constellations. We first consider the role of partnerships.

Different decades see the appearance of new institutional champions for development—the developmental state in the 1960s and 1970s, free market concepts in the 1980s and 1990s, and public–private partnerships (PPPs) in the 2000s. PPPs range from the global to the local in scale, and take many forms. Utting and Zammit (2006) see them as part of the 'pragmatic turn' in the post-Soviet era, in which the public sector is urged to focus on 'what works'. The United Nations became a major promoter of business partnerships in the late 1990s, when it came under severe budgetary pressure. Commented Secretary General Kofi Annan in 1998:

> If reform was the dominant theme of my first year in office, the role of the private sector in economic development was a strong sub-theme. A fundamental shift has occurred. The United Nations once dealt only with governments. By now we know that peace and prosperity cannot be achieved without active partnerships involving governments, international organizations, the business community and civil society. In today's world we depend on each other. The business of the United Nations involves the businesses of the world.
>
> (quoted in Zammit, 2009: 30)

At the World Economic Forum in Davos the following year, Annan announced the Global Compact. Businesses were encouraged to sign up to principles of corporate social responsibility, and to become partners in global development projects. The UN is, of course, only one amongst a wide range of actors which have actively promoted partnerships. Many national and local level governments have also done so.[21] Like targeting and lifelong learning, it is difficult to oppose the concept of 'partnership', and like lifelong learning, the notion of partnership is vague and fungible. But PPPs have also proved controversial, with critics claiming the risks are shifted to the public side, and benefits to the private side.

PPPs have sometimes been framed in terms of 'new social policy', which combines pluralism in provisioning with decentralization of services and community participation (Razavi, 2009). In developing countries, however, the reality has often been 'participation without resources'; or local communities being called on to supply funds, labour and other in-kind contributions for educational necessities, including school maintenance and teacher salaries. As a result, access

[21] On ePPPs (PPPs in education) see Robertson et al. (2012); Verger (2012).

to education on the part of poor communities is often impeded (Klees, 2008; Tomasevski, 2003).

Donors channelling funds through nongovernmental actors require not just milestones and accountability, but visible progress. This requires complex social issues like poverty to be broken into components and recast as solvable according to predictable timetables. Overall, the result has been fragmentation, in which 'gaps are filled by providers that offer services of varying quality which cater and are accessible to different segments of the population' (Razavi, 2009: 12). In this circular process of 'microization' (Tendler, 2004), decentralization and multi-actor participation lead to 'projectification', in which social issues are structured as projects to encourage stakeholder participation, including that of NGOs. Projects are able to target bottlenecks, and mobilize a range of resources, human included, but there is mixed evidence that they produce superior results.

An additional, crucial set of actors in this mix are *policy entrepreneurs*, who are typically based in international organizations, think tanks, universities, or big consultancy firms; 'located at the interstices of business, government and academia' (Verger, 2012: 111), who frame and present their ideas in ways that make them appear familiar, feasible and superior, using 'bricolage, transposition and translation' (112). Policy entrepreneurs work with international organizations to legitimize their innovations and to package them in a way that they might be sold to clients in developing countries. Networks encompass advocates in developing countries. An example is Vietnam where, through conferences and similar mechanisms organized by the World Bank, hitherto cautious Vietnamese leaders were socialized into the idea of quickly building world class universities, and boosting the competitiveness of Vietnamese universities in the international arena, with the support of leading US institutions. The result was a shift in Vietnamese higher education policy towards a greater emphasis on efficiency and effectiveness through decentralization of administration and finances, as well as privatization (Dang, 2009: 89).[22]

And finally, there are broader networks of advocates and enterprises. In his study of the Indian Education Reform Movement, Ball (2016) found policy ideas circulating within a network of advocates, with a neoliberal rationality that included investment efficiency, business innovation, and performance management. Entrepreneurs saw themselves as part of a movement to bring private sector solutions to education problems which the state was slow to address. They articulated this in the form of 'crisis and reform'. In the constantly evolving and mutating network, ideas circulated—internationally—not as a complete package,

[22] Facilitating the globalization of higher education is the general agreement of trade in services (GATS), which came into force in 1995. For a discussion of GATS and education, see for example Verger (2008); Robertson, Bonal, and Dale (2002). While this discussion is focused on higher education, Vietnam has also received a plethora of advice from the World Bank on how to industrialize in the context of GVCs (e.g. Hollweg, Smith, and Taglioni, 2017).

but in terms of policy prototypes, experiments and units which were constantly reconfigured to suit the proposed destination. 'Artefacts, schemes, programmes, ideas, propositions, and "programmatic" ideas... move through these network relations, at some speed, gaining credibility, support, and funding as they move, mutating and adapting to local conditions at the same time—often treated separately and re-assembled on-site' (Ball, 2016: 558).

Active in such networks or spaces are venture capital-backed enterprises, like Bridge International Academies which advertises its 'evidence-based, data driven and technology-enabled' methods to students and governments in developing countries. Using this data and technology, the company adopts a standardized approach to both curriculum and how it is taught, down to the last detail, which includes monitoring of teachers through their tablet use.[23] Standardized testing opens the door for other participants in developed and developing countries, including media companies producing textbooks for the tests, and companies (e.g. Pearson, and Brookings) that aggregate test results for use in big data analysis so they can offer 'solutions' like 'adaptive learning'. The World Bank operates similar programmes.[24] Remarkably, where many countries had serious reservations about the application of the 1995 General Agreement of Trade in Services to education (particularly primary-level education), the combination of human capital concepts, testing, and 'evidence-based' policy have opened the door wider, and more quickly, than even its strongest advocates would have foreseen in the mid-1990s. Such educational entrepreneurship is implicitly justified by 'government failure', which it ironically might help to create by directing education funds into private hands. The creation of coherent and/or universalized policy becomes more difficult, as policy stretch is intensified.[25]

[23] Its activities have been highly controversial; in November 2016 Uganda's high court ordered the company to close sixty-three schools because it had opened branches without permission. Such aggressive practices have invited comparisons with Uber (*The Economist*, 28 January 2017). There has been criticism of the UK government for using development aid to finance such enterprises (*New Internationalist*, 11 November 2018). <https://www.economist.com/news/business/21715695-its-biggest-challe...y-well-be-financial-bridge-international-academies-gets-high-marks>, accessed 8 September 2017. <https://newint.org/features/2018/09/11/uk-must-stop-aid-failing-private-schools>, accessed 2 October 2019.

[24] The World Bank's SABER (systems approach for better education results)–EMIS (education management information systems) 'brings education policymakers and stakeholders closer to a higher level of system knowledge and insight by providing a comprehensive framework based on a thorough review of global evidence as well as a methodology to evaluate an EMIS; aiding countries in analysing their education systems through diagnosis, dialogue, and reform; enhancing the global knowledge base on effective EMIS policies; involving key system leaders and stakeholders in identifying reform priorities'.

[25] Ollila (2005: 3) summarizes for health policy: 'Health policy-making has become increasingly fragmented and verticalized, with the increasing emphases on selected interventions, the increasing number of partnerships, and especially because of the founding of new entities for various health issues. Little emphasis has been put on comprehensive infrastructure building. These trends are in contrast to the stated aims of integrating health policy making with the broader development agenda or with comprehensive health sector planning.'

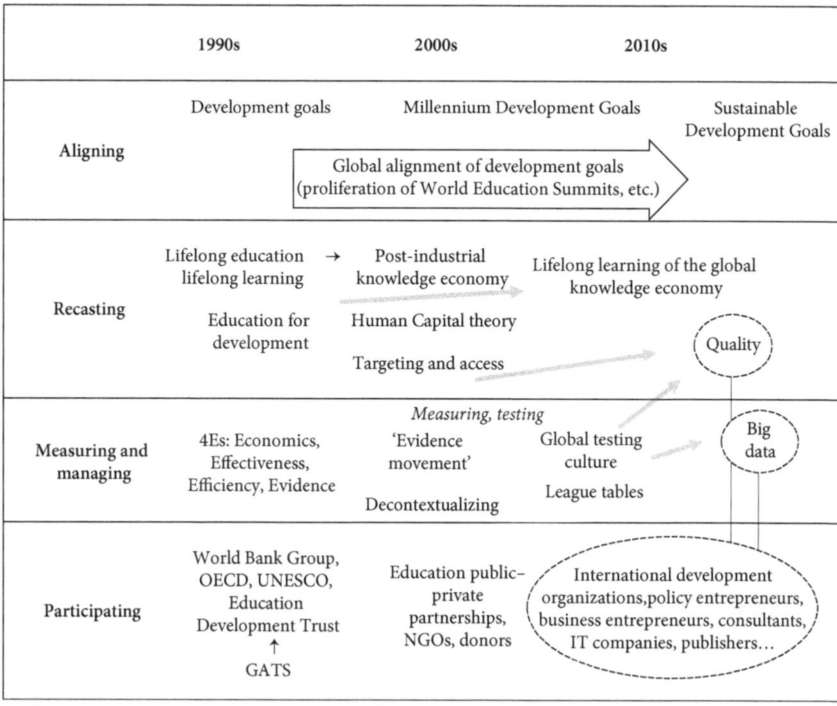

Figure 7.3 Transformation of education policy, practice, and participation

Figure 7.3 summarizes the developments we have just discussed. The first row presents the alignment of development and education goals over time, at an international level. The second row shows how the double challenges have been recast by era influences; higher education at the top as 'lifelong learning for the global knowledge economy', and primary or basic education below into 'education for development', through targeting and access, towards 'quality'. This is assured by means of measuring and testing, depicted in the next row, which is in the process of yielding big data that can be used by a range of actors, old and new. The emergence and proliferation of new actors occupies the final row. It should be emphasized that not all countries have been equally caught up in these trends, and less-developed countries are not necessarily passive participants. This can be seen in the case of China, to which we now turn.

Chinese education challenges revisited

Compression and 'era' factors play out differently in different countries, shaped by politics and geopolitics, legacies and endowments. In China formal PPPs have not been prominent, at least in education, due in part to the complexities of business-state interaction, local officials' preference for interacting with SOEs, uncertainty, and limited profitability.[26] International networks of policy entrepreneurs have also played a relatively limited role compared to India and a number of African countries. Nevertheless, many of the 'era' influences we have described also apply to China, and can be seen in the challenges of education.

Basic education in China: education for development

China's mid-1980s education reforms featured decentralization, funding diversification, and increased flexibility (Liu and Dunne, 2009). Local governments and non-state actors were encouraged to assume more responsibility for financing and provision. By 2004 there were over 70,000 *minban* (non-state-run schools), enrolling almost 18 million students (Mok et al., 2009: 506). The reforms also led to a variety of hybrid arrangements, characterized as *guoyou minban* (state-owned and non-state-run).

Not surprisingly, decentralization and funding diversification increased regional and local disparities. Rong and Shi (2001: 120) calculated that in 1996 per capita expenditure on children aged 6–14 was six times higher in type 1 (coastal, urban) regions than type 4 (inner, rural) regions. In some inner rural areas there were as many as 120 students per classroom (Pingping, 2008). Variability was particularly acute when it came to education of females and minorities. Zhang and Kanbur (2005: 201) lamented that many local governments, especially in poor regions, had effectively 'withdrawn from their role in investing in human development'. According to one calculation, 37.5 per cent of expenditure on education in China in 2017 came from non-state (i.e. household) sources.[27]

As household expenses for education rose—markedly for extra-school classes—so did those for health, sometimes forcing a trade-off between payment for medical treatment and education.[28] The World Bank (2009: 24–5) reported that a relatively small proportion of rural households were persistently poor between 2001 and 2003, but a much higher proportion were poor in either one or two of the years. Unexpected income or health 'shocks' might be enough to interrupt schooling, and when this happened, the break was often permanent. Thus, school *completion* rates in China remained problematic (UNDP, 2005).

[26] *China Daily*, 5 September 2017 ('State Promotes Public-Private Partnerships'); *Bloomberg News*, 27 February 2017 ('In China, Public-Private Partnerships Are Really Public-Public').

[27] From the China Institute for Education Finance Research, Peking University, cited by Feng (2018: 281).

[28] One estimate saw a six-fold increase in out-of-pocket household medical expenditure between 1994 and 2004 (World Bank, 2009: 168), with a proportionately steeper increase in rural areas (Zhang and Kanbur, 2005). These expenses came on top of sharp rises in house prices in many areas.

Such problems were noted by the central government. Concerned with rising social unrest and problems accompanying economic growth, it increased spending on social policies from the early 2000s under the banner of 'building a harmonious society'. The proportion of GDP expended on employment and social security, education, and healthcare rose from 4.69 per cent in 2003 to 7.20 per cent in 2011 (Ngok and Huang, 2014). Compulsory education was ostensibly made free. Support for poor households, especially in rural areas, was introduced at the same time, with fee and textbook exemptions and boarding subsidies (the so-called 'two exemptions and one subsidy' policy). However, the policy was not implemented evenly; it, too, depended on local budgets, and onerous and stigmatizing application procedures. Local administrative capacity, already under strain, was further stretched (Zhang, 2008).

Advanced education: lifelong learning for the global knowledge economy

Meanwhile, the proportion of 18–22 year olds in tertiary education surged, from just 4 per cent in 1990 to 21 per cent in 2005, skewed sharply towards those in urban areas. It had doubled again by 2015, to 43 per cent. Although the proportion of central government education expenditure allocated to tertiary education also rose considerably, it did not keep up with growth, creating space for private sector provision in higher education. By the late 1990s the number of private institutions easily outnumbered the number of public institutions (Cao and Levy, 2015).

For economic growth, and for youth life chances, increasing expectations were placed on the tertiary sector, encompassing not just universities and colleges, but (higher) vocational education and training and adult education institutions (of variable quality). These were brought together under the umbrella concept of lifelong learning (Xiong, 2006; Huang and Shi, 2008), which emerged as a key concept for China's socioeconomic transformation in the late 1990s, not long after it had gained prominence in developed countries facing postindustrial transitions (Xiong 2006; Huang and Shi, 2008). Lifelong learning was seen as crucial for economic growth in a rapidly changing global environment, as well as the building of a harmonious society (Sun, 2007). Indeed, it was tasked with reconciling economic growth and its resulting tensions, including inequality.

Far from being a passive or reluctant participant in the global alignment of education policy and lifelong learning, the Chinese state played a major role in APEC's human resources development activities, for example in the 'Beijing Initiative' of 2001 (Haworth, 2013). China has also been a major player in the internationalization of higher education (Chapter 4). In addition to large numbers of students studying abroad, in 2014, some 600 Chinese universities were working with foreign partner institutions, offering over 1100 joint programmes.[29] The flow of students has not only been outward, moreover, as China aims to increase the number of inbound students to 500,000 by 2020. China has also set its sights on emerging education technologies, such as those creating and deploying big data and distance learning.[30]

To sum up, education has played a major role in China's socioeconomic transformation, not simply by providing human resources, but as an arena for negotiation of international engagement, and of shifting state–market relations. As elsewhere, education has been tasked with playing a key role in building a knowledge economy and incubating indigenous innovation, as well as youth sorting, and (perhaps ironically) 'building a harmonious society'. Overall, the state has maintained its overseer role, and fragmentation has not spiralled out of control, but policy stretch has created tensions and gaps, especially through decentralization.

Policy stretch and policy integration

Compressed developers face double challenges in the social sphere, in both health and education. This comes on top of the challenges of coordinating economic and social policy (Chapter 6), in which the social tends to become an 'afterthought' which is 'added on' to economic policy, particularly at the macro level (Tendler, 2004).

Addressing double challenges with limited resources results in 'policy stretch'. This increases the attractiveness of era-related solutions, including decentralization, projectification, internationalization, and PPPs. These, however, create new challenges of coordination in turn. As Ollila (2005) notes, health partnerships in developing countries are rarely synchronized with processes aimed at developing national health systems. They can bypass broader institutional development (McCarthy and Rose, 2010), and indeed undermine it by absorbing public funds and dividing the domestic constituency for effective social policy, precisely at the moment when new public sector capabilities are needed. Tasks such as choosing the right form of project or PPP, and negotiating, monitoring, and enforcing contracts, are acknowledged to be difficult in developed countries, but in less-

[29] China Education Association for International Exchange, cited in *The Guardian*, 12 October 2015.

[30] In 2014 China's Ministry of Education and IBM entered into a $100 million big data collaboration. 'IBM's latest agreement with China's Ministry of Education, dubbed "IBM U-100," is intended to create a generation of data scientists among young people, reaching 40,000 students per year. The program has three aspects: setting up "big data and analytics" technology centers in 100 universities, implementing academic programs at 30 institutions, and creating centers of excellence at five schools. At the same time, the company will be working with a Chinese firm to develop massive open online courses (MOOCs) to extend the big data instruction' (Schaffhauser, 2014).

developed countries, they can be especially challenging, and create new pathways for corruption.

The combined effect is to intensify a challenge which goes by various names, including policy coordination, policy integration, joined-up policy, and joined-up government.[31] Meijers and Stead summarize the general challenge well:

> Some of these trends are toward globalization and greater centralization of decision-making, whilst other trends are toward fragmentation and decentralization of decision-making. A variety of factors have increased the number of actors involved in the policy process, such as the emergence of the information society, greater emphasis on public participation and the increasing role of non-governmental organizations, pressure groups and agencies in the decision-making process. All these developments make policy integration increasingly difficult but more compelling to achieve. (2004: 1)

The challenge arises from the emergence of issues which are 'increasingly "cross-cutting," and do not fit the ministerial boxes into which governments, and policy analysts, tend to place policies' (Peters, 1998: 296). In another example of a double challenge, conventional ('old') agriculture and food policy addresses the need to increase agricultural productivity to produce sufficient food for an urbanizing population. This serves health needs as well. But problems emerged from the resulting agri-food regimes in the form of food-borne pathogens, and lifestyle and dietary diseases (Waltner-Toews and Lang, 2000). Such 'advanced-country' food-related issues affect less-developed countries as well, sometimes in more extreme form, while they are still implementing 'old' policies at the same time. Ultimately, governments need to 'strengthen national institutional capability and capacity to integrate social, economic, developmental and environmental issues', as UNCED noted as far back as the 1992 Earth Summit in Rio de Janeiro.[32] This challenge is compounded by compression and the era-related features of compressed development.

Concluding comments

The UN's MDGs and SDGs have raised awareness of the role of social (and environmental) policy in development, potentially countering a growing

[31] Challis et al. (1988); Geerlings and Stead (2003). Policy integration at one level of government, moreover, does not ensure it is reflected at other levels.

[32] UNCED (1992: paragraph 8.2), cited in Steurer (2009: 5), who notes: 'The guiding model of sustainable development is one of the most important "cross-cutting" issues of our time because it is essentially about better integrating economic, social and environmental aspects in order to avoid unintended consequences (or external effects), such as climate change through greenhouse gas emissions.'

disconnect with economic and technological development (Chapter 6). As we have seen in this chapter, however, the global alignment of social policy and other era-related developments pose new challenges for developing countries, which might facilitate or mitigate against any such rapprochement. What is clear is that the combination of compression and such era-related influences have powerfully reshaped social policy and social development.

We have focused on three constellations of factors, namely the insertion of human capital theory into education (bringing education closer to capitalist principles and tools), the 'evidence-based policy' movement and its derivatives ('hard', context-free numerical data used for comparison, modelling, and targeted policy interventions), and a host of new actors (ePPPs, policy entrepreneurs, business entrepreneurs, etc,), which are associated with 'centrifugal' forces of decentralization and projectification. These three constellations have been instrumental in transforming education into a field of new business opportunities and frontier of compression, and, consequently, an arena for the renegotiation of state–market relations.

The 'evidence-based policy' movement promised to take politics out of social policy, bringing the sharp edge of scientific rigour to cut through persistent problems and government failure and corruption. By identifying best practice and modelling its causal relationships, and by focusing resources on critical areas, development would be hastened. In reality, the movement, whose banners are constantly changing, is far from technocratic and apolitical. 'Evidence' relies on standardization and assumptions of transportability across contexts, or breaking complex problems into manageable projects with linear milestones. This both exposes and creates new issues—'crises'—to address by policy entrepreneurs. The rise of the 'global testing culture', which has paved the way for the use of big data, is a central part of this milieu. It strengthens the power of those who control the data, and opens the way for new private and public sector solutions and problem identification.

The way that compression and era factors or influences have unfolded varies from country to country, of course. Some countries have embraced the changes enthusiastically; others much more cautiously. China has been able to harness era-related institutions to address compression, and to accelerate development, although not without problems. This may be largely because of the strength of the central state, and central–local government relations, which we will explore in the next chapter.

Ultimately, it is not just that developing countries face new tensions between economic and social development, or that social policy space has become compressed in the way we suggested in Chapter 2. What we have described in this chapter may also be seen as Polanyian disembedding in the social sphere, a marketization which blurs the distinctions between the economic and the social. This should not be surprising, as the distinctions are, after all, historical, as well as conceptual. As Deutschmann (2019) argues, disembedded markets are not simply an economic subsystem, a part of a whole, but a product of capitalism with an overarching or transcendent narrative of how to best—practically, as well as normatively—organize the social relations of that whole.

Yet, on the other hand, it may be that such disembedding provokes a Polanyian counter-movement, or new civil society movements which attempt to re-create a nonmarketized sphere of public and social relations. Civil society, largely missing from our analysis so far, and notably from our state–market dyad, needs to be brought into the picture. This will be taken up in the next chapter.

PART 3

NAVIGATING COMPRESSED DEVELOPMENT

8
The Adaptive (Developmental) State

Introduction

This chapter brings the state to the fore of our analysis of compressed development. In Chapter 2 we proposed the co-evolution—and co-dependence—of states and markets. Nation-state building and modern economic development, with capitalism harnessing technologies from the industrial revolution, went hand in hand. Both were strongly influenced by the wider economic, technological, and geopolitical systems of successive eras, shaped by the dominant powers Britain and then the United States from the late-eighteenth century onward. The state has played, and continues to play, a crucial role in the evolution of markets and creation and diffusion of technology by organizing and financing innovation, as Mazzucato (2013) reminds us.

But the co-evolutionary relationship between states and markets is not necessarily balanced, or mutually supportive. The state may overwhelm markets, as it did in former socialist countries, even as it promoted (heavy) industrialization. And arguably the reverse has happened more recently, with markets encroaching on spaces created by the state under embedded liberalism, and indeed changing the nature of the state itself. We described two aspects of this in Chapter 2—financialization and the compression of policy space—and the transformation of education and education policy in Chapter 7.

The state–market dyad needs further elaboration, however, and this chapter brings a new actor into the discussion. Civil society has been seen as the intermediate realm between the family and the state, and alternatively as the realm outside or between states and markets, influenced by both, and potentially influencing them as well.[1] Combining these views, Heller (2013: 2) defines 'civil society' as 'the full range of voluntary associations and movements that operate outside the market, the state and primary affiliations, and that specifically orient themselves to shaping the public sphere'. Conceptually, we can add civil society to our state–market dyad, as in Figure 8.1.

The relationships between civil society and states and markets are varied. Our concern here is the role of civil society in the era of compressed development. On

[1] The state can dominate civil society (most dramatically in fascist regimes, as can the market in very liberal regimes), while civil society can influence both the state and the market, as in embedded liberalism and in the social democratic welfare state.

Compressed Development: Time and Timing in Economic and Social Development. D. Hugh Whittaker, Timothy J. Sturgeon, Toshie Okita, and Tianbiao Zhu, Oxford University Press (2020). © D. Hugh Whittaker, Timothy J. Sturgeon, Toshie Okita, and Tianbiao Zhu. DOI: 10.1093/oso/9780198744948.001.0001

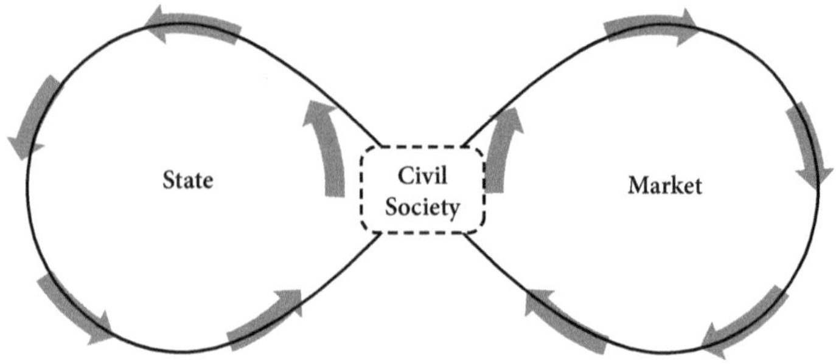

Figure 8.1 States, markets, and civil society

the one hand, as in late developers such as South Korea and Taiwan (and prewar Japan), the state may suppress civil society in the pursuit of economic growth. On the other, it may woo or sponsor civil society organizations in order to address double burdens and policy stretch, while also trying to contain them. Civil society organizations come in many forms, and are active at multiple levels, from the local to the global.[2] As in business, the global and the local are increasingly interacting: contributing to 'actor proliferation', but also to solutions for compressed development.

The chapter has three sections. In the first section we revisit the developmental state, to consider whether it has been dismantled or transformed in the era of compressed development. This is in part a definitional question. From our perspective (Chapter 2) the British state was developmental, and there is no categorical divide in the developmental orientation between early and late developers in this orientation, even though strategies and institutions changed. Nor is the developmental state limited to East Asia, or indeed the global South.[3] But the state faces a number of challenges that we have identified so far, which necessarily take it in new directions. These include:

- Navigating international treaty obligations (often with neoliberal foundations), and global integration;
- Creating coalitions with domestic and international actors, at national and subnational levels;

[2] Kaldor (2003: 590) traces the rise of 'global civil society' in the 1990s. She defines it as 'a platform inhabited by activists (or post-Marxists), NGOs and neoliberals, as well as national and religious groups, where they argue about, campaign for (or against), negotiate about, or lobby for the arrangements that shape global developments'.

[3] O'Riain (2000) for Ireland; Block (2008) and Lazonick (2008) for the US. Levi-Faur, too, critiques the developmental versus regulatory state dichotomy, and argues that 'the definition of the developmental state should not be associated with a region, a stage of development or a successful growth performance... the term "developmental state" should not be associated with particular industrial strategies' (2012: 9).

- Creating an 'innovation/technology system' conducive to global engagement, learning, and upgrading, especially where manufacturing and innovation have been separated;
- Addressing different (historical) 'stage' targets simultaneously: a new dimension to forward and backward linkages;
- Addressing double burdens and challenges with limited resources; and
- Dealing more explicitly with the interrelationships and balance between economic, social, and environmental policies.[4]

We will argue that in order to be developmental, the state must be increasingly adaptive, at multiple levels. When we consider how the state is changing, moreover, we must consider the subnational level, as well as the dynamics of multilevel governance. Local level initiatives, coalition building, and civil society engagement may enact central government objectives or undermine them. Indeed, compressed developers face the further double challenge of (nation) state building, historically associated with political and administrative centralization, and decentralization, in part due to the centrifugal forces described in Chapter 7. A widely cited survey in the early 1990s showed that all but twelve out of seventy-five developing and transitional countries with a population above 5 million had embarked on some form of political decentralization (Dillinger, 1994: 8), and that in the 2000s, over 80 per cent of developing countries had adopted some form of decentralized governance (Gaynor, 2016: 198).[5] We will consider the specific case of China.

Relatedly, and expanding our focus to include India, we will consider the proliferation of 'smart cities' as subnational developmental projects, including their governance features. They have been dubbed 'fast cities' by Datta and Shaban (2017), and are in many ways an expression of the paradoxes of compressed development. First, a state's responses to policy stretch and the challenges of compressed development push it towards flexibility, yet this makes it more difficult to achieve policy coherence and integration at a time when these have become increasingly necessary. Second, the politics of speed and promotion of rapid growth tend to marginalize social development and the environment, even as they become increasingly urgent issues.

In the final section we return to the 'embedded autonomy' of the developmental state and consider the increasing need for, and difficulties of, creating dynamic state–civil society relations. In the postwar decades, these were typically seen in terms of relations between the state, big business and (to varying degrees) organized labour, or

[4] Whittaker et al. (2010).

[5] In the same time period, more than two-thirds of sub-Saharan African countries implemented one or more decentralization policy reforms (Awortwi, 2010: 348). For Latin America, almost every country had already embarked on some form of decentralization by the late 1990s (West, 2015: 46).

in terms of class coalitions and compromise. But compression and the drive for flexibility and speed heighten the importance of the state interacting with a wider range of actors, from civil society, and from business, both domestic and external, to address its simultaneous challenges. (The importance of civil society is ultimately not a function of its cooperation with the state, of course, or with markets. And it is possible for both state and 'markets' to act together to undermine quality of life, freedom of citizens, and, ultimately, both social and economic development.)

Developmental challenges, as Hirschman (1958, 1971) reminds us, can bring forth new capabilities and solutions. Our goal in this chapter is not to seek a model as such, but to understand how states have been influenced by, and are attempting to navigate, the challenges of compressed development.

The developmental state: dismantled or transformed?

> 'Despite the limitations of the public sector, it is...hard to imagine ways to unleash a virtuous circle of productivity development without a government that builds consensus on a national project of industrial transformation, encourages investment in human capital, accelerates the emergence of an entrepreneurial class, builds trust and helps to organize producers, and reforms a range of other formal and informal institutions.'
>
> (Altenberg and Lütkenhorst, 2015: 178)

It is hard to argue with this statement. The tasks of a developmental state are complex, the challenges great, and success stories relatively few. Questioning why some countries successfully develop while others languish, Weiss and Hobson (1995) identify the need for a 'long term commitment to a developmental project', and behind this a 'will to develop'. This will, they suggest, was stronger in Japan, South Korea, and Taiwan than in Latin American countries, because the East Asian Three faced far greater existential threats to their national independence and security.[6] The threats to Latin American countries, by contrast, were internal rather than external, weakening their ability to build strong state infrastructural power and development coalitions. Others point to the need for disciplining alliances, such as Chibber (2003), who contrasts the Korean state's ability to

[6] Here Weiss and Hobson are drawing on Dore (1990), and Wade (1990). It was not simply the existence of strong, proximate enemies that mattered. The Koumintang in Taiwan was initially focused on retaking mainland China, and pursued a strategy of heavy industrialization rather than catch-up industrialization. The announcement by the United States in 1963 that it would cut its aid in two years' time forced a reorientation towards catch-up industrialization, as it did in South Korea (Weiss and Hobson, 1995).

discipline capital with that of India, whose attempts to build a postwar developmental state were undermined by its capitalists.[7]

But is it possible to have a developmental state in the era of compressed development? The answer to this question depends in part on how we define it, which broadly speaking, may be in terms of (a) basic state orientations, will to develop, for instance; or (b) specific political or institutional configurations or policies. In the first case, concrete institutions or policies may change, but the state may still be considered developmental (rather than predatory, for example). In the second case significant institutional or policy change would mean the end of a developmental state. Our conceptual framework leads us to the former position, as we have noted. Without concrete institutional and policy manifestation, of course, any stated 'will to develop' is in itself is vacuous, but we argue that these may take various forms, and that they will be influenced by the era, compression, as well as country specificities. Here, we present the debate about the fate of the developmental state in a way that highlights these changing forms.

The 'demise' view

A good case for the demise of the developmental state is made in Carroll and Jarvis (2017). Carroll (2017) sees the developmental state as being replaced by the 'variegated market state' (after Brenner, Peck, and Theodore, 2010).[8] He views the developmental state as being historically contingent in the evolution of capitalism, based on the interests of different fractions of capital and capitalist system dynamics. Historical contingencies have changed, and the state has become subject to global market discipline and capitalist competition.

Central to the transition is the relationship between the spatial reorganization of capital—'from Fordist nationally oriented regimes of accumulation to "flexible," transnational regimes'—and successive waves of neoliberal policies and agendas that '*seek to reorder state and society along liberal market lines and instil market discipline*' (95, emphasis in the original). In other words, changes in both states and markets, and their interrelationships, have undermined the developmental state. Embedded autonomy (Evans, 1995) and governed interdependence (Weiss and Hobson, 1995) have given way to something more amorphous and fluid, and attempts to enact developmental policies such as market protectionism,

[7] Davis (2004), too, argues that the state must attain the will and capacity to discipline both capital and labour, and contrasts the disciplining alliance of state and 'rural middle class' in South Korea and Taiwan with Latin American examples.

[8] There are commonalities with Cerny's (1997) 'competition state', in which the 'domestic rationale of the state is over time being supplanted by a not-so-new but increasingly overarching goal – maintaining and promoting competitiveness in a world market place and multi-level political system' (Cerny, 2010: 6). The competition state is a product of economic and political globalization.

capital controls, and industrial policy run the risk of incurring national pariah status, with 'higher borrowing costs, capital flight and marginalization from global markets' (108).

Carroll illustrates his argument with the transformation of South Korea after the Asian Financial Crisis. Its conversion into a variegated market state came through a combination of external imposition by the United States and multilateral institutions, and domestic contestation between those aligned with neoliberal interests, and those opposed. The *chaebol*, once champions of the national developmental project, were transformed into transnational champions, accountable to global shareholders rather than the Korean state and its citizens.

The 'transformation' view

By contrast, neo-developmental-state writing stresses the continued importance of the nation state, possibilities for an agentic state, and evolutionary adaptation to changes in markets and technology. Just as networks became a dominant organizational paradigm from the 1990s (Chapter 3; Bodrožić and Adler, 2017), there have been parallels in state development: Ansell (2000) proposes a 'networked polity' that is 'functionally and territorially disaggregated, but nevertheless linked together and linked to society through a web of interorganizational and intergovernmental relationships' (303). Rather than hierarchically organized on a 'one-to-many' basis, the networked polity is multipolar and organized on a 'many-to-many' basis. At least three types and levels of organization interact organically and flexibly—non-state, public agencies, and macro-state organizations—typically on a project basis, transcending public and private. Authority is diffused, and service provision is decentralized.

More immediately, O'Riain (2000, 2004) sees the tightly coupled 'developmental bureaucratic state' (DBS) giving way to a loosely coupled 'developmental network state' (DNS; or 'flexible developmental state'), whose embedded autonomy derives less from a coherent bureaucracy than from flexibility of the state structure. The DNS attempts to nurture networks of production and innovation within global investment flows. Working with a range of local and global actors, the state itself is more decentralized and flexible.[9] This is the other side of the actor-proliferation and policy-space-compression coins which reveals multiple actors' attractiveness to states as potential aids to state activities rather than simple constraints.

Rather than the demise of the South Korean developmental state, writers from this perspective depict its evolution—for Larson and Park (2014), from a DBS to a

[9] 'The decentralization of state agencies enables them to become deeply embedded in their clients/constituencies, even though they are often dealing with a wide range of individuals and organizations across widely dispersed networks' (O'Riain, 2000: 167).

DNS. This occurred in tandem with the emergence of information and communications technology (ICT) and the subsequent shift to mobile networks and international digital platforms, which limited the power of the state to orchestrate sectoral development. In response, the state hired returnees and consulting firms with technological knowledge and connections to international networks, moving it from bureaucracy to network engagement.[10]

In passing, Japan's developmental state has undergone change, as well, although it has not necessarily become a DNS. On the one hand, the belief that Japan had to devote more resources to basic research, and to coordinate science and technology policy across ministries better, led to a centralization of science and technology policy. On the other, the belief that Japan needed a more diverse and decentralized innovation system led to US-inspired legislation attempting to bring universities into the system, and the promotion of clusters and start-ups. In the aftermath of the 'triple disaster' (earthquake, tsunami, and nuclear) in March 2011, there was a shift towards a 'human-centred, open, sustainable, inclusive and experimentation-driven' vision (Carraz and Harayama, 2019). Decentralization and regional rejuvenation have been key themes since the 2000s.

Both demise and transformation advocates see changes to developmental-state institutions, but differ when it comes to the scope for state agency or autonomy. These differences might derive more from different theoretical starting points than from different empirical observations. From a yet different theoretical perspective, Yeung (2014, 2018) sees the ability of the South Korean, Taiwanese and Singaporean states to orchestrate economic transformation becoming circumscribed from the 1990s, as firms became disembedded from their respective developmental states and re-embedded in global production networks aligned with lead firms, a process he calls 'strategic coupling'. In parallel to this firm disembedding and strategic coupling, states themselves have undergone change through domestic political and economic liberalization. Yeung concludes:

> While the state in these East Asian economies has actively repositioned its role in this changing governance, it can no longer be conceived as the dominant actor in steering domestic industrial transformation. The developmental trajectory of these national economies becomes equally, if not more, dependent on the successful articulation of their domestic firms in global production networks spearheaded by lead firms. In short, the dynamics of global production networks tend to trump state-led initiatives as one of the most critical conditions for economic development. (2014: 74)

[10] The DNS concept has been applied more generally, for example to Chile's attempts to diversify and upgrade its agro-industrial exports. Negoita and Block (2012) propose that network forms of governance are particularly effective in such settings because of increasing uncertainty and risk from competing in a global economy with many nimble, sophisticated competitors, and that this applies to both developing and developed countries.

Not dead in this view, but relegated to playing the role of 'catalyst' of public and private interaction, especially for the development of new technologies. Even here, however, success has been elusive, at least in biotechnology, according to Wong's (2011) study of the same three countries that Yeung focuses on. Confronted with the reality of being unable to manage the uncertainties of biotechnology R&D in spite of massive investments, the respective states reverted to previously successful formulae—comprehensive and complementarity-forming R&D in the case of South Korea, small bets on niches in the case of Taiwan, and attracting global biomedical firms in the case of Singapore. These strategies were not notably successful.

Indeed, the quest for effective industrial and innovation policy took on a new urgency in the wake of the Global Financial Crisis, but success has been elusive (Chapter 5).[11] Interest is particularly focused on technologically dynamic industries in which challenges tend to be greatest. These include biomedical technologies, as noted, but have come to encompass advanced digital technologies such the Internet of Things (IoT), big data, artificial intelligence, and emerging technologies associated with alternative drivetrain and autonomous vehicles and urban mobility.

As we saw in Chapter 5, the temptation to pursue traditional industrial policies aimed at replicating entire value chains remains strong. China is a special case, not just because of its great power ambitions, but also because it has funds (not least through its exports) to make large investments across this gamut of technologies, and in higher-value segments across value chains. 'Made in China 2025' projects a strong emphasis on indigenous innovation and self-sufficiency (Wübbeke et al., 2016). There *may* be fully domestic industries in which traditional industrial policy nurturing SOE 'national champions' can be effective, especially in regulated sectors such as energy (Brandt and Rawski, 2019), and in sectors where the state is a main purchaser. However, it is very risky when technologies are fast-moving, and where filling in all segments of the smiling curve (Chapter 3) can mean huge investments for meagre returns.

In other cases the most promising approach is for policy to focus on niche strategies in GVCs. But even these may be difficult to sustain as such niches by definition operate in global value chain (GVC) markets where competition may be intense, and winner-take-all or winner-take-most dynamic economies might prevail. In brief, while the importance of a state with developmental objectives is undiminished, traditional industrial policy is difficult to sustain, even in countries with large markets. Not only must policies change, but the way they are devised

[11] We use 'industrial policy' in a broad sense here, as 'any type of intervention of government policy that attempts to improve the business environment or to alter the structure of economic activity towards sectors, technologies or tasks that are expected to offer better prospects for economic growth or societal welfare than would occur in the absence of such intervention' (Warwick, 2013: 16).

and implemented must change as well. We see this as bringing about a transformation of the developmental state, rather than its demise.

Cerny (1997) points to the 'relativization' of the embedded nation state as a result of economic and political globalization, stressing supra-national processes in transforming the welfare state into the 'competition state'. But we must also consider transformations *within* nation states, and particularly whether elements of the developmental state have been reconstructed at subnational levels as a result of political, administrative, and economic decentralization. It is to this possibility that we now turn, with a focus in the first instance on China.

Multilevel governance and local developmentalism: the case of China

China is a developmental state according to our orientation-based (rather than institution-specific) perspective. From the standpoint of state–market relations, it is closer to Taiwan and further from Japan and South Korea in the sense that the state has preferred to work with and through SOEs rather than private enterprises in implementing industrial policy, particularly in strategic and upstream industries (Zhu, 2000; Eaton, 2016). This is not surprising, given the common historical roots of the Chinese Communist Party and Koumintang. Reflecting its era of integration into the global economy, moreover, China may also be characterized as a flexible or adaptive developmental state (Zhu, 2012).[12]

However, to focus on the national level alone is to give an incomplete picture of the developmental state in China, and the sources of its flexibility or adaptiveness. Of these, we can point to at least three types of adaptiveness: in the central state's ability to adjust strategic directions and incentive structures; in flexible strategy and policy implementation, particularly at subnational levels; and in diversity generated by local experimentation. On the one hand, therefore, the central state has engaged in the supra-national processes depicted by Cerny, attempting to navigate the 'welter of international governmental and non-governmental associations' and 'huge global consulting industries that instruct national states, organizations and procedures for properly agentic actorhood' (Meyer, 2000: 241). On the other hand, China has combined the central state's agenda and incentive control with decentralization and 'local developmentalism' (Su and Tao, 2017). Indeed, multilevel governance has become a core state capability.

[12] Other designations are possible. 'Developmental', 'entrepreneurial', 'corporatist', 'market-facilitating', 'regulatory', and 'rent-seeking' (Howell, 2006: 282) are just some of the terms that have been used to describe the Chinese state, not to mention a plethora of adjectives modifying 'authoritarian' and 'developmental', suggesting the difficulty of accommodating China to existing models.

We begin this section with some brief comments about management of China's integration into the global economy, reprising some of the discussion in Chapter 5 but from the perspective of politics rather than (re-)industrialization, however our main focus is on subnational rather than supra-national levels of governance. After considering these, we turn to state–civil society relations.

Opening the door—carefully

The major rebalancing of China's state–market dyad, and its (re)industrialization, has taken place in an era of globalization, which has political dimensions, expressed well by Cerny:

> Globalization as a political phenomenon basically means that the shaping of the playing field of politics itself is increasingly determined not within insulated units, i.e. relatively autonomous and hierarchically organized structures called states; rather it derives from a complex congeries of multilevel games played on multi-layered institutional playing fields, above and across, as well as within, state boundaries. These games are played out by *state actors*, as well as market actors and cultural actors. Thus globalization is a process of political *structuration*.
>
> (Cerny, 1997: 253)

China's compressed, multifaceted, and multilevel journey of reform transformation was embarked on cautiously. The initial challenge of international engagement and integration into the global (political) economy was in essence two-fold: overcoming internal resistance to change on the one hand, and ensuring that the influx of external influences did not undermine state development goals on the other. Realizing that a sudden dismantling of regulations controlling global linkages would have been met with enormous resistance by threatened government officials, specific locations, sectors, universities, and even enterprises were deregulated, in what Zweig (2002) called 'segmented deregulation'. Gatekeepers were assigned to manage and monitor opening. When funds for the gatekeepers were cut in the 1990s, they turned their roles into a source of revenue, becoming advocates for further opening, but at the same time maintaining their pursuit of national interests, such as, in the official development assistance field, trying to stop donors from employing foreign advisors.[13] They became adept at leveraging the politics of aid agencies and donors from different countries, similar to the way the central state did when it mediated multinational corporation (MNC) access to

[13] 'From the state's perspective, CPAs [counterpart agencies] protected national security and the prestige of China; monitored the flow of foreign exchange, technology, and foreign values; forced donors to conform to China's national priorities; and limited foreign interests' (Zweig, 2002: 220).

local authorities, firms, and markets, for example, by mandating joint ventures (Zweig, 2002). Thus, the state managed to retain considerable autonomy, even as it was embedded externally through integration with the global (political) economy.

A specific challenge was maintaining that autonomy in the financial sector after China joined the WTO. China's negotiators were under heavy and persistent pressure to open the sector up to foreign participation, not only as a condition of WTO membership, but also internally as a means for rapidly modernizing the sector, and for help in restructuring the bad loans which had mushroomed in the wake of the Asian Financial Crisis (AFC). Equally, however, the country's political and financial leaders viewed the AFC as a cautionary lesson in rapid opening up, and took the path of reforming the sector using the prospect of opening as a lever, thereby forcing through domestic changes. They used foreign consultants, but resisted all-out liberalization (Williams, 2019). These choices should be seen in the context of a state which views money, and finance, as integrally linked to state power. Indeed, the Chinese government has subsequently inserted itself deeply into the information flows of financial intermediation through the social credit system (Selmier, 2019).

The central state was of course not the sole mediator and regulator of the processes of opening up and integration. Tsai (2016) urges us to both disaggregate the state, and deterritorialize the range of actors that constitute society, noting that China and India have the world's largest diaspora populations of 55 and 25 million respectively. She compares three regional/local state and diaspora networks from each country. Actively fostered by the local governments and their overseas offices, the diasporas of Wenzhou and Surat helped to create the 'World's Largest Supermarket for Small Commodities' and the 'Diamond Hub of the World' respectively. As centres of high tech—especially ICT—entrepreneurship, Zhongguancun (a district of Beijing) and Bangalore 'rely on blended domestic and diasporic networks of human, intellectual and social capital' (12). Capital from a multigenerational diaspora played a major role in Guangdong's emergence, while remittances have played an important role in Kerala. Tsai concludes that the combination of local state agency, migratory circulation, and diasporic reinvestment has been crucial to the development of these six localities, and that stretching our conception of state–society relations 'downwards' and 'outwards' is crucial to understand both China and India's integration with the global economy.

China's multilevel governance and adaptive experimentation

Stretching our conception of the Chinese state and state–society relations downwards also adds a crucial dimension to our understanding of the transformation of the developmental state, which in China's case results from selective drawing on the past (Zhu, 2012), trial and error—'feeling for the stones'—and perhaps 'Mao's invisible hand'.[14] China's 'local state corporatism' (Oi, 1992) or 'local developmentalism' (Su and Tao, 2017) is a product of oscillating central–provincial–local state relations.

The gradualist and decentralized 'growing out of the plan' (Naughton, 1995) approach weakened the dominance of the state sector, and central state control. Central state revenues declined markedly during the 1980s, while the July Fourth Tiananmen Square protests were seen as a direct challenge to the state itself. In their wake the state introduced a number of rebalancing measures, including a 'new-style development planning system' in 1993:

> The decentralization of economic decision making and policy implementation of the 1980s served to mobilize local knowledge and to promote policy innovation. But it threatened Beijing's control over macroeconomic policy. New style planning tackled this problem by creating a dynamic, nested hierarchy of political authority. (Heilmann and Melton, 2013: 583)

Decentralization in China rested on the dual mechanisms of what Heilman and Melton call the 'plan-cadre nexus'; state development planning through a hierarchy of policy types, and hierarchical control of Chinese Communist Party (CCP) officials. The combination was critical. Tax reforms increased the central government's share, but left local and regional governments struggling to meet centrally imposed targets. They were given discretion over how to meet those targets, however, and successfully meeting them paved the way for officials' upward promotion in the personnel 'tournament' (Zhou, 2004; Li et al., 2017). Through 'fiscal contracting' and the control exercised through the CCP personnel system, higher levels of government were able to focus on priority challenges, monitoring, and appropriating and diffusing promising local and regional innovations (Zhu, 2012, 2017).[15]

Significantly, the reforms of the early 1990s changed local governments from 'asset owners' (of town and village enterprises and SOEs) to 'tax collectors' (Su and Tao, 2017). Rather than protecting their 'children', local governments competed to attract business, including foreign business, for which they made huge infrastructure investments (including in industrial parks and trade infrastructure, as discussed in Chapter 5). The lynchpin in 'local developmentalism', according to Su and Tao, was (publicly owned) land, which provided a major source of extra-

[14] This refers to the Chinese Communist Party's origins as a guerrilla movement and its need to adapt to local contingencies (Heilmann and Perry, 2011).

[15] 'The incorporation of experimental programs into macro-plans, a tiered hierarchy of policy oversight, newly introduced mid-course evaluations, and systematic top-level policy review have allowed Chinese planners to play a central role in economic policy making without succumbing to the rigidity traps that debased traditional planned economies' (Heilmann and Melton, 2013: 580).

budgetary revenue through leases and land development. These revenues 'enabled regional governments to subsidize incentive packages, including cheap land and tax exemptions, to attract footloose manufacturing capital' (242; Rithmire, 2017).

Local officials had a strong incentive both to appropriate land, and to push real estate values higher. This caused bubbles, rising debt levels, and ghost cities, as well as evictions, while young urbanites were often unable to afford housing, with knock-on effects on marriage and childbirth rates. It also caused environmental degradation.[16] To counter the negative effects, and to achieve greater standardization, 'soft centralization' was reimposed by the central government. Administrative regulation, financial regulation and commodity management were assigned to the *provincial* level (Mertha, 2005).

Provincial governments, meanwhile, developed their own projects crossing metropolitan boundaries, drawing on special funds from the central government (Jaros, 2016a, 2016b). Such funds were also available for cross-provincial projects. Heilmann and Melton (2013) observe that in addition to promoting regional development and policy coordination, regional plans created a policy space which enabled local officials to address problems creatively, and find solutions appropriate for local conditions which could then be adopted nationally. Thematic 'special plans', cutting across departments and jurisdictions, played a similar role.

In sum, by circumstances, trial and error, China evolved a system of multilevel governance combining bottom-up economic dynamism and top-down framework setting, with competition at multiple levels. The balance changed over time; early decentralization was modified in the 1990s, but it provided new incentives to metropolitan and provincial governments, based on 'creative' policy interpretation and implementation, with land as a key resource. The system was based on a hierarchy of regulations and plans with different degrees of compulsion and permissiveness. Jurisdictions overlapped, and creative interpretations were tacitly encouraged, but central control was maintained through the parallel personnel promotion system. The inter-urban and inter-province competition encouraged by this loose governance structure led to speculative over-extensions in infrastructure and urban development, as well as environment degradation, but helped to fuel China's rapid growth. The past tense is used because the system continues to evolve, with Xi Jinping's ascent marking a new phase of centralization.

In seeking to retain oversight and to focus on system design and implementation, the central state has been a developmental state. But it is very different from those of East Asian late developers, and all the while it has been stretched, and has struggled in terms of policy integration. Balancing the excesses of local developmentalism

[16] By some estimates, between 40–50 million peasants had lost their land by the 2000s (Huang, 2009: 17).

with social and environmental issues remains an ongoing challenge, and it has been an important motivation for China's industrial policies promoting solar power and electric vehicles.

State–society relations and social corporatism

China's local developmentalism was focused on economic growth. Su and Tao (2017: 247) lament the growth coalition of local governments, manufacturers, financial institutions, and real estate developers that 'has gradually formed to perpetuate this unsustainable path', and conclude that 'local governments in China have become one major force behind the destruction of society'. But could society fight back? Could 'civil society' in China play a role in shaping socioeconomic outcomes?

In fact, in Howell's (2012) view, in order to promote the market—capitalist development—the state *had to* promote civil society, while also seeking to constrain it. The 'two-pronged approach of control and engagement' by central and local governments 'is driven by the need to facilitate the emergence of a civil society that will advance capitalist interests and maintain political stability' (272). Old institutions of intermediation proved insufficient for the challenges of economic growth and the increasing complexity of society, so the state had to promote the formation of various associations and create a more open space for intellectuals, but also cracked down when it feared these were getting out of control (Howell, 2012). The state was incapable of meeting all the challenges of its reforms, and facilitated the growth of civil society organizations to provide support, especially in areas of social welfare and services to migrant workers.

In other words, because of compression-induced policy stretch, the state encouraged civil society, while also seeking to control it. It did so by using the system of hierarchical control used for business organizations, with different types of organization overseen by different levels of state according to their strategic importance, their ability to challenge the government, and the value of the public goods they provide (Kang and Han, 2008). Nonetheless, Howell is critical of situating civil society organizations in a state corporatist framework, noting that many—most—organizations are not registered, despite a formal requirement to do so.

Han (2016) analyzes three categories of social organization in China; 'social associations' (SAs) which are membership-based and often organized by the state;[17] nonprofit organizations (NPOs), which are bottom-up social service providers and grassroots organizations; and public and private foundations,

[17] These seem to equate with government-organized NGOs, or GONGOs.

specialized in fund raising and grant making. Using Schmitter's (1974) distinction, he argues that SAs represent the face of 'state corporatism', while the rise of the latter categories indicates the emergence of 'social corporatism', marked by independent initiation and leadership, uptake of members' interests, and attempts to influence policy. Significantly, the number of NPOs increased almost fifty-fold between 1999 and 2014, from 6000 to 292,000, while the number of SAs only doubled, from 135,000 to 300,000. In 1999 the proportion of SAs to NPOs was 96:4, but by 2014 the ratio had shifted to 51:48, while the number of private foundations outnumbered public foundations by almost 2:1.

Although limited in their ability to challenge state power, civil society organizations in China are sometimes able to 'exploit the regulations to use the supervisory agency as an access point to policymakers whom they otherwise could not reach' (Teets, 2017: 1). The policymakers, in turn, gain access to 'bottom-up' information, and support when ideas, and not just interests, overlap (Teets, 2017). Such organizations thus provide feedback and services to the state at various levels. When it becomes protest, the state may try to placate protestors, or failing that, to compensate victims, and to suppress those seen as rebels.

Summing up, as Heilmann and Melton (2013: 617) note, 'it is clear that the Chinese planning system is not capable of dealing with everything it claims to address at once'. This is the reality of policy stretch. But through adaptive processes and incentive structures the Chinese state created a system which unlocked local energies—with both positive and negative results—and enabled the central government to maintain overall control, and focus its energies on pressing, core issues. It is a distinctive 'embedded autonomy' which has prioritized economic goals over social policy, albeit with some rebalancing. The state also built an external facing 'embedded autonomy' which leveraged external resources and technologies for change, without being over-run by them. The multilevel and local governance system, and the role of civil society organizations, continue to evolve in the Xi Jinping era.

'Fast cities'

Local developmentalism is closely linked to rapid urbanization, or what Zhang and Chen (2010) refer to as China's 'compressed urbanization'. In fact, in parts of the global South urbanization has come to be seen as a (financialized) substitute for industrialization.[18] This is evident in 'smart' city projects. From East Asia to the Middle East, Africa and Latin America, there has been a vogue for eco-city,

[18] Goodfellow (2017), and earlier Lefebvre (1970), and Harvey's (1978, 1985) theorization of a 'secondary circuit of capital'. Gollin, Jedwab, and Vollrath (2016) depict 'urbanization without industrialization'.

smart-city, and related transformation projects in recent years.[19] Some are literally designed from scratch, with a master plan assuming a blank 'canvas' outside or between existing cities. Smart cities are marketed on the prospect of leapfrogging into the future, and of leaving behind traditional problems of urbanization such as overcrowding, traffic congestion, and pollution. Technology is invoked as the solution to social and environmental problems, as well as an accelerant of economic development. Such projects tend to bring together governments at multiple levels, and networks of international actors. Public–private partnerships (PPPs) are common, and public–private distinctions are blurred in the project management corporations set up to oversee implementation.

By early 2017, almost 300 cities in China had registered to become smart cities, and had signed contracts with major IT companies, and by the end of the year, most provincial capitals and prefecture-level cities had done the same.[20] The figures were similar for eco cities.[21] The allure of such projects is strong, even though some of the early projects have run into trouble.[22]

Impressed by the urban growth he observed in Shenzhen, (then) Gujarat State Chief Minister Narendra Modi returned to India to launch the Gujarat International Finance Tec-City, to be built in five years. Modi also proposed the construction of Dholera, and, subsequently, as Prime Minister, started the India '100 Smart City Mission' in 2015. Although Dholera does not exist yet—its basic infrastructure projects were started in 2018—the scale of the plan is staggering.[23] Designed by UK-based Halcrow, the master plan envisages a city of over 900 square kilometres by 2040; twice the size of present-day Mumbai, and larger than Singapore. Another colossal project is Amaravati, a new state capital for Andhra Pradesh designed by UK-based Foster and Partners, loosely modelled on Singapore (and Venice for the obligatory canals). It, too, was originally meant to be built in five years.

Rapid urbanization, urban utopianism, and techno-urbanism are by no means new. However: 'What is different in Dholera today is that it is driven by a sense of urgency . . . which justifies the speeding up of law-making, regulations and politics to enable a new city to quickly materialize' (Datta, 2015: 5). Speed has become a

[19] See, for example, Watson (2014) for African cities. As of early 2017, eleven countries had joined the Smart Africa Initiative, which signed a partnership agreement with Ericsson to promote connectivity and knowledge-based society in Africa. Smart cities have proliferated in Latin America, with backing from the Inter-American Development Bank, amongst others. A G20 Global Smart Cities Alliance was formed in 2019.

[20] <http://www.chinadaily.com.cn/china/2017–04/21/content_29024793.htm>, accessed 9 August 2017.

[21] <http://www.citymetric.com/skylines/can-hundreds-new-ecocities-solve-chinas-environmental-problems-1306>, accessed 9 August 2017.

[22] Troubled cases include Caofeidian, and Dongtan, which was slated to become the world's first eco city under plans drawn up by London-based Arup in 2005, under an agreement with Shanghai Industrial Investment Corporation. Even Tianjin Eco-city, with strong public support from the central Chinese and Singaporean governments, has struggled. See Morera (2017).

[23] Ahmedabad-Dholera is itself just one of eight special investment regions and one of sixteen 'nodes' in the massive Delhi Mumbai Industrial Corridor project.

modus operandi, a justification in itself for changing laws, cutting through red tape, streamlining approval processes, favouring certain parties, and silencing others. Datta and Shaban (2017) label this modus operandi 'fast cities'.

> Speed continues to be a prerequisite to conceptualizing and legitimizing these cities as 'solutions' to the crises of urbanization, migration and climate change. Speed builds upon the rhetorics of urgency but takes it further in producing a range of visions, imageries and fantasies of time-space compression that expedite the circulation of global capital and its materialization into new cities in different regions. (Datta, 2017: 3)

Speed and the 'rhetorics of urgency' are a means to bypass the 'failures' of existing megacities. Fast is contrasted with the 'slow' way of doing things in the past. To deliver speed, governments have to become more involved rather than less, but through quasi private corporations which transact with international and domestic private businesses on a commercial (though not necessarily transparent) basis. Fast city projects concentrate the tensions and contradictions of compressed development. Beneath the promise of technological solutions, enterprise and efficiency is the reality of land, its acquisition, and commercialization. 'Empty' land typically contains villages and farms, meaning that dispossession, corruption, and the silencing of inconvenient claims are common.[24] In Dholera's case, the 'blank canvas' has been home to roughly 40,000 local residents, mainly farmers.[25] Not surprisingly, a grass roots land-rights movement has been protesting against this and other smart cities in the region.

It is possible that 'bottlenecks' caused by protests will encourage governments to seek early citizen engagement. There are signs of this in China, which may be further along the smart-city learning curve. But the current reality in many developing countries is that civil society organizations are expected to deal with the consequences, rather than to play a meaningful part in the planning, implementation, and review processes. Fast and smart cities bring the tensions between economic and social development, and paradoxes of the developmental state under compressed development, into sharp relief.

Bringing civil society in

Our use of the term 'civil society' might be questioned. The examples from China and India are a long way from the understanding of civil society which evolved in

[24] D'Costa's (2014) capital intensive and primitive accumulation aspects of 'compressed capitalism'. His third aspect—the informal sector—does not feature in the plans, but by implication it will be present, servicing the needs of the aspiring and connected professionals.

[25] The low population density is related to periodic flooding; in fact 1cm of local coastline is lost to the sea every day (*The Guardian*, 17 April 2014).

the European context from the eighteenth century, contributing both to the growth of liberal democracy, as well as the welfare state (Powell, 2007). In our examples, states have a strong influence over civil society, and civil society organizations do not necessarily press for either liberal democracy or universal social welfare.[26] In particular, the governments of East Asian late developers were reluctant to divert resources and energy from economic development into building substantial public welfare provision, with the partial exception of Japan in the postwar period (Chapter 6). When forced by political or labour movements to make concessions, they did so hesitantly, rather than with universal policies, sometimes using civil society organizations, or government-organized nongovernmental organizations (GONGOs). The resulting 'welfare gap' was exposed in the wake of the AFC, and has become critical with rapid individualization and demographic ageing (Kamimura, 2018).[27]

Compression also contributes to the differences in the role of civil society. Sandbrook et al. (2007) identify two sets of impediments to the development of independent civil society and especially social democracy in developing countries in recent decades that map onto our compression and era factors. The impediments have caused promising movements to degenerate into ethnic conflict, coups, populism, corruption, or economic decline.

The first set is external pressures, or what we have called 'era' influences, which have been the subject matter of preceding chapters, and need little elaboration here. The second is compression. Here the authors cite industrialization, democratization, and social citizenship, which unfolded sequentially over a century in now-developed countries, from industrialization in the mid-nineteenth century, through democratization in the late-nineteenth and early twentieth centuries, to social citizenship in the postwar era. The simultaneity of the three in contemporary developing countries means that class compromises are pursued before industrialization has created a strong material base for their stability. Hence 'social-democratic pacts or class compromises, if forged, will be more complicated and fragile in the global periphery'.[28]

In his case studies of civil society in Brazil, India, and South Africa, Heller (2013) notes the shared problem that top-down central state developmental policies are often ineffective at the local level, and as with the Chinese state, the

[26] There are, to be sure, wide variations in civil society engagement with local developmentalism in India, but in many cases, civil society leaves untouched the 'massive neglect of the interests of the unprivileged' (Dreze and Sen, 2011: 10). Indeed, civil society participation itself can be used to justify 'a communitarian ethic that leaves the structures of intra-group inequalities intact' (Mahajan, 1999: 1194).

[27] Kamimura additionally notes that families remained the primary welfare unit in East Asia, limiting the growth of European-style civil society, and, ultimately, the welfare state. On the importance of civil society organizations in Japan's economic growth and postwar recovery, see for example: Garron (1998, 2003); Schwartz and Pharr (2003); Kage (2011).

[28] Sandbrook et al. (2007: 21).

three countries have tried to strengthen local civil society and citizen participation. This has been an important motivation for decentralization, in fact. But while compressed developers may have more of a developmental need to promote civil society than late developers, they also typically attempt to restrain it. The result in China's case has been cycles of encouragement and restraint, and elsewhere, inconsistencies.

There are exceptions in which civil society movements have helped to create 'social democratic developmental states' (SDDS). Sandbrook et al. (2007) cite four such cases: Kerala in India, Costa Rica, Mauritius, and (post-1990) Chile. Preconditions for the SDDS, they argue, include early and deep integration into the global capitalist economy, which transforms pre-capitalist social relations, weakening of the power of landlords and strengthening of working and middle classes, and the growth of a robust civil society; as well as critical junctures in which social actors come together to form coalitions, such as small farmers and workers combining with discipline, but not ultimately threatening private property of the business elite (Sandbrook et al., 2007).

This is a difficult juggling and balancing act. Even in Europe, social democracy has undergone significant change, if not deterioration. The postwar welfare state has gradually transformed into the 'social investment state', with redistribution curtailed in favour of enabling economic participation.[29] New challenges loom, such as new social divisions and inequalities associated with the digital economy, and environmental degradation and climate change. Once again, compressed developers will be forced to address these more quickly, and with fewer resources, heightening the need for a vibrant civil society and state–civil society engagement. In fact, in these new challenges, civil society is important for another reason, namely the potential for states and market actors to collude against their citizens, in digital surveillance of citizens, for example, or when states fail to react quickly enough to climate change. Civil society will play an important role in both rebalancing of the digital economy and the re-embedding of markets, both in developed and developing countries (Chapter 9).

Concluding comments

Whether the developmental (nation) state has been dismantled or transformed depends on one's definition and theoretical perspective. Certainly, the states of East Asian late developers have changed, and the states of developing and transition countries are quite different from the classical developmental states. That is only to be expected; economic and geopolitical systems, organizational

[29] Ferrara (2010); Leoni (2016); Busemeyer et al. (2018).

paradigms, and technologies are different in the era of compressed development than in earlier eras. All the while compression has posed extra challenges for countries that engage in developmentalism. The need for flexibility or adaptiveness is greater than ever.

We have considered how China and to some extent India have navigated the challenges of growth through integration into the global economy, without presenting either as a model. The two countries are in some ways unique, given their size, but they—especially China—show that adaptiveness is partly derived from multilevel governance structures and incentives. Actor proliferation and the politics of speed, evident in smart-city projects, highlight the possibilities and problems of compressed development. Local developmentalism and flexible state–business interaction may promote growth, but they also create new problems. They embody twin paradoxes, that its responses to policy stretch and the challenges of compressed development push the state towards flexibility, yet this makes it more difficult to achieve policy coherence and integration (at a time when these have become increasingly necessary); and second, that the politics of speed and promotion of rapid growth tend to marginalize social development and the environment, even as they become more critical.

States may turn to civil society to ease these paradoxes, and may also seek to control it at the same time. Civil society contributes both to actor proliferation and the problem of policy coherence and integration, and to addressing the double burdens and simultaneous challenges of compressed development. There is an especially urgent need for social and environmental issues to be addressed through expanded state–civil society concertation. But there is also a need for civil society to hold both states and markets to account, and to push towards a new 're-embedding' of markets. Just what this re-embedding might look like will depend on other factors, including geopolitics, which we turn to in Chapter 9.

9
Are We All Compressed Developers?

Introduction

In 2016 the World Bank stopped using the term 'developing country' in its World Development Indicators and policy documents. The world cannot meaningfully be divided into developed and developing groups, it reasoned. Differences *within* less-developed countries (LDCs) have become more pronounced, while, by some indicators, differences between developing and developed countries have closed markedly in the past half century. This thinking is also evident in the transition in 2015 from the United Nations Millennium Development Goals, which focused on developing countries, to the Sustainable Development Goals (SDGs), which were conceived more globally. 'The SDG views every country as needing development, and it's universal.'[1] Indeed, many contemporary economic, social, public health and environmental challenges are global in both cause and effect. On the other hand, income differences between countries remain stark and seemingly intractable, as suggested by Figure 0.1; from an entirely different perspective, terms like 'developing' and 'emerging' could also be seen as problematic, as they suggest inevitable progress.

None of these distinctions—convergence on some indicators, continued divergence on others, and the emergence of new global challenges—contradict the fact that world *has* become more interconnected. We start this chapter by turning the lens around to consider the effects of compressed development on now-developed (industrialized, high income) countries. We do so from two perspectives. The first is co-evolution. Influences flow not only from developed to LDCs, but in the reverse direction as well. Simply put, the production systems described in this book are co-evolutionary; the new roles taken up by recent developers are related to, and to some extent triggered by, changes in the roles played by developed countries, and *vice versa*. With technology as an accelerant, a global 'Red Queen' effect has come into play, in which nearly *all* countries have to run faster even to stay in the same place. Where LDCs have to contend with *thin* industrialization, in a system with high levels of global integration, developed countries face selective *de*industrialization and job-light vertical specialization in the innovation segments of GVCs.

[1] Umar Serajuddin, Senior Economist, World Bank, cited in Fernholz (2016).

Compressed Development: Time and Timing in Economic and Social Development. D. Hugh Whittaker, Timothy J. Sturgeon, Toshie Okita, and Tianbiao Zhu, Oxford University Press (2020). © D. Hugh Whittaker, Timothy J. Sturgeon, Toshie Okita, and Tianbiao Zhu. DOI: 10.1093/oso/9780198744948.001.0001

Second, being forced to run faster and face postindustrial transitions sooner means constant structural change and seemingly intractable institutional pressures that call for new policy responses and adjustments. Andrioni and Chang (2018: p. 11) cogently frame contemporary pressures on developmental industrial policy in this way: '(T)he economic system will be in a never-ending condition of disequilibrium. Within this framework industrial policies will be necessary for addressing at different stages of development (not just underdevelopment!), various structural tensions, institutional bottlenecks and dualisms.' This applies equally to developing as well as developed countries. Industrial policies the world over increasingly require constant coordination and adjustment across a range of governmental and nongovernmental actors, which is extremely challenging for all. In addition, these issues must be addressed with institutions developed in different eras and adjusting at different speeds. In these two senses—co-evolution, and temporal adjustment and coordination—we might say that '*we are all compressed developers now*'.

In the first section of this chapter, therefore, we consider how the forces of co-evolution and compression are being experienced in the United States and Japan, and how these experiences are being shaped by developments in China, in particular. We then turn towards the future and consider whether it is reasonable to talk of a historic 'great convergence' between North and South, as information and communications technology (ICT) has enabled an unbundling of production stages to where they can be carried out most cost effectively, which is often in the global South (Baldwin, 2016), or if the dualisms and inequalities of uneven development will be maintained, or further deepen.[2] We do this by returning to our dyads. In the second section we consider how the digital economy might unfold. In particular, we look at implications for the geographic distribution of economic activity—whether manufacturing will continue to be relocated to the global South, or whether it will be 'reshored'. A notable aspect of the evolution of GVCs has been the geographic separation of production and innovation, with production progressively outsourced and offshored, and innovation at both ends of the 'smiling curve' remaining at 'home'. We therefore look at the implications of new technologies and tools in the digital economy for production and innovation separately, as well as together. Could either or both of these could undergo significant geographical reconfiguration? We also consider how the digital economy and platform organizational paradigm may unfold in the near future, specifically the prospects for a new 'balancing cycle'.

Next, we look at changes to the state–market dyad, and potential upheavals in state–market relations. As well, from recent events, it seems clear that geopolitics will re-emerge as a major influence on the development trajectories of both

[2] See also Spence, 2012; Grinin and Koroteyev (2015); Mahbubani (2013, 2018).

developed and LDCs. A number of concurrent and interlocking crises could trigger a rebalancing, or a new Polanyian 're-embedding'. The crises are political (Trump and Brexit to start with);[3] financial (shocks, scandals, and tax-haven abuse); technological (abuse of data and monopoly positions by 'Big Tech'); and environmental (dislocations from climate change). Liberal market capitalism (LMC) shrugged off a challenge to the World Trade Organization (WTO) Ministers Meeting in Seattle in 1999, and survived the Global Financial Crisis (GFC) in 2007–2008, but there has been a belated recognition, even in LMC heartlands, that drastic reform is necessary. Consider the following, all in August and September 2019:

- The US Business Roundtable (a bastion of LMC) issued a statement, signed by most of its members, that the corporation's role goes beyond making profits for its shareholders to encompass customers, employees, suppliers and communities.
- The UK's *Financial Times* (an information hub of LMC) called for a 'better form of capitalism' under the banner 'Capitalism: Time for a Reset'.
- The International Monetary Fund (IMF) co-produced a report lamenting that 40 per cent of foreign direct investment (FDI) in 2017—some $15 trillion—flowed into 'phantom' special purpose entity shells in tax havens (Damgaard, 2019).
- A bipartisan group of forty US state attorneys general announced an anti-trust investigation into tech giants Facebook and Google, an indication that the age of lax regulation of Big Tech was coming to an end.
- In California a bill was passed that requires Uber, Lyft, and other gig companies to treat their workers as employees.
- A global 'climate strike' preceding the UN Climate Summit (21–23 September 2019), and further strikes after the summit, signalled a growing global civil society movement which is certain to have an impact on how business is conducted in the future.

Finally, and perhaps most significantly, the ongoing trade war between the United States and China—a struggle between the existing dominant global power and a rising power respectively—is casting a pall over the global economy, with very high stakes for the future. What sense do we make of these crises? Have we worked to define compressed development only to find, at the end, that we are writing its obituary? Given that some of the crises are reminiscent of the chaotic

[3] Connecting to our discussion in Chapter 6, the circumstances leading to the election of Trump and the 'leave' result of the Brexit referendum may be linked to a thinning and weakening of the middle class, a trend which has been particularly severe in liberal market or welfare regime countries such as the United States and UK (Pressman, 2007; OECD, 2019), but it forms a backdrop to the growing waves of protests in many countries.

period between early late development and late-late development, might we be entering a period of transition towards 'late compressed development', or simply a descent into chaos and conflict?

Co-evolution and compression: the United States and Japan

Global economic integration, the increasing involvement of multilateral institutions and nongovernmental organizations (NGOs) in the development process, and the growing influence of international consultancies in the formulation of social policy have all historically been driven by powerful actors centred in OECD countries, especially the United States. The continuation of a postwar geopolitical stance based not only on US military power but on the notion that global conflict could be avoided by lifting the 'developing world' out of poverty was bound to become frayed as large LDCs advanced in both economic and military terms. Supporting huge transformational efforts such as China 2025 and the Belt and Road Initiative through development institutions such as the United Nations Industrial Development Organization and the World Bank was bound to become controversial, particularly given the resources being deployed by the Chinese state to challenge the technological leadership of OECD countries and project economic power across large swathes of the globe. Just as compressed development has changed the calculus for the developmental state, it seems only a matter of time before the engines of the world economy have to reckon with a more multipolar world, and be forced to adapt, not only to the rise of new competitors—which has happened before with the postwar ascendency of Japan and Germany—but with competitors whose economies are deeply woven into GVCs. In this section, we briefly sketch out these processes for the United States and Japan, and how the rise of China in particular has had domestic consequences for both countries. These include social polarization in the United States, as well as in Japan, albeit in less extreme form.

The United States: the 'new model' under pressure

Michael Best (2018) attributes the United States' rise to global dominance to its ability to combine mass production and innovation. Although the seeds were sewn earlier, during and after World War II the United States developed the remarkable capability of applying mass production to military hardware and to innovation in weaponry at the same time. Germany had advantages in innovation, but not in mass production. Thus:

> [The United States'] unmatched performance can be measured by comparing national rates of expansion in munitions production over the period from 1935–39

> to 1944: it was 7 times in Germany, 10 times in the Soviet Union, 15 times in Japan, 22 times in the United Kingdom, and *140 times in the United States.*
>
> (Best, 2018: 25, emphasis in the original)

This highly productive mass production-with-innovation system was carried over into the postwar period, encapsulated in the large, vertically integrated enterprises discussed in Chapter 3. The 'Fordist' organizational paradigm produced waves of new products conceived in central research laboratories and delivered to markets through a linear innovation-production process. Combined with the Bretton Woods system, stable oil prices, and high marginal tax rates that kept government coffers full, it helped to create a 'golden era' for the United States and its allies, which lasted until the late 1960s.

Things changed from the 1970s and 1980s, as outlined in Chapters 2 and 3. The age of cheap oil ended; domestic firms internationalized;[4] imports increased; trade deficits climbed; and enemies-turned-pupils-and-allies Germany and Japan began to challenge US dominance in a progression of industries. Profitability in US corporations declined, and investors started to chafe. By the mid-1980s the 'Fordist' age was all but over, and it appeared as if US manufacturing was in decline, perhaps terminally. But in fact, it was undergoing systemic change towards the network organizational paradigm, a trend that was driven by and fostered further financialization.

The 'new American model' (Sturgeon, 2002) had four interconnected elements—financialization, a focus on seeking competitive advantage from intellectual property and intangible rather than fixed assets, the adoption and diffusion of information technology, and the global projection of these elements via global value chains (GVCs). Under pressure to raise profits, US companies began to strip out equity in exchange for debt (Mazzucato, 2018), focus on intangible assets at both ends of the 'smiling curve' (design and high-value components in the upstream end of the value chain and marketing and retailing on the downstream end) and to outsource and offshore the lower-value-yielding segments in between, particularly manufacturing. This was dependent on the effective governance of GVCs, which became a new source of competitiveness. The effective governance of GVCs was in turn enabled by product, process, and value-chain modularity and new uses of ICT. A potential danger in this system was the loss of intellectual property or its devaluing from the standardization needed to support modularity (Chesbrough and Kusunoki, 2001). Hence, intellectual property rights (IPR) became increasingly prominent in new trade agreements, the nature of which shifted from traditional trade restrictions to

[4] Large US companies that had closed or had their foreign affiliates nationalized during the war 're-internationalized' afterwards.

regulatory standards convergence and IPR protection (Durand and Milberg, 2019; Manger, 2014).

The wave of outsourcing and offshoring that came with the network organizational paradigm, accompanied by domestic and cross-border consolidation at the lead firm and key supplier level, led to a geographic separation of innovation from production in key industries, as described in Chapter 3. While the US trade balance in services (including technology licences) remained positive, the deficit with China in goods soared to US $382 billion in 2018 (see Figure 9.1).

This trend was important—and much discussed—throughout the 1990s, but the historically unprecedented surge came after China's accession to the WTO in December 2001. Not coincidentally, this came on the heels of the bursting of the 'technology bubble', which sent US manufacturers scrambling to cut costs and access 'big emerging markets' in China, India, and Brazil, moves than often came with requirements to set up local production and (reluctantly and partially, at best) transfer technology to local joint venture partners, as detailed in Chapter 5.

The social impact in the United States was enormous. Wealth accumulation in the few postal codes hosting the new titans of the digital economy (mainly in Silicon Valley and Seattle) was both extreme and conspicuous, while adjustment pain was severe across deindustrialized states in the Midwest where Fordist enterprises and their captive supply chains had reigned supreme—regions largely ignored by politicians and coastal pundits. At the same time the benefits of China trade were broadly diffused across the country as low consumer prices, making them hard to detect and blunting their political potency.

In this way, the 'China shock' set the stage for the political upheavals of 2016 and beyond. Autor et al. (2016, abstract) note:

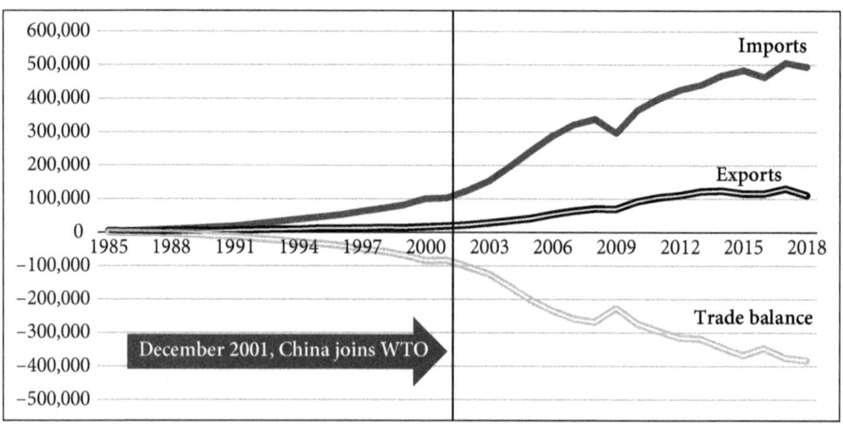

Figure 9.1 US goods trade with China, 1985–2019

Note: Figures are in US million dollars on a nominal basis, not seasonally adjusted.

Source: US Census Bureau: <https://www.census.gov/foreign-trade/balance/c5700.html>.

> China's emergence as a great economic power has induced an epochal shift in patterns of world trade. Simultaneously, it has challenged much of the received empirical wisdom about how labour markets adjust to trade shocks. Alongside the heralded consumer benefits of expanded trade are substantial adjustment costs and distributional consequences. These impacts are most visible in the local labour markets in which the industries exposed to foreign competition are concentrated. Adjustment in local labour markets is remarkably slow, with wages and labour-force participation rates remaining depressed and unemployment rates remaining elevated for at least a full decade after the China trade shock commenced. Exposed workers experience greater job churning and reduced lifetime income. At the national level, employment has fallen in U.S. industries more exposed to import competition, as expected, but offsetting employment gains in other industries have yet to materialize.

When they have materialized, they have been less secure jobs in the service sector, and increasingly in the digitally mediated 'gig economy'. At the same time, the United Sates' position at the frontier of innovation accelerated as more companies adapted to and drove the network model. A novel feature of the new, networked forms of innovation were systems of 'open innovation' (Chesbrough, 2003; Von Hippel, 2017), which featured the pre-competitive pooling of R&D activities and generic design criteria. Gibbons et al. (1994) argue that these changes are part of a fundamental shift, in which the production of new knowledge has become more fluid and less encapsulated by single institutions or disciplines, and trans-disciplinary and trans-institutional teams come together for short periods to solve specific problems and develop urgently needed applications. Importantly, both the restructured production system and the new innovation system were financialized. Indeed, finance played a key role in shifting resources between the two, for example when US manufacturers were rewarded by institutional investors for selling factories to contract manufacturers to focus on competing via their intangible assets (Lazonick, 2009).

While the network model worked well for the principal actors for a time, with financialized growth in the United States and industrial growth in places like China, it is a Red Queen system, with successful compressed developers that have mastered mass production now seeking to leverage the global technologies and open innovation resources, supply chains and logistics infrastructures, and open financial (and investment) markets put in place to support GVCs. The social and political tensions from this interplay have been laid bare since the GFC of 2007–2008, and even more notably since 2016, as the rise of neo-nationalism has become apparent. As of this writing there is an ongoing trade and techology war between the United States and China, with the Trump Administration's 'America First' policies mirrored by China's techno-nationalist 'China 2025' industrial policies that have the stated goal of challenging the West's technological dominance in short order.[5]

Japan: between the United States and emerging Asia, and between paradigms

Japan's postwar rise was based on its mastery and extension of mass production techniques, combined with quality, in a 'productionist' system. It was complemented by 'patient capital' and lifetime employment, macroeconomic stability, and a range of supportive government financial, industrial, and social policies which achieved a high degree of fit, or 'institutional interlock' and 'motivational congruence' (Dore, 1987). In hindsight this fit, and its very success, created rigidities—a 'Stinchcombe effect'—which arguably made it difficult for Japan to change when its environment changed. This featured the emergence of the new US network organization paradigm and its heavy reliance on ICT, and also an emerging Asia, especially China's integration into the global economy. Sandwiched in between, Japan did in fact change, but this weakened the systemic fit of its component institutions.

We left Japan in Chapter 4 at about 1980, determined to end the 'catch-up' phase of its development and to chart a new path, not only in education policy, but in finance and industry as well. In practice, the 1980s were marked by intensifying trade friction and massive currency appreciation.[6] The desire for change and external pressures came together in the Maekawa Report (1986), which envisaged a structural shift towards domestic demand, and called for Japan to become a 'giant in living', as well as in production. The accompanying policy changes, and partial liberalization by the Nakasone administration, began to unwind the postwar system.

Unsurprisingly, one result of trade friction and appreciation of the yen was a surge in outward foreign direct investment, mostly to North America and Europe, but adding to Japan's existing footprint in Southeast Asia, as well, especially in the machine industries.[7] Hatch and Yamamura (1996: 7) note that: 'As of 1994, there were 800 Japanese affiliates in Asia manufacturing electrical machinery. There were 413 in the United States and Europe combined.' Many of the features that characterized domestic Japanese business, including tight linkages to group

[5] Nissan et al. (2018). The conflict has also been cast as an 'AI Arms Race' or 'AI Cold War': Thompson and Bremmer (2018).

[6] Following the Plaza Accord in 1985 the Yen-Dollar rate surged from roughly ¥240:$1 to ¥160:$1 less than a year later, and it kept climbing to ¥79:$1 in 1995.

[7] This designation includes autos and machinery, but Japanese factories of the period were also mass producing household appliances as a way to jump over tariff walls and serve and build brand loyalty among local consumers that in many cases were buying such 'modern' products for the first time.

suppliers, the authors argue, were reproduced on an Asia-wide scale. Asia, especially Southeast Asia, was 'in Japan's embrace', albeit temporarily.

Japan's postwar developmental state objectives required that finance serve industry, and traditional industrial policy could not function without it. The financial sector was gradually liberalized, under the influence of economists who believed that a 'liberalized environment was required in order to promote decentralized innovation and more diverse corporate organization . . . This vision . . . served as the intellectual background of the evolution of state apparatus in general' (Lechevalier et al., 2017: 8). At the corporate level, the increasing presence of foreign shareholders and activist funds put pressure on managers to devote more time to investor relations and to raise returns on equity. But any moves towards wholesale embrace of the 'new American model' were blunted. There was resistance to shareholder interest *maximization*, and to abandoning what propelled Japan to postwar prominence, namely excellence in manufacturing, or *monozukuri*, and tight linkages to group suppliers in the interest of in-group complementarities. This resistance, or attachment, was also at the root of Japan's partial adoption the other elements of the 'new American model'. The challenge from US companies that had fully embraced the network model such as Dell and Apple posed a series of difficult questions for managers of Japanese IT companies, captured in a series of interviews by Sturgeon (2006, p. 62):

> Suppose we do away with all of our plants and fire all of our workers? If we were driven to this we might do it, but in Japan you can't do this. It is our policy to protect jobs. It is part of our mission as a company. So, we must continue to develop products that cannot easily be outsourced. Putting parts together is the job of a trading company. We are not a trading company. This is why we cannot do what Apple has done (Japanese electronics executive, March 2004).

Emerging competition from Korean, Taiwanese, and then mainland Chinese companies in industries such as consumer electronics and home appliances also took its toll, with formerly dominant brands (Sony, Panasonic, Toshiba, etc.) suffering from high prices through over-engineering and excessive quality, and sometimes from continued reliance on high-cost domestic manufacturing, forcing a retreat or focus on high-value material, components, and machinery. Sharp was the first mass producer of flat panel displays, and was the world's leading photovoltaic (PV) solar cell producer from 2000–2007, just as the Chinese PV industries were being established. By 2010 China's Suntech was the world's largest producer of solar panels, and Sharp itself was acquired by Taiwan's Hon Hai Precision Industry (Foxconn) in 2016. Even in motorcycles, where Japan's global dominance in many segments was once undisputed: 'Across the region, Japanese companies are finding themselves playing catch-up. In Mandalay, Myanmar's second-largest city, hardly any Hondas or Yamahas can be found among the multitudes of motorbikes, nearly all of which come from China...'[8] And even paragons of catch-up industrialization and innovation such as Toyota ran afoul of mega-recalls.[9] Products such as mobile phones also lost relevance because handsets were over-engineered and failed to adhere to global standards, and Japan's domestic market did not provide firms with enough market power to *set* global standards.

The employment and social consequences of being sandwiched between the 'new American model' and emerging Asia, as well as its own partial financialization, have been profound. The share of non-standard workers in Japan surged from roughly 20 per cent in 1990 to almost 40 per cent by 2015. Relative poverty also surged, and a 'working poor' emerged.[10] As the labour share of income dropped, and the population began to decline as a result of accelerated demographic ageing, companies increasingly invested abroad, embarking on a 'second internationalization', with a strategic emphasis on mergers and acquisitions (M&A) and alliances, and in Asia, in a more horizontal type of integration.[11]

In sum, both the United States and Japan have been profoundly influenced by the co-evolutionary processes we have described in this book. The social tension and polarization which has resulted has brought the countries closer to developing countries, in some respects, in what D'Costa (2011) describes as a 'perverse convergence' (Chapter 1). Put differently, in terms of the erosion of social cohesion and Red Queen effects, we could say that 'we are all compressed developers now'.

The digital economy: winner take most, or lowering barriers to innovation?

In Chapter 3 we inserted the 'digital economy' (right-hand column of Table 3.1) to suggest we have entered the revolutionary phase of a new techno-economic period, with its attendant 'platform organizational paradigm' and 'platform-innovation'

[8] *Nikkei Weekly*, 14 January 2013.

[9] In the automobile industry, a big unknown is which parts Japanese companies will continue to dominate in an era of alternative fuels and autonomous driving. Given the competence in materials science in Japan, batteries are one possibility, but competition from China is especially fierce given the huge lead that country has in the adoption of electric vehicles; about 400,000 electric buses are in operation in China, representing nearly 99 per cent of the world's total (Margolis, 2019).

[10] '(T)he government's reliance on the availability of jobs to maintain the social protection system justified the creation of low-paid jobs as preferable to the alternative of mass unemployment' (Miura, 2012: 90).

[11] Asia's visibility in Japan grew in other ways in the 2010s, notably a huge rise in tourists, and in 'guest' workers: the number of foreign workers in Japan quadrupled between 2007 and 2018 to 1.3 million, the majority coming from China, Vietnam, and the Philippines (*Nikkei Asian Review*, 4–10 June 2018), while in 2018, the government launched a scheme to attract another 500,000 'unskilled' workers by 2025.

business model. One question that arises is how the application of advanced digital technologies in manufacturing will affect the geography of production and trade. Another is if it will reverse, accelerate, or alter the geographic separation of innovation and production that arose in the context of GVCs. We examine these possibilities for the future geography of (advanced) manufacturing and innovation, first separately, and then together. Needless to say, our views are speculative.

The economic geography of manufacturing and innovation in the digital economy

The role of manufacturing in the digital economy has been discussed in terms of 'industry 4.0' in Germany and 'advanced manufacturing' in the United States (Bonvillian, 2012, 2017). Features commonly mentioned include additive manufacturing (or 3D printing), intelligent and adaptive robots (or cobots), ubiquitous measurement with sensor-laden equipment, high levels of traceability in the supply chain, real-time monitoring and adjustment of production lines, and the development of new material and processes. But what can be said, *in general*, about the likely role and characteristics of manufacturing in the digital economy, and critically, of its location?

Trade-offs in production scale, product variety, and unit costs/labour hours are summarized in Figure 9.2, which also assumes that advanced manufacturing (industry 4.0) could change these trade-offs.[12] Starting on the upper-left quadrant, we see a rationale for high-volume, low-mix production in places (e.g. China) where scale is large, product variety is low, and where labour costs are low, leading to low unit costs relative to other locations. In the lower-right quadrant, we see the opposite end of the spectrum, with low-volume, customized manufacturing of customized products, and medium-volume, high-mix factories in the centre (higher cost locations, closer to demand). Smaller factories with higher unit costs are a durable part of the manufacturing landscape, since mass markets do not exist for all products, rapid replenishment is sometimes required, and cost sensitivity is not always high (Reynolds, 2017). Low-volume production can be for bespoke products, and for one-off items, such as prototypes.

In Figure 9.2 the arrows depict possible convergence of these three types of factories towards an advanced digital model, where automation renders labour

[12] These variables are not the only determinants of manufacturing location. Fragmentation has been less prevalent where cutting-edge manufacturing processes are required, where frequent engineering changes or process alterations are needed, or where regulations might require domestic manufacturing (as in military hardware). Nonetheless, a change in this calculus will have implications for the geography of manufacturing.

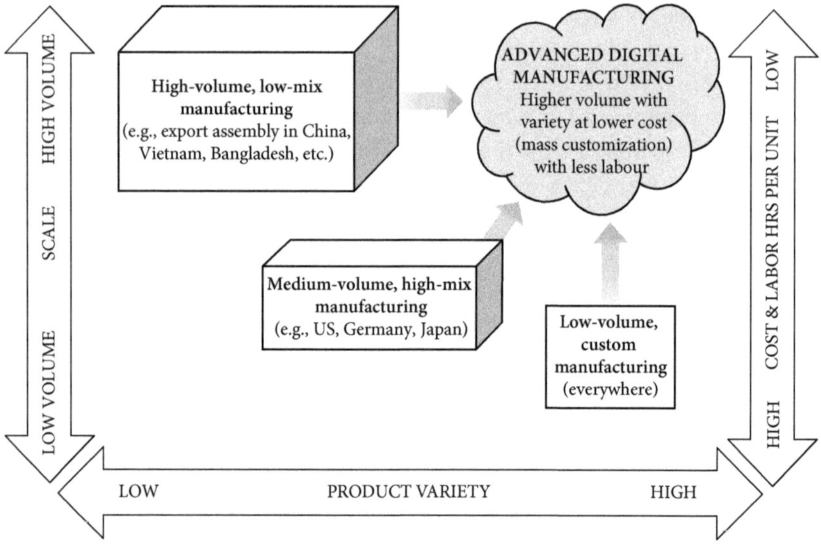

Figure 9.2 Shifting trade-offs with the emergence of advanced manufacturing; scale, product variety, and costs and labour hours per unit
Source: Adapted from UNCTAD (2017).

costs and scale less important, while product variety is either maintained or increased. If this scenario has any validity, then the question becomes what will happen to the location of production. Some anticipate that the digital economy will result in the 'reshoring' of higher-volume production, with factories located closer to end-consumers, similar to a farm-to-table model in food, in what Sanjay Sarma envisions as linked networks of 'distributed virtual factories' (Markowsky, 2012). In this somewhat utopian vision, jobs will migrate closer to end markets; transportation costs and CO_2 emissions will be lower; inventory requirements will shrink; and consumers will have their needs and desires met with a wide variety of products produced specifically for them as needed.

But the increased flexibility promised by advanced digital manufacturing, and the high cost of initial deployment, could have the *opposite* effect, by increasing product variety in large-scale manufacturing. Large-scale production units have the enduring advantage of purchasing power (for components, electric power, and logistics services, for example), which in turn incentivizes high responsiveness and even co-location of suppliers, investments in highly efficient transportation and infrastructure, and proximate institutional supports such as domain-specific education and training. Thus, it is also possible to imagine that advanced digital manufacturing will be deployed mainly in places where mass production is currently taking place, such as China and other export-oriented economies.

There is a third possibility. The deployment of advanced digital technologies in manufacturing could be a more general, secular trend, with new systems deployed without dramatically altering the location of production. This would see a leap in productivity, quality, and traceability in all sorts of manufacturing facilities—mass, high mix, and customized—with a global decrease in demand for direct manufacturing labour. This possibility, especially if it arrives without sufficient time for labour market adjustment, worries some observers of the digital economy, such as McAfee and Brynjolfsson (2016); see also UNCTAD (2017).

Next, let us consider innovation. The first thing to note is the increasing richness of digital tools supporting innovation in the digital economy, as suggested in Figure 9.3, which offer new ways to access finance, labour, inputs and production services, customer service, sales channels, and marketing. Given this toolkit, the potential of the digital economy for innovation and entrepreneurship could be profound. Will this usher in new opportunities for innovation in developing countries? Or, as with earlier rounds of globalization, will there be counter-trends to fragmentation, and continued concentration in technology clusters such as Silicon Valley, where the systems that underpin the digital economy are developed, standards battles are waged, and digital platform ownership is concentrated (Sturgeon, 2003)?

It is not yet clear if the geographic concentration of core platform ownership derives from the youth of the digital economy, or from the winner-take-all nature of platform competition. Still, artificial intelligence (AI)–assisted digital design tools could reduce the need for iterative engineering work, along with the expertise required to design new products, generating additional demand for highly skilled skilled labour in core platform owners, with many fewer highly skilled engineers and workers needed in firms that *use* the systems. Much of the expertise required to design, test, and validate new product designs would be embedded in software platforms.

When the lens is shifted from core platforms to higher-level platforms, platform complementors, and platform users, however, the possibilities open up significantly. The resources listed in Figure 9.3 point to a growing set of digital resources that could be used by start-up, smaller, and globally remote companies to innovate, grow, improve operations, and connect to markets. These tools create possibilities, and they exist not *despite* the biggest technology firms and core platform owners, but *because* of them. So, platform innovation that takes place downstream, close to customers—not innovation in core platforms, but in new platforms and products created by and around them—could lead to an *upturn* in

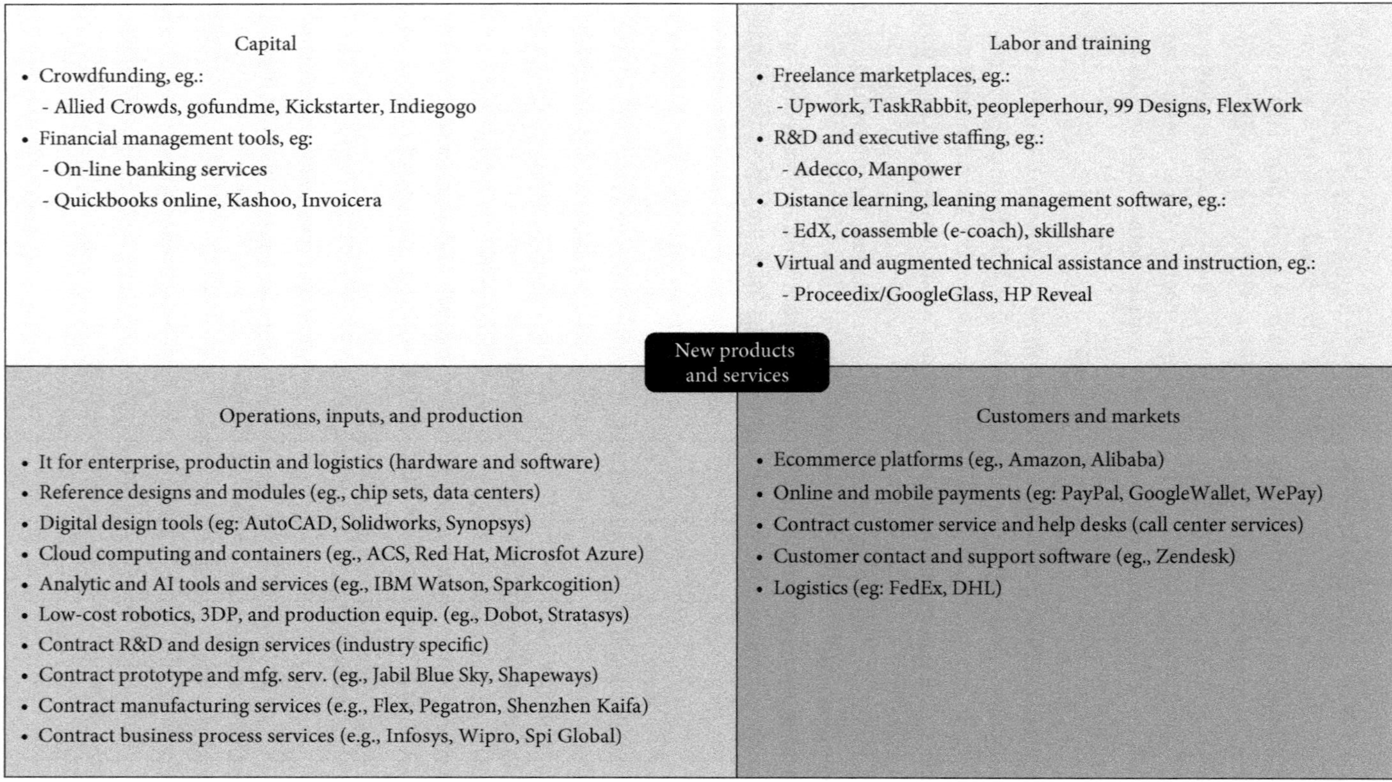

Figure 9.3 Examples of tools for the emerging innovation ecosystem in the digital economy

Source: Adapted from UNCTAD (2017).

innovation outside the heartland of the digital economy as products tailored to local markets are developed and produced more easily, quickly, and inexpensively.

Finally, a crucial question, alluded to in Chapter 3, is how tightly innovation will be geographically tied to production in the digital economy. When there is no well-defined, modular break-point between innovation and production, successful innovation might require manufacturing and innovation to be co-located. Yet, as seen in important industries such as electronics, software, and motor vehicles, effective modular linkages between the innovation and production stages of the value chain can facilitate geographic de-linking: global industries may continue to co-evolve as geographically separated technology and production clusters.

In short, while evidence suggests that there will be variation across industries (Sturgeon and Memedovic, 2010), and that firms will have strategic choices in regard to business models (Berger et al., 2005), it is reasonable to think that a maturing digital economy will lead to a further loosening of spatial ties between many business functions including innovation, production, logistics, marketing, distribution, and after-sales service. The emergent features of the digital economy appear poised to extend the organizational and geographical fragmentation of work into new realms, including formerly indivisible and geographically rooted activities that reside at the front end of GVCs (and edges of the smiling curve), especially R&D, product design, and other knowledge-intensive and innovation-related business functions. Changes to the regulatory environment, however, could change locational incentives dramatically. We will consider such possibilities next.

Scenarios for less-developed countries in the digital economy

Given the scenarios just outlined, what impacts is the digital economy likely to have on LDCs? As we have seen with manufacturing, there are three broad scenarios for developing countries in the digital economy. First, routine business functions such as manufacturing, software coding, and back office services could be 'reshored' or even eliminated by advanced manufacturing and automation. Indeed, AI and automated software testing may already be taking the bloom off the rose of IT offshoring in places such as India and the Philippines. This could drive a retreat from GVCs and cause social disruptions in recent developers. In a second scenario, the tools of the digital economy could empower developing-country firms to move up the value chain, become less dependent on the innovation and coordination functions of lead firms in GVCs, and produce globally competitive and compatible products on their own.[13] A third scenario would see

[13] Rehnberg and Ponte (2017) depict this scenario, using the example of 3D printing, as a possible flattening of the value chain curve from 'smiling to smirking'.

little distributional change as both scenarios gain traction. Indeed, these scenarios assume that lead firms in GVCs are principally headquartered in the North, and produce in the South. However, a growing number of lead firms are now located in LDCs, and with a related increase in South-South trade, the mixing of these scenarios is also possible, and indeed likely.

Crisis and rebalancing?

The digital economy creates opportunities, tensions, and risks. A positive, somewhat utopian vision sees it as ushering in a newly equitable and environmentally sustainable growth model based on the maximization of human empowerment and wellbeing rather than maximization of profits and resource extraction and utilization (Ercoskun, 2011). Even with a more sober assessment, there are real and potential benefits such as tracking the timing and location of disease outbreaks though real-time analysis of public search terms (McAfee and Brynjolfsson, 2016).

On the other hand, there are palpable worries that the digital economy is introducing frightening new risks in both developed countries and LDCs. For workers, large and sudden productivity increases enabled by advanced digital technologies could shorten the employment adjustment period in comparison with earlier rounds of automation. The penetration of computerization and AI into knowledge-intensive services could also mean that many more jobs will be at risk of disappearing, even as output and productivity rise (McAfee and Brynjolfsson, 2016). Jobs suitable for on-demand work, such as copyediting, data cleaning, moderation of online content, transcription, and even driving, could be the most vulnerable to replacement by AI and autonomous systems. Even if many more intellectually stimulating and satisfying jobs are created, rising inequality, potential for worker abuse, and downward pressure on wages are all worrying aspects of the digital economy.

For consumers, there are also risks. Data flows to platform owners underpin, at least theoretically, ongoing enhancements and upgrades to digital products and services, but the price for these services is users who passively, and often unknowingly, provide app makers and platform owners with very fine-grained information about their whereabouts, finances, and personal habits.[14] Aggregation of personal and consumer data can be used for the purposes of segmenting the

[14] For example, Facebook collects user data that includes city, gender, age, IP address, and a full record of the platform's users linked to and how they tag content (when logged in). In addition, the company combines information and assumptions about users harvested from their online activity with information from public sources and data brokers to assemble dossiers on users with nearly one hundred variables (job title, parents' birthdays, etc.) to help target advertisements more precisely (Dewey, 2016).

quality of customer service, price discrimination, and social control. Customer lifetime value scores refer to rankings surreptitiously used by companies to gauge the potential long-term financial value of customers: those with low scores are not offered discounts or can wait longer for customer service (Safdar, 2018). Indeed, automated-decision making, data mining, and predictive analytics are widely used to discriminate against the poor (Eubanks, 2017; O'Neil, 2016). In addition to data exploitation, there is a growing awareness of addiction problems, particularly affecting but not limited to children using social media. Whatever the advantages of the digital economy for average consumers, greater advantages accrue to those with the capability and authority to accumulate, access, and analyse big data.[15]

Risks to citizenship are also profound. Using images from cameras located on streets and in other public spaces, authorities can use a combination of big data and AI to almost instantaneously identify individuals from their faces, gaits, and other characteristics for the purposes of public safety—and social control. While many public spaces are currently surveilled in this way, and there are arguably justifiable benefits from the use of such systems in some contexts (e.g. airport security), there are obvious risks in the broader realms of privacy and opportunities for democratic association. These risks are particularly great in authoritarian states, but exist whatever form of government.

For companies, organizations, and governments, we have already seen the vulnerability—to hacking, identity theft, espionage, larceny, ransoming, and even industrial sabotage—that comes with connecting private communications, industrial systems, and public infrastructure to the Internet (Hampson and Jardine, 2016). The 2016 'Brexit' referendum in the UK and the US presidential election were subjected to massive waves of divisive political messaging and false news micro-targeted with information gleaned from Facebook and other social media platforms, and amplified by 'gaming' Google search algorithms (Cadwalladr, 2016).

But such negative outcomes are not set in stone. In the words of MIT's president, commenting on a recent report about work of the future: 'Fortunately, the harsh societal consequences that concern us all are not inevitable. Technologies embody the values of those who make them, and the policies we build around them can profoundly shape their impact. Whether the outcome is inclusive or exclusive, fair or laissez-faire, is therefore up to all of us' (Dizikes, 2019). As the dark sides of the digital economy become clearer, we have seen a mounting backlash that could mark the beginning of the 'balancing cycle' of the digital economy. Elements of a balancing cycle could include strengthened regulations on data privacy and new business models based on data democracy and meritocracy (paying people for their data and contributions to open innovation

[15] Zuboff (2019) characterizes the appropriation of 'behavioural surplus' as a new form of 'accumulation by dispossession' which is integral to surveillance capitalism pioneered by Google and Facebook in the early 2000s.

systems), as well as a growing emphasis on cyber-security at all levels. We cannot at this stage predict how such a balancing cycle will take shape, or whether it will supplant or, true to the form of compressed development, overlay and co-evolve with an ongoing revolutionizing cycle. Such questions bring us to the evolving relationship between states and markets, to which we now turn.

States, markets, and geopolitics

The relationship between states and markets changed dramatically from the postwar late-late-development era to the (early) compressed-development era. There are good reasons to believe they may be about to change again, in the direction of a new 're-embedding' of markets, which might eventually find expression in a new era of late compressed development. In other words, the institutional environment for compressed developers could change in quite dramatic ways. In this section we look at possible directions of change, starting with the institutions of LMC, followed by 'de-coupling' and 'de-globalization', and finally, geopolitics. We will conclude the chapter, and the book, with a brief assessment of what these changes mean for compression, and compressed development.

Just as liberalism and the gold standard survived until 1931, neoliberalism survived the protests that derailed the WTO Ministers Meeting in Seattle in 1999 and the GFC. But by the late 2010s, calls for reform were coming from its very core, including the US Business Roundtable, as mentioned in the chapter's introduction. Reform of LMC, or its 're-embedding', may be gaining momentum. But what forms might it take?[16]

Underlying both of our dyads (state–market and organization–technology), but not depicted directly in them, are finance and financialization. The nation state's ability to collect taxes without undermining economic vitality was fundamental in its emergence, as well as the emergence of capitalism (see Chapter 2). States' ability to do so in a world of 'phantom' investments and tax havens, sophisticated corporate transfer pricing mechanisms, and downward pressure through competitive deregulation, has been brought into question. The base erosion profit shifting (BEPS) measures and Common Reporting Standard are coordinated attempts to address the problems, but in the face of powerful vested interests (from both states and markets) they have not been notably successful as yet, as the IMF's lament in this chapter's introduction suggests. States have also been

[16] Recall that for Polanyi, embedding has a political or institutional dimension, as well as an ideational or moral dimension (Block and Somers, 2014). Collier (2019) makes a strong case for moral or ethical re-embedding, through pragmatism and the *rejection* of ideology.

deprived of tax revenues by sophisticated fraud, such as the €60 billion 'cum-ex'[17] scandal, described by Le Monde as the 'robbery of the century'. In addition, complex and opaque financial products create systemic risk, as was the case with the GFC. Transparency is further undermined, and a tiny group of insiders rewarded, by the decentralization of exchanges and trading platforms combined with high-speed trading (Mattli, 2019). The threat to both states and markets—and democracy—is tangible.

The digital economy has provided rocket fuel for financialization, while becoming financialized itself. In 2016, in the largest ever tax case, the European Commission ordered Apple to pay the Irish government €13 billion, ruling that their tax agreement was illegal.[18] In 2019 France unveiled plans for a 3 per cent 'GAFA tax' (so-called for its targeting of Google, Amazon, Facebook, and Apple) on digital economy companies with global revenues of over €750 million and above €25 million in France, and the OECD unveiled a scheme to allow countries to levy tax on corporate income earned from e-commerce sales in their territories.

Taxation is not the only front on which the digital giants are being challenged by states. The stirrings of a new antitrust measures after decades of hiatus can also be seen. Google was fined a total of €8.2 billion by the EU over three years (2017–2019) for manipulating search results for shopping, abusing market dominance, and forcing customers of its AdSense to shun advertising from rival search engines.[19] In the United States, too, a bipartisan group of forty state Attorneys General launched an antitrust investigation into tech giants Facebook and Google in 2019, an indication that the age of lax regulation of monopoly power in that country is coming to an end. In addition, challenges to the surreptitious appropriation and combination of 'user-profile information' will continue, and no doubt heighten.

The challenge to LMC goes beyond a rebalancing of state–market relations, to the targeting of corporate behaviour, incentives, and ethics. After advocating shareholder primacy for over two decades, the US Business Roundtable issued a revisionist 'Statement on the Purpose of the Corporation' in August 2019, signed by 181 CEOs, stating—perhaps with a nod to 'America First', or to growing criticism of income inequality, or both—that the purpose of the corporation was to serve 'all Americans': It called for 'delivering value to our customers, investing in our employees, dealing fairly and ethically with our suppliers, supporting the

[17] 'Cum-ex' involved a system in which (borrowed) shares with ('cum') and without ('ex') dividend rights were rapidly traded before payout day amongst a vast network of players to achieve double tax reclaims. By some estimates tax authorities in Europe were defrauded of 60 billion euros from the mid-2000s until the fraud was discovered in 2017. Two former bankers went on trial for their part in the scheme in September 2019. <https://www.theguardian.com/business/2019/sep/20/the-men-who-plundered-europe-city-of-london-practices-on-trial-in-bonn>, accessed 21 September 2019.

[18] At the time of writing, Apple was appealing the ruling.

[19] <https://www.theverge.com/2019/3/20/18270891/google-eu-antitrust-fine-adsense-advertising>, accessed 27 September 2019.

communities in which we work, and generating long term value for our shareholders'—*in that order*, and with the insertion of '*long-term*' (rather than short-term) value![20] If this is matched by actual corporate behaviour, it would indeed represent a major shift. Changes might also be forced by social unrest and legislators. Some platform companies—including Lyft and Amazon—have experienced strikes coinciding with their IPOs, or in Amazon's case, its Prime Day (offering special discounts to paying members). In September 2019 in digital heartland California, a bill was passed that requires Uber, Lyft, and other 'gig' companies to treat their workers as employees. The ripple effects could be extensive.

Finally, climate change and other facets of environmental degradation (loss of habitat and water shortages from unchecked development...) might prove most consequential of all, giving birth to both local and global civil society movements of hitherto unseen proportions. The 'climate strikes' which preceded the UN Climate Summit in September 2019, and followed it, may be a portent of things to come, like the labour movement in the early twentieth century. The movement is certain to have an impact on how business is conducted in the future, perhaps radically so, as well as on how we live, work, and consume.

Yet neo-nationalist upsurges could create very different scenarios. Although not always, they tend to emerge from the right wing of the political spectrum. So far they have shown little enthusiasm for regulating capitalism per se—often quite the reverse—but they do seek to unravel elements of globalization, including migration, and GVCs through 'reshoring'. At the same time, the left's long-standing antipathy toward the network model's outsourcing and off-shoring is gaining momentum. It seems that either way GVCs are likely to be entering a period of rebalancing and reconfiguration.

There are other expressions of dissent, as well, directed against governments. Sometimes protesters are angry that governments have not protected them from the vicissitudes of markets, but there have been a wide range of other causes, in which a common theme is that governments have lost touch with the daily lives of ordinary citizens. Some protest movements have been leaderless, and employ mobilization by encrypted messaging apps like WhatsApp and Telegram. They push for political change. On top of this, moreover, we cannot ignore geopolitical tensions.

New geopolitical tensions

Our conceptual framework draws our attention beyond individual state–market and civil society relations to consider the changing geopolitical context, and to

[20] In case anyone was left in doubt about the statement's stakeholder orientation, it concludes: 'Each of our stakeholders is essential. We commit to deliver value to all of them, for the future success of our companies, our communities and our country.'

three important questions. First, how do we interpret the rise of China, and the simmering trade and technology conflict with the United States? Is China destined to usurp the role of the United States as the dominant power, will the United States reassert its dominance, or something else? Second, does this conflict, and the rise of neo-nationalism, represent a turning point in the tide of globalization, and a retreat into national borders or blocs, with a corresponding fragmentation of the Internet?[21] Third, which we will consider in our concluding comments, what does this mean for compression, and the era of compressed development?

Regarding the first question of dominant powers, our conceptual framework points to parallels—and differences—with the early twentieth century, when tensions were stoked, not just by those around the Great Power table, but by others agitating to join it, especially Germany, Italy, and Japan. Today, the challenger is undoubtedly compressed developer China, with its historical grievances and chafing at the imbalance between its growing economic might and the influence it has been able to wield in existing international institutions.

One of China's responses has been to try to build new transnational institutions of its own. The Belt and Road Initiative (BRI) provides a platform for this. Projects which have been rolled into the BRI predate 2013, and it was initially seen as a solution for chronic overcapacity in Chinese domestic state-owned-enterprises (SOEs) (especially steel and concrete producers), but it has become a strategic economic and geopolitical vehicle for China's regional ambitions. One part, the Silk Road Economic Belt, has expanded west into Central Asia and beyond as far as Europe, transforming remote outposts of the old Silk Road into logistic and commercial hubs. South, it seeks to extend Chinese influence into the poorer ASEAN countries of Laos, Cambodia, and Myanmar, as well as into Pakistan and on to the Indian Ocean through the China Pakistan Economic Corridor. The sheer size of Chinese investment and trade, coming at a time when other sources have dwindled, and especially to landlocked countries long peripheral to world trade, has drawn many countries on these land routes into closer ties with China. The Belt is complemented by the twenty-first-century Maritime Silk Road (MSR), with its string of strategic ports ('pearls') stretching to Africa, and indeed Europe.[22] As well as enhancing sea transportation, the MSR, too, encompasses railway, highway, air- and seaport, pipeline, special economic zones, and other

[21] Mueller describes this rather as 'alignment'—'an attempt to force the round peg of global communications into the square hole of territorial states . . . It is about partitioning cyberspace to subordinate it to sovereign states.' Pressure for alignment, he notes, does not just come from authoritarian governments: <https:/www.cfr.org/blog/internet-fragmentation-exists-not-way-you-think>, accessed 8 October 2019; also Mueller (2017).

[22] Not all of this expansion is state-sponsored. Sun (2017) highlights the presence of doughty private Chinese factory owners in Africa, projecting that they will turn Africa into the 'next factory of the world'.

hard infrastructure, as well as 'soft' aspects such as people-to-people exchange and training (Blanchard and Flint, 2017).

China is creating new funding institutions and regional organizations as well. The former include the Silk Road Fund, and the multilateral Asia Infrastructure Investment Fund (AIIB), launched in 2015 immediately prior to the announcement of the BRICS New Development Bank. The Shanghai Five became the Shanghai Cooperation Organization in 2002, and has expanded its membership since. It creates a framework for cooperation and conflict resolution in Central Asia, and China and Russia find common cause in condemning US activities in the region. The 'sixteen plus one' grouping of China and central and east European countries takes China into present day Europe as well.

These initiatives have not been without friction. There is a delicate balance in Central Asia between China's growing economic influence and Russia's traditional cultural and military influence. India faces the dilemma of how much to cooperate in the Bangladesh-China-India-Myanmar Economic Corridor (BCIM-EC), while potentially being encircled by land and sea with facilities which could threaten its own interests. The EU is wary of how China might leverage its growing influence in Eastern Europe. Territorial disputes have been activated in the South China Sea.

But the biggest tension is between China and the incumbent dominant power, the United States. The tension escalated in 2018, with the United States imposing tariffs on $34 billion worth of imports from China, citing its massive trade deficit, as well as other grievances such as intellectual property appropriation. By September 2019 tariff coverage had increased to $360 billion, while China had imposed tariffs on $110 billion of imports from the United States. The United States trade deficit with China fell as a result, but at the cost of more than $4.5 billion worth of exports from 2018 to 2019 (see Figure 9.1). This is not a simple conflict over trade, however. It has spilled into investment, and even more fundamentally into technology. The US president has attempted to cajole US companies to abandon China and 'reshore' their manufacturing, while China has become more determined than ever to reduce its technological dependence on the United States, especially following US actions against Huawei (which led to its inclusion in the US Entity List, banning it from US communications networks), and its pressure on other countries to follow suit.

At the point of writing, it is unclear how this multifaceted conflict will play out. An academic industry has grown up trying to predict whether the United States is a hegemon in decline, or China is one on the rise, or not. US dominance—and adaptiveness—has proved more durable than many predicted, and China, despite its size and growing technological strengths, has weaknesses that we have noted such as thin industrialization, layered dualism in labour markets, policy stretch, and premature demographic ageing. But China is *already* a major regional power, and in all likelihood, we are, at least, heading into an era of multipolarity that will be different from the Cold War era, which was tense, but involved reasonably clear demarcations between US and Soviet interests, with conflict on the fringes. The new multipolarity, which includes Russia and the EU, as well as emerging India, Iran, and so on, is more complex, and in part the complexity reflects the rise, not just of China, but of the South.

A multipolar world will also be one of 'polycentric trade' (Horner and Nadvi, 2018). On the one hand, China's dominance in GVCs may have partially deindustrialized other developing (and developed) countries, similarly to peripheral European and non-European countries in the nineteenth century (see Chapter 2). Its massive supply of labour with basic education shifted the comparative advantage of other developing (and some developed) countries towards, for example, primary production (Wood and Mayer, 2009). But as China's economy and skill base develop, opportunities for labour-intensive production reopen elsewhere. The South—China and elsewhere—accounts for a growing proportion of global trade, *and* a growing number of lead firms in GVCs coordinating that trade.

This brings us to our second question, namely whether the tide of globalization has turned, and the US–China conflict will usher in a period of retreat into national borders or regional blocs, fuelled by neo-nationalist movements. It was widely anticipated that global trade would decline after the GFC, but it rebounded, especially for LDCs, although growing at a much slower pace. Trade is a rough indicator, however. As we have argued, the network and platform organizational paradigms valorize intangible intellectual and technology assets over fixed assets, and trade statistics are best at tracking the flow of goods. Taking the example of mobile phone handsets, US-based companies are suppliers of key components and software, while China is the largest producer and exporter of finished handsets, by far (accounting for about 86 per cent of world exports in 2016). Chinese telecom companies, including those at the very centre of the trade conflict such as Huawei and ZTE, are heavily reliant on components and software imported from the United States. This was put into stark relief in May of 2018, when ZTE was forced to cease production in a matter of days when it was denied access to US semiconductors and software (Lee, 2018).

Although the Chinese government is actively supporting capital and technology investments to substitute for such imports (e.g. through its China 2025 policy), there are likely to be significant barriers over the short, or even medium terms, for Chinese companies to engage in import substitution while remaining internationally competitive. Key inputs directly imported by China include both the proprietary and difficult-to-replicate technologies and technology platforms directly embedded in components, and a set of indirect and difficult-to-quantify contributions from (increasingly global) ecosystems of third-party firms, especially for software (e.g. operating systems and compatible apps in mobile phones) and finance. China's dependences on global technology ecosystems and services—for example in digital technology–intensive industries such as telecom, automotive electronics, and consumer electronics—run deeper than simple reliance on imported components and are therefore difficult to quantify.

There are risks for US firms as well. These most obviously include access to the Chinese consumer market (the largest in the world), and access to the highly efficient and effective 'fast manufacturing' ecosystem that has emerged in Southern China to support the production and export of electronic goods in high volumes, with great responsiveness and product variety. This ecosystem, which has allowed China to dominate world mobile phones and consumer electronics production and exports by a wide margin, would be difficult to substitute, as suggested by the mostly failed experiments of 'reshoring' assembly to the United States.

The complex technology ecosystems underlying the trade flows that emerged to support GVCs have created a large and complex network of interlocking dependencies, not only in terms core technologies, but on expansive ecosystems of third-party contributors at every stage of the value chain. Given this, we have to ask if it is even possible to maintain the production and use of modern goods and services without a very significant and sustained level of global integration.

A short answer is that the depth of interconnection and integration of financial, business, and technology ecosystems make it unlikely that the genie can be put back into national bottles. GVCs, and many of the institutions which support them, are unlikely to be fully unwound. In addition, many of the other challenges noted earlier in this chapter—of globalized (and virtualized) finance and environmental protection, for example—*cannot* be dealt with effectively by individually competing nation states. New forms of supra-national governance are needed, although their scope could be more expansive or more limited, and global or fragmented into blocs. Also, any 're-embedding' of markets and digital technologies cannot simply be national. Postwar multilateral institutions can be adapted, as some were repurposed to serve neoliberalism in the (early) compressed-development era, and new ones might be created, one would hope without decades of political, economic, and military strife in between. Still, none of this forecloses the development of new trading blocs and spheres of influence, which could be part of a multipolar world of polycentric trade.

Conclusion: on convergence and compression

In sum, a transition from early compressed development to a new era of late compressed development, if that is indeed what we are witnessing, will hopefully be very different from the violent transition from early late development to postwar late-late development. New forms of embedding are needed, of markets, and mechanisms for accumulation and regulation in the digital economy. State–

market relations are on the cusp of change, as the 'externalities' of unfettered markets provoke mounting damage and indignation. Such problems will require multilevel responses, including global responses to matters such as tax evasion and climate change. At best we will be moving in the direction of a (peaceful) multipolar world, in which LDCs can engage with a diversity of institutions, models, and partners.

Rather than marking an end to compressed development, the next development era will likely take the structures, systems, and ideologies of the (early-) compressed-development era as a starting point and, therefore, retain many of its (compressed) features. As such—and if catastrophe can be avoided—compressed development will endure, at least in the near-to-medium term, as a co-evolving cluster of era-related development features with strong yet unforeseeable interaction effects.

But a new era of late compressed development is also bound to be different from earlier eras. Part of the reason is compression itself. Techno-economic periods and era effects increasingly merge and interact, creating complex new challenges—and hopefully solutions—virtually simultaneously in the North and South. In that respect, we are all compressed developers. This is a kind of convergence, but whether it avoids being the 'perverse convergence' of 'low-road' capital accumulation converging with a downward slide of mature capitalism (D'Costa, 2011; Chapter 1) depends on the paths these transitions take, the extent to which we can recognize our common humanity, and protect the earth that sustains us.

Afterword

The End of Compressed Development?

The onset of the Covid-19 pandemic has been traced to early December 2019, just as we were submitting our completed manuscript for publication. We were tempted to comb through the manuscript for ways to address what has rapidly emerged as an unprecedented global public health crisis, economic crisis, and more. But, we decided to leave the text be for several reasons. The first is the ongoing nature of the pandemic and its fallout. The scope of the damage and its long-term social, economic, and political effects will not be fully visible for years, and we are resistant to the business of prognostication. The second is that we believe the book, as it stands, can help make sense of some of the distinctive features of the pandemic, including its unprecedented speed of transmission to all corners of the globe and the economic chaos engendered by the disruption of industries embedded in the elaborate global supply chains and technology ecosystems that comprise GVCs. Third, it is very likely that the pandemic will intensify, if not actually cause, the overlapping and interacting crises that we depicted in Chapter 9. Capping our analysis at December 2019 creates a useful starting point for analysis of what comes next; a natural experiment of a sort.

So far, the virus appears to be capricious in terms of where outbreaks catch hold, who contracts severe forms of the disease, and with what symptoms. Attempts to generalize about climate, culture, form of government, or any other factor to explain where severe outbreaks have been experienced or avoided tend to break down under scrutiny. It will be years before the path of the virus can be fully understood and explained.

That said, we have seen the abject failure of institutions and infrastructures in some countries to respond to the crisis effectively, not least in the Anglo-American heartlands of liberal market capitalism, where markets have been encouraged to penetrate and reshape spaces formerly occupied by the state and the institutions of civil society. This has happened through budget cuts, privatization, outsourcing, and requirements for lowest cost (often global) procurement, which are all features of the compressed development era. Financialization and the network model, including outsourcing and offshoring, have been embraced by states as well as businesses. The ideology of 'new public management'—exacerbated, in the United States in particular, by a wilful disdain for experts and evidence with politically inconvenient messages—has left the ability to effectively respond in tatters, while more regulated market economies (in terms of the Varieties of Capitalism literature), including social democracies and the newly developed states in East Asia, appear to have done somewhat better.

With Covid-19, we see with extreme clarity that compression has been allowed to gain traction in recent decades without the potential risks and costs factored in. The pandemic has laid these vulnerabilities bare in a quick and brutal fashion. It has exposed fragilities in our societies, from supply chains to social safety nets, and threatens to deepen many longstanding and more recent divides. We see fragility of states from thirty years of tax cuts and privatization, and the fragility of vulnerable groups in societies with rising inequality and ongoing social inequities and various forms of discrimination, especially racial discrimination. Those suffering the most in the pandemic include immigrants, people of colour, the elderly, people in jail and prison, and indigenous peoples. Those doing gig work and face-to-face services are either out of a job and unable to pay for food or housing, or have been deemed 'essential' and put on the 'front lines' where they are more likely to contract the virus. Inequality is far from new, but for those of us who have not had to live out its deprivations and injustices, it suddenly has a more vivid face: the working poor, the uninsured, the undocumented.

In regard to the business systems underlying compressed development, it now seems quite reasonable to ask if the financialized strategies of lean and just-in-time production, supply chain consolidation, and low-cost global sourcing laid out in this book have been taken too far. In fact, supply-chain interruptions from unforeseen events occur with regularity, and GVCs have proven to be remarkably adaptable and resilient in the past. Examples include labour actions at facilities residing in supply-chain pinch points, fires at factories making most, if not all, of the world's supply of a specialized component or material, as well as earthquakes, tsunamis, and floods that take key manufacturing regions offline for a time. In most of these cases, the effects have been felt narrowly and resolved quickly, due in large part to the ability of companies to quickly repurpose existing facilities—and often excess capacity—to produce scarce materials, parts, and products. Because GVCs include a large dose of market consolidation and multinational companies as key players, production locations can sometimes be substituted in short order. Advances in information technology and the nascent tools of the digital economy can make this easier. As we discussed in Chapter 9, and depict in the centre box of Figure 9.2, medium-volume, high-mix manufacturing is common in many places, and such facilities can change their product mix in response to rapid shifts and surges in demand. These adaptive capabilities are now being put to the test as factories try to pivot to the manufacture of scarce ventilators and personal protective equipment (PPE).

Perhaps because of the demonstrated ability of GVCs to adapt and economies to recover from earlier 'black swan' events, if sometimes slowly and incompletely, prior post-crisis responses have been, as often as not, to return to business as usual, or even to double down on GVCs that deliver at the lowest cost in an attempt to recoup losses suffered during the crisis. Thus, even as global trade began to slow in 2011, China retained and even consolidated its central position in a range of GVCs, including, it turns out, for personal protective equipment such as masks, face shields, and surgical gowns; parts for key medical equipment such as ventilators; and a very large share of the world's active pharmaceutical ingredients. With even the most adaptive production systems unable to cope with the spike in demand caused by the pandemic (and lack of adequate preparation for it) policymakers have in some cases tried to take over the governance of global (and national) value chains for critical products, commandeering shipments, banning exports, and leaving global suppliers suddenly blocked from serving their long-standing international customers. The result has been a spike in international conflict and bellicose protectionism at a time when cooperation and coordination is needed most.

The Covid-19 pandemic is clearly not the same as previous 'black swan' or *force majure* events. It is affecting the entire world at once, seeded by international travellers moving at speeds and in numbers undreamt of in 1919, when Spanish influenza ravaged the planet. Moreover, the surge in global demand for some products and services (like medical equipment) and the nearly complete collapse in demand for others (such as air travel and hospitality) has truly been unprecedented given the current scale of these industries. It is unlikely that we will return to business as usual, either in developed or less-developed countries.

Then what? Our analysis in the final chapter suggests a turning point from an era of early-compressed development to late-compressed development. We expected a series of overlapping challenges and crises to contribute to this turn, including many of those which have been exposed and exacerbated by the pandemic. We will almost certainly see the acceleration and cementing of existing trends: remote work, consolidation in large firms at the expense of the small and independent, greater inequality, and further pressure on the institutions of global governance. We might also the see reversal of other trends: high reliance on China for export production, a reduction in global travel and tourism, and a loosening of just-in-time supply chains. Trends and experiments accelerated or launched during the pandemic, such as working from home and the Emergency Basic Income payments being made in Brazil, could accelerate or become permanent after the pandemic, ushering in a reconfiguration of urban spaces and the institutionalization of Universal Basic Income in more places.

We are set to test the concept of 'decoupling', but can GVCs really be unwound? Probably not without extreme difficulty and discomfort. If they cannot, the moment will call for greater international cooperation and coordination and a stronger role for the institutions of global governance. While is impossible to predict what the responses will be in terms of both corporate strategy and geopolitics, or social policy and what form a new Polanyian 're-embedding' might take, from the current vantage point it appears that geopolitical frictions and economic and technological nationalism are only being further stoked, which bodes ill. If any moment demands an adaptive policy response, including cross-border cooperation and reliance on key international institutions *and* intelligent consideration of domestic production and stockpiling, it is the current one. If and when a vaccine or vaccines are developed, even greater international cooperation will be needed to coordinate its production, distribution, and administration; avoiding 'vaccine nationalism' while balancing care on the home front.

Whether the pandemic triggers such a turn, or indeed something more fundamental—an *end* to compressed development—may depend on whether attitudes toward *time* have changed. As we wrote in the chapters of the book, it was difficult to envision how policy makers, managers, and entrepreneurs—or citizens and consumers—might accept a slowing down of a hot-running, just-in-time, globally-integrated, low-cost global economy. The compression of development has not happened through any law of nature or impersonal 'progress', but by policy-makers and managers attempting to bring about development more and more quickly using the tools, business models, and ideologies of the compressed development era, and by expectations from citizens and consumers that they do so. Perhaps a pandemic with unprecedented reach and impact is one of the few events which might conceivably prompt a reversal or change in course. What is impossible to say at this time is if such a slowdown would be benign or brutal, for whom, and where.

Finally, the likely origins of the pandemic, as with the climate crisis, point to the need to fundamentally reassess our relationship with nature, and not just in compressed developers. The limitations of pursuing growth at all costs, and indeed of putting 'nature on the rack' and 'torturing it to reveal its secrets' (expressions rightly or wrongly attributed to Francis Bacon) have been laid bare. Perhaps we have not paid sufficient attention to this in our analysis. Be that as it may, we hope the book will provide a useful starting point for making sense of future changes.

References

Acemoglu, D. and Robinson, J. (2012), *The Origins of Power, Prosperity and Poverty: Why Nations Fail*, New York: Crown Publishers.

Acemoglu, D. and Autor, D. (2010), 'Skills, Tasks and Technologies: Implications for Employment and Earnings', NBER Working Paper No.16082.

Acemoglu, D. and Robinson, J. (2002), 'The Political Economy of the Kuznets Curve', *Review of Development Economics*, 6(2), 183–203.

Adler, P. (2001), 'Market, Hierarchy, and Trust: The Knowledge Economy and the Future of Capitalism', *Organization Science*, 12(2), 215–34.

Aghion, P., Caroli, E., and Garcîa-Peñalosa, C. (1999), 'Inequality and Economic Growth: The Perspective of the New Growth Theories', *Journal of Economic Literature*, 37 (4), 1615–60.

Ahamed, L. (2009), *Lords of Finance: 1929, The Great Depression, and the Bankers Who Broke the World*, London: Windmill Books.

Aiyar, S., R. Duval, D. Puy, Y. Wu and L. Zhang (2013), 'Growth Slowdowns and the Middle Income Trap', IMF Working Paper WP/13/71.

Akamatsu, K. (1961), 'A Theory of Unbalanced Growth in the World Economy', *Weltwirtschaftliches Archiv*, 86, 196–217.

Akyüz, Y. (2009), 'Multilateral Disciplines and the Question of Policy Space', Third World Network, TWN Trade and Development Series Working Paper 38.

Alavi, M. and Leidner, D. (2001), 'Review: Knowledge Management and Knowledge Management Systems: Conceptual Foundations and Research Issues', *MIS Quarterly*, 25(1), 107–36.

Ali-Yrkkö, J., Rouvinen, P., Seppälä, T., and Ylä-Anttila, P. (2011), 'Who Captures Value in Global Supply Chains? Case Nokia N95 Smartphone', *Journal of Industry, Competition and Trade*, 11, 263–78.

Altenburg, T. and Lütkenhorst, W. (2015), *Industrial Policy in Developing Countries: Failing Markets, Weak States*, Cheltenham: Edward Elgar.

Amano, I. (2011), *The Origins of Japanese Credentialism*, Melbourne, Australia: Trans Pacific Press (orig. in Japanese, 1982).

Ambaras, D. (2018), *Japan's Imperial Underworlds: Intimate Encounters at the Borders of Empire*, Cambridge: Cambridge University Press.

Amsden, A. (2007), *Escape from Empire: The Developing World's Journey Through Heaven and Hell*, Cambridge, MA: MIT Press.

Amsden, A. (1989), *Asia's Next Giant: South Korea and Late Industrialization*, New York: Oxford University Press.

Andrews, M. Pritchett, L., and Woolcock, M. (2017), *Building State Capability: Evidence, Analysis, Action*, Oxford: Oxford University Press.

Andrioni, A. and Chang, H-J. (2019), 'The Political Economy of Industrial Policy: Structural Interdependencies, Policy Alignment and Conflict Management', *Structural Change and Economic Dynamics*, 48(March), 136–50.

Aneesh, A. (2006), *Virtual Migration: The Programming of Globalization*, Durham, NC: Duke University Press.

Anglade, C. and Fortin, C. (1990), 'Accumulation, Adjustment and the Autonomy of the State in Latin America', in C Anglade and C Fortin (eds.) *The State and Capital Accumulation in Latin America*, Vol. 2, Basingstoke: Macmillan, pp. 211–40.

Anievas, A. and Nisancioglu, K. (2015), *How the West Came to Rule: The Geopolitical Origins of Capitalism*, London: Pluto Press.

Ansell, C. (2000), 'The Networked Polity: Regional Development in Western Europe', *Governance*, 13(3), 303–33.

Arcand, J-L. Berkes, E., and Panizza, U. (2012), 'Too Much Finance?', IMF Working Paper WP/12/161.

Asia Development Bank (2013), *Key Indicators for Asia and the Pacific, 2013*, Manila, ADB.

Asia Development Bank (2011), *Asia Development Outlook 2011: Preparing for Demographic Transition*, Manila, Philippines: ADB.

Autor, D. (2015), 'Why Are There Still So Many Jobs? The History and Future of Workplace Automation', *Journal of Economic Perspectives*, 29 (3), 3–30.

Autor, D., Dorn, D., and Hanson, G. (2016), 'The China Shock: Learning from Labor Market Adjustment to Large Changes in Trade', NBER Working Paper No. 21906.

Autor, D., Dorn, D., Katz, L., Patterson, C., and van Reenen, J. (2017), 'The Fall of the Labour Share and the Rise of Superstar Firms', NBER Working Paper 23396.

Avirgan, T., Bivens, S., and Gammage, J. (eds.) (2005), *Good Jobs, Bad Jobs, No Jobs: Labour Markets and Informal Work in Egypt, El Salvador, India, Russia and South Africa*, Washington, DC: Economic Policy Institute.

Awortwi, N. (2010), 'The Past, Present, and Future of Decentralization in Africa: A Comparative Case Study of Local Government Development Trajectories of Ghana and Uganda', *International Journal of Public Administration*, 33(12–13), 620–34.

Babb, S. and Chorev, N. (2016), 'International Organizations: Loose and Tight Coupling in the Development Regime', *Studies in Comparative International Development*, 51(1), 81–102.

Baldwin, R. (2016), *The Great Convergence: Information Technology and the New Globalization*, Cambridge, MA: Belknap/Harvard University Press.

Ball, S. (2016), 'Following Policy: Networks, Network Ethnography and Education Policy Mobilities', *Journal of Education Policy*, 31(5), 549–66.

Banister, J. and Cook, G. (2011), 'China's Employment and Compensation Costs in Manufacturing Through 2008', *Monthly Labor Review*, March, 39–52.

Barley, S. and Kunda, G. (1992), 'Design and Devotion: Surges of Rational and Normative Ideologies of Control in Managerial Discourse', *Administrative Science Quarterly*, 37(3), 363–99.

Barnard, J. (1983), *Walter Reuther and the Rise of the Auto Workers*. Boston: Little, Brown.

Barrientos, S. (2013), '"Labour Chains": Analyzing the Role of Labour Contractors in Global Production Networks', *The Journal of Development Studies*, 49(8), 1058–71.

Barrientos, S., Gereffi, G., and Rossi, A. (2010), 'Economic and Social Upgrading in Global Production Networks: Developing a Framework for Analysis', Capturing the Gains Working Paper 2010/03.

Bartley, T., Soener, M., and Gershenson, C. (2019), 'Power at a Distance: Organizational Power Across Boundaries.' *Sociology Compass*. 13(10), https://doi.org/10.1111/soc4.12737.

Becattini, G. (1978), 'The Development of Light Industry in Tuscany: An Interpretation', *Economic Notes*, 3, 107–23.

Beck, U. and Beck-Gernsheim, E. (2001), *Individualization: Institutionalized Individualism and Its Social and Political Consequences*, London: Sage.

Beck, U. and Sznaider, N. (2006), 'Unpacking Cosmopolitanism for the Social Sciences', *British Journal of Sociology*, 57(1), 381–403.

Berg, A. and Ostry, J. (2011), 'Inequality and Unsustainable Growth: Two Sides of the Same Coin?' IMF Staff Discussion Note SDN/11/08.

Berger, S. and the MIT Industrial Performance Center (2005), *How We Compete*, New York: Doubleday.

Bergsten, F, Ito, T., and Noland, M. (2001), No More Bashing: Building a New Japan-United States Economic Relationship, Washington, DC: Peterson Institute for International Economics.

Berman, M. (1982), *All That Is Solid Melts into Air: The Experience of Modernity*, New York: Simon and Schuster.

Bernanke, B. (2015), *The Courage to Act: A Memoir of a Crisis and Its Aftermath*, New York: Norton.

Bernard, M. and Ravenhill, J. (1995), 'Beyond Production Cycles and Flying Geese: Regionalization, Hierarchy, and the Industrialization of Asia', *World Politics*, 47(2), 171–209.

Bernhardt, A., Batt, R., Houseman, S., and Applebaum, E. (2016), 'Domestic Outsourcing in the US: A Research Agenda to Access Trends and Effects on Job Quality', Institute for Research on Labour and Employment, IRLE Working Paper No.102–16.

Best, M. (2018), *How Growth Really Happens: The Making of Economic Miracles by Production, Governance, and Skills*, Princeton, NJ: Princeton University Press.

Bhattacharya, A. (2017), '56,000 Layoffs and Counting: India's IT Bloodbath This Year May Just Be the Start', *Quartz India*, December 26. https://qz.com/india/1152683/indian-it-layoffs-in-2017-top-56000-led-by-tcs-infosys-cognizant/.

Biao, X. (2006), *Global 'Body Shopping': An Indian Labour System in the Information Technology Industry*, Princeton, NJ: Princeton University Press.

Blanchard, J-M. and Flint, C. (2017), 'The Geopolitics of China's Maritime Silk Road Initiative', *Geopolitics*, 22(2), 223–45.

Block, F. (2003), 'Karl Polanyi and the Writing of "The Great Transformation"', *Theory and Society*, 32(30), 275–306.

Block, F. (2008), 'Swimming Against the Current: The Rise of a Hidden Developmental State in the United States', *Politics and Society*, 36(2), 169–206.

Block, F. and Somers, M. (2014), *The Power of Market Fundamentalism: Karl Polanyi's Critique*, Cambridge, MA: Harvard University Press.

Bloom, D., Canning, D., and Malaney, P. (2000), 'Population Dynamics and Economic Growth in Asia', *Population and Development Review*, 26 supplement, 257–90.

Blyde, J. (ed.) (2014), *Synchronized Factories: Latin America and the Caribbean in the Era of Global Value Chains*, Heidelberg, New York, Dordrecht, London: Springer Open.

Blyth, M. (2002), *Great Transformations: Economic Ideas and Institutional Change in the Twentieth Century*. Cambridge: Cambridge University Press.

Bodrožić, Z. and Adler, P. (2017), 'The Evolution of Management Models: A Neo-Schumpeterian Theory', *Administrative Science Quarterly*, 63(1), 85–129.

Boltanski, L. and Chiapello, E. (2007), *The New Spirit of Capitalism*, London: Verso (orig. *Le nouvel esprit du capitalism*, Editions Gallimard, 1999).

Bonal, X. (2007), On Global Absences: Reflections on the Failings in the Education and Poverty Relationship in Latin America, *International Journal of Educational Development*, 27(1), 86–100.

Bonizzi, B. (2014), 'Financialization in Developing and Emerging Countries', *International Journal of Political Economy*, 42(4), 83–107.

Bonvillian, W. (2017), 'Advanced Manufacturing: A New Policy Challenge', *Annals of Science and Technology Policy*, 1(1), 1–131.

Bonvillian, W. (2012), 'Reinventing American Manufacturing: The Role of Innovation', *Innovations*, 7(3), 97–125.

Bord, V. and Santos, J. (2012), 'The Rise of the Originate-to-Distribute Model and the Role of Banks in Financial Intermediation', *FRBNY Economic Policy Review*, July, 21–34.

Borg, C. and Mayo, P. (2005), 'The EU Memorandum on Lifelong Learning: Old Wine in New Bottles?', *Globalisation, Societies and Education*, 3(2), 203–25.

Brandt, L. and Rawski, T. (eds.) (2019), *Policy, Regulation, and Innovation in China's Electricity and Telecom Industries*. Cambridge: Cambridge University Press.

Brenner, N., Peck, J., and Theodore, N. (2010), 'Variegated Neoliberalization: Geographies, Modalities, Pathways', *Global Networks*, 10(2), 182–222.

Broadberry, S. and Irwin, D. (2004), 'Labour Productivity in the United States and the United Kingdom in the Nineteenth Century', NBER Working Paper No.10364.

Brusco, S. (1986), 'Small Firms and Industrial Districts: The Experience of Italy', in D. Keeble and E. Wever (eds.) *New Firms and Regional Development in Europe*, Beckenham and Kent: Croom Helm, pp. 184–202.

Buckley, P. and Casson, M. (1976), *The Future of the Multinational Enterprise*, Basingstoke and London: Macmillan.

Budowski, M., Tillmann, R., Keim, W., and Amacker, M. (2010), 'Conceptualizing "Precarious Prosperity": Empirical and Theoretical Elements for Debate', *International Journal of Comparative Sociology*, 51(4), 268–88.

Busemeyer, M., de la Porte, C., Garritzmann, J., and Pavolini, E. (2018), 'The Future of the Social Investment State: Politics, Policies and Outcomes', *Journal of European Public Policy*, 25(6), 801–9.

Butollo, F. (2014), *The End of Cheap Labour? Industrial Transformation and 'Social Upgrading' in China*, Campus Verlag: Frankfurt.

Cadwalladr, C. (2016), 'Google, Democracy and the Truth about Internet Search', *The Guardian*. https://www.theguardian.com/technology/2016/dec/04/google-democracy-truth-internet-search-facebook.

Cai, F. (2006), 'Choosing a Growth Pattern that Suits the Present Development Stage', *China Economist*, July, 80–8.

Cai, F. (2014a), 'Approaching a Neoclassical Scenario: The Labour Market in China After the Lewis Turning Point', in Y-P Huang and F. Cai eds, *Debating the Lewis Turning Point in China*, London: Routledge, pp. 1–16.

Cai, F. (2014b), 'Demographic Transition, Demographic Dividend and the Lewis Turning Point in China', in Y-P Huang and F. Cai eds, *Debating the Lewis Turning Point in China*, London: Routledge, pp. 17–29.

Cain, P. and Hopkins, A. (1993), *British Imperialism: Innovation and Expansion 1688–1914*, White Plains, NY: Longman.

Cain, P. and Hopkins, A. (1980), 'The Political Economy of British Expansion Overseas, 1750-1914', *The Economic History Review*, New Series, 33(4), 463–90.

Cao, Y. and Levy, D. (2015), 'China's Private Higher Education: The Impact of Public-sector Privatization', *International Higher Education*, Fall, 14–15.

Cardoso, A. (2004), 'Industrial Relations, Social Dialogue and Employment in Argentina, Brazil and Mexico', ILO Employment Strategy Papers, July.

Cardoso, F. and Faletto, E. ([1969] 1979), *Dependency and Development in Latin America*, Berkeley: University of California Press.

Carlson, L. (2005), The Current State of Advertising to Children, *International Journal of Advertising*, 24(3), 395–405.

Carraz, R. and Harayama, Y. (2019), 'Japan's Innovation Systems at the Crossroads: Society 5.0', *Panorama: Insights Into Asian and European Affairs*, 1, January, 33–45.

Carroll, T. (2017), 'Late Capitalism and the Shift from the "Developmental State" to the Variegated Market State', in T. Carroll and D. Jarvis (eds.) *Asia after the Developmental State: Disembedding Autonomy*, Cambridge: Cambridge University Press, pp. 93–123.

Carroll, T. and Jarvis, D. (eds.) (2017), *Asia after the Developmental State: Disembedding Autonomy*, Cambridge: Cambridge University Press.

Castells, M. ([1993] 2009), *The Rise of the Network Society*, 2nd edn., London and New York: Wiley-Blackwell.

Castells, M. (1996), *The Rise of the Network Society, The Information Age: Economy, Society and Culture Vol. I*, Cambridge, MA, and Oxford: Wiley-Blackwell.

Cerny, P. (2010), 'The Competiton State Today: From Raison d'Etat to Raison de Monde', *Policy Studies*, 31(1), 5–21.

Cerny, P. (1997), 'Paradoxes of the Competition State: The Dynamics of Political Globalization', *Government and Opposition*, 32(2), 251–74.

Challis, L., Fuller, S., Henwood, M., Klein, R., Plowden, W., Webb, A., Whittinghan, P., and Wistow, G. (1988), *Joint Approaches to Social Policy: Rationality and Practice*, Cambridge: Cambridge University Press.

Chamberlin, E. (1933), *The Theory of Monopolistic Competition*, Cambridge, MA: Harvard University Press.

Chan, A. (1997), 'Chinese Danwei Reforms: Convergence With the Japanese Model?', in X. Lü and E. Perry (eds.) *Danwei: The Changing Chinese Workplace in Historical and Comparative Perspective*, New York: M.E. Sharpe, pp. 91–113.

Chandler, A. (1990), *Scale and Scope: The Dynamics of Industrial Capitalism*, Cambridge, MA: Belknap Press.

Chandler, A. (1977), *The Visible Hand: The Managerial Revolution in American Business*, Cambridge, MA: Belknap/Harvard University Press.

Chandler, A. (1962), *Strategy and Structure: Chapters in the History of American Industrial Enterprise*, Cambridge, MA: MIT Press.

Chang, H-J. (2002a), *Kicking Away the Ladder: Development Strategy in Historical Perspective*, London: Anthem Press.

Chang, H-J. (2002b), 'The Role of Social Policy in Economic Development: Some Theoretical Reflections and Lessons From East Asia', Prepared for UNRISD, Geneva.

Chang, K-S. (2019), *Developmental Liberalism in South Korea: Formation, Degeneration, and Transnationalization*, London: Palgrave Macmillan.

Chang, K-S. (2010a), *South Korea Under Compressed Modernity: Familial Political Economy in Transition*, London: Routledge.

Chang, K-S. (2010b), 'The Second Modern Condition? Compressed Modernity as Internalized Reflexive Cosmopolitanization', *The British Journal of Sociology*, 61(3), 444–64.

Chang, K-S. (1999), 'Compressed Modernity and Its Discontents: South Korean Society in Transition' in *Economy and Society*, 28(1), pp. 30–55.

Chang, K-S. and Song, M-Y. (2010), 'The Stranded Individualizer Under Compressed Modernity: South Korean Women in Individualization Without Individualism', *The British Journal of Sociology*, 61(3), 539–64.

Chapman, D. and Chien, C-L. (2014), 'Expanding Out and Up: What Are the System-Level Dynamics? Case Study of Malaysia and Thailand', in UNESCO Institute for Statistics, (eds.) *Higher Education in Asia, Expanding Out and Up: The Rise of Graduate Education and University Research*, Montreal, Canada: Expanding Up, pp. 37–48.

Chen, M. (2012), 'The Informal Economy: Definitions, Theories and Policies', WIEGO Working Paper No.1, Cambridge, MA.

Chernilo, D. (2011), The Critique of Methodological Nationalism: Theory and History', *Thesis Eleven*, 106(1), 98–117.

Chesbrough, H. (2003), *Open Innovation: The New Imperative for Creating and Profiting From Technology*, Boston: Harvard Business School Press.

Chesbrough, H. and Kusunoki, K. (2001), 'The Modularity Trap: Innovation, Technology Phase Shifts, and the Resulting Limits of Virtual Organizations', in I. Nonaka and D. Teece (eds.) *Managing Industrial Knowledge*, London: Sage Press, pp. 202–30.

Chesbrough, H., Vanhaverbeke, W., and West, J. (eds.) (2006), *Open Innovation: Researching a New Paradigm*, Oxford: Oxford University Press.

Cheung, T. M. (2014), *Forging China's Military Might: A New Framework for Assessing Innovation*, Baltimore, MD: Johns Hopkins University Press.

Chibber, V. (2003), *Locked in Place: State Building and Late Industrialization in India*, Princeton, NJ: Princeton University Press.

Chipidzaa, W. and Leidnerb, D. (2019), 'A Review of the ICT-enabled Development Literature: Towards a Power Parity Theory of ICT4D', *The Journal of Strategic Information Systems*, 28, (2), 145–74

Choi, S. and Peng, Y. (2015), 'Humanized Management? Capital and Migrant Labour in a Time of Labour Shortage in South China', *Human Relations*, 68(2), 287–304.

Christensen, C. and Raynor, M. (2003), 'Why Hard-Nosed Executives Should Care About Management Theory', *Harvard Business Review*, 81(9), 66–74.

Chu, R., Fortunati, L., Law, P-L., and Yang, S. (eds.) (2012), *Mobile Communication and Greater China*, London: Routledge.

Cibils, A. and Allami, C. (2013), 'Financialization vs Development Finance : The Case of the Post-Crisis Argentine Banking System', *Revue de la regulation* (En Ligne) 13/1er semester/Spring, 1–23

Cingano, F. (2014), 'Trends in Income Inequality and its Impact on Economic Growth', OECD Social, Employment and Migration Working Papers No. 163, OECD Publishing.

Clark, C. ([1940] 1951), *The Conditions of Economic Progress*. London: Macmillan.

Cole, R. (1978), 'The Late-Developer Hypothesis: An Evaluation of Its Relevance for Japanese Employment Practices', *The Journal of Japanese Studies*, 4(2), 247–65.

Collier, P. (2019), *The Future of Capitalism: Facing the New Anxieties*, New York: Harper Collins.

Colpan, A. and Hikino, T. (2010), 'Foundations of Business Groups: Towards an Integrated Framework', in A. Colpan, T. Hikino, and J. Lincoln (eds.) *The Oxford Handbook of Business Groups*, Oxford: Oxford University Press, pp. 15–66.

Corbridge, S., Harriss, J., and Jeffrey, C. (2014), '"Lopsided", "Failed", or "Tortuous": India's Problematic Transition and Its Implications for Labour', in D. Davin and B. Harriss-White (eds.) *China and India: Pathways of Economic and Social Development*, Oxford: Oxford University Press/The British Academy, pp. 157–72.

Córdova, E. (1986), 'From Full Time Wage Employment to Atypical Employment: A Major Shift in the Evolution of Labour Relations?', *International Labour Review*, 125(6), 641–57.

Crouch, C. (2011), *The Strange Non-death of Neoliberalism*, Cambridge: Polity Press.

CSOT (2017), 'Company Profile of Shenzhen China Star Optoelectronics Technology Co., Ltd (CSOT)', PowerPoint presentation.

Cumings, B. (1989), 'The Political Economy of China's Turn Outward', in S. Kim (ed.) *China and the World: New Directions in Chinese Foreign Relations* (2nd edition), Boulder, CO: Westview Press, pp. 203–36.

Cumings, B. (1984), 'The Origins and Development of the Northeast Asian Political Economy: Industrial Sectors, Product Cycles, and Political Consequences', in F. Deyo (ed.) *The Political Economy of the New Asian Industrialism*, Ithaca, NY: Cornell University Press, pp. 44–83.

Cusso, R. (2006), 'Restructuring UNESCO's Statistical Services – The "Sad Story" of UNESCO's Education Statistics: Four Years Later', *International Journal of Educational Development*, 26, 532–44.

Cusso, R. and D'Amico, S. (2005), 'From Development Comparatism to Globalization Comparativism: Towards More Normative International Education Statistics', *Comparative Education*, 41(2), 199–216.

Cusumano, M. (1989), 'Scientific Industry": Strategy, Technology and Entrepreneurship in Prewar Japan', in W. Wray (ed.) *Managing Industrial Enterprise: Cases From Japan's Prewar Experience*. Cambridge, MA: Harvard University Press, pp. 269–315.

Dale, R. (2000), 'Globalization and Education: Demonstrating a "Common World Educational Culture" or Locating a "Globally Structured Educational Agenda"?', *Educational Theory*, 50(4), 427–48.

Dallas, M., Ponte, S., and Sturgeon, T. (2019), 'Power in Global Value Chains', *Review of International Political Economy*, 26(4), 666–94.

Damgaard, J., Elkjaer, T., and Johannesen, N. (2019), 'The Rise of Phantom Investments: Empty Corporate Shells in Tax Havens Undermine Tax Collection in Advanced, Emerging Market, and Developing Economies', *Finance & Development*, 56(3). https://www.imf.org/external/pubs/ft/fandd/2019/09/the-rise-of-phantom-FDI-in-tax-havens-damgaard.htm.

Dang, Q-A. (2009), 'Recent Higher Education Reforms in Vietnam: The Role of the World Bank', Working Papers on University Reform 13, Danish School of Education (DPU), University of Aarhus.

Dannreuther, R. (2007), 'War and Insecurity: Legacies of Northern and Southern State Formation', *Review of International Studies*, 33(2), 307–26.

Dasgupta S. and Singh, A. (2006), 'Manufacturing, Services and Premature De-industrialization in Developing Countries: A Kaldorian Analysis', UNU-WIDER Research Paper 2006/49.

Dasgupta S. and Singh, A. (2005), 'Will Services Be the New Engine of Indian Economic Growth?', *Development and Change*, 36(6), 1035–58.

Datta, A. (2017), 'Introduction: Fast Cities in an Urban Age', in A. Datta and A. Shaban (eds.) *Mega-Urbanization in the Global South: Fast Cities and the New Urban Utopias of the Postcolonial State*, London: Routledge, pp. 1–27.

Datta, A. (2015), 'New Urban Utopias of Postcolonial India: "Entrepreneurial Urbanization" in Dholera Smart City, Gujarat', in *Dialogues in Human Geography*, 5 (1), 3–22.

Datta, A. and Shaban, A. (eds.) (2017), *Mega-Urbanization in the Global South: Fast Cities and the New Urban Utopias of the Postcolonial State*, London: Routledge.

Davidow, W. (1992), *The Virtual Corporation: Structuring and Revitalizing the Corporation for the 21st Century*, New York: Harper Collins.

Davis, D. (2004), *Discipline and Development: Middle Classes and Prosperity in East Asia and Latin America*, Cambridge: Cambridge University Press.

Davis, D., Kaplinsky, R., and Morris, M. (2018), 'Rents, Power and Governance in Global Value Chains', *Journal of World-Systems Research*, 24(1), 43–71.

Davis, L., Paulo, J., de Souza, A., and Hernandez, G. (2019), 'An Empirical Analysis of Minsky Regimes in the U.S. Economy', *Cambridge Journal of Economics*, 43(3), 541–83.

D'Costa, A. (2014), 'Compressed Capitalism and Development: Primitive Accumulation, Petty Commodity Production, and Capitalist Maturity in India and China', *Critical Asian Studies*, 46(2), 317–44.

D'Costa, A. (2011), 'Compressed Capitalism and Development: Primitive Accumulation, Petty Commodity Production, and Capitalist Maturity in India and China', paper presented to 'Rethinking Development in an Age of Scarcity and Uncertainty' conference, University of York, 19–22 September.

Deacon, B. (2005), 'The Governance and Politics of Global Social Policy', *Social Policy and Society*, 4(4), 437–45.

Deacon, B. and Cohen, S. (2011), 'From the Global Politics of Poverty Alleviation to the Global Politics of Social Solidarity', *Global Social Policy*, 11(2–3), 233–49.

Deacon, B., Hulse, M., and Stubbs, P. (1997), *Global Social Policy*, London: Sage.

Deakin, S. (2005), 'The Comparative Evolution of the Employment Relationship', University of Cambridge Centre for Business Research Working Papers No.317.

Deakin, S. and Wilkinson, F. (2005), *The Law of the Labour Market: Industrialization, Employment and Legal Evolution*, Oxford: Oxford University Press.

Dedrick, J., Kraemer, K., and Linden, G. (2010), 'Who Profits from Innovation in Global Value Chains? A Study of the iPod and Notebook PCs', *Industrial and Corporate Change 19*(1), 81–116.

Dedrick, J. and Kraemer, K. (1998), *Asia's Computer Challenge: Threat or Opportunity for the United States and the World?* Oxford: Oxford University Press.

Defoe, D. (1728), *A Plan of the English Commerce*, published by C. Rivington, republished by Basil Blackwell, 1928.

Demir, F. (2007), 'The Rise of Rentier Capitalism and the Financialization of Real Sectors in Developing Countries', *Review of Radical Political Economics*, 39(3), 351–9.

Dertouzos, M., Lester, R., and Solow, R. (1989), *Made in America: Regaining the Productive Edge*, Cambridge, MA: MIT Press.

deTreville, S. and Antonakis, J. (2006), 'Could Lean Production Job Design be Intrinsically Motivating? Contextual, Configurational, and Levels-of-analysis Issues', *Journal of Operations Management*, 24(2), 99–123

Deutschmann, C. (2019), *Disembedded Markets, Economic Theology and Global Capitalism*, Abingdon: Routledge.

Dewey, C. (2016), '98 Personal Data Points that Facebook Uses to Target Ads to You', *Washington Post, The Intersect*, August 19.

Dillinger, W. (1994), 'Decentralization and Its Implications for Service Delivery', UNDP/UNCHS/World Bank Urban Delivery Programme, Urban Management and Municipal Finance Paper 16, Washington, DC: World Bank.

Distelhorst, G., Hainmueller, J., and Locke, R. (2015), 'Does Lean Improve Labour Standards? Capability Building and Social Performance in the Nike Supply Chain', SSRN/Watson Institute for International Studies Research Paper No.2013–09.

Dizikes, P. (2019), 'MIT Report Examines How To Make Technology Work For Society; Task Force Calls for Bold Public and Private Action to Harness Technology for Shared Prosperity', *MIT News*, September 4.

Doner, R. and Schneider, B. (2016), 'The Middle-income Trap: More Politics Than Economics', *World Politics*, 68(4), 608–44.

Dore, R. (2008), 'Financialization of the Global Economy', *Industrial and Corporate Change*, 17(6), 1097–112.

Dore, R. (1990), 'Reflections on Culture and Social Change', in G. Gereffi and D.L. Wyman (eds.) *Manufacturing Miracles: Paths of Industrialization in Latin America*, Princeton, NJ: Princeton University Press, pp. 353–67.

Dore, R. (1987), *Taking Japan Seriously: A Confucian Perspective on Leading Economic Issues*, London: Athlone, and Stanford, CA: Stanford University Press.

Dore, R. (1976), *The Diploma Disease: Education, Qualification and Development*, London: Allen and Unwin.

Dore, R. (1973), *British Factory—Japanese Factory: The Origins of National Diversity in Industrial Relations*, Berkeley: University of California Press.

Dore, R. (1966), 'On the Possibility and Desirability of a Theory of Modernization', in Asiatic Research Centre, Korea University (ed.) *International Conference on the Problems of Modernization in East Asia: Report*, Seoul: Korea University, pp. 157–62.

Dore, R. (1963), *Education in Tokugawa Japan*, London: Routledge.

Dore, R. (1959), 'Japan: Country of Accelerated Transition (A Review Article)', *Population Studies*, 13(1), 103–11.

Dreze, J. and Sen, A. (2011), 'Putting Growth in Its Place', *Outlook*, 14 November, 1–23.

D'Souza, D. (2019), 'The Impact of Trump's H-1B Visa Crackdown in 5 Charts,' *Investopedia*, 27 June. https://www.investopedia.com/news/impact-trumps-h1b-visa-crackdown-5-charts/.

Duke, B. (1973), *Japan's Militant Teachers: A History of the Left-wing Teachers' Movement*, Honolulu: University Press of Hawaii.

Dunning, J. (1988), 'The Eclectic Paradigm of International Production: A Restatement and Some Possible Extensions', *Journal of International Business Studies*, 19(1), 1–31.

Durand, C. and W. Milberg (2019), 'Intellectual Monopoly in Global Value Chains', *Review of International Political Economy*, 27(2), 404–429.

Dutz, M. (2018), *Jobs and Growth: Brazil's Productivity Agenda*, International Development in Focus Series, Washington, DC: World Bank Group.

Easterly, W., Islam, R., and Stiglitz, J. (2000), 'Shaken and Stirred, Explaining Growth Volatility', in *Annual Bank Conference on Development Economics*, Washington, DC: World Bank, pp. 1–13.

Eaton, S. (2016), *The Advance of the State in Contemporary China: State-Market Relations in the Reform Era*, Cambridge: Cambridge University Press.

Eichengreen, B., Park, D., and Shin, K. (2012), 'When Fast-Growing Economies Slow Down: International Evidence and Implications for China', *Asian Economic Papers*, 11(1), 42–87.

Epstein, G. (2005), 'Introduction', in G. Epstein (ed.) *Financialization and the World Economy*, Cheltenham: Edward Elgar, pp. 3–16.

Ercoskun, O. (ed.) (2011), 'Green and Ecological Technologies for Urban Planning: Creating Smart Cities', *IGI-Global*. https://www.igi-global.com/book/green-ecological-technologies-urban-planning/55271.

Ericson, S. (1989), 'Railroads in Crisis: The Financing and Management of Japanese Railway Companies During the Panic of 1890', in W. Wray (ed.) *Managing Industrial Enterprise: Cases From Japan's Prewar Experience*, Cambridge, MA: Harvard University Press, pp. 121–82.

Eriksen, S. (2017), 'State Effects and the Effects of State Building: Institution Building and the Formation of State-centred Societies', *Third World Quarterly*, 38(4), 771–86.

Esping-Andersen, G. and Billari, F. (2015), 'Retheorizing Family Demographics', *Population and Development Review*, 41(1), 1–31.

Eubanks, E. (2017), *Automating Inequality: How High-tech Tools Profile, Police, and Punish the Poor*, New York: St Martin's Press.

Evans, P. (1995), *Embedded Autonomy: States and Industrial Transformation*, Princeton, NJ: Princeton University Press.

Evans, P. and Staveteig, S. (2008), 'The Changing Structure of Employment in Contemporary China', in D. Davis and W. Feng (eds.) *Creating Wealth and Poverty in Postsocialist China*, Stanford, CA: Stanford University Press, pp. 69–82.

Fan, S., Zhang, L., and Zhang, X. (2002), 'Growth, Inequality, and Poverty in Rural China: The Role of Public Investments', International Food Policy Research Institute (IFPRI) Research Report 125, Washington, DC.

Farole, T. and Akinci, G. (2011), *Special Economic Zones: Progress, Emerging Challenges, and Future Directions*, Washington, DC: World Bank.

Federation of Indian Chambers of Commerce and Industry (FICCI), National Association of Software and Service Companies (NASSCOM) and Ernst and Young (2017), 'Future of Jobs in India: A 2022 Perspective', FICCI, NASSCOM, and EY.

Feenstra, R. and Hamilton, G. (2006), *Emerging Economies, Divergent Paths: Business Groups and Economic Organization in South Korea and Chinese Taipei*, New York: Cambridge University Press.

Felipe, J. (2012), 'Tracking the Middle-Income Trap: What Is It, Who Is in It, and Why, Part 1?', Asian Development Bank Working Paper No.306, March.

Felipe, J., Mehta, A., and Rhee, C. (2014), 'Manufacturing Matters... But It's the Jobs That Count', ADB Economics Working Paper Series, No. 420.

Feng, X. (2018), *The Making of Labour Precariousness in Post-1949 China*, DPhil thesis, University of Oxford.

Feng, X. (2009), 'The Emergence of Temporary Staffing Agencies in China', in J. Fudge and K. Strauss (eds.) *Temporary Work, Agencies and Unfree Labour: Insecurity in the New World of Work*, London: Routledge, pp. 143–63.

Ferguson, N. (2008), *The Ascent of Money: A Financial History of the World*, New York: Penguin.

Fernández-Macías, E. and Hurley, J. (2008), *ERM Report, 2008: More and Better Jobs: Patterns of Employment in Europe*, Dublin, Ireland: European Foundation for the Improvement of Living and Working Conditions.

Fernholz, T. (2016), 'The World Bank Is Eliminating the Term "Developing Country" from Its Data Vocabulary', *Quartz*, May 17. https://qz.com/685626/the-world-bank-is-eliminating-the-term-developing-country-from-its-data-vocabulary/.

Ferrera, M. (2010), 'From the Welfare State to the Social Investment State', LPF Working Paper No.1, centro Einaudi, ISSN 2036–1246.

Fine, C. (1998), *Clockspeed—Winning Industry Control in the Age of Temporary Advantage*, New York: Perseus Books.

Fisher, A.G.B. (1935), *The Clash of Progress and Security*, London: MacMillan.

Flaaen, A., Ghani, E., and Mishra, S. (2013), 'How to Avoid Middle-income Traps? Evidence From Malaysia', The World Bank Economic Policy and Debt Unit Policy Research Working Paper 6427.

Flechtner, S. and Panther, S. (2013), 'Middle-income Traps, Growth and Inequality', paper presented to ECAFE Annual Conference.

Fligstein, N. (2002), *The Architecture of Markets: An Economic Sociology of Twenty-first Century Capitalist Societies*, Princeton, NJ: Princeton University Press.

Florida, R. and Kenney, M. (1993), *Beyond Mass Production: The Japanese System and Its Transfer to the U.S.*, New York: Oxford University Press.

Florida, R. and Kenney, M. (1991), *The Breakthrough Illusion*, New York: Basic Books.

Fourastié, J. (1949), *Le Grand Espoir du XXe Siècle*, Paris: Presses Universitaires de France.

Fox, A. (1985), *History and Heritage: The Social Origins of the British Industrial Relations System*, London: Allen and Unwin.

Freeman, C. and Soete, L. (1997), *The Economics of Industrial Innovation*, 3rd edition, Cambridge, MA: MIT Press.

Freeman, R. (2006), 'The Great Doubling: America in the New Global Economy', Usery Lecture, 8 April, Georgia State University.

Freeman, R. (2014), 'A Labour Market With Chinese Characteristics', in G.C. Chow (ed.) *The Routledge Handbook of the Chinese Economy*, Princeton, NJ: Routledge, Chapter 7.

Freeman, R. (2005), 'What Really Ails Europe (and America): The Doubling of the Global Workforce', *The Globalist*, 3 June. http://www.theglobalist.com/StoryId.aspx?StoryId=4542.

Freeman, J., Carroll, G., and Hannan, M. (1983). 'The Liability of Newness: Age Dependence in Organizational Death Rates', *American Sociological Review* 48(5), 692–710.

Friedman, E. and Kuruvilla, S. (2015), 'Experimentation and Decentralization in China's Labour Relations', *Human Relations* 68(2), 181–95.

Friedman, T. (2005), *The World Is Flat: A Brief History of the Twenty-first Century*, 1st edn., New York: Farrar, Straus and Giroux.

Fröbel, F., Heinrichs, J., and Kreye, O. (1980), *The New International Division of Labour: Structural Unemployment in Industrialised Countries and Industrialisation in Developing Countries*, Cambridge: Cambridge University Press.

Fu, X., Woo, W-T., and Hou, J. (2016), 'Technological Innovation Policy in China: The Lessons, and the Necessary Changes Ahead', *Economic Change and Restructuring*, 49(2–3), 139–57.

Fuchs, V. (1968), 'The Service Economy', NBER General Series No. 87

Fuller, D. (2015), *Paper Tigers, Hidden Dragons: The Political Economy of China's Technological Development*, Oxford: Oxford University Press.

Galbraith, James K. (2008), *The Predator State: How Conservatives Abandoned the Free Market and Why Liberals Should Too*, New York: Free Press.

Galbraith, John K. (1967), *The New Industrial State*, Boston: Houghton Mifflin.

Gallagher, K. and Zarsky, L. (2007), *The Enclave Economy: Foreign Investment and Sustainable Development in Mexico's Silicon Valley*, Cambridge, MA: The MIT Press.

Garron, S. (1998), *Molding Japanese Minds: The State in Everyday Life*, Princeton, NJ: Princeton University Press.

Garten, J. (1997), *The Big Ten: The Big Emerging Markets and How They Will Change Our Lives*, New York: Basic Books.

Gaynor, N. (2016), 'Challenges to Decentralization in the Democratic Republic of the Congo: Beyond the Political Settlement', *Journal of International Development*, 28, 198–213.

Geerlings, H. and Stead, D. (2003), 'The Integration of Land Use Planning, Transport and Environment in European Policy and Research', *Transport Policy*, 10(3), 187–96.

Gereffi, G. (1994), 'The Organization of Buyer-driven Global Commodity Chains: How U.S. Retailers Shape Overseas Production Networks', in G. Gereffi and M. Korzeniewicz (eds.) *Commodity Chains and Global Capitalism*, Westport, CN: Greenwood Press, pp. 95–122.

Gereffi, G., Humphrey, J., and Sturgeon, T. (2005), 'The Governance of Global Value Chains', *Review of International Political Economy*, 12(1), 78–104.

Gereffi, G. and Lee, J. (2016), 'Economic and Social Upgrading in Global Value Chains and Industrial Clusters: Why Governance Matters', *Journal of Business Ethics*, 13(3), 25–38.

Gereffi, G. and Sturgeon, T. (2013), 'Global Value Chain-Oriented Industrial Policy: The Role of Emerging Economies', in D. Elms and P. Low (eds.) *Supply Chains in a Changing World*, Geneva, Singapore, and Hong Kong: WTO in cooperation with the Fung Global Institute and the Temasek Centre for Trade and Negotiations, pp. 329–60.

Gerschenkron A. (1962), *Economic Backwardness in Historical Perspective: A Book of Essays*, Cambridge, MA: Harvard University Press.

Gibbons, M., Limoges, C., Nowotny, H., Schwartzman, S., Scott, P., and Trow, M. (1994), *The New Production of Knowledge; the Dynamics of Science and Research in Contemporary Societies*, London: Sage Publications.

Giddens, A. (1990), *The Consequences of Modernity*, Cambridge: Polity Press.

Godin, B. (2006), 'The Knowledge-based Economy: Conceptual Framework or Buzzword?', *Journal of Technology Transfer*, 31, 17–30.

Goldscheider, F., Bernhardt, E., and Lappegård, T. (2015), 'The Gender Revolution: A Framework for Understanding Changing Family and Demographic Behaviour', *Population and Development Review*, 41(2), 207–39.

Goldstein, A., Bonaglia, F., and Mathews, J. (2006), 'Accelerated Internationalization by Emerging Multinationals: The Case of White Goods'. https://www.oecd.org/dev/36317032.pdf.

Gollin, D. (2014), 'The Lewis Model: A Sixty Year Retrospective', *The Journal of Economic Perspectives*', 28(3), 71–88.

Gollin, D., Jedwab, R., and Vollrath, D. (2016), Urbanization With and Without Industrialization', *Journal of Economic Growth*, 21(1), 35–70.

Goodfellow, T. (2017), 'Urban Fortunes and Skeleton Cityscapes: Real Estate and Late Urbanization in Kigali and Addis Ababa', *International Journal of Urban and Regional Research*, 41(5), 786–802.

Goodman, R., White, G., and Kwon, H-J., (eds.) (1998), *The East Asian Welfare Model: Welfare Orientalism and the State*, London: Routledge.

Gooptu, N. (2007), 'Economic Liberalization, Work and Democracy: Industrial Decline and Urban Politics in Kolkata', *Economic and Political Weekly*, 43(21), 1922–33.

Gooptu, N. (2013), 'Servile Sentinels of the City: Private Security Guards, Organized Informality, and Labour in Interactive Services in Globalized India', *IRSH*, 58, 9–38.

Gordon, A. (1985), *The Evolution of Labour Relations in Japan: Heavy Industry, 1853–1955*, Cambridge, MA: Harvard University Press.

Gospel, H. (1992), *Markets, Firms and the Management of Labour in Modern Britain*, Cambridge: Cambridge University Press.

Gourevitch, P., Bohn, R., and McKendrick, D. (2000), 'Globalization of Production: Insights from the Hard Disk Drive Industry', *World Development* 28, 301–17.

Grimes, S. (2015), 'Some Thoughts on China's Integration Into the Global Value Chain (GVC) of ICT', PPT from the Whitaker Institute, National University of Ireland, Galway, presented at East China Normal University, Shanghai, China.

Grinin, L. and Koroteyev, A. (2015), *Great Divergence and Great Convergence: A Global Perspective*, Basel: Springer International.

Grossman, G. and Rossi-Hansberg, E. (2008), 'Trading Tasks: A Simple Theory of Offshoring,' *American Economic Review*, 98(5), 1978–97.

Grove, A. ([1996] 1999), *Only the Paranoid Survive: How to Exploit the Crisis Points That Challenge Every Company and Career*, Chicago and New York: Currency Doubleday.

Grunwald, J. and Flamm, K. (1985), *The Global Factory: Foreign Assembly and International Trade*, Washington, DC: The Brookings Institution.

Hall, J. (1986), *Powers and Liberties*, Harmondsworth: Penguin.

Hallak, J. (1990), *Investing in the Future*, Paris: Pergamon Press.

Hamilton, G. and. Kao, C-S. (2017), *Making Money: How Taiwanese Industrialists Embraced the Global Economy*, Stanford, CA: Stanford University Press.

Hampson F. and Jardine, E. (2016), *Look Who's Watching*, Waterloo, ON, Canada: Centre for International Governance Innovation.
Han, J. (2016), 'The Emergence of Social Corporatism in China: Nonprofit Organizations, Private Foundations, and the State', *China Review*, 16(2), 27–53.
Han, S-J. and Shim, Y-H. (2010), 'Redefining Second Modernity for East Asia: A Critical Assessment', *British Journal of Sociology*, 61(3), 465–88.
Hansen, M. and Woronov, T. (2013), 'Demanding and Resisting Vocational Education: A Comparative Study of Schools in Rural and Urban China', *Comparative Education*, 49(2), 242–59.
Hao, H., Ou, X., et al. (2014), 'China's Electric Vehicle Subsidy Scheme: Rationale and Impacts.' *Energy Policy* 73, 722–32.
Haraguchi, N., Cheng, C.F.C., and Smeets, E. (2017), 'The Importance of Manufacturing in Economic Development: Has This Changed?', *World Development*, 93, 293–315.
Harrison, B. (1994), *Lean and Mean: the Changing Landscape of Corporate Power in the Age of Flexibility*, Cambridge, MA: Harvard University Press.
Harvey, D. (1989), *The Condition of Postmodernity: An Enquiry Into the Origins of Cultural Change*, Cambridge, MA: Blackwell.
Harvey, D. (1985), *The Urbanization of Capital: Studies in the History and Theory of Capitalist Urbanization*, Baltimore, MD: Johns Hopkins University Press.
Harvey, D. (1978), 'The Urban Process Under Capitalism: A Framework for Analysis', *International Journal of Urban and Regional Research*, 2.1(4), 101–31.
Hatch, W. and Yamamura, K. (1996), *Asia in Japan's Embrace: Building a Regional Production Alliance*, Cambridge: Cambridge University Press.
Haworth, N. (2013), 'Compressed Development: Global Value Chains, Multinational Enterprises and Human Resource Development in the 21st Century', *Journal of World Business*, 48(2), 251–9.
Hazama, H. (1960), 'Keiei kazoku-shugi no ronri to sono keisei katei' ('Logic and Emergence of Managerial Familism'), *Shakaigaku hyōron*, 11(1), 2–18.
Heilmann, S. and Melton, O. (2013), 'The Reinvention of Development Planning in China, 1993–2012', *Modern China*, 39(6), 580–628.
Heilmann, S. and Perry, E. (2011), 'Embracing Uncertainty: Guerilla Policy Style and Adaptive Governance in China', in S. Heilmann and E. Perry (eds.) *Mao's Invisible Hand: Adaptive Governance in China*, Cambridge, MA: Harvard University Press, pp. 1–29.
Heller, P. (2013), 'Challenges and Opportunities: Civil Society in a Globalizing World', UNDP Human Development Report Office Occasional Paper 2013/06.
Henderson, J. and Hooper, M. (2019), 'China and European Innovation: Dynamics, Logics and Consequences of Corporate Acquisitions', Paper presented at the China in Europe Research Network workshop, European Union Cooperation in Science and Technology Association (COST), Brussels, Belgium, 7 November.
Herrigel, G. (1996), *Industrial Constructions: The Sources of German Industrial Power*, New York: Cambridge University Press.
Hershatter G. (2007), *Women in China's Long Twentieth Century*. Berkeley: University of California Press.
Hilferding, R. ([1910] 1981), *Finance Capitalism*, London: Routledge and Kegan Paul.
Hinchliffe, K. (1993), 'Neo-liberal Prescriptions for Education Finance: Unfortunately Necessary or Inherently Desirable?', *International Journal of Educational Development*, 13(2), 183–7.

Hirschman, A. (1981), *Essays in Trespassing: Economics to Politics and Beyond*, Cambridge: Cambridge University Press.
Hirschman, A. (1971), *A Bias for Hope: Essays on Development and Latin America*, New Haven, CT: Yale University Press.
Hirschman, A. (1958), *The Strategy of Economic Development*, New Haven, CT: Yale University Press.
Hobsbawm, E. ([1962] 1988), *The Age of Revolution, 1789–1848*, London: Weidenfeld and Nicolson.
Hoekman, B. and Djankov, S. (1997), 'Determinants of the Export Structure of Countries in Central and Eastern Europe', *The World Bank Economic Review*, 11(3), 471–91.
Hoffmann, W.G. ([1931] 1958), *The Growth of Industrial Economics*, Oxford: Oxford University Press (orig. in German).
Hollweg, C. Smith, T., and Taglioni, D. (eds.) (2017), *Vietnam at a Crossroads: Engaging in the Next Generation of Global Value Chains*, Directions in Development—Trade. Washington, DC: World Bank.
Horner, R. and Nadvi, K. (2018), 'Global Value Chains and the Rise of the Global South: Unpacking Twenty-first Century Polycentric Trade', *Global Networks*, 18(2), 207–37.
Hou, J., Gelb, S., and Calabrese, L. (2017), 'The Shift in Manufacturing Employment in China', Supporting Economic Transformation programme, Overseas Development Institute, UK.
Howell, J. (2012), 'Civil Society, Corporatism and Capitalism in China', *Journal of Comparative Asian Development*, 11(2), 271–97.
Howell, J. (2006), 'Reflections on the Chinese State', *Development and Change*, 37, 273–97.
Howeth, L.S. (1963), *History of Communications-electronics in the United States Navy*, Washington, DC: US Government Printing Office.
Hu, D., Reardon, T., Rozelle, S., Timmer, P., and Wang, H. (2004), 'The Emergence of Supermarkets With Chinese Characteristics: Challenges and Opportunities for China's Agricultural Development', *Development Policy Review*, 22(5), 557–86.
Huang, J. and Shi, W. (2008), 'Policies and Practices of Lifelong Learning in China', *International Journal of Lifelong Education*, 27(5), 499–508.
Huang, P. (2009), 'China's Neglected Informal Economy', *Modern China*, 35(4), 405–38.
Huang, Y-P. and Cai, F. (eds.) (2014), *Debating the Lewis Turning Point in China*, London: Routledge.
Huitfeldt, H. and Jütting, J. (2009), 'Informality and Informal Employment', in OECD (ed.) *Promoting Pro-Poor Growth: Employment*, Paris: OECD, pp. 95–108.
Humphrey, J. (2000), 'Assembler-Supplier Relations in the Auto Industry: Globalisation and National Development', *Competition and Change*, 4, 245–71.
Humphrey, J. and Schmitz, H. (2002), 'How Does Insertion in Global Value Chains Affect Upgrading in Industrial Clusters?', *Regional Studies*, 36(9), 1017–27.
Hymer, S. (1976), *The International Operations of National Firms: A Study of Direct Foreign Investment*, Cambridge, MA: MIT Press.
Imai, K. and Shiu, J.M. (2010), 'Value Chain Creation and Reorganization: The Growth Path of China's Mobile Phone Handset Industry', in M. Kawakami and T. Sturgeon (eds.) *The Dynamics of Local Learning in Global Value Chains: Experiences from East Asia*. Basingstoke: Palgrave Macmillan, pp. 43–67.
Imbs, J. and Wacziarg, R. (2003), 'Stages of Diversification', *American Economic Review*, 93(1), 63–86.
Inagami, T. and Whittaker, D.H. (2005), *The New Community Firm: Employment, Governance and Management Reform in Japan*, Cambridge: Cambridge University Press.

Ingham, G. (2004), *The Nature of Money*, Cambridge: Polity Press.
Ingham, G. (1984), *Capitalism Divided? The City and Industry in British Social Development*, Basingstoke: Palgrave Macmillan.
International Labour Organization (2019), '*Helping the Gig Economy Work Better for Gig Workers*', ILO Office for the United States.
International Labour Organization (2016), *Non-standard Employment Around the World: Understanding Challenges, Shaping Prospects*, Geneva: ILO.
International Labour Organization (2015), *Non-standard Forms of Employment*, Geneva: ILO.
International Labour Organization (1999), *Decent Work*, Geneva: ILO.
Iqbal, M. (2019), 'Pokémon GO Revenue and Usage Statistics (2019)', *Business of Apps*, May 10. https://www.businessofapps.com/data/pokemon-go-statistics/.
Iriye, A. (1989), 'Japan's Drive to Great Power Status', in M. Jansen (ed.) *The Cambridge History of Japan, Volume 5 the Nineteenth Century*, Cambridge: Cambridge University Press, pp. 721–82.
Islam, S.N. (2015), 'Will Inequality Lead China to the Middle-income Trap?', UN Department of Social and Economic Affairs DSEA Working Paper No.142, New York.
Jacobs, H. (2018), 'Inside "iPhone City," The Massive Chinese Factory Town Where Half of the World's iPhones Are Produced', *Business Insider*, 7 May. https://www.businessinsider.com/apple-iphone-factory-foxconn-china-photos-tour-2018-5?r=US&IR=T.
Jacobides, M. (2006), 'The Architecture and Design of Organizational Capabilities', *Industrial and Corporate Change*, 15(1), 151–71.
Jacoby, S. ([1985] 2004), *Employing Bureaucracy: Managers, Unions and the Transformation of Work in the 20th Century*, revised edn., Mahwah, NJ: Lawrence Erlbaum Associates.
Jain-Chandra, S., Kinda, T., Kochlar, K., Shi, P., and Schauer, J. (2016), 'Sharing the Growth Dividend: Analysis of Equity in Asia', IMF Working Paper WP/16/48.
Jakobi, A. (2009), 'Global Education Policy in the Making: International Organizations and Lifelong Learning', *Globalisation, Societies and Education*, 7(4), 473–87.
Jaros, K. (2016a), 'Forging Greater Xi'an: The Political Logic of Metropolitanization', *Modern China*, 42(6), 638–73.
Jaros, K. (2016b), 'Rethinking Subnational Government Capacity in China', *Journal of Chinese Governance*, 14, 633–53.
John, D. (1999), 'Consumer Socialization of Children: A Retrospective Look at Twenty-Five Years of Research', *Journal of Consumer Research*, 26(3), 183–213.
Johnson, C. (1982), *MITI and the Japanese Miracle: The Growth of Industrial Policy, 1925–1975*, Stanford, CA: Stanford University Press.
Jomo, K.S. (2003), 'Globalization, Liberalization and Equitable Development: Lessons From East Asia', UNRISD Overarching Concerns Paper No.3.
Jütting, J. and De Laiglesia, J. (eds.) (2009), *Is Informal Normal? Towards More and Better Jobs in Developing Countries*, Paris: OECD.
Kage, R. (2011), *Civic Engagement in Postwar Japan: The Revival of a Defeated Society*, Cambridge: Cambridge University Press.
Kaldor, M. (2003), 'The Idea of Global Civil Society', *International Affairs*, 79(3), 583–93.
Kaldor, N. (1967), *Strategic Factors in Economic Development*, Ithaca, NY: Cornell University Press.
Kaldor, N. (1966), *Causes of the Slow Rate of Economic Growth of the United Kingdom*, Cambridge: Cambridge University Press.

Kamens, D. and McNeely, C. (2010), 'Globalization and the Growth of International Educational Testing and National Assessment', *Comparative Education Review*, 54(1), 5–25.

Kamimura, Y. (2018), 'Welfare Gap in East Asia: A Comparative Sociological Reflection on Family and State', paper presented at the International Conference on Global Dynamics of Social Policy, Bremen University, Bremen, 25–6 November.

Kang, X. and Han, H. (2008), 'Graduated Controls: The State-Society Relationship in Contemporary China', *Modern China*, 34(1), 36–55.

Karabarbounis. L. and Neiman, B. (2013), 'The Global Decline of the Labor Share', *Quarterly Journal of Economics*, 129 (1), 61–103.

Kariya, T. (forthcoming), 'Japan's Catch-up Modernity: Educational Transformation and Its Unintended Consequences', in H. Takeda and M. Williams (eds.) *Routledge Handbook of Contemporary Japan*, London: Routledge.

Kariya, T. (2018), 'Meritocracy, Modernity, and the Completion of Catch-up: Problems and Paradoxes', in A. Yonezawa, Y. Kitamura, B. Yamamoto, and T. Tokunaga (eds.) *Japanese Education in a Global Age: Sociological Reflections and Future Directions*, Basel: Springer.

Kasahara, S. (2004), 'The Flying Geese Paradigm: A Critical Study of Its Application to East Asian Regional Development', UNCTAD Discussion Papers No.169.

Kässi, O. and Lehdonvirta, V. (2016), 'Online Labour Index: Measuring the Online Gig Economy for Policy and Research', Oxford Internet Institute, MPRA Paper No. 74943.

Kasza, G. (2018), 'Gerschenkron, Amsden, and Japan: The State in Late Development', *Japanese Journal of Political Science*, 19(2), 146–72.

Kattan, R. (2006), 'Implementation of Free Basic Education Policy' Washington, DC: World Bank.

Kawakami, M. (2011), 'Inter-firm Dynamics of Notebook PC Value Chains and the Rise of Taiwanese Original Design Manufacturing Firms', in M. Kawakami and T. Sturgeon (eds.) *The Dynamics of Local Learning in Global Value Chains: Experiences from East Asia*, Basingstoke: Palgrave Macmillan, pp. 16–42.

Kay, C. (2002), 'Why East Asia Overtook Latin America: Agrarian Reform, Industrialisation and Development' *Third World Quarterly*, 23(6), 1073–102.

Kerr, C., Dunlop, J., Harbison, F., and Myers, C. (1960), *Industrialism and Industrial Man: The Problems of Labour and Management in Economic Growth*, Cambridge, MA: Harvard University Press.

Kharas, H. and Kohli, H. (2011), 'What is the Middle-income Trap, Why Do Countries Fall Into It, and How Can It Be Avoided?', *Global Journal of Emerging Market Economies*, 3, 281–9.

Kim, H-K., Muramatsu, M., Pempel, T.J., and Yamamura, K. (eds.) (1995), *The Japanese Civil Service and Economic Development: Catalysts of Change*, Oxford: Oxford University Press.

Kimura, S. (2007), *The Challenges of Late Industrialization: The Global Economy and the Japanese Commercial Aircraft Industry*, London: Palgrave Macmillan.

King, K., McGrath, S., and Rose, P. (2007), 'Beyond the Basics: Educating and Training Out of Poverty', *International Journal of Educational Development*, 27(4), 349–57.

King, K., Palmer, R., and Hayman, R. (2005), 'Bridging Research and Policy on Education, Training and Their Enabling Environment', *Journal of International Development*, 17(6), 803–17.

King, R. and Levine, R. (1993), 'Finance and Growth: Schumpeter Might be Right', *The Quarterly Journal of Economics* 108(3), 717–37.

Kinzley, D. (1991), *Industrial Harmony in Modern Japan: The Invention of a Tradition*, London: Routledge.

Klees, S. (2008), 'Reflections on Theory, Method, and Practice in Comparative and International Education', *Comparative Education Review*, 52(3), 301–28.

Knight, J., Deng, Q., and Li, S. (2010), 'The Puzzle of Migrant Labour Shortage and the Rural Labour Surplus in China', University of Oxford DoE Working Paper Series No.494.

Kohli, A. (2004), *State-directed Development: Political Power and Industrialization in the Global Periphery*, Cambridge: Cambridge University Press.

Koike, K. (1981), *Nihon no jukuren (Skills in Japan)*, Tokyo: Yuhikaku.

Kojima, K. (1977), *Direct Foreign Investment: A Japanese Model of Multinational Business Operations*, London: Croom Helm.

Konishi, S. (2013), *Anarchist Modernity: Cooperatism and Japanese-Russian Intellectual Relations in Modern Japan*, Cambridge, MA: Harvard University Asia Centre.

Koopman, R. Wang, Z., and Wei, S-J. (2008), 'How Much of Chinese Exports is Really Made in China? Assessing Domestic Value-Added When Processing Trade Is Pervasive', NBER Working Paper Series, No. 14109, Cambridge, MA.

Krätke, S. (1999), 'Regional Integration or Fragmentation? The German-Polish Border Region in a New Europe', *Regional Studies*, 33(7), 631–41.

Kregel, J. (2004), 'External Financing for Development and International Financial Instability', G-24 Discussion Paper Series No.32, New York: United Nations.

Krippner, G. (2005), 'The Financialization of the American Economy', *Socio-Economic Review*, 3, 173–208.

Krugman, P. (1991a), *Geography and Trade*, Cambridge, MA: MIT Press.

Krugman, P. (1991b), 'Increasing Returns and Economic Geography', *Journal of Political Economy*, 99(3), 483–99.

Kuznets, S. (1971), *Economic Growth of Nations: Total Output and Production Structure*, Cambridge, MA: Belknap Press.

Kuznets, S. (1955), 'Economic Growth and Income Inequality', *American Economic Review*, 45(1), 1–28.

Lai, K. and Daniels, J. (2015), 'Banking on Finance in Singapore: The State-Led Financialization of Banking Firms', NUS Global Production Networks Centre, GPN2015-002.

Lakhani, T., Kuruvilla, S., and Avgar, A. (2013), 'From the Firm to the Network: Global Value Chains and Employment Relations Theory', *British Journal of Industrial Relations*, 51(3), 440–72.

Lall, S. (2000), 'The Technological Structure and Performance of Developing Country Manufactured Exports, 1985–98', *Oxford Development Studies*, 28(3), 337–69.

Lall, S. (1993), 'Promoting Technology Development: The Role of Technology Transfer and Indigenous Effort', *Third World Quarterly*, 14(1), 95–108.

Lapavitsas, C. (2019), *The Left Case Against the EU*, Cambridge: Polity Press.

Lapavitsas, C. (2011), 'Theorizing Financialization', *Work, Employment and Society*, 25(4), 611–26.

Lapavitsas, C. (2009), 'Financialization Embroils Developing Countries', *Papeles de Europa*, 19, 108–39.

Larson, J. and Park, J. (2014), 'From Developmental to Network State: Government Restructuring and ICT-led Innovation in Korea', *Telecommunications Policy*, 38, 344–59.

Lazonick, W. (2015), 'Stock Buybacks: From Retain-and-reinvest to Downsize-and-distribute', Brookings Centre for Effective Public Management report, April.

Lazonick, W. (2009), *Sustainable Prosperity in the New Economy?: Business Organization and High-Tech Employment in the United States*, Kalamazoo, MI: W.E. Upjohn Institute.

Lazonick, W. (2008), 'Entrepreneurial Ventures and the Developmental State: Lessons From Advanced Economies', UNU-Wider Discussion Paper 2008/01, Helsinki.

Lazonick, W. and O'Sullivan, M. (2000), 'Maximizing Shareholder Value: A New Ideology for Corporate Governance', *Economy and Society*, 29(1), 13–35.

Leamer, E. and Storper, M. (2001), 'The Economic Geography of the Internet Age', *Journal of International Business Studies*, 32(4), 641–65.

Leathers, C. and Raines, P. (2004), 'The Schumpeterian Role of Financial Innovations in the New Economy's Business Cycle', *Cambridge Journal of Economics*, 28(5), 667–81.

Lee, C-H., Brown, W., and Wen, X. (2014), 'What Sort of Collective Bargaining is Emerging in China?', *British Journal of Industrial Relations*, 54(1), 214–36.

Lee, K. (2013), *Schumpeterian Analysis of Economic Catch-up: Knowledge, Path-Creation and the Middle-income Trap*, Cambridge: Cambridge University Press.

Lee M-J., Popkin, B., and Kim, S. (2002), 'The Unique Aspects of the Nutrition Transition in South Korea: The Retention of Healthful Elements in Their Traditional Diet', *Public Health Nutrition*, 5(1A), 197–203.

Lee, T. (2018), 'The Trump Administration Just Forced Smartphone Maker ZTE to Shut Down', *Ars Technica*, May 6. https://arstechnica.com/tech-policy/2018/05/the-trump-administration-just-forced-smartphone-maker-zte-to-shut-down.

Lechevalier, S., Debanes, P., and Shin, W. (2017), 'Financialization and Industrial Policies in Japan and Korea: Evolving Institutional Complementarities and Loss of State Capabilities', *Structural Change and Economic Dynamics*, 48(March), 69–85.

Lefebvre, H. (1970), *La Révolution Urbaine (The Urban Revolution)*, Paris: Gallimard.

Leoni, T. (2016), 'Social Investment as a Perspective on Welfare State Transformation in Europe', *Intereconomics*, 51(4), 194–200.

Lewis, A. (1954), 'Economic Development With Unlimited Supplies of Labour', *The Manchester School of Economic and Social Studies*, 22, 139–91.

Levi-Faur, D. (2012), 'States Making and Market Building for the Global South: The Developmental State vs. the Regulatory State?', Jerusalem Papers in Regulation and Governance, Working Paper No.44.

Levy-Orlik, N. (2014), 'Financialization and Economic Growth in Developing Countries: The Case of the Mexican Economy', *International Journal of Political Economy*, 42(4), 108–27.

Li, X., Liu, C., Weng, X., and Zhou, L.A. (2017), 'Target Setting in Tournaments: Theory and Evidence From China', https://papers.ssrn.com/sol3/papers.cfm?abstract_id=2937195., accessed 6 August 2018.

Li, M., Xue, H., Wen, M., Wang, W., and Wang, Y. (2016), 'Nutrition and Physical Activity Related School Environment/Policy Factors and Child Obesity in China: A Nationally Representative Study of 8573 Students in 110 Middle Schools', *Pediatric Obesity*, 12(6), 485–93.

Lima de Oliveira, R. and Zylberberg, E. (2019), 'A Tale of Two Industries: Collective Action and Industrial Policy in Brazil,' manuscript submitted to *World Development.*

Lima-de-Oliveira, R. and Sturgeon, T. (2017), 'From Resource Extraction to Knowledge Creation: Oil-Rich States, Oil Companies and the Promotion of Local R&D', MIT-IPC Working Paper 17–003.

Linden, G. Kraemer, K., and Dedrick, J. (2009), 'Who Captures Value in a Global Innovation System? The Case of Apple's iPod', *Communications of the ACM*, 52(3), 140–4.

Lindtner, S., Greenspan, A., and Li, D. (2015), 'Designed in Shenzhen: Shanzhai Manufacturing and Maker Entrepreneurs', Paper presented at the Fifth Decennial Conference on Critical Alternatives, 17–21 August, Aarhus, Denmark.

Lipietz, A. (1987), *Mirages and Miracles*, London: Verso.

Liu, G. (2014), 'Private Employment Agencies and Labour Dispatch in China', ILO Sector Working Paper No.293, Geneva.

Liu, Y. (2016), *Higher Education, Meritocracy and Inequality in China*, Singapore: Springer.

Liu, Y. and Dunne, M. (2009), 'Educational Reform in China: Tensions in National Policy and Local Practice', *Comparative Education*, 45(4), 461–76.

Locke, R., Amengual, M., and Mangla, A. (2009), 'Virtue Out of Necessity? Compliance, Commitment, and the Improvement of Labor Conditions in Global Supply Chains', *Politics & Society*, 37(3), 319–51.

Lockheed, M., Jamison, D., and Lau, L. (1980), 'Farmer Education and Farm Efficiency', *Economic Development and Cultural Change*, 29(1), 37–76.

Lüthje, B., Luo, S., and Zhang, H. (2013), *Beyond the Iron Rice Bowl: Regimes of Production and Industrial Relations in China*, Frankfurt: Campus Verlag.

Machlup, F. (1962), *The Production and Distribution of Knowledge in the United States*, Princeton, NJ: Princeton University Press.

Mahajan, G. (1999), 'Civil Society and Its Avatars: What Happened to Freedom and Democracy?', *Economic and Political Weekly*, 34(20), 1188–96.

Mahbubani, K. (2018), *Has the West Lost It? A Provocation*, London: Allen Lane.

Mahbubani, K. (2013), *The Great Convergence: Asia, the West and the Logic of One World*, Philadelphia: PublicAffairs.

Maier, C. (2012), *Leviathan 2.0: Inventing Modern Statehood*, Cambridge, MA: Harvard University Press.

Manger, M. (2014), 'The Economic Logic of Asian Preferential Trade Agreements: The Role of Intra-Industry Trade', *Journal of East Asian Studies*, 14(2), 151–84.

Mann, M. (1984), 'The Autonomous Power of the State: Its Origins, Mechanisms and Results', *European Journal of Sociology*, 25(2), 185–213.

Margolis, J. (2019), 'China Dominates the Electric Bus Market, but the US Is Getting on Board', PRI's *The World*, October 8. https://www.pri.org/stories/2019-10-08/china-dominates-electric-bus-market-us-getting-board.

Markowsky, E. (2012), 'Welcome to the Virtual Factory: American Manufacturing in the 21st Century', *ILP Institute Insider*, May 10. http://ilp.mit.edu/newsstory.jsp?id=18006.

Marshall, A. ([1890] 1961), *Principles of Economics*, London: Macmillan.

Massey, D. (1994), 'A Global Sense of Place', in *Space, Place, and Gender*, Minneapolis: University of Minnesota Press, pp. 146–56.

Mathews, J. (2006), 'Catch-up Strategies and the Latecomer Effect in Industrial Development', *New Political Economy*, 11(3), 313–36.

Mathews, J. (2002), 'Competitive Advantages of the Latecomer Firm: A Resource-based Account of Industrial Catch-up Strategies', *Asia Pacific Journal of Management*, 19, 467–88.

Mattli, W. (2019), *Darkness By Design: The Hidden Power in Global Capital Markets*, Princeton, NJ: Princeton University Press.

Mazzucato, M. (2018), *The Value of Everything: Making and Taking in the Global Economy*, London: Allen Lane.

Mazzucato, M. (2013), *The Entrepreneurial State: Debunking the Public vs. Private Myth in Risk and Innovation*. London and New York: Anthem Press.

McAfee, A. and Brynjolfsson, E. (2016), 'Human Work in the Robotic Future: Policy for the Age of Automation', *Foreign Affairs*, 95(4), 139–50.

McAfee, A., Brynjolfsson, E., and Spence, M. (2014), 'New World Order: Labor, Capital, and Ideas in the Power Law Economy', in G. Rose (ed.) *The Fourth Industrial Revolution: A Davos Reader*, New York: Council on Foreign Relations, pp. 44–53.

McCarthy J. and Rose, P. (eds.) (2010), *Values-based Health and Social Care: Beyond Evidence-based Practice*, London: Sage.

McCormick, K. (2000), *Engineers in Britain and Japan: Education, Training and Employment*, London: Routledge.

McMahon, W. (2003), 'Lifelong Learning in Developing Countries: An Analysis with Estimates of Private Returns and Externalities', Washington, DC: World Bank.

Meijers, E. and Stead, D. (2004), 'Policy Integration: What Does It Mean and How Can It Be Achieved? A Multi-disciplinary Review', Paper presented at the Berlin Conference on the Human Dimensions of Global Environmental Change: Greening of Policies—Interlinkages and Policy Integration.

Menon, J. and Melendez-Nakamura, A. (2009), 'Aging in Asia: Trends, Impacts and Responses', *ADB Working Paper Series on Regional Economic Integration*, No.25, February.

Mertha, A. (2005), 'China's "Soft" Centralization: Shifting *Tiao/Kuai* Authority Relations', *The China Quarterly*, 184, 791–810.

Meyer, J. (2000), 'Globalization: Sources and Effects on National States and Societies', *International Sociology*, 15, 233–48.

Milanovic, B. (2016), *Global Inequality: A New Approach for the Age of Globalization*, Cambridge, MA: Harvard University Press.

Minami, R. (1994), *The Economic Development of China: A Comparison with the Japanese Experience*, Basingstoke: Macmillan.

Minami, R., Kim, K., Makino, F., and Seo, J-H., (1995), 'Japanese Experience in Technology: A Survey', in R. Minami, K. Kim, F. Makino, and J-H. Seo (eds.) *Acquiring, Adapting and Developing Technologies: Lessons From the Japanese Experience*, London: Macmillan, pp. 1–29.

Minami, R. and Ma, X. (2014), 'The Lewis Turning Point of Chinese Economy: Comparison With Japanese Experience', in Y-P. Huang and F. Cai (eds.) *Debating the Lewis Turning Point in China*, London: Routledge, pp. 71–87.

Mingat, A. (1998), 'The Strategy Used by High-performing Asian Economies in Education: Some Lessons for Developing Countries', *World Development*, 26(4), 695–715.

Mingat. A. and Tan, J-P. (1985), 'Subsidization of Higher Education Versus Expansion of Primary Enrolments: What Can a Shift of Resources Achieve in Sub-Saharan Africa?', *International Journal of Educational Development*, 5(4), 259–68.

Minsky, H. (1992), 'Schumpeter and Finance', in S. Biasco, A. Roncaglia, and M. Salvati (eds.) *Market and Institutions in Economic Development: Essays in Honour of Paulo Sylos Labini*, London: Macmillan, pp. 103–15.

Minsky, H. (1988), 'Schumpeter: Finance and Evolution', paper prepared for Evolution of Technology and Market Structure in an International Context, conference sponsored by the International Schumpeter Society and Universita degli Studi di Siena, Siena, 24–27 May.

Mishra, S. (forthcoming), 'Examining the Status of Migrant Workers Across the Industrial Landscape of Delhi New Capital Region', DPhil thesis, University of Oxford.

Mitchener, K. Shizume, M., and Weidenmier, M. (2004), *A Bitter Revolution: China's Struggle With the Modern World*, Oxford: Oxford University Press.

Mitchener, K. Shizume, M., and Weidenmier, M. (2010), 'Why Did Countries Adopt the Gold Standard? Lessons From Japan', *The Journal of Economic History*, 70(1), 27–56.

Mitter, R. (2004), *A Bitter Revolution: China's Struggle with the Modern World*, Oxford: Oxford University Press.

Miura, M. (2012), *Welfare Through Work: Conservative Ideas, Partisan Dynamics and Social Protection in Japan*, Ithaca, NY: Cornell University Press.

Mkandawire, T. (ed.) (2004), *Social Policy in a Development Context*, Basingstoke: Palgrave and Geneva: UNRISD.

Mok, K.H. (2003), 'Similar Trends, Diverse Agendas: Higher Education Reform in East Asia', *Globalization, Societies and Education*, 1(2), 201–21.

Mok, K.H., Wong, Y.C., and Zhang, X. (2009), 'When Marketization and Privatization Clash with Socialist Ideals: Educational Inequality in Urban China', *International Journal of Educational Development*, 29(5), 505–12.

Morera, B. (2017), 'Planning New Towns in the Peoples' Republic: The Political Dimensions of Eco-city Images in China', in A. Datta and A. Shaban (eds.) *Mega-urbanization in the Global South: Fast Cities and the New Urban Utopias of the Postcolonial State*, London: Routledge, pp. 188–204.

Moriguchi, C. (2000), 'The Evolution of Employment Relations in the U.S. and Japanese Manufacturing Firms, 1900-1960: A Comparative Historical and Institutional Analysis', NBER Working Paper Series No.7939, Cambridge, MA.

Morikawa, H. (1989), 'The Increasing Power of Salaried Managers in Japan's Large Corporations', in W. Wray (ed.) *Managing Industrial Enterprise: Cases From Japan's Prewar Experience*, Cambridge, MA: Harvard University Press, pp. 27–51.

Morland, P. (2019), *The Human Tide: How Population Shaped the Modern World*, London: John Murray.

Mortensen, N.H. (2019), 'How the Global Electronics Industry Came to Rely on Forced Labour and Debt Bondage', *DanWatch*, 28 June. https://danwatch.dk/en/undersoegelse/how-the-global-electronics-industry-came-to-rely-on-forced-labour-and-debt-bondage/.

Mueller, M. (2017), *Will the Internet Fragment? Sovereignty, Globalization and Cyberspace*, Cambridge: Polity Press.

Mundy, K., Green, A., Lingard, B., and Verger, A. (eds.) (2016), *Handbook of Global Education Policy*, Chichester: Wiley.

Nahm, J. and Steinfeld, E. (2014), 'Scale-up Nation: China's Specialization in Innovative Manufacturing', *World Development*, 54, 288–300.

Nakamura, T. (1988), 'Depression, Recovery, and War 1920-1945', in P. Duus (ed.) *The Cambridge History of Japan, Volume 6 The Twentieth Century*, Cambridge: Cambridge University Press, pp. 451–93.

Naughton, B. (2007), *The Chinese Economy: Transitions and Growth*, Cambridge, MA: MIT Press.

Naughton, B. (1995), *Growing Out of the Plan: Chinese Economic Reform 1978–1993*, Cambridge: Cambridge University Press.

Naughton, B. and Tsai, K. (2015), *State Capitalism, Institutional Adaptation, and the Chinese Miracle*, New York: Cambridge University Press.

Neary, I. (2019), *The State and Politics in Japan*, 2nd edn., Cambridge: Polity Press.

Nee, V. and Opper, S. (2012), *Capitalism From Below: Markets and Institutional Change in China*, Cambridge, MA: Harvard University Press.

Negoita, M. and Block, F. (2012), 'Networks and Public Policies in the Global South: The Chilean Case and the Future of the Developmental Network State', *Studies in Comparative International Development*, 47(1), 1–22.

Neilson, J. and Pritchard, B. (2009), *Value Chain Struggles: Institutions and Governance in the Plantation Districts of South India*, Chichester: John Wiley and Sons.

Ngok, K-L. and Huang, G. (2014), 'Policy Paradigm Shift and the Role of the State: The Development of Social Policy in China Since 2003', *Social Policy and Society*, 13(2), 251–61.

Nilsson, M., Jordan, A., Turnpenny, J., Hertin, J., Björn, N., and Russel, D. (2008), 'The Use and Non-use of Policy Appraisal Tools in Public Policy Making: An Analysis of Three European Countries and the European Union', *Policy Science*, 41, 335–55.

Nishiguchi, T. (1994), *Strategic Industrial Sourcing*, New York: Oxford University Press.

Nissan, C., Gronager, J. Metzger, R., and Rishikof, H. (2018), 'Deliver Uncompromised: A Strategy for Supply Chain Security and Resilience in Response to the Changing Character of War', The MITRE Corporation.

Noguchi, Y. (1998), 'The 1940 System: Japan under the Wartime Economy', *American Economic Review*, 88(2), 404–7.

Nolan, P. (2001), *China and the Global Economy*, Basingstoke: Palgrave.

Ocampo, J. and. Ros, J. (2012), 'Shifting Paradigms in Latin America's Economic Development', in J. Ocampo and J. Ros (eds.) *The Oxford Handbook of Latin American Economics*, Oxford: Oxford University Press, Chapter 1.

Ochiai, E. (2014), 'Leaving the West, Rejoining the East? Gender and Family in Japan's Semi-compressed Modernity', *International Sociology*, 29(3), 209–28.

Ochiai, E. (2011), 'Unsustainable Societies: The Failure of Familialism in East Asia's Compressed Modernity', *Historical Social Research* (*Historiche Sozialforschung*), 36(2), 219–45.

O'Dwyer, L. (2003), 'A Systematic Literature Review of Evidence-Based Policy: Introduction and Review Protocol', AHURI Positioning Paper No. 45.

OECD (2019), *Under Pressure: The Squeezed Middle Class: Overview and Main Findings*, Paris: OECD.

OECD (2011), 'Global Value Chains: Preliminary Evidence and Policy Issues', Directorate for Science, Technology and Industry. Paper presented to the Committee on Industry, Innovation and Entrepreneurship, CIIE meeting, 31 March–1 April.

OECD/Japanese Ministry of Education, Culture, Sports, Science and Technology (2006), *OECD Thematic Review of Tertiary Education: Country Background Report of Japan*, Paris: OECD.

OECD/P.R. of China Ministry of Education (2007), *OECD Thematic Review of Tertiary Education: Background Report for the P.R. of China*, Paris: OECD.

Office of the World Health Organization Representative in China and Social Development Department of China State Council Development Research Centre (OWHORC/EDDC) (2006), *China: Health, Poverty and Economic Development 7*, Beijing: OWHORC/EDDC.

Ohno, K. (2009), 'Avoiding the Middle-income Trap: Renovating Industrial Policy Formulation in Vietnam', *ASEAN Economic Bulletin*, 26(1), 25–43.

Oi, J. (1992), 'Fiscal Reform and the Economic Foundations of Local State Corporatism in China', *World Politics*, 45(1), 99–126.

Okazaki, T. (2018), 'Developmental State Evolving: Japan's Graduation From a Middle-income Country', Centre for International Research on the Japanese Economy Working Paper CIRJE-F-1086, University of Tokyo.

Okazaki, T. and Okuno-Fujiwara, M. (eds.) (1999), *The Japanese Economic System and Its Historical Origins*, Oxford: Oxford University Press.

Ollila, E. (2005), 'Global Health Priorities: Priorities of the Wealthy?', *Globalization and Health*, 1(6), doi:10.1186/1744-8603-1-6.

O'Neil, C. (2016), *Weapons of Math Destruction: How Big Data Increases Inequality and Threatens Democracy*, New York: Crown.

O'Riain, S. (2004), *The Politics of High-tech Growth: Developmental Network States in the Global Economy*, Cambridge: Cambridge University Press.

O'Riain, S. (2000), 'The Flexible Developmental State, Globalization, Information Technology and the "Celtic Tiger"', *Politics and Society*, 28(2), 157–93.

Ozawa T. (2008), 'History Repeats Itself: Evolutionary Structural Change and TNC Involvement in Infrastructure Overseas, Flying Geese Style', Working Paper 261, Centre on Japanese Economy and Business, Colombia Business School.

Ozawa T. (1979), 'International Investment and Industrial Structure: New Theoretical Implications From the Japanese Experience', *Oxford Economic Papers*, 31(1), 72–92.

Packard, D. (2006), *The HP Way: How Bill Hewlett and I Built Our Company*, New York: Harper Collins, Collins Business Essentials.

Pahl, S. and Timmer, M. (2019), 'Do Global Value Chains Enhance Economic Upgrading? A Long View', *Journal of Development Studies*, DOI: 10.1080/00220388.2019.1702159.

Palacios, M. (2003), *Options for Financing Lifelong Learning*, Washington, DC: World Bank.

Palma G. (2005), 'Four Sources of Deindustrialization and a New Concept of the Dutch Disease', in J. Ocampo (ed.) *Beyond Reforms: Structural Dynamics and Macroeconomic Vulnerability*, Stanford, CA: Stanford University Press, pp. 71–116.

Parker, G., Van Alstyne, M., and Choudary, S. (2016), *Platform Revolution: How Networked Markets Are Transforming the Economy—And How to Make Them Work for You*, New York: W. W. Norton and Company.

Perez, C. (2002), *Technological Revolutions and Financial Capital: The Dynamics of Bubbles and Golden Ages*, Cheltenham: Edward Elgar.

Perrow, C. (1981), 'Markets, Hierarchies, and Hegemony: A Critique of Chandler and Williamson', in A. Van de Ven and W. Joyce (eds.) *Perspectives on Organizational Design and Behavior*, New York: Wiley, pp. 371–87.

Peters, G.B. (1998), 'Managing Horizontal Government: The Politics of Co-ordination', *Public Administration*, 76(Summer), 295–311.

Phongpaichit, P. and Benyaakipul, P. (2012), 'Locked in the Middle-income Trap: Thailand's Economy Between Resilience and Future Challenges', Friedrich-Ebert-Stiftung occasional paper, Bangkok, Thailand.

Piketty, T. (2014), *Capital in the Twenty First Century*, Cambridge, MA: Harvard University Press.

Pine, J.P. and Davis, S. (1999), *Mass Customization, the New Frontier in Business Competition*, Cambridge, MA: Harvard Business School Press.

Pingping, H. (2008), 'Perfect the System, Increase Input and Promote a More Equitable Education: Thoughts after the Implementation of the New Mechanism for Assured Funding for Rural Compulsory Education', *Chinese Education and Society*, 41(1), 69–74.

Piore, M. and Sabel, C. (1984), *The Second Industrial Divide*, New York: Basic Books.

Polanyi, K. (1944), *The Great Transformation: The Political and Economic Origins of Our Time*, New York: Farrar and Rinehart.

Pomeranz, K. (2000), *The Great Divergence: China, Europe, and the Making of the Modern World Economy*, Princeton, NJ: Princeton University Press.

Ponte, S. and Sturgeon, T. (2013), 'Explaining Governance in Global Value Chains: Towards a Broader Analytical Framework', *Review of International Political Economy*, 21(1), 195–223.

Popkin, B. (2002), 'The Shift in Stages of the Nutrition Transition in the Developing World Differs from Past Experiences!', *Public Health Nutrition* 5(1A), 205–14.

Powell, F. (2007), *The Politics of Civil Society: Neoliberalism or Social Left?* Bristol: Polity Press.

Powell, W. (1990), 'Neither Market Nor Hierarchy: Network Forms of Organization Research', *Organizational Behavior*, 12, 295–336.

Powell, W. (1987), 'Hybrid Organizational Arrangements: New Form or Transitional Development?', *California Management Review*, Fall, 67–87.

Pozsar, Z., Adrian, T. Ashcraft, A., and Boesky, H. (2010), 'Shadow Banking', Federal Reverse Bank of New York Staff Reports, No. 458, July.

Prahalad, C.K. and Hamel, G. (1990), 'The Core Competence of the Corporation', *Harvard Business Review*, May–June (3), 79–91.

Prebisch, R. (1950), *The Economic Development of Latin America and Its Principal Problems*, New York: United Nations.

Preece, J. (2005), 'Conceptualising Lifelong Learning: North-South Divides', Working Paper 2, Centre for Research and Development in Adult and Lifelong Learning, University of Glasgow.

Prentice A. (2006), 'The Emerging Epidemic of Obesity in Developing Countries', *International Journal of Epidemiology*, 35, 93–9.

Pressman, S. (2007), 'The Decline of the Middle Class: An International Perspective', *Journal of Economic Issues*, 41(1), 181–200.

Principe, A., Davies, A., and Hobday, M. (eds.) (2003), *The Business of Systems Integration*, Oxford: Oxford University Press.

Pritchett, L., Woolcock, M., and Andrews, A. (2010), 'Capability Traps? The Mechanisms of Persistent Implementation Failure', Centre for Global Development Working Paper 234.

Pritchett, L. and Summers, L. (2014a), 'Asiaphoria and Regression to the Mean', NBER Working Paper No.20573.

Pritchett, L. and Summers, L. (2014b), 'Growth Slowdowns: Middle-income Trap vs. Regression to the Mean', VOX, CEPR, 11 December.

Psacharapoulos, G. (1985), 'Returns to Education: A Further International Update and Implications', *The Journal of Human Resources*, 20(4), 583–97.

Qian, Y. and Xu, C. (1993), 'Why China's Economic Reforms Differ: The M-form Hierarchy and Entry/Expansion of the Non-state Sector', *Economics of Transition*, 1(2), 135–70.

Qiu, G., Zhang, S., and Liu, W. (2019), 'Trafficking of Myanmar Women for Forced Marriage in China', *Crime, Law and Social Change*, 72(1), 35–52.

Quan, X. and Chesbrough, H. (2009), 'Hierarchical Segmentation of R&D Process and Intellectual Property Protection: Evidence From Multinational R&D Laboratories in China', *IEEE Transactions on Engineering Management*, 57(1), 9–21.

Quinn, J. and Hilmer, F. (1994), 'Strategic Outsourcing', *Sloan Management Review*, 35(4), 43–55.

Radaelli, C. (2004), The Diffusion of Regulatory Impact Analysis: Best Practice or Lesson-drawing?', *European Journal of Political Research*, 43, 723–47.

Ramamurti, R. (2012), 'Competing With Emerging Market Multinationals', *Business Horizons*, 55, 241–9.

Ranis, G. and Fei, J. (1961), 'A Theory of Economic Development', *American Economic Review*, 51(4), 533–65.

Ratigan, K. (2017), 'Disaggregating the Developing Welfare State: Provincial Social Policy Regimes in China', *World Development*, 98, 467–84.

Razavi, S. (2009), 'Revisiting Progress on "Social Integration": Some Change and Much That Remains the Same', *Global Social Policy*, 9(9), 9–13.

Reardon, T. (2011), 'The Global Rise and Impact of Supermarkets: An International Perspective', Keynote address to The Supermarket Revolution in Food: Good, Bad or Ugly for the World's Farmers, Consumers and Retailers Conference, Canberra, 14–16 August.
Rehnberg, M. and Ponte, S. (2017), 'From Smiling to Smirking? 3D Printing, Upgrading and the Restructuring of Global Value Chains', *Global Networks*, Early View, 20 June.
Reynolds, E. (2017), 'The New Face of Manufacturing Jobs', *Boston Globe*, Opinion, February 13. https://www.bostonglobe.com/opinion/2017/02/13/the-new-face-manufacturing-jobs/jsozWRgDPwiXo5yJwA3z2M/story.html.
Reynolds, E., Schneider, B., and Zylberberg, E. (2019), *Innovation in Brazil: Advancing Development in the 21st Century,* London: Routledge Series in Innovation, Organization, and Technology.
Rio Times (2019), 'Uber Celebrates Five Years in Brazil With 2.6 Billion Trips', 18 July.
Rithmire, M. (2017), 'Land Institutions and Chinese Political Economy: Institutional Complementarities and Macroeconomic Management', *Politics and Society*, 45(1), 123–53.
Roberts, J. (2009), 'The Global Knowledge Economy in Question', *Critical Perspectives on International Business*, 5(4), 285–303.
Robertson, S. (2005), 'Re-imagining and Rescripting the Future of Education: Global Knowledge Economy Discourses and the Challenge to Education Systems', *Comparative Education*, 41(2), 151–70.
Robertson, S., Bonal, X., and Dale, R. (2002), 'GATS and the Education Service Industry: The Politics of Scale and Global Reterritorialization', *Comparative Education Review*, 46(4), 472–96.
Robertson, S., Mundy, K., Verger, A., and Menashy, F. (eds.) (2012), *Public Private Partnerships in Education: New Actors and Modes of Governance in a Globalizing World*, Cheltenham: Edward Elgar.
Rodrik, D. (2016), 'Is Liberal Democracy Feasible in Developing Countries?', *Studies in Comparative International Development*, 51(1), 50–9.
Rodrik, D. (2015), 'Premature Deindustrialization', unpublished paper, Institute for Advanced Study, Princeton, NJ.
Rodrik, D. (2013), 'The Past, Present, and Future of Economic Growth', Global Citizen Foundation Working Paper No.1, Geneva.
Romano, L. and Traù, F. (2017), 'The Nature of Industrial Development and the Speed of Industrial Change', *Structural Change and Economic Dynamics*, 42, 26–37.
Romer, P. (1993), 'Idea Gaps and Object Gaps in Economic Development', *Journal of Monetary Economics,* 32(3), 543–73.
Rong, X-L. and Shi, T-J. (2001), 'Inequality in Chinese Education', *Journal of Contemporary China*, 10(26), 107–24.
Rose, G. (ed.) (2016), *The Fourth Industrial Revolution: A Davos Reader*, New York: Council on Foreign Relations.
Rosling, H., with Rosling, O., and Rosling Rönnlund, A. (2018), *Factfulness: Ten Reasons We're Wrong About the World, and Why Things Are Better Than You Think*, New York: Flatiron Books.
Rostow, W. (1960), *The Stages of Economic Growth: A Non-communist Manifesto*, Cambridge: Cambridge University Press.
Rousseau, P. (2002), Historical Perspectives on Financial Development and Economic Growth', NBER Working Paper 9333.
Rousseau, P. and Wachtel, P. (2011), 'What is Happening to the Impact of Financial Deepening on Economic Growth?', *Economic Inquiry* 49(1), 276–88.

Rowthorn R. and Coutts, K. (2004), 'De-industrialization and the Balance of Payments in Advanced Economies', *Cambridge Journal of Economics* 28, 767–90.

Rowthorn, R. and Wells, J. (1987), *De-industrialization and Foreign Trade*, Cambridge: Cambridge University Press.

Ruggie, J. (1982), 'International Regimes, Transactions, and Change: Embedded Liberalism in the Post-war Economic System', *International Organization*, 36(2), 379–415.

Rydell, A. and Bremberg, S. (2006), *Television Consumption and Children's Health and Adjustment: A Systematic Review*, Stockholm: Swedish National Institute of Public Health.

Sabel, C. (1989), 'Flexible Specialisation and the Re-emergence of Regional Economies', in P. Hirst and J. Zeitlin (eds.) *Reversing Industrial Decline?* New York: St. Martin's Press, pp. 17–69.

Sahay, R., Čihák, M., N'Diaye, P., Barajas, A., Bi, R., Ayala, D., Gao, Y., Kyobe, A., Nguyen, L., Saborowski, C., Svirydzenka, K., and Yousefi, S. (2015), 'Rethinking Financial Deepening: Stability and Growth in Emerging Markets', IMF Staff Discussion Note SDN15/08.

Samuels, R. (2003), *Machiavelli's Children: Leaders and Their Legacies in Italy and Japan*, Ithaca, NY: Cornell University Press.

Samuels, R. (1994), *Rich Nation, Strong Army*, Ithaca, NY: Cornell University Press.

Sandbrook, R., Edelman, M., Heller, P., and Teichman, J. (2007), *Social Democracy in the Global Periphery: Origins, Challenges, Prospects*, Cambridge: Cambridge University Press.

Sassen, S. (ed.) (2002), *Global Networks, Linked Cities*, New York and London: Routledge.

Sassen, S. (1990), *The Mobility of Labor and Capital: A Study in International Investment and Labor Flow*, Cambridge: Cambridge University Press.

Saxenian, A. (1994), *Regional Advantage: Culture and Competition in Silicon Valley and Route 128*, Cambridge, MA: Harvard University Press.

Schaffhauser, D. (2014), 'IBM and China Make Large-Scale Commitment to Big Data Education', *Campus Technology*, July 9. https://campustechnology.com/articles/2014/07/09/ibm-and-china-make-large-scale-commitment-to-big-data-education.aspx.

Schettkat, R. and Yocarini, L. (2003), 'The Shift to Services: A Review of the Literature', IZA Discussion Paper No.964, Bonn.

Schmitter, P. (1974), 'Still the Century of Corporatism?', *The Review of Politics*, 36(1), 85–131.

Schoenberger, E. (2008), 'The Origins of the Market Economy: State Power, Territorial Control, and Modes of War Fighting', *Comparative Studies in Society and History*, 50(3), 663–91.

Schumpeter, J. ([1934] 1983), *The Theory of Economic Development*, Cambridge, MA: Harvard University Press.

Schumpeter, J. (1942), *Capitalism, Socialism, and Democracy*, New York: Harper and Brothers.

Schwab, K. (2018), *The Fourth Industrial Revolution*, New York: Crown Business.

Schwab, K. (2015), 'The Fourth Industrial Revolution: What It Means and How to Respond', *Foreign Affairs*, 12 December. https://www.foreignaffairs.com/articles/2015-12-12/fourth-industrial-revolution.

Schwartz, H. (2010), *States Versus Markets: The Emergence of a Global Economy*, 3rd edn., Basingstoke: Palgrave.

Schwartz, F. and Pharr, S. (eds.) (2003), *The State of Civil Society in Japan*, Cambridge: Cambridge University Press.

Seabrooke, L. and Wigan, D. (2017), 'The Governance of Global Wealth Chains', *Review of International Political Economy*, 24(1), 1–29.

Seabrooke, L. and Wigan, D. (2014), 'Global Wealth Chains in the International Political Economy', *Review of International Political Economy*, 21(1), 257–63.

Segal, A. (2003), *Digital Dragon: High-Technology Enterprises in China*, Ithaca, NY: Cornell University Press.

Seki, M. (2004), *Beyond the Full Set Industrial Structure: Japan in the New Age of East Asia*, Tokyo: LTCB International Library Foundation.

Selmier, T. (2019), 'Conflict, Contention and Cooperation in China's New Model of Financial Intermediation Monitoring', paper presented to Society for the Advancement of Socio-economics (SASE) conference, The New School, New York, 27–29 June.

Selwyn, B. (2011), 'Trotsky, Gerschenkron and the Political Economy of Late Capitalist Development', *Economy and Society*, 40(3), 421–50.

Semiconductor Equipment and Materials International China (SEMI) (2017), 'China IC Industry Environment', International Roadmap Committee (IRC), slide presentation, March. http://stg7.semi.org/en/marketinfo/semi-china-ic-industry-outlook.

Semiconductor Industry Association, (2015), 'Databook', *semiconductors.org*. https://www.semiconductors.org/data-resources/market-data/sia-databook/.

Sen, A. (1999a), *Development as Freedom*, Oxford: Oxford University Press.

Sen, A. (1999b), 'Beyond the Crisis: Development Strategies in Asia', Paper at JCIE Conference: Second Intellectual Dialogue on Building Asia's Tomorrow: Promoting Sustainable Development and Human Security, 12–13 July, Singapore.

Sharman, J. (2012), 'Canaries in the Coal Mine: Tax Havens, the Decline of the West and the Rise of the Rest', *New Political Economy*, 17(4), 493–513.

Sharman, J. (2010), 'Offshore and the New International Political Economy', *Review of International Political Economy*, 17(1), 1–19.

Shen, J. (2019), 'Beijing Begins Introducing Measures to Protect Gig-Economy Workers, Starting With Delivery Drivers', *Technode*, 20 February.

Siegel, K. and Stuckler, D. (2011), 'Comparative Case Studies From Brazil, China, India, Mexico, and South Africa', in D. Stuckler and K. Siegel (eds.) (2011), *Sick Societies: Responding to the Global Challenge of Chronic Disease*, Oxford: Oxford University Press, pp. 217–90.

Singer, H. (1970), 'Dualism Revisited: A New Approach to the Problems of the Dual Society in Developing Countries', *Journal of Development Studies*, 7(1), 60–75.

Singh A. (1977), U.K. Industry and the World Economy: A Case of De-industrialization', *Cambridge Journal of Economics* 1(2), 113–36.

Smeyers, P. and Depaepe, M. (2008), 'Introduction – Pushing Social Responsibilities: The Educationalization of Social Problems', in Smeyers, P. and M. Depaepe (eds.) *Educational Research: The Educationalization of Social Problems*, Gent: Springer, pp. 1–11.

Smith, C. and Chan, J. (2015), 'Working for Two Bosses: Student Interns as Constrained Labour in China', *Human Relations*, 68(2), 305–26.

Smith, T., Sonnenfeld, D., and Pellow, D. (2006), *Challenging the Chip*, Philadelphia: Temple University Press.

Smith, W. (2016), 'An Introduction to the Global Testing Culture', in W. Smith (ed.) *The Global Testing Culture: Shaping Education Policy, Perceptions, and Practice*, Oxford: Symposium Books, pp. 7–23.

Smith, W. (2015), *The Global Testing Culture: Shaping Education Policy, Perspective and Practice*, Oxford: Oxford University Press.

Spence, M. (2012), *The Next Convergence: The Future of Economic Growth in a Multispeed World*, New York: Picador.

Staley, O. (2019), 'Whatever Happened to Six Sigma?' *Quartz at Work*, 3 September. https://qz.com/work/1635960/whatever-happened-to-six-sigma/.

Staritz, C. and Whitfield, L. (2019), 'Local Firm-level Learning and Capability in Global Value Chains', in S. Ponte, G. Gereffi, and G. Raj-Reichert (eds.) *Handbook on Global Value Chains*, Cheltenham: Edward Elgar, Chapter 24.

Steinberg, J. (2008), 'Was the Russo-Japanese War World War Zero?', *The Russian Review*, 67, 1–7.

Steurer, R. (2009), 'Sustainable Development as Governance Reform Agenda: An Aggregation of Distinguished Challenges for Policy-making', InFER Discussion Paper 2009/1, Vienna.

Stinchcombe, A. (1965), 'Social Structure and Organizations', in J. March (ed.) *Handbook of Organizations*, Chicago: Rand McNally, pp. 142–93.

Storper, M. and Scott, A. (1988), 'The Geographical Foundations and Social Regulation of Flexible Production Complexes', in J. Wolch and M. Dear (eds.) *The Power of Geography*, Boston: Allen and Unwin, pp. 21–39.

Streeck, W. (2009), 'Institutions in History: Bringing Capitalism Back in', MPIfG Discussion Paper 09/8, Max Planck Institute für Gesellschaftsforschung.

Streeck, W. (2016), *How Will Capitalism End?*, London: Verso.

Streeck, W. and Thelen, K. (2005), *Beyond Continuity: Institutional Change in Advanced Political Economies*, Oxford: Oxford University Press.

Stringer, C., Hughes, S., Whittaker, D.H., Haworth, N., and Simmons, G. (2016), 'Labour Standards and Regulation in GVCs: The Case of the New Zealand Fishing Industry', *Environment and Planning A*, 48(10), 1910–27.

Stringer, C., Whittaker, D.H., and Simmons, G. (2016), 'New Zealand's Turbulent Waters: The Use of Forced Labour in the Fishing Industry', *Global Networks: A Journal of Transnational Affairs*, 16(1), 3–24.

Stuckler, D. and Basu, S. (2011), 'Evaluating the Health Burden of Chronic Diseases', in D. Stuckler and K. Siegel (eds.) (2011), *Sick Societies: Responding to the Global Challenge of Chronic Disease*, Oxford: Oxford University Press, pp. 1–25.

Sturgeon, T. (2019), 'Upgrading Strategies in the Digital Economy', *Global Strategy Journal*, special issue on Strategies in the Global Digital Economy, published online 7 November. https://doi.org/10.1002/gsj.1364.

Sturgeon, T. (2007), 'How Globalization Drives Institutional Diversity: The Japanese Electronics Industry's Response to Value Chain Modularity', *Journal of East Asian Studies*, 7(1), 1–34.

Sturgeon, T. (2003), 'What Really Goes on in Silicon Valley? Spatial Clustering Dispersal in Modular Production Networks', *Journal of Economic Geography*, 3(April), 199–225.

Sturgeon, T. (2002), 'Modular Production Networks: A New American Model of Industrial Organization', *Industrial and Corporate Change*, 11(3), 451–96.

Sturgeon, T. Chagas, L., and Barnes, J. (2017), 'Inovar Auto: Evaluating Brazil's Automotive Industrial Policy to Meet the Challenges of Global Value Chains', background paper for the report 'Um Ajuste Justo: Analise da eficiência e equidade do gasto público no Brasil', World Bank, October.

Sturgeon, T. and Florida, R. (2004), 'Globalization, Deverticalization, and Employment in the Motor Vehicle Industry', in M. Kenny with Richard Florida (eds.) *Locating Global Advantage; Industry Dynamics in a Globalizing Economy*, Palo Alto, CA: Stanford University Press, pp. 52–81.

Sturgeon, T., Gereffi, G. Guinn, A., and Zylberberg, E. (2013), 'O Brasil nas Cadeias Globais de Valor: Implicações para a Política Industrial e de Comércio', *Fundação Centro de Estudos do Comércio Exterior* (FUNCEX), RBCE Nº 115, April–June.

Sturgeon, T. and Kawakami, M. (2011), 'Global Value Chains in the Electronics Industry: Characteristics, Crisis, and Upgrading Opportunities for Firms from Developing Countries', *International Journal of Technological Learning, Innovation and Development*, 4(1/2/3), 120–47.

Sturgeon, T. and Lee, J.R. (2005), 'Industry Co-evolution: A Comparison of Taiwan and North American Electronics Contract Manufacturers', in S. Berger and R.K. Lester (eds.) *Global Taiwan: Building Competitive Strengths in a New International Economy*, Armonk, NY: M.E. Sharpe, pp. 33–75.

Sturgeon, T. and Lester, R. (2004), 'The New Global Supply-Base: New Challenges for Local Suppliers in East Asia', in S. Yusuf, A. Altaf, and K. Nabeshima (eds.) *Global Production Networking and Technological Change in East Asia*, Oxford: Oxford University Press, pp. 35–87.

Sturgeon, T. and Memedovic, O. (2010), 'Mapping Global Value Chains: Intermediate Goods Trade and Structural Change in the World Economy', UNIDO Working Paper 05/2010. United National Industrial Development Organization, Vienna.

Sturgeon, T. with Levy, F., Brown, C., Jensen, J.B., and Weil, D. (2006), *Why We Can't Measure the Economic Effects of Services Offshoring: The Data Gaps and How to Fill Them*, report from the MIT Industrial Performance Center's Services Offshoring Working Group. Issued as Industrial Performance Center Working Paper 06–006, 10 September, Boston.

Sturgeon, T. and Thun, E. (2018), *China: New Drivers of Growth, Case Studies of China's Automotive and ICT Hardware Sector*, paper prepared as a background study for the World Bank Group, 24 January.

Sturgeon, T. and Van Biesebroeck, J. (2010), 'Global Value Chains in the Automotive Industry: An Enhanced Role for Developing Countries?', *International Journal Technological Learning, Innovation and Development*, 4(1), 181–205.

Sturgeon, T., Van Biesebroeck, J., and Gereffi, G. (2008), 'Value Chains, Networks, and Clusters: Reframing the Global Automotive Industry', *Journal of Economic Geography*, 8 (3), 297–321.

Su, F. and Tao, R. (2017), 'The China Model Withering? Institutional Roots of China's Local Developmentalism', *Urban Studies*, 54(1), 230–50.

Suehiro, A. (2008), *Catch-up Industrialization: The Trajectory and Prospects of East Asian Economies*, Singapore: NUS Press.

Sumner, A. (2012), 'The Bouyant Billions: How "Middle Class" Are the New Middle Classes in Developing Countries? (Any Why Does It Matter?)', London: Centre for Global Development Working Paper 309.

Sun, I.S. (2017), *The Next Factory of the World: How Chinese Investment is Reshaping Africa*, Boston: Harvard Business Review Press.

Sun, Q. (2007), 'A Critical View on Building Learning Cities in China: Lifelong Learning as a Vehicle Towards a Harmonious Society', *Convergence*, XL(1–2), 95–115.

Sun, Y., von Zedtwitz, M., and Simon, D. (2007), 'Globalization of R&D and China: An Introduction', *Asia Pacific Business Review*, 13(3), 311–19.

Suraj, S. (2018), 'The Gig Economy and Skills Traps in Indonesia', *The Jakarta Post*, 21 November.

Szirmai, A. (2009), 'Is Manufacturing Still the Main Engine of Growth in Developing Countries?', UNU-WIDER *Angle Newsletter*, May, pp.1–3.

Szirmai, A. and Verspagen, B. (2015), 'Manufacturing and Economic Growth in Developing Countries, 1950–2005', in *Structural Change and Economic Dynamics*, 34, 46–59.

Tan, J., Li, S., and Xia, J. (2007), 'When Iron Fist, Visible Hand, and Invisible Hand Meet: Firm-level Effects of Varying Institutional Environments in China', *Journal of Business Research*, 60, 786–94.

Tan, J-P., Jimenez, E., and Psacharapoulos, G. (1986), *Financing Education in Developing Countries: An Exploration of Policy Options*, New York: World Bank.

Tarabini, A. (2007), 'The Spread of Targeted Educational Policies in Latin America: Global Thesis and Local Impacts', *International Studies in Sociology of Education*, 17(1–2), 21–43.

Tasker, P. (2015), 'China and the Three Japans', author website. http://www.petertasker.asia/articles/china-and-the-three-japans/.

Tayal, P. (2016), 'China Gaining Position in the Global Semiconductor Market', *Market Realist.*

Teets, J. (2017), 'The Power of Policy Networks in Authoritarian Regimes: Changing Environmental Policy in China', *Governance*, doi: 10.1111/gove.12280.

Thelen, K. (2014), *Varieties of Liberalization and the New Politics of Social Solidarity*, Cambridge: Cambridge University Press.

Thobani, M. (1984), 'Charging User Fees for Social Services: Education in Malawi', *Comparative Education Review*, 28, 402–23.

Thomas, C. (2015), 'A New World under Construction: China and Semiconductors', McKinsey and Co. https://www.mckinsey.com/featured-insights/asia-pacific/a-new-world-under-construction-china-and-semiconductors.

Thomas, M. Burt, M., and Parkes, J. (2010), 'The Emergence of Evidence-based Practice, in J. McCarthy and P. Rose (eds.) *Values-Based Health and Social Care: Beyond Evidence-Based Practice*, London: Sage, pp. 3–24.

Thompson, W. (1929), 'Population', *American Journal of Sociology*, 34(6), 959–75.

Thun, E. (2006), *Changing Lanes in China: Foreign Direct Investment, Local Governments, and Auto Sector Development*, New York: Cambridge University Press.

Thun, E. and Sturgeon, T. (2019), 'When Global Technology Meets Local Standards: Reassessing China's Mobile Telecom Policy in the Age of Platform Innovation', in L. Brandt and T. Rawski (eds.) *Policy, Regulation and Innovation in China's Electricity and Telecom Industries*, Cambridge: Cambridge University Press, pp. 177–220.

Thünen, J.H. von ([1826] 1966), *The Isolated State*, P. Hall (ed.) and C. Wartenberg (trans.), New York: Pergamon Press.

Tilly, C. (1990), *Coercion, Capital, and European States*, AD 990–1990, Oxford: Blackwell.

Tilly, C. (1985), 'War Making and State Making as Organized Crime', in P. Evans, D. Rueschemeyer, and T. Skocpol (eds.) *Bringing the State Back In*, New York: Cambridge University Press, pp. 161–91.

Timmer, M., de Vries, G., and de Vries, K. (2015), 'Patterns of Structural Change in Developing Countries', in J. Weiss and M. Tribe (eds.) *Routledge Handbook of Industry and Development*, London: Routledge, pp. 65–83.

Tomasevski, K. (2003), 'School Fees as Hindrance to Universalizing Primary Education', Background study for EFA Global Monitoring Report, Paris: UNESCO.

Trotsky, L. ([1932] 2017), *History of the Russian Revolution*, London: Penguin Books.

Trotsky, L. ([1906] 1969), *The Permanent Revolution and Results and Progress*, New York: Merit Publishers.

Tsai, K. (2016), 'Cosmopolitan Capitalism: Local State-Society Relations in China and India', *The Journal of Asian Studies*, 75(2), 335–61.

Tse, E. (2010), *The China Strategy: Harnessing the Power of the World's Fastest-Growing Economy*, New York: Basic Books.

Tsutsui, W. (1998), *Manufacturing Ideology: Scientific Management in Twentieth-Century Japan*, Princeton, NJ: Princeton University Press.

Tylecote, A., Cai, J., and Liu, J. (2010), 'Why Do Mainland Chinese Firms Succeed in Some Sectors and Fail in Others? A Critical View of the Chinese System of Innovation', *International Journal of Learning and Intellectual Capital*, 7(2), 123–44.

UNCTAD (2017), *The 'New' Digital Economy and Development*, New York: UNCTAD.

UNCTAD (2016), *World Investment Report, 2016*, New York: United Nations.

UNCTAD (2015a), *Trade and Development Report, 2015*, New York: United Nations.

UNCTAD (2015b), *International Trade in ICT Services and ICT-enabled Services; Proposed Indicators from the Partnership on Measuring ICT for Development*, Division on Technology and Logistics; Science, Technology and ICT Branch; ICT Analysis Section, Technical Note No.3, TN/UNCTAD/ICT4D/03, October.

UNCTAD (2008), *World Investment Report: Transnational Corporations and the Infrastructure Challenge*, New York: UNCTAD.

UNCTAD (2006), *World Investment Report*, New York: United Nations.

UNCTAD (2002), *World Investment Report*, New York: United Nations.

UNDP (2005), *China Human Development Report 2005*, New York: UNDP.

UNESCO (2016), 'c7p4'. http://uis.unesco.org/en/country/cn?theme=education-and-literacy.

UNICEF (2008), 'Bridging the Gap: The Role of Monitoring and Evaluation in Evidence-based Policy Making', Evaluation Working Papers Issue 12, New York: UNICEF.

UNICEF (2009), *Country-led Monitoring and Evaluation Systems: Better Evidence, Better Policies, Better Development Results*, New York: UNICEF.

UN Statistics Division (2016), *Manual for the Classification by Broad Economic Categories, Revision 5*. United Nations Department of Economic and Social Affairs, Statistics Division, Statistical Papers, Series M, No.53, Rev.5.

Useem, M. (1996), *Investor Capitalism: How Money Managers are Changing the Face of Corporate America*, New York: Basic Books.

Utting, P. and Zammit, A., (2006), 'Beyond Pragmatism: Appraising UN-Business Partnerships', UNRISD Markets, Business and Regulation Programme Paper No. 1, Geneva: UNRISD.

Van Alstyne, M. (2016), 'Platform Shift: How New Biz Models Are Changing the Shape of Industry', Presentation to the ICT Industry Roundtable, MIT Industrial Performance Center Accelerating Innovation in Brazil Project, Sao Paulo, Brazil, 10 May.

Van Dijk, T., Bhide, A., and Shitare, V., (2016), 'When a Participatory Slum Sanitation Project Encounters Urban Informality: The Case of the Greater Mumbai Metropolitan Region', *International Area Studies Review*, 19(1), 45–59.

Vanek, J., Chen, M., Carré J. Heintz, F., and Hussmanns, R. (2014), 'Statistics on the Informal Economy: Definitions, Regional Estimates and Challenges', WIEGO Working Paper (Statistics) No.2, Cambridge, MA.

Varghese, N., Chien, C-L., Montjourides, P., Tran, H., Sigdel, S., Katayama, H., and Chapman, D. (2014), 'The Reshaping of Higher Education Across Asia', in UNESCO Institute for Statistics (ed.) *Higher Education in Asia: Expanding Out, Expanding Up*, Montreal, Canada: UNESCO.

Veblen, T. (1919), *The Place of Science in Modern Civilization and Other Essays*, New York: Huebsch.
Veblen, T. (1915), *Imperial Germany and the Industrial Revolution*, New York: Macmillan.
Vercelli, A. (2014), 'Financialization in a Long-run Perspective', *International Journal of Political Economy*, 42(4), 19–46.
Verger, A. (2012), 'Framing and Selling Global Education Policy: The Promotion of Public–private Partnerships for Education in Low-income Contexts', *Journal of Education Policy*, 27(1), 109–30.
Verger, A. (2008), 'Measuring Educational Liberalization: A Global Analysis of GATS', *Globalization, Societies and Education*, 6(1), 13–31.
Vernon, R. (1971), *Sovereignty at Bay: The Multinational Spread of U.S. Enterprises*, New York: Basic Books.
Vernon, R. (1966), 'International Investment and International Trade in the Product Cycle', *Quarterly Journal of Economics*, 80(2), 190–207.
Vlcek, W. (2008), 'From Road Town (BVI) to Shanghai: FDI, IBCs and Global Capital Flows', paper presented to the Ocean Conference on International Studies, Brisbane, Australia, 2 July.
Vogel, S. (2018), *Marketcraft: How Governments Make Markets Work*, Oxford: Oxford University Press.
Von Hippel, E. (2017), *Free Innovation*. Cambridge, MA: MIT Press.
Wade, R. (2018), 'Escaping the Periphery: The East Asia "Mystery" Solved' in D. Nayyar (ed.) *Asian Transformations: An Inquiry into the Development of Nations*, New York: UNU-WIDER, Chapter 1.
Wade, R. (2012), 'Return of Industrial Policy?', *International Review of Applied Economics*, 26(2), 223–39.
Wade, R. (2003), 'What Strategies Are Viable for Developing Countries Today? The World Trade Organization and the Shrinking of "Development Space"', *Review of International Political Economy*, 10(4), 621–44.
Wade, R. (1990), *Governing the Market: Economic Theory and the Role of Government in East Asian Industrialization*, Princeton, NJ: Princeton University Press.
Walker, R.A. (1974), 'Urban Ground Rent: Building a New Conceptual Framework', *Antipode*, 6(1), 51–8.
Waltner-Toews, D. and Lang, T. (2000), 'A New Conceptual Base for Food and Agriculture: The Emerging Model of Links between Agriculture, Food, Health, Environment and Society', *Global Change and Human Health*, 1(2), 116–30.
Wang, J-H. (2006), 'China's Dualist Model on Technological Catching Up: A Comparative Perspective', *The Pacific Review*, 19(3), 385–403.
Wang, M. (2014), 'The Rise of Labour Cost and the Fall of Labour Input: Has China Reached the Lewis Turning Point?', in Y-P. Huang and F. Cai (eds.) *Debating the Lewis Turning Point in China*, London: Routledge, pp. 46–62.
Wang, Y. (2015), 'The Rise of the Shareholding State: Financialization of Economic Management in China', *Socio-Economic Review*, 13(3), 603–25.
Wang, Y., Sperlinga, D., Tala, G., and Fang, H. (2017), 'China's Electric Car Surge', *Energy Policy*, 102, 486–90.
Warr, P. (1989), 'Export Processing Zones: the Economics of Enclave Manufacturing', *The World Bank Research Observer*, 4(1), 65–88.
Warwick, K. (2013) *Beyond Industrial Policy: Emerging Issues and New Trends,* OECD Science, Technology and Industry Policy Papers No. 2, OECD Publishing.

Watson, V. (2014), 'African Urban Fantasies: Dreams or Nightmares?', *Environment and Urbanization*, 26(1), 215–31.

Weil, D. (2014), *The Fissured Workplace: Why Work Became So Bad for So Many and What Can be Done to Improve It*, Cambridge, MA: Harvard University Press.

Weiss, L. and Hobson, J. (1995), *States and Economic Development: A Comparative Historical Analysis*, Cambridge: Polity Press.

Welch, L.S. and Luostarinen, R. (1988), 'Internationalisation: Evolution of a Concept', *Journal of General Management*, 14(2), 34–55.

West, K. (2015), 'Decentralization, the Inclusion of Ethnic Citizens, and Support for Democracy in Latin America', *Latin American Research Review*, 50(3), 46–70.

White and Case (2017), *China's Rise in Global M&A: Here to Stay*, New York: White and Case.

Whittaker, D.H. (1997), *Small Firms in the Japanese Economy*, Cambridge: Cambridge University Press.

Whittaker, D. H. (1990), *Managing Innovation: A Study of British and Japanese Factories*, Cambridge: Cambridge University Press.

Whittaker, D.H., Sturgeon, T. and Song, L. (2016), 'Compressed Development, Business Systems, and Innovation: The Importance of Timing and Agency in Economic and Institutional Development and Change', in R. Whitley and X. Zhang eds., Changing Asian Business Systems: Globalization, Socio-Political Change, and Economic Organization, Oxford: Oxford University Press.

Whittaker, D.H., Zhu, T., Sturgeon, T., Tsai, M.H., and Okita, T. (2010), 'Compressed Development', *Studies in Comparative International Development*, 45(3), 439–67.

Wilkinson, A. (2005), 'Downsizing, Rightsizing or Dumbsizing? Quality, Human Resources and the Management of Sustainability', *Total Quality Management and Business Excellence*, 16(8–9), 1079–88.

Wilkinson, R. and Pickett, K. (2009), *The Spirit Level: Why More Equal Societies Almost Always do Better*, London: Allen and Lane.

Williams, G. (2019), *The Evolution of China's Banking System, 1993–2017*, Abingdon: Routledge.

Williamson, O. (1981), 'The Modern Corporation: Origins, Evolution, Attributes', *Journal of Economic Literature*, 19, 1537–68.

Wimmer, A. (2018), *Nation Building: Why Some Countries Come Together While Others Fall Apart*, Princeton, NJ: Princeton University Press.

Wimmer, A. and Glick Schiller, N. (2002), 'Methodological Nationalism and Beyond: Nation-state Building, Migration and the Social Sciences', *Global Networks*, 2, 301–34.

Womack, J., Jones, D., and Roos, D. (1990), *The Machine that Changed the World*, New York: Rawson Associates.

Wong, J. (2011), *Betting on Biotech: Innovation and the Limits of Asia's Developmental State*, Ithaca, NY: Cornell University Press.

Woo-Cumings, M. (ed.) (1999), *The Developmental State*, Ithaca, NY: Cornell University Press.

Wood, A. and Mayer, J. (2009), 'Has China De-industrialized Other Developing Countries?', Working Paper 175, Queen Elizabeth House, University of Oxford.

World Bank (2015a), *Live Long and Prosper: Aging in East Asia and Pacific*, Washington, DC: World Bank.

World Bank (2015b), 'Global Value Chains', Brief, IBRD/IDA, 16 July.

World Bank (2013), *China 2030: Building a Modern, Harmonious and High-income Society*, Washington, DC: World Bank.

World Bank (2009), *From Poor Areas to Poor People: China's Evolving Poverty Reduction Agenda: An Assessment of Poverty and Inequality in China*, Beijing: World Bank.

World Bank (2003), *Lifelong Learning for the Global Knowledge Economy: Challenges for Developing Countries*, New York: World Bank.

World Bank (1993), *The East Asian Miracle: Economic Growth and Public Policy*, New York: Oxford University Press.

World Economic Forum (2018), *The Future of Jobs 2018, Insight Report*, Geneva: Centre for the New Economy and Society. *s Report*

World Health Organization (2013), *World Tuberculosis Report, 2013; 2016*, Geneva: WHO.

Woronov, T. (2016), *Class Work: Vocational Schools and China's Youth*, Stanford, CA: Stanford University Press.

Wray, L.R. (2009), 'The Rise and Fall of Money Manager Capitalism: A Minskian Approach', *Cambridge Journal of Economics*, 33, 807–28.

Wübbeke, J., Meissner, M., Zenglein, M., Ives, J., and Conrad, B. (2016), 'Made in China 2025: The Making of a High-tech Superpower and Consequences for Industrial Countries, Mercator Institute for Chinese Studies MERICS Papers on China 2.

Xiang, B. and Shen, W. (2009), 'International Student Migration and Social Stratification in China', *International Journal of Educational Development*, 29, 513–22.

Xiong, J. (2006), 'Establishing a Lifelong Learning System by Developing Higher Vocational Education: A Case of China', occasional paper, University of Alberta.

Xing, Y. (2019), 'Global Value Chains and the Innovation of the Chinese Mobile Phone Industry', National Graduate Institute for Policy Studies (GRIPS) Discussion Paper 19–14, Tokyo.

Xu, F. (2016), 'Temporary Work in China: Precarity in an Emerging Labour Market', in J. Fudge and K. Strauss (eds.), *Temporary Work, Agencies and Unfree Labour: Insecurity in the New World of Work*, New York: Routledge, Chapter 1.

Xue, X-Y. and Liu, G-L. (2005), 'Global Risk World: Present and Future', *Marxism and Reality*, 1, 44–55 (in Chinese).

Yeung, H. (2018), *Strategic Coupling: East Asian Industrial Transformation in the New Global Economy*, Ithaca, NY: Cornell University Press.

Yeung, H. (2014), Governing the Market in a Globalizing Era: Developmental States, Global Production Networks and Inter-firm Dynamics in East Asia', *Review of International Political Economy*, 22(1), 70–101.

Yoo, T., de Wysocki, M., Cumberland, A., and Cisco Corporate Affairs (2018), *Country Digital Readiness: Research to Determine a Country's Digital Readiness and Key Interventions*, Research: Modeling an Inclusive Digital Future. https://www.cisco.com/c/dam/assets/csr/pdf/Country-Digital-Readiness-White-Paper-US.pdf.

Young, A. (1929), 'Increasing Returns and Economic Progress', *Economic Journal*, 38, 527–42.

Zalewski, D.A. and Whalen, C.J. (2010), 'Financialization and Income Inequality: A Post Keynesian Institutionalist Analysis', *Journal of Economic Issues*, 44(3), 757–77.

Zammit, A. (2009), 'Development at Risk: Rethinking UN-Business Partnerships, South Centre and UNRISD.

Zhang, G-F. (2006), 'Reflexive Modernization and Risk Society', *Marxism and Reality*, 1, 130–5 (in Chinese).

Zhang, J. and Chen, H. (2010), 'China's Compressed Urbanization and Urban Planning Responses', *Cnki.com*. http://en.cnki.com.cn/Article_en/CJFDTOTAL-CXGH201006005.htm.

Zhang, R. (2008), 'Preliminary Legal Exploration of the "Two Exemptions and One Subsidy" (TEOS) Program', *Chinese Education and Society*, 41(1), 17–22.

Zhang, X-B. and Kanbur, R. (2005), 'Spatial Inequality in Education and Health Care in China', *China Economic Review*, 16, 189–204.

Zhang, Y. (2001), 'System, Empire and State in Chinese International Relations', *Review of International Studies*, 27(5), 43–63.

Zhou, L.A. (2004), 'Jinsheng boyi zhong zhengfu guanyuan de jili yu hezuo' ('The Incentive and Cooperation of Government Officials in the Political Tournament'), *Jingji yanjiu (Journal of Economic Research)*, 6, 1– 9.

Zhu, T. (2017), 'China's State Capacity in the Context of Multilayered Government-Business Relations', paper presented to International Workshop on Chinese State Capacity, Institute for Advanced Studies in Humanities and Social Sciences, Zhejiang University.

Zhu, T. (2015), 'International Context and China's Government-Business Relations', *Economic and Political Studies*, 3(2), 3–29.

Zhu, T. (2012), 'Compressed Development, Flexible Practices, and Multiple Traditions in China's Rise', in P. Katzenstein (ed.) *Sincization and the Rise of China: Civilizational Processes Beyond East and West*, London and New York: Routledge, Chapter 4.

Zhu, T. (2000), *Consistent Threat, Political-Economic Institutions, and Northeast Asian Developmentalism*, Ph.D. thesis, Government Department, Cornell University.

Zhuang, J-Z. (2012), 'How China Can Avoid the Middle-income Trap', *South China Morning Post*, 12 November.

Zuboff, S. (2019), *The Age of Surveillance Capitalism: The Fight for a Human Future at the New Frontier of Power*, London: Profile Books.

Zucman, G. (2015), *The Hidden Wealth of Nations: The Scourge of Tax Havens*, Chicago: University of Chicago Press.

Zweig, D. (2002), *Internationalizing China: Domestic Interests and Global Linkages*, Ithaca, NY: Cornell University Press.

Zylberberg, E. (2017), *Industrial Policy Refraction: How Corporate Strategy Shapes Development Outcomes in Brazil*, DPhil Thesis, Saïd Business School, University of Oxford.

Zylberberg, E., (2016), 'Redefining Brazil's Role in Information and Communication Technology Global Value Chains', MIT Industrial Performance Center Working Paper Series No. 16–003.

Index

For the benefit of digital users, indexed terms that span two pages (e.g., 52–53) may, on occasion, appear on only one of those pages.